THE GOSPEL ACCORDING TO MARK.

BY

JOHN PETER LANGE, D.D.,

PROFESSOR OF THEOLOGY AT THE UNIVERSITY OF BONN.

REVISED FROM THE EDINBURGH TRANSLATION, WITH ADDITIONS,

BY

WILLIAM G. T. SHEDD, D.D.,

PROFESSOR IN UNION THEOLOGICAL SEMINARY, NEW YORK.

SIXTH EDITION.

Wipf & Stock
PUBLISHERS
Eugene, Oregon

Wipf and Stock Publishers
199 W 8th Ave, Suite 3
Eugene, OR 97401

The Gospel according to Mark
an Exegetical and Doctrinal Commentary
By Lange, John Peter
ISBN 13: 978-1-55635-402-1
ISBN 10: 1-55635-402-9
Publication date 4/4/2007
Previously published by Charles Scribner, 1866

II.

THE GOSPEL ACCORDING TO MARK;

BEING THAT OF THE NEW AND DIRECT MANIFESTATION OF CHRIST FROM HEAVEN, OF HIS ALL-CONQUERING DIVINE POWER, AND OF HIS DIVINE VICTORY.

(SYMBOLIZED BY THE LION.)

INTRODUCTION.

1. DISTINCTIVE CHARACTERISTICS OF THE SECOND GOSPEL.

The Gospel by Mark, like that of Matthew, presents the *theocratic* side of the life and acts of Christ; while Luke and John bring out prominently their *universal bearing*, or application to mankind generally. On this common ground, however, it occupies a position distinct from that of Matthew. Matthew sets forth our Saviour as the New Testament King of the Jews, in whom the Old Testament has been completely and throughout fulfilled; Mark, on the other hand, exhibits Him in His independent Personality, as that new and absolute manifestation of the Deity in Israel which the whole Old Testament was designed only to pre-announce and make ready for. Matthew presents the history of the Lord as that of the true Prophet, Priest, and King, in His conflict with the spurious representations of these set up by traditionalism; while Mark shows how all the powers existing in the world, representing as they did the various phases of unbelief, rose in opposition to the Lord, and how all were vanquished by His absolute, victorious power. Hence, in the narrative of Matthew, the history of Jesus is presented as the summing up and culminating of the martyrdom of all the Old Testament worthies and prophets, as that deepest and fullest suffering which, through the Spirit of all grace, becomes and forms the expiatory service of the great High-Priest; in the Gospel of Mark, on the other hand, the element of victory and of triumph (Isa. ix.) appears, and is scarcely kept in the background, even amidst the scenes of intensest suffering. In the narrative of Matthew, Christ enters upon the scene in order to remove the conditions and limitations which had hitherto beset the course of history, and from His own infinite vantage-ground to transform it, and give it new direction; in the Gospel by Mark, the coming of Christ is presented as the absolute breaking up of the former state of things, by which the elements of the old broken world are reduced to subservient material out of which the new kingdom of salvation and of liberty is constructed. The first Evangelist delineates for us the life of Jesus in its theocratic aspect, and as bearing upon universal history; the second shows that, besides this human bearing, the life of Jesus, both in its nature and working, carries the direct impress of divinity. Thus the Gospel of history is followed by the history of the Gospel; the Gospel which details mighty suffering, by the Gospel which delineates mighty achievement; the Gospel which has appropriately been symbolized by the sacrificial bullock, by that to which even antiquity attached the symbol of the lion. (*See* the *Introduction to the New Testament*, p. 26.)

Hence, in tracing the Gospel history, Mark seems to have viewed his subject mainly in the light of that prophecy of the patriarch Jacob: "Judah is a young lion" (Gen. xlix. 9)—a prediction taken up once more by Hosea (xi. 10) and by Amos (i. 2), and swelling into a note of triumph in the last pages of Scripture (Rev. v. 8). Accordingly, although the great adversary of that Lion, even Satan himself, goeth about like a roaring lion (1 Pet. v. 8), he is not a lion in the genuine and spiritual sense. The simile applies only allegorically, in reference to his bold appearance in the open persecution of believers; in its higher symbolical meaning, that title belongs to the Lord Himself. In this respect, Peter has well described the agency of Christ (Acts x. 38) as "healing all that were oppressed of the devil." Mark delineates Christ as, from first to last, pre-eminently the victorious Conqueror of all Satanic powers. He has left us a record of the manifestation of Christ's power, when that great Lion seized upon the ancient world, and of His brief but decisive victory, after which only the ruins of the ancient world are left, which in turn furnish the materials for the new one.

This Gospel of the intrinsic power and life of Christ, in its original freshness, as it is reflected in the kindred soul of the Evangelist, possesses a great variety of distinguishing characteristics, both of a negative and positive kind. It is on the ground that it springs out into record from his own peculiar individual life, that we account for the conciseness of this the briefest of the Gospels, and not primarily on that of the historical occasion for its composition (Mark, one of Peter's Evangelists, relating the events of evangelical history by way of explaining his preaching). We can understand thus, why there is apparent in it no deliberate leisurely contemplation of things and events; why meditation gives place to rapid and picturesque description; why he omits the longer discourses of Jesus, and, when he does record any of His discourses, selects those burning words of controversy, denunciation, judgment, or triumph; why, occasionally, there is an indulgence in hasty, dashing expression (such as not to "put on two coats," ch. vi. 9); and towards the close he even breaks off abruptly and begins again (ch. xvi. 9); and why the arrangement of his material, though distinct, is so often obscured by the rapid succession of the great events described, that Papias suggested that Mark had not written in the order of succession, such as he conceived it to have been (οὐ τάξει, Euseb. iii. 39).

These negative traits owe their origin to the positive characteristics of this Gospel. The deeds of divine heroism which it describes, find, as it were, an appropriate body in peculiarities of expression, whether by an accumulation of strong negatives (οὐκέτι, οὐδείς) and by rapid transitions, or by rapid succession in the narrative. In fact, the word εὐθέως may be designated as the appropriate watch-word of our Gospel. While Matthew transports us gradually into the events of his time, as he relates what "came to pass in those days," the peculiar expression "immediately," "forthwith," "straightway," employed by Mark, hurries us from one event to another. So frequently, indeed, does the term occur, that ancient copyists not unfrequently questioned its authenticity, and in Codex D it is even omitted in several instances. (*See* Credner, *Introd.* i. p. 102.) It is this vividness of description also that leads to the frequent use of the present tense in the narrative (ch. i. 21, 40, &c.), and to the introduction of the very language used by individuals (ch. iv. 38, v. 8, &c.). On the same ground also, the identical Aramæan words are introduced which were employed in the actual occurrence (ch. iii. 17, 22, v. 41), and the new, customary, or popular expressions of the time are used (δηνάριον; κεντυρίων). But while the Evangelist rapidly sketches his great picture, he also greatly delights to dwell on those particular events which form its essential features. That enthusiasm and vividness of realization which account for the brevity, rapidity, and somewhat dramatic tone of the narrative, also explain the introduction of details which seem to give life to the scene. Thus we have certain graphic touches of description,—such as Christ being in the wilderness among wild beasts; the cursed fig-tree withering to the root; Jesus asleep on a pillow in the hinder part of the vessel while crossing the lake. Along with those lifelike touches of the historian's pencil, which appear in the delineation of that beautiful simile in ch. iv. 26, or in that of the gradual cure of the blind man in ch. viii. 22, we also find a freshness and accuracy of recollection, as in recalling, for example, the name of Bartimæus, the son of Timæus, the blind beggar on the road to Jericho, and a childlike affectionateness, leading to the frequent use of diminutive forms of expression, such as "little daughter," "little child," &c. Lastly, from the same causes there is a marked accuracy of details in reference to the persons introduced on the scene, the particulars of time and place, numbers, secondary circumstances, and other small points, more especially when the Evangelist describes the miraculous cures performed by the Lord. (*See* CREDNER, p. 103 *seq.*) Thus the second Gospel may be characterized as that of a rapt beholding of the Son of God manifesting His divine power by His divine working. The victorious work of Christ passes before us in a series of great life-pictures, rapidly succeeding each other. His mission of pardon and grace is accomplished in a few great stages, each the result of deepest energy and zeal, and the manifestation of His inmost life. It is as if the heavens were rent asunder, and were eternally pouring down their richest showers of blessing. Hence, also, both the attractive and the repelling influence of Christ are sharply and decisively set before us; the enmity of unbelievers rises immediately into mortal hatred, while the people, on the contrary, gather around Him in thronging crowds, bearing with them those who need His help. Sometimes there is not even room to stand, nor leisure so much as to eat. "Nay, His active love shines forth in such bright effulgence, and kindles such enthusiasm among the multitudes which surround Him, that on one occasion His kinsmen were about forcibly to remove Him from the throng, from an apprehension that He was beside Himself (ch. iii. 21). He produces the deepest impression on the people; they are filled with wonder, astonished beyond measure, and dismayed, wherever He makes His appearance to manifest His power and love." The effects produced correspond to the influence felt. "He healed many, insomuch that they rushed upon Him for to touch Him, as many as had plagues." Wherever His arrival is announced, the sick are brought from all the neighborhood, and laid in the street on their couches; and they beseech Him that they might touch if it were but the hem of His garment, "and as many as touched Him were made whole." Even His appearance among them causes the people to be greatly amazed, so that they tremble for joy and awe (ch. ix. 15). But every deed He performs is a victory over the hostile powers. Mark's Gospel is, not so deeply pervaded by the anticipation of death as that of Matthew. Even of Christ's last words on the cross, only these are recorded: "My God, My God, why hast Thou forsaken Me?"—as if in this hour of agony, also, we were to hear only the Lion's cry of woe. In the same manner, in the history of the resurrection, only its astounding features are prominently brought forward. In their distress, the disciples believe not the tidings of His resurrection, whether from the lips of Mary Magdalene, or from those of the two disciples to whom He had appeared by the way. But as soon as Christ Himself appears among them, and upbraids them with their unbelief, they are completely changed; they are now ready to receive the commission to preach the Gospel to every creature. A continued manifestation of His power attends, after His resurrection and ascension, the messengers of Christ, and confirms the word. Thus characteristically closes the Gospel by Mark, even as, throughout his narrative, his eye was mainly fixed on those miraculous and healing manifestations of divine power by which the world was shaken and transformed. In this respect his narrative is unique; it exhibits the life of Christ as divine power pervading the world. Throughout, it presents the history of Christ as the working, manifestation, and influence of the God-man. From the pages of Mark we gather how, at the time, He touched every chord of feeling in the souls of the people—amazement, fear, confidence, hope, joy, and delight; and how He adapted His divine power to those varying states of emotion, whether by reproof, healing, or sanctification. The rapidity with which the Saviour achieved such immense results, the impetuous enthusiasm which characterizes that day's work in which He pervaded the world with the power and efficacy of His name, and the victorious strength with which He triumphed over the bondage of the world and the sorrows of the grave, and rose to His throne of glory, are here presented as the grand characteristics of the divine Redeemer, who accomplishes His work of redemption by a series of rapid victories. At the same time, this glorious life of work and victory is to serve as a symbol, in the light of which we are to view and to understand every deed wrought in the name of the Lord, every awakening and vivifying operation in hearts divinely moved, every triumph of christological power, every lion-like bound, shout, and victory of faith on earth,—in short, every outgoing of that eternal energy which proceeds from the throne of the Son of God. (*See* LANGE, *Life of Jesus*, i. p. 248.)

Another peculiarity of our Gospel deserves special mention. It will readily be noticed that the Evangelist lays emphasis on the periods of pause and rest which rhythmically intervene between the several great victories achieved by Christ. Each fresh advance, each new contest and victory, is preceded by a period of retirement. Thus, the Saviour, at the commencement of His work, leaves the obscure abode of His humiliation at Nazareth, that by humble submission to the baptism of John, He might insure His victorious progress. Thence He retires into the wilderness; again and again He repairs into the desert, to issue forth anew and to achieve ever larger conquests. Even His ascension is presented at the close of our Gospel under the peculiar aspect of Christ retiring in order to conquer, by His power and blessing, the whole world, through the instrumentality of His ambassadors. (*See* this feature fully brought out in Section 5.)

[To this sketching of LANGE may be added the remarks of a thoughtful English critic, which strikingly agree with it. "There are many, again, whose sympathies are entirely with the present, who delight in the activity and warmth of daily life, who are occupied with things around them, without looking far beyond their own age and circle. To them St. Mark addresses a brief and pregnant narrative of the ministry of Christ, unconnected with any special recital of His birth and preparation for His work, and unconnected, at least in its present shape, with the mysterious history of the Ascension. . . . It seems natural to find in St. Mark a characteristic fitness for his special work. One whose course appears to have been marked throughout by a restless and impetuous energy was not unsuited for tracing the life of the Lord, in the fresh vigor of its outward power. The friend alike of St. Paul and St. Peter, working in turn in each of the great centres of the Jewish world, at first timidly sensitive of danger, and afterwards a comforter of an imprisoned apostle, himself 'of the circumcision,' and yet writing to Gentiles, St. Mark stands out as one whom the facts of the Gospel had moved by their simple force to look over and beyond varieties of doctrine in the vivid realization of the actions of the 'Son of God.' For him teaching was subordinate to action; and every trait which St. Peter preserved in his narrative would find a faithful recorder in one equally suited to apprehend and to treasure it." WESTCOTT, *Study of the Gospels*, pp. 205, 213, 214.—*Ed.*]

§ 2. HISTORY OF MARK THE EVANGELIST.

In the Book of Acts, the writer of our Gospel is first designated as John Mark (ch. xii. 12, 25), then as John (ch. xiii. 5, 13), and lastly as Mark (ch. xv. 39). Comp. Col. iv. 10; 2 Tim. iv. 11; Philem. 24. Originally he seems to have borne the Jewish name of John; but it must not be imagined that on entering upon the duties of an Evangelist, he arbitrarily adopted the Roman name of Mark. His familiarity with the Latin, which may be gathered from the circumstance that he afterwards became "the interpreter of Peter" (his ἑρμηνεύτης, according to Papias in Euseb. iii. 39, Iren. iii. 1 *et alia;* also Tertullian, Jerome); may have been due to some connection between his family and Italy. His father, or some other of his relatives, may have been a proselyte from Rome; or else a wealthy family like that of Mark may have had other reasons for giving him, along with the Hebrew, a Roman name. Certain it is that, in his capacity of companion to the Apostles, he is generally designated Mark, just as Saul took the name of Paul when engaged in his great work. Later ecclesiastical tradition has in the present, as in other instances, availed itself of this circumstance to transform our Evangelist into two or three saints. The Evangelist Mark was represented as being a different personage from John Mark; and again, these two as distinct from the relative of Barnabas (compare the art. *Mark* in WINER, *Real Encycl.*). Among later divines, Grotius, Calovius, and Schleiermacher (*Stud. u. Krit.* for 1832), and still more recently Kienlen (*Stud. u. Krit.* for 1843, p. 423), have endeavored, though unsuccessfully, to maintain the existence of two biblical personages of the name of

Mark,—the one a companion of Peter, the other of Paul. The fact that Mark acted as Evangelist alternately in connection with Paul and with Peter, is readily accounted for, both from the vitality and mobility of his temperament and character, and from the mutual understanding and accord between the two Apostles themselves. Nor is there more solid reason for including Mark among the seventy disciples,—upon the conjecture that he was one of those who were offended by the saying of Christ, about the necessity of eating His flesh and drinking His blood (John vi. 53, 60), but was afterwards restored through the admonitions of Peter. Stronger probability attaches to the supposition that Mark himself was the young man, of whom he relates in his Gospel (ch. xiv. 51), that on the night of the Lord's betrayal he followed Him clothed in a light night-dress, which he left in the hands of the officers when he fled from them (Comp. OLSHAUSEN, LANGE, *Life of Jesus*, i. p. 245, and our comment on this passage). From the Book of Acts, we gather that the mother of Mark was a wealthy proprietress; and the supposition does not appear far-fetched, that she may have owned a country-house in the valley of the Kidron, at the foot of the Mount of Olives,—perhaps even the garden of Gethsemane. At any rate, there is a striking resemblance between the character of that young man and the life of Mark, in whose quick and ardent, but mobile and inconstant disposition sin required to be especially met and conquered by sovereign grace. Thus we find that, while Mark boldly accompanied Paul on his first missionary journey, he suddenly forsook him, but afterwards again recovered himself, and offered his services in other expeditions of the same kind. For further particulars respecting the young man mentioned in ch. xiv. 51, *see* the Notes below.

As already noticed, Mark was the son of an influential Christian matron of Jerusalem, called Mary, in whose house the disciples were wont to meet for united worship, according to the custom of those days (Acts xii. 12). Mary had wholly devoted herself to the cause and service of Christ; for at a time when James the Elder had just fallen by the sword of Herod Agrippa, and Peter lay in prison awaiting a doom from which he was only delivered by a miracle, she risked her all by converting her house, so to speak, into the principal church of Jerusalem. Indeed, so well was this understood, that after his miraculous liberation from prison, Peter at once directed his steps to her house, as the great centre and meeting-place of the disciples. The son of such a woman—a worthy companion of the other heroic Maries of the Gospels—could not but be early acquainted with the blessed truths of Christianity. From the expression in 1 Pet. v. 13 (υἱός μου), it has been inferred that the Apostle Peter had been the instrument of his conversion. That his religious convictions, however, depended not on those of any man in particular, is evidenced by the fact, that his peculiar relation towards Peter did not prevent him from joining Paul and Barnabas on their return from Jerusalem to Antioch, probably with a view to that missionary tour on which he afterwards accompanied them in the capacity of an evangelist or minister (ὑπηρέτης, Acts xiii. 5). But this step was probably taken, mainly at the suggestion of his uncle Barnabas (Mark was ἀνεψιός to Barnabas, Col. iv. 10). We are not informed on what ground our Evangelist deserted the mission at Perga in Pamphylia, and returned to Jerusalem. Luke is silent on the point; although Paul regarded the conduct as so blameworthy, that when he and Barnabas resolved to undertake a second missionary tour (Acts xv. 36), he firmly refused to accept the proffered assistance of Mark (Acts xv. 38). Nay, of such importance did he deem the matter, that, when Barnabas insisted on allowing his nephew to accompany them, Paul, rather than yield, separated from his old companion, and that, too, although he was in many respects under considerable obligations to one who, under the influence of that love which thinketh no evil, had first introduced him to the Apostles at Jerusalem, and afterwards, with an unselfishness truly Christian, had brought him to Antioch, to share in the work going on in that city. We cannot doubt that Barnabas had spiritual grounds for his conduct in reference to Mark, beyond a mere natural feeling for his young relative, and that large-hearted charity of which he otherwise had given proof (*See* Acts iv. 36). Still, it may be supposed that the well-merited reproof administered by Paul, proved of greater use to Mark in after-life than the apology offered for him by Barnabas. It is just possible that, at the time, some of the views on which Paul acted in his missionary labors had appeared too liberal to the young convert from Jerusalem. Even Barnabas does not seem to have always felt equally confident on the subject (Gal. ii.). Suffice it that the presence of Mark was the occasion of "sharp contention" and separation between the two missionaries, who now took up different fields of labor. Paul went from Syria directly to Cilicia; while Barnabas took ship for Cyprus, his native island, where also, on his first journey he had commenced a mission. It deserves special notice, that while Paul was in the habit of commencing a missionary tour by revisiting the place where on a former occasion he had first labored, he this time ceded it to Barnabas. It is on this occasion, that Luke for the first time designates our Evangelist simply by the name of Mark (Acts xv. 39). But the spirit of apostolic peace soon overcame the temporary misunderstanding and disagreement. Hence, we afterwards find Mark among the assistants of Paul during the time of his first captivity at Rome (Col. iv. 10; Philem. 24), *i. e.*, about the year 62. At a somewhat later period, however, he seems to have been with Peter at Babylon (1 Pet. v. 13), whence the Apostle, addressing the disciples in Asia Minor, sends salutations from Marcus his son. For we regard the following as settled points: First, that Babylon means the place of that name, and not Rome, as it could have served no rational purpose to conceal the name of a place under a mystical title, which might so readily be misunderstood; secondly, that the First Epistle of Peter bears evident marks of having been composed at the time when the persecution of Christians throughout the Roman Empire was just beginning, and the Jews were preparing for their last great war of nationality, *i. e.*, some time after the year 62. But as, during his second captivity, Paul charged Timothy (2 Tim. iv. 11) to bring Mark with him to Rome (probably from Asia Minor), the supposition is probable, that our Evangelist was at the time returning from Babylon. It is easily supposable, that in those great and portentous days—when, in rapid succession, the Epistle of James, that to the Hebrews, and the First Epistle of Peter were addressed to Jewish Christians, with the view of warning them against the danger of apostasy, and of entreating them to bear with patience the trials and sufferings which were approaching—Mark had been employed as the medium of special communication between Paul and Peter. At any rate, there is nothing strange in an interchange of service in the common work of the Lord, just as Silas was both a companion of Paul, and also engaged with Peter in the work of the Lord. Such special missions would be peculiarly in consonance with the bold and valiant character of Mark; and hence, we do not wonder to find him ranged by the side of the chief Apostles, like a young lion, at the most dangerous points of attack, now at Babylon, and now again at Rome. But from this commission of Paul to Timothy, it does not necessarily follow that the latter was in circumstances to obey it. In all probability, Peter arrived at Rome about the same time as Mark; as there is sufficient evidence of the fact, that Peter suffered martyrdom at Rome along with Paul, about the year 68. This fact, again, is the foundation for the other statements of antiquity (Papias in Euseb. iii. 39; Iren. iii. 1, and others), to the effect, that Mark acted as interpreter (ἑρμηνεύτης) to Peter. Nor is it necessary to suppose, with Kuinoel, that, according to this statement, Mark translated into Greek what Peter spoke in Aramæan; nor, with Meyer (who quotes from Jerome a statement evidently marked with a dogmatic bias), that the expression Hermeneutes merely meant a secretary, whose duty it was to put on paper the oral communications of the Apostle (Comp. MEYER, *Introd. to the Gospel of Mark*, p. 2). It is evident that Mark, who was familiar with the manners and language of Rome, could render important assistance to Peter in Italy, as "interpreter" in the strictest sense, and that too, notwithstanding the apostolic gift of tongues. It is also sufficiently well attested (Euseb. vi. 14; Clemens Alex. *Hypot.* 6) that Mark was with Peter at Rome,—a statement wholly unconnected with the ecclesiastical hypothesis, according to which the Babylon of 1 Pet. v. 13 means the city of Rome (Euseb. ii. 15; Hieron. *Vir. Ill.* 8). The Gospel of Mark presents evidence of a protracted intercourse with Peter, as plainly as that of Luke shows that this Evangelist must have enjoyed continued intercourse with Paul. It is indeed true, that the New Testament idea of the kingdom of God is not so fully developed in the Gospel of Mark as in the Epistles of Peter; yet the narrative of the Evangelist presents Christ chiefly as the Lord of that kingdom, and as the conqueror of Satan and his legions,—and that in so marked a manner, as if the sacred historian had adopted for his motto the testimony of Peter, Acts x. 28. Similarly, also,

Irenæus (iii. 1; comp. Eusebius v. 8) records that, after the death of the Apostles Paul and Peter at Rome, Mark, as the disciple and interpreter of Peter, wrote down the statements of that Apostle. According to the testimony of Clemens Alexandrinus (*Hypot.* 6; *see* Euseb. vi 14), Mark composed his Gospel during the lifetime of Peter, in accordance with the request of that Apostle's converts, and Peter, who was cognizant of the fact, did not interpose in the matter. (For other similar testimonies, *see* CREDNER, p. 113.) In that case, we must, of course, not confound the first draft with the final revision of the work. According to the unanimous testimony of antiquity, Mark went, after the death of Peter, to Alexandria, where he founded a Christian church (Euseb. iii. 39), became its first bishop, and suffered martyrdom (Epiphan. *Hæres.* li. 6; Euseb. ii. 16; Hieron. *Vir. Illust.* ii. 8, and others). The city of Venice, it is well known, has selected St. Mark as its patron-saint, and consecrated the renowned church of St. Mark to his name.

There is an entire correspondence between the character of Mark, and that of his Gospel. And this is another evidence of the fact, that the human form and aspect of a Gospel depended on the individuality of the Evangelist, and on the point of view which he took, deciding him in selecting, arranging, and presenting the historical material at his command. It may yet require some time before views like these will prevail in the schools, and the common error be discarded, that the auxiliaries and aids which the writer had enjoyed were the main thing, and the mental characteristics of the historian only secondary, if, indeed, at all to be taken into account. Mark the Evangelist, ardent and energetic (a kindred companion to Peter), kindly, warm-hearted, and affectionate (a nephew of Barnabas, in the spiritual sense also), liberal and original in his views (a friend of Paul), was called by the Lord to transmit unto the Church a Gospel, in which it is shown how the Lion of the tribe of Judah became the Lamb of God, and how all human heroism finds both its harmony and transfiguration in the glorious achievements and conquests of the God-man. Thus the Gospel of actual personal suffering, follows that of history and of historical suffering. [Lange's thought seems to be, that Mark represents the God-man in his concrete and actual personality, almighty both in his miracles and his passion, while Matthew presents him more as an object of prophecy.—*Ed.*]

§ 3. COMPOSITION AND INTEGRITY OF THE GOSPEL.

The oldest testimony as to the origin of the second Gospel is that of Papias, Bishop of Hierapolis, dating from the first half of the second century, and communicated by Eusebius (*Hist. Eccles.* iii. 39): "Mark, being the interpreter * of Peter, wrote down with great accuracy whatever he interpreted (in other words, what Peter stated), though he recorded not in the order (οὐ μέντοι τάξει) in which it was spoken or done by the Lord (*i. e.*, as Matthew, who arranged and combined together the sayings and the history of the Saviour); for he neither heard nor followed our Lord (as His disciple), but, as before said, he was afterwards the companion of Peter, who arranged his instructions as was necessary (for popular teaching *i. e.*), but did not give a history of our Lord's discourses (which was one of Matthew's main objects). Wherefore Mark has not erred in any way by writing some things as he remembered them. For he was careful of one thing, not to omit anything of what he had heard, or to falsify (or add) anything in these accounts." It appears to us, that in his excessive anxiety to vindicate the apostolic authority of this Gospel, Papias has represented the undoubted fact of a connection between Mark and Peter, as if the Evangelist had been merely the penman of the Apostle. Hence the other ancient testimony, derived by Clement of Alexandria from primitive tradition, and recorded in extracts from the Hypotyposes (in Euseb. vi. 14), must be regarded as supplementary of this account. According to the statement of Clement, a great number of those who had heard Peter proclaiming the word of God at Rome requested Mark, who had followed the Apostle for a long time, and well remembered what he had said, to reduce to writing what the Apostle had declared. It is added that Peter was cognizant of this, and

* [Lange translates by the word *gedolmetscht.* The original is ἐμνημόνευσε, and denotes what Peter related from memory.—*Ed.*]

encouraged it (the work as a whole); while, at the same time, he abstained from all active interference, either in the way of directing or restraining (in its individual parts). We leave it to others to translate the passage so as to mean that he neither hindered nor encouraged (προτρεπτικῶς) the matter. His encouragement of the work as a whole (προτρεπτικῶς) consisted in this, that he did not find it necessary to omit anything from, or to add unto, its individual portions. It was the approbation of a work bearing evidence of independent authorship. This view of the passage agrees with the earlier account in Eusebius (ii. 15). In both cases, the ostensible reason assigned for the work is the same. We are told that Peter was cognizant of the fact that Mark had composed the Gospel by the revelation of the Holy Spirit, and that he rejoiced in the zeal of those who solicited the Gospel; finally, that he gave his authority to the work in order that it might be read in the churches. On these grounds the earlier Fathers were warranted in designating our Gospel as that of Peter, so far as its substance is concerned, without thereby invalidating the originality of Mark, so far as the style and arrangement of material are concerned. (Justin, *c. Tryph.*: τὰ ἀπομνημονεύματα Πέτρου; Tertull. *c. Marc.* 4, 5: "Marcus, quod edidit Evangelium Petri adfirmetur, cujus interpres Marcus"; Euseb. ii. 15; Hieronym. *Vir. Ill.* 8.)

A very slight examination will suffice to convince the student, that in the third Gospel the distinctive mental characteristics of Luke coincided with the views of the Apostle Paul, and exactly met the wants of well-educated Grecian inquirers and converts. Similarly, in our Gospel we note how the mental characteristics of Mark corresponded with the manner in which Peter presented the truth, while at the same time they also harmonized with the wants of Roman Christians, and were peculiarly suited to the popular mind in the capital. This fact, along with the special occasion for the composition of the Gospel, must be regarded as giving its tone to the narrative. But before proceeding to consider this factor, we must refer to, and refute, some of the more popular theories on the subject. These are: 1. Mark was merely a compiler, who derived his Gospel from those of Matthew and of Luke, if not from the former alone. 2. The Gospel of Mark was the original record from which the other two were copied. 3. The Gospel of Mark and those of the other two Evangelists were equally derived from a primitive Gospel or tradition. 4. The Gospel of Mark was written for a special purpose (*Tendenzschrift*). Lastly, 5. The special notion of those who carry their views of inspiration so far as to ignore throughout Scripture, and in our Gospel also, all human individuality.—The first of these views was propounded in its most extreme form,—*viz.*, that Mark was merely the *pedisequus et breviator* of Matthew,—by Augustine, *De consensu Evang.* 1, 2, and after him by Euthym. Zigadenus and Michaelis. In a less extreme manner, Michaelis, Griesbach, Saunier (*On the sources of the Gospel of Mark*, 1825), Theile, Strauss, Von Ammon, and others, maintain that our Evangelist made use of Matthew and Luke. To this we reply, 1st, That Mark introduces a number of things not mentioned at all in the other Gospels (ch. iii. 20, 21, iv. 26–29, vii. 31–37, viii. 22–26, ix, 11–14, xiv. 51, 52, xvi. 9–11); and that he is marked by a peculiar way of presenting matter which he has in common with the others (ch. i. 42, v. 4, 5, vii. 3, 4, ix. 21–26, x. 24, 34, 49, xii. 32–34). 2. The Gospel of Mark commences and closes in an independent manner, and the material which it has in common with Matthew and Luke (39 sections), with Matthew alone (23 sections), or with Luke alone (18 sections), is presented in an independent form. Hence, these critics felt it necessary to modify the original hypothesis of Augustine as stated above.—The second hypothesis, that the Gospel of Mark contains the original and primitive record from which the other narratives were derived, was first propounded by Herder, and adopted by Storr, Wilke, Weisse, Reuss, and Ewald. Of late, critics have even gone further, and assigned to our Evangelist the authorship of the Book of Revelation (HITZIG, *On John Mark; or, which John was the author of the Book of Revelation?* Zürich, 1843). But it is evident that the other two Evangelists furnish too many details of their own—such as the history of Christ's infancy, the longer discourses of Jesus, &c.,—to warrant us in supposing that their narrative was derived from Mark. Add to this the consideration, that they also have their peculiar manner of presenting and arranging the evangelical history.—The third hypothesis, of the existence of some primitive Gospel, from which the canonical Gospels were derived, may now be regarded as finally discarded. The Aramæan Matthew, to which Papias refers, could not have been that primitive Gospel, as Corrodi and others suggest (*see* EBRARD, *Evangelien Kritik*, p. 5), since our first Gospel is itself a Greek version of it. The same objection applies to the Gospel of the Hebrews (Niemeyer and others), which was merely a Judæo-Christian and interpolated edition of Matthew; while the hypothesis of Herder and of Eichhorn, of an original Gospel now wholly lost, is evidently a baseless fiction. Greater importance attaches to the supposition of the existence of an original evangelical *oral tradition* which, in some considerable degree, became fixed in a written form (Eckermann, Gieseler) Nor is it a sufficient objection to this hypothesis, that the Apostles at an early period became separated from each other; for each original witness told and retold the evangelical narrative of and by himself. There was a mutual and unceasing narration of the same history. Moreover, we gather from Luke i. 1, that at a very early period there existed individual sketches, memorabilia, relating to events in the history of our Lord. It will be readily understood how witnesses of such events would feel constrained to write down these glorious facts; nor is it improbable that such narratives may have been disseminated, until they were incorporated into, or superseded by, the four Gospels. But this hypothesis of an original Gospel must be modified in its application, in three respects: 1. The first, second, and fourth Gospels are evidently derived from the personal recollection of the Apostles; and the third Gospel, at least indirectly. 2. The unique style of the Gospels, their peculiar apostolic simplicity, could have been produced only by the continuous influence of the apostolic spirit. 3. So far as the form is concerned, the mental individuality of the Evangelists constituted a most important element in shaping the historical materials at their command.—In reply to the fourth hypothesis, defended by Baur, Schwegler, Köstlin, and others, that the Gospel of Mark was written with a special object, it is sufficient to say, that this has fallen to the ground along with the peculiar notions about Ebionism upon which it was reared. The main source whence the Gospel narratives were derived was the vivid recollection of the Apostles, deepened, strengthened, and purified by the Spirit of God. Thus Mark depended on the narrative of Peter, which shaped itself in accordance with the peculiar point from which that Apostle viewed the facts of the Gospel. As a secondary source of information, our Evangelist, no doubt, drew from that general evangelical tradition, which had in particular instances been chronicled by eye-witnesses. As to the origin of this tradition, it is of great importance to bear in mind, that both the evangelical narratives themselves, and the peculiar form in which they were couched, originated in evangelical faith and feeling, and that their integrity, affectionateness, and simplicity were due to the inspiration of these writers. Thus, our Evangelist drew his materials from subjective recollection (on the part of Peter), which in turn rested on the more general basis of objective recollection (in apostolic tradition). This material took form in agreement with his particular charisma; *i. e.*, objectively under the influence of inspiration by the Spirit, and subjectively under that of his mental idiosyncrasy.

According to the statement of Irenæus (iii. 1), Mark published his Gospel after the death of Peter and Paul (ἔξοδον, not their departure, as Mill, Grabe, Ebrard, and others render it). There is no contradiction between this and the statement of Clement of Alexandria, to the effect that this narrative had been composed during the lifetime of Peter, as Irenæus refers not to the commencement, but to the close of its composition. For the purpose of introducing the apocryphal story of the victory of Peter over Simon Magus at Rome, Eusebius has fixed the time of the Apostle's stay in the capital in the third year of the Emperor Claudius (A. D 43), evidently post-dating it. The publication of Mark's Gospel must have taken place between the year 68 and 70. That it was written prior to the destruction of Jerusalem, we gather from the circumstance that in ch. xiii. the Evangelist relates the prediction of that event without referring to its fulfilment. Hence it must have been composed about the same time as that by Matthew and probably that by John; the Gospel of Luke having been published several years earlier.

According to the testimony of Clement, Eusebius, Jerome, and others, the Gospel of Mark as composed at Rome—a tradition which is credited by most modern theologians. Richard

Simon and others, on the strength of a statement by Chrysostom that Mark's Gospel was written at Alexandria, have conjectured that it existed in a twofold recension. A comparison of the notice in ch. xv. 21 with Acts xi. 20, led Storr to adopt the untenable hypothesis that it was composed in Antioch.

As our Gospel was, in the first place, intended for Roman Christians, it naturally addressed itself mainly to such as had formerly been Gentiles. Still, it cannot be inferred, from the total absence of Old Testament proof passages (with one or two exceptions), that it was exclusively designed for Gentile Christians (Meyer). We have already seen that it is one of the characteristics of Mark, to evince Christ to be the Son of God by His immediate divine working. That Mark introduces no Judaizing elements (Köstlin), is a trait which he has in common with all the New Testament writers. On the other hand, it cannot be doubted that, when the ardent Evangelist found himself addressing Latin readers, this may have influenced his style, as in the choice of Latin expressions (ch. vi. 27, vii. 4, 8, xv. 39, 44), in giving explanation (ch. xii. 42, xv. 16), and in making certain additions (ch. x. 12, xv. 21).

There is the strongest historical evidence in favor of the genuineness of Mark. Besides the general ecclesiastical testimonies, commencing with Justin Martyr's Memorabilia and Tatian's Diatessaron, and those of Irenæus, Clement, and Tertullian, we have a sufficiently clear quotation in Justin and the primitive testimony of Papias in his favor, as in that of Matthew. But, just as the testimony of Papias in favor of Matthew has been turned against him by putting a peculiar meaning upon the words *τὰ λόγια*,* so in the present instance also it has been sought to invalidate the evidence in favor of our Gospel by an appeal to the expression *οὐ τάξει*, used by Papias. This view was first propounded by Schleiermacher in the *Studien und Kritiken* (1832), and for a time adopted by Credner, although that writer has since discarded this interpretation. The criticism of Schleiermacher was based on the ungrounded hypothesis, that Mark's Gospel was written in chronological order. Meyer refers the expression *οὐ τάξει* to the first outlines of notices which Mark had made after hearing the discourses of Peter, and which were afterwards revised and arranged. In our opinion, the language of Papias refers more particularly to the contrast between the Gospel of Mark and the careful arrangement adopted by Matthew (of whom he had previously spoken), especially in recording the Lord's discourses. Baur, as might be expected, supposes that the original Gospel of Mark was a work similar in character to the Clementines; Köstlin speaks of an original Gospel by Peter; while other writers indulge in similar fancies. In support of such freaks of critical imagination, each of these critics appeals to the *οὐ τάξει* of Papias, no matter whether it was originally well or ill founded, or is at present properly or improperly interpreted. Others, such as De Wette, have cast doubts upon the testimony of Papias, in order thus to invalidate the authenticity of Mark. According to Ewald, there were many recensions of Mark, which underwent different variations. All these suggestions are sufficiently refuted by a proper appreciation of the internal testimony of Mark's Gospel itself concerning its authorship.

The conclusion of ch. xvi. 9–20 has given rise to critical difficulties and doubts, which are better founded than any of those above referred to. Eusebius did not admit the authenticity of this passage (ad Marin. Quæstio I.), remarking, that in almost all manuscripts Mark's Gospel closed with a description of the flight of the women from the sepulchre. Jerome (though not uniformly), Gregory of Nyssa, and Euth. Zigabenus make the same statement. Besides, the passage is wanting in the Vatican codex B.; † and the Syriac Philoxeniana adds, that the close of the Gospel was different in other codices. Credner points out certain divergences in this paragraph from the ordinary modes of expression employed in this Gospel. He asserts that, while the distinctive characteristics of Mark are wanting in this passage, others not found throughout his Gospel may be traced there. Among the latter, are such expressions as *πᾶσα κτίσις, γλώσσαις καιναῖς λαλεῖν*, etc.

On the other hand, it should be noticed: 1. That Irenæus (adv. Hæres. iii. 10, 6) was acquainted with the present conclusion of our Gospel, as appears from the following passage:

* See LANGE, on *Matthew*, p. 42; [FISHER: *Essays on the Supernatural Origin of Christianity*. Scribner, New York, 1866.]
† [Also in *Codex Sinaiticus*.—*Ed.*]

In fine autem Evangelii ait Marcus (xvi. 19): *Et quidem dominus Jesus, postquam locutus est eis, receptus est in cœlos et sedet ad dexteram Dei.* Considering how much older and more important the testimony of Irenæus is than that of Eusebius, we are naturally led to suppose it more likely that our present conclusion of the Gospel was originally found in all manuscripts, but was afterwards left out from ecclesiastical prejudices (because the Apostles were reproved in it, etc.), than that it was afterwards added. 2. In opposition to those codices in which this portion was wanting, we have the evidence of other codices in which it existed. 3. While the fact that minor characteristics of Mark—such as the expressions εὐθέως, πάλιν—are wanting in this section, is prominently brought forward by opponents, the leading features of the passage are overlooked. But these are quite characteristic of our Evangelist, and show the conclusion of his Gospel to be quite in unison with the total narrative itself. Among these we reckon the fundamental idea of the section, that the risen Saviour overcame the unbelief of His disciples, and the promise of the Lord, that those who believed on Him should triumph over devils and serpents, and over the powers of death. The form and contents of the section, also, correspond with the idea of the Gospel generally. The strong expression, "*Preach the Gospel to every creature,*" is in keeping with the statement at the beginning of the Gospel, "*Jesus was with the wild beasts;*" as are also the closing words, "*The Lord confirming the word with signs following.*" Add to this, that the Gospel could not have closed with verse 8, without being fragmentary. Still, we cannot ignore the fact, that at an early period the Gospel of Mark seems to have existed in twofold recension or form. This we have, in another place (LANGE, *Leben Jesu*, i. 166) explained by the supposition that an incomplete work of the Evangelist may have circulated among the Christian public before our present and complete Gospel. A certain degree of probability attaches to this hypothesis from the circumstance, which the Fathers record, that the Roman Christians were very anxious to obtain Mark's Gospel. "This rapid compilation and publication, followed by delay and hesitation in view of new materials, and, lastly, the final completion of the work, are so many traits in accordance with the general character of Mark, as it is otherwise known to us." Nor should it be forgotten that, as hierarchical views gradually spread in the Church after the third century, the fragment in question may have excited greater interest from the fact that the Apostles had been presented by Mark in an unfavorable light in his narrative of the resurrection. Considerations like these may have weighed with such men as Eusebius. Thus, it would almost seem as if the very characteristics of the Evangelist, appearing in the passage, had given rise to the doubts about its authenticity. In this paragraph, as in his Gospel generally, Mark seems mainly bent upon presenting the risen Saviour in the full majesty of His power, as He transforms, by one stroke, the remaining unbelief of His followers into a faith that overcomes the world.—The authenticity of this section has been impugned by Michaelis, Griesbach, Credner, Ewald, Hitzig (who, however, ascribes its composition to Luke), and many others; among them Meyer, who designates the passage as an "apocryphal fragment." Its authenticity is defended by Richard Simon, Wolf, Bengel, Kuinoel, Hug, Guerike, and others.

In consequence of the supposition that Mark had composed his Gospel at Rome, and for Romans, the idea was broached in the Syrian Church, that he had originally written it in Latin. Hence the subscription of the old Syriac Peshito runs in these words: Completion of the Holy Gospel, the announcement of Mark; which he uttered and proclaimed at Rome. This view reappears in the Philoxeniana and some Greek manuscripts. Baronius availed himself of it in his Annals (ad ann. 45), for the purpose of adding to the authority of the Vulgate, and he was followed by others. Since the time of Richard Simon, however, the hypothesis has been abandoned, even by Romanist writers. A supposed Latin autograph of Mark's Gospel at Venice has been found to be a fragment of the Vulgate. The older Fathers partly imply, and partly expressly state, that Mark wrote in Greek.

§ 4. THEOLOGICAL AND HOMILETICAL WORKS ON THIS GOSPEL.

For those exegetical and homiletical works which treat of the Gospel of Mark along with other smaller or larger sections of the New Testament, we refer the reader to the General Introduction, and the remarks prefatory to the Gospel by Matthew.* To the writings there enumerated, we would add, the *Commentary on the Scriptures of the Old and New Testament,* by Drs. VAL. LOCH and W. REISCHL (Roman Catholic), Regensb., 1827; and *Luther's Exposition of the Gospels,* edited by EBERLE, Stuttg., 1857. Besides these, we would mention BESSER'S *Bible-Hours* (*Bibel-Stunden*) HARMS' and JOSEPHSON'S works on the *Sermon on the Mount.* For the older commentaries on the Gospel by Mark, *see* LILIENTHAL'S *Evangelium secundum Marcum;* DANZ'S *Universal-Wörterbuch,* Art. *Markus;* and WINER'S *Handbuch,* i. 247. ROLLE, J. B. KOPPE, and WILKE, have written in defence of the originality of Mark's Gospel; while the opposite view, that he was dependent upon Matthew, has been maintained chiefly by GRIESBACH and H. SAUNIER. Compare also the works of KNOBEL, HITZIG, BAUR, and others. Of homiletical works, we specially mention those by SCHLEIERMACHER (Berlin, 1835), C. BRIEGER (Berlin, 1856), and W. L. BAUER (Dillenb. 1859).

§ 5. FUNDAMENTAL IDEA AND ARRANGEMENT OF THE GOSPEL ACCORDING TO MARK.

We find the motto of this Gospel in the declaration of Peter in Acts x. 38,—"Jesus of Nazareth, anointed by God with the Holy Ghost and with power, who went about doing good, and healing all that were oppressed of the devil, for God was with Him."

Jesus, the mighty God (אֵל גִּבּוֹר, Isa. ix. 6), who broke through all fetters and bonds, appeared as a Divine Person, both in His origin, mission and preparation, and as Prince of the kingdom of heaven engaging in warfare with, and achieving the victory over, Satan and his powers. Throughout, the narrative presents to view a continuous series of victorious onslaughts, like the leaps of a lion, followed by withdrawals on the part of Christ. Each victory is succeeded by a withdrawal with the acquired booty, which serves as preparation for fresh progress. The ascension of the Lord forms His last withdrawal, which is to be followed by His final onset and absolute victory.

Part First.

Grand preparation. Royal appearance of Jesus *by the side of* John the Baptist. First manifestation, when He quits the retirement of His humiliation at Nazareth, and first withdrawal.—In principle and germ all the succeeding contests are now decided. (Ch. i. 1–13.)

1st Section.—John (vers. 1–8).

2d Section.—Christ (vers. 9–13).

Part Second.

Royal appearance of Christ *after* the Baptist. His conflicts and victories in Galilee, in the old Jewish Church. (Ch. i. 14–ix. 50.)

1st Section.—Announcement of the kingdom of heaven (ch. i. 14, 15).

2d Section.—Conquest of the first disciples at Capernaum, victory over the demons in that city, and withdrawal into the wilderness (vers. 16–35).

3d Section.—Conquest of disciples in Galilee, victory over the demons in the country, and withdrawal into the wilderness (vers. 36–45).

4th Section.—Attracting and repelling influence of the Lord. The multitude filled with enthusiasm; the traditionalists offended. Conflicts with the powers of evil under the form of traditionalism. Hardening, and mortal hatred of the hostile party, and withdrawal of

* LANGE, on *Matthew*, pp. 19, 42, 43.

Jesus into a ship. (The preaching in synagogues gives place to that on the sea-shore.) (Ch. ii. 1–iii. 12.)

5th Section.—Conflict of Jesus with the unbelief of His countrymen, and withdrawal into the villages (ch. iii. 13–vi. 6).

6th Section.—Conflict between Jesus and the hostility of Herod. Calling and mission of the Apostles. Beheading of John, and withdrawal into the wilderness on the other side of he lake (vers. 7–45).

7th Section.—Contest between Jesus and the scribes of Jerusalem, and withdrawal into the Pagan country about Tyre, and into the region of Decapolis (ch. vi. 46–viii. 9).

8th Section.—Decisive conflict between Jesus and the Pharisees in Galilee, and withdrawal to the mountains east of the lake. The preparation for the new Church (ch. viii. 10–ix. 29).

9th Section.—Retirement of Jesus in Galilee, preparatory to His journey to Peræa and Jerusalem. Further preparation for the new Church (vers. 30–50).

Part Third.

Conflicts and victories of the Lord in Peræa. Transition from the old to the new Church. Withdrawal of the Lord for the purpose of collecting the disciples for His last journey. (Ch. x. 1–34.)

1st Section.—Carnal views of the Pharisees, and spiritual law of the Lord, concerning marriage.

2d Section.—Rabbinical notions of the disciples, and theocratic and New Testament arrangements of the Lord (vers. 13–16).

3d Section.—Temporal riches of the world, and poverty of believers (vers. 17–31).

4th Section.—Solemn gathering of the disciples on the road to impending sufferings (vers. 32–34).

Part Fourth.

Conflicts and victories of the Lord in Judæa. Christ founding the new Church. (Ch. x. 35–xv. 47.)

1st Section.—The departure and the triumphal entry of Jesus into Jerusalem (ch. x. 35–xi. 26).

2d Section.—Decisive conflict of Jesus with His enemies at Jerusalem, and withdrawal of the Saviour to the Mount of Olives (ch. xi. 27–xiii. 37).

3d Section.—The Saviour's conflict of suffering, and His rest in the grave. Withdrawal into the realm of the dead (ch. xiv. 1–xv. 47).

Part Fifth.

Resurrection of the Lord. The great victory, and appearance of the Victor in the midst of the Apostles for the purpose of completely establishing the new Church. Ascent to heaven (or last withdrawal), to achieve His victory throughout the whole world. (Ch. xvi.)

1st Section.—The risen Saviour victorious *for* the Church; or, preparation for belief in the resurrection. The three Easter messages: the angel, the woman, the two men (vers. 1–12).

2d Section.—The risen Saviour victorious *in* the Church, sweeping away the unbelief of the disciples, perfecting their faith, and giving them their glorious message and commission (vers. 13–18).

3d Section.—The risen Saviour ascending to heaven victorious *with* the Church, confirming the "word" and message of the disciples throughout the world (vers. 19, 20).

These periods of rest and withdrawal on the part of the Saviour, preparatory to fresh progress and victory, are also noticed by the other Evangelists, but not in so striking a manner as in Mark's Gospel. In two instances, indeed, they appear less clearly, showing that, while it was the leading idea of Mark to indicate these contrasts, his Gospel was nevertheless not strictly and uniformly constructed or arranged upon such a plan. We subjoin a brief survey of the Gospel, with the view of setting more clearly before the reader these contrasts of withdrawal and renewed progress.

The Prelude: John in the wilderness; John arousing the whole country.

Fundamental Fact: Jesus (the Son of God) concealed in Nazareth; glorified in consequence of His baptism in the river Jordan.

1. Sojourn of Jesus in the wilderness; His appearance in room and stead of John; conquest of Capernaum.

2. Retirement of the Saviour into the wilderness; evangelization of Galilee until the preliminary conflict with traditionalism, ch. i. 40, &c.

3. Retirement of Jesus into the wilderness (ch. i. 45); commencement and completion of the conflicts in Galilee.

4. Retirement (from intercourse with the synagogue) to the ship, and commencement of the open-air sermons (ch. iii. 7); and also, of the contest of the Saviour, in fellowship with His disciples, with the unbelief of the people.

5. Retirement to the villages in the mountains (ch. vi. 6); and reappearance of the Saviour, to enter, in fellowship with His disciples, into conflict with the enmity of Herod—in the way of healing and feeding the people.

6. Retirement into the wilderness on the other side of the Lake of Galilee (ch. vi. 30); and reappearance of the Saviour to enter into conflict with the scribes of Jerusalem. Preliminary separation from Judaism.

7. Retirement into the Gentile border-land of Tyre and Sidon, and to Decapolis (ch. vi. 24, &c.); and decisive conflict with Pharisaism in Galilee. Final separation from the hierarchical party.

8. Retirement to the mountains on the other side of the Lake of Galilee, and secret sojourn in Galilee (ch. viii. 13–ix. 50); journey to Peræa.

9. Gathering of the disciples on the journey to Jerusalem (ch. x. 32), triumphal entry into the city, and decisive conflict in Jerusalem. Separation from the temple and the ancient theocracy.

10. Retirement of Jesus to the Mount of Olives (ch. xiii. 1), and reappearance to enter on His conflict of suffering.

11. Rest and concealment of Jesus in the grave (ch. xv. 42), and reappearance in the personal victory and triumph of His resurrection. Victory over the realm of the dead.

12. Ascension of Jesus; being His personal retirement from this earth and His reappearance in the victories achieved by His Church. Victory over the world.

We conceive that there is scarcely any room for questioning the correctness of this arrangement, except perhaps so far as sections 5 and 9 are concerned. But section 5 certainly bears a special mark in the calling of the Twelve, which was preceded by solitude and prayer. And if it be objected that the theme of section 9 holds no very prominent place in Mark's Gospel, we reply that it occupies a highly prominent one in the Gospel of John, as the last sojourn of Jesus preparatory to His triumphal entry into Jerusalem (John xi. 54 etc.). And even in Mark's Gospel it is indicated with sufficient distinctness, provided we attach their full and proper meaning to those important words in ch. x. 32: "καὶ ἦν προάγων, etc., καὶ ἀκολουθοῦντες ἐφοβοῦντο," "καὶ παραλαβὼν πάλιν τοὺς δώδεκα," etc. Meyer rightly observes: "Hitherto the disciples had only partially and timidly followed Him; most of them, filled with consternation, had left Him by the way. But now the Saviour halted on His journey, and again called the Twelve around Him. This event marks the gathering of the disciples of Jesus in the wilderness of Ephraim for the solemn and avowed purpose of surrender to the final entry into Jerusalem, and all that it implied." In this progressive series of victorious conflicts, the four chosen Apostles form the first conquest of Jesus—the final subjection and possession of the whole world, His last triumph!

THE

GOSPEL ACCORDING TO MARK.

PART FIRST.

GRAND Preparation. Christ's kingly appearing *by the side of* John the Baptist. First Victory and First Withdrawal. The virtual Decision of all subsequent Conflicts and Victories (CH. I. 1–13).

FIRST SECTION.

JOHN THE BAPTIST.

CHAPTER I. 1–8.

(Parallels: Matt. iii. 1-12; Luke iii. 1-20; John i. 19-28.)

1, 2 The beginning of the Gospel of Jesus Christ, the Son of God: As it is written in
the prophets,[1] Behold, I send my messenger before thy face, which shall prepare thy
3 way before thee;[2] The [A] voice of one crying in the wilderness [desert], Prepare ye
4 the way of the Lord, make his paths straight. John did baptize in the wilderness, and
5 preach the baptism of repentance for the remission of sins. And there went out unto
him all the land of Judea, and they of Jerusalem [the Jerusalemites], and were all[3] bap-
6 tized of [by] him in the river of Jordan, confessing their sins. And John was clothed
with camel's hair, and with a girdle of a skin about his loins; and he did eat locusts
7 and wild honey; And [he] preached, saying, There cometh one mightier than I after
8 me, the latchet of whose shoes I am not worthy to stoop down and unloose. I indeed
have baptized you with water: but he shall baptize you with the Holy Ghost.

[1] Ver. 2.—We regard the testimony of Irenæus and other fathers, with Codd. A., P., as sufficient to establish the reading ἐν τοῖς προφήταις, against the reading of Codd. B., D., L., and others, ἐν Ἠσαΐᾳ τῷ προφήτῃ, which Griesbach and most recent critics would prefer on their authority. That the text was changed into the form which it has in our reading is scarcely conceivable; on the other hand, the reading "in Esaias" might have been inserted from the second citation through an inexact reminiscence, especially as Mark is not elsewhere accustomed to quote minutely (ch. xi. 17; xii. 10; xiv. 27). If the reading "in Esaias the prophet" be preferred, the passage of Malachi must be regarded as a further development of the main passage in Isaiah, which is made prominent as the first announcement of the forerunner.

[2] Ver. 2.—Ἔμπροσθέν σου is not sufficiently supported.

[3] Ver. 5.—The πάντες belongs to the inhabitants of Jerusalem, according to the best MS., and does not come after ἐβαπτίζοντο.

EXEGETICAL AND CRITICAL.

Ver. 1. **The beginning of the Gospel.**—The superscription includes from vs. 1 to 3, closing with the words, "make his paths straight." The Evangelist designs by both passages (vs. 2 from "behold," etc., and vs. 3) to indicate the forerunnership of John. Hence the beginning goes on, according to Meyer, to vs. 8, and not, as Ewald says, to vs. 15. There is an analogous superscription in Matt. i. 1. When Mark points to John the Baptist as the beginning of the Gospel, he refers to its whole development, and this logically leads to and includes the narrative of the Infancy. But he does not include in his design generally, *processes* and *means:* hence John also must come upon the scene as the mature man. In this concise and sudden introduction, the Evangelist himself appears before us in all his own peculiarity. Indeed, this beginning of the Gospel was in the apostolical age the customary commencement of evangelical tradition, and as such always accompanied the apostolical preaching. It always started with the appearance of John the Baptist. The history of the Infancy and the doctrine of the Logos followed later for the initiated, the believers.—**Of Jesus Christ** (genitive of the object), **the Son of God.**—Matthew: The Son of David. In Mark, the theocratic relation of Jesus recedes, as he wrote especially for Gentile Christians.

Ver. 3. **In the wilderness.**—*See* on Matthew iv. 1. So also Luke iv. 1.—**The baptism of repentance.**—Baptism as not only obliging to change of mind (μετάνοια), but also exhibiting and symbolizing it.—**For the remission of sins.**—Meyer rightly: To be received from the Messiah; and not, as Hoffmann in the *Schriftbeweis* asserts, as assured by John's baptism. Thus it denotes the preparatory reference of John's baptism to Christ, or to the baptism of the Holy Ghost.

Ver. 5. **All the land of Judea, and** (even) **all they of Jerusalem.**—Peculiar to Mark, is this strong expression. But it is so far not hyperbolical, as the Baptist had at this crisis overpowered and led captive, not only the consciousness of the people, but that of the hierarchy also.

Ver. 6. **And John was clothed.**—*See* on Matthew iii. 4.

Ver. 7. **There cometh one mightier than I after me.**—Present. Decision and vigor of the Baptist, reflecting itself in the view of the Evangelist. Christ is already in the company.—**To stoop down.**—Pointing to his self-depreciation and humility. In this picturesqueness, peculiar to Mark.

Ver. 8. **With the Holy Ghost.**—As Mark does not record the severity of John's preaching, and his announcement of the judicial work of Jesus, he omits the clause "and with fire." Thus the omission proves nothing against the genuineness of the clause.

DOCTRINAL AND ETHICAL.

1. Jesus the Christ, and Christ the Son of God, n the full apostolical meaning. Thus the Gospel of the manifestation of the Mighty One of God is described and opened.

2. The Baptist is here, as in the Gospel of John, ch. i., the representative and final expression of the whole Old Testament. But the Old Testament itself, terminating in him, becomes one great forerunner, and the voice of the Spirit of God in the wilderness, which proclaims the manifestation of Christ; that is, it becomes a compendious introduction to the original New Testament, springing from heaven.

3. John appears here as at once summing up his office as forerunner: 1. Himself the preparer of the way; 2. and the voice summoning to prepare the way. For the prophecies of Isaiah and Malachi, *see* on *Matthew* iii. 3.

4. The great baptism of John: its seemingly slight, but yet great and decisive, results.

5. John in the desert as a hermit; John arousing the land: preludes of the Lord's self-humiliation and withdrawals, and of His victorious comings forth into the world.

HOMILETICAL AND PRACTICAL.

The beginning of the Gospel of Christ in the manifestation of the Baptist: 1. In his appearance, as described by the prophets; 2. in his vocation (preaching and baptism); 3. in his demeanor; 4. in his alarming influence; 5. in his reference to Christ.—The two Testaments, as they concurrently glorify Christ as the Lord.—How far the Lord will have a way prepared for Him, and how far He makes a path for Himself.—Repentance and faith a miraculous path through the wilderness.—The confession of sin, and its significance for piety: 1 Oftentimes, alas! nothing, or less than nothing; 2. oftentimes very much; 3. oftentimes everything.—John's great renunciation of the world, the silent condition of his great influence.—The hermit and the shaken land.—Collectedness in secret, victory in the world.—The two strong men, with whom the kingdom of heaven breaks into the world: 1. John, the strong man; and 2. Christ, the stronger than he.—The anointing of the Holy Ghost: the consummation of the baptism of Christ.—The greatness of John the Baptist, that he always, and in all things, points out of and beyond himself: 1. A preparer of the way, who summons his people to prepare their own way; 2. baptizing, and preaching the baptism of repentance; 3. the overcomer of the people, who predicts Christ as overcoming himself; 4. pointing from his own water-baptism to the baptism of the Spirit.—The baptism of water and the baptism of Spirit.—The heroic constancy and decision of John in his work, a symbol for all believers.

Starke:—Thus the last messenger of the old covenant points to the first of the new. Thus truth agrees with truth.—The New Testament looks back to the Old.—The wilderness in which the Baptist appeared, a shadow of this world.—Word and sacrament the two essential elements of the preaching office.—Preachers furnished with the Spirit and power may have great concourse around them; but Israel soon becomes weary of the manna, John vi. 66.

Gerlach:—John's baptism as the conclusion, and consequently also the epitome, of all that the legal economy contained in itself.—It was not itself to communicate forgiveness of sins, but prepare the way for it.—Even Christians should not despise such preparations through the law for the Gospel.—In times of great declension in morals, the servants of the Lord appear with a special self-renunciation even in external things. So the ancient Elijah, 2 Kings i. 8.—Gossner:—A preacher should be only a messenger who proclaims the coming of the Lord and Saviour.—W. L. Bauer:—The man of humility, who aimed only to prepare the way.

SECOND SECTION.

CHRIST.

Chapter I. 9–13.

(Parallels: Matt. iii. 13—iv. 11; Luke iii. 21—iv. 13; John i. 29–42.)

9 And it came to pass in those days, that Jesus came from Nazareth of Galilee, and
10 was baptized of [by] John in Jordan. And straightway coming up out of [from, απο[1]]
the water, he saw the heavens opened [parted], and the Spirit, like a dove, descending
11 upon him. And there came a voice from heaven, *saying*, Thou art my beloved Son, in
12 whom[2] I am well pleased. And immediately the Spirit driveth him into the wilderness.
13 And he was there in the wilderness forty days tempted of Satan; and was with the
wild beasts; and the angels ministered unto him.

[[1] Ver. 10.—The reading of the Received Text is ἀπό, which is also adopted by Scholz, and agrees, moreover, with Matt. iii. 16. But Lachmann, Tischendorf, and Meyer, following B., D., L., and the Gothic Version, read ἐκ. Griesbach also favored this reading. The English Version "out of" accords with the latter reading, but not with the former. The use of the two prepositions is seen in Luke ii. 4: "And Joseph also went up from (ἀπό) Galilee, out of (ἐκ) the city of Nazareth," &c. "Beyond doubt," remarks Winer, "ἐκ indicates the closest connection; ὑπό, one less strict; παρά, and more especially ἀπό, one still more distant."—*Ed.*]

[2] Ver. 11.—After B., D., &c., Lachmann and Tischendorf read ἐν σοί, "in Thee."

EXEGETICAL AND CRITICAL.

Ver. 10. **Straightway,** εὐθέως.—Mark's watchword, constantly recurring from this time onwards. But here it means that Jesus only in a formal sense submitted to the act, and therefore did not linger in it. Much in the same way as Luke hastily passes over the circumcision of our Lord.—**He saw the heavens.**—Not John (as Erasmus and others), but Jesus is the subject of the seeing (Meyer): yet the concurrent and mediate beholding of the Baptist is not excluded; *see* John i. That the occurrence should not have been only an external one, but also an internal (*Leben Jesu*, ii. 1, S. 182), Meyer calls "fantasy." But it is certain that without the fantasy of theological spiritual insight we cannot penetrate the internal meaning of the text, and must fall now into mere dogmatism, and now into rationalistic perversions.

Ver. 12. **And immediately the Spirit driveth Him.**—Ἐκβάλλει is stronger than the ἀνήχθη of Matthew and the ἤγετο of Luke.

Ver. 13. **And He was there forty days tempted of Satan.**—According to Meyer and others, Mark (with Luke) is here out of harmony with Matthew. This difficulty springs from neglecting to distinguish, 1. between real difference and less exactitude, and 2. between the being tempted generally of Satan, and the being tempted in a specifically pregnant and decisive manner. But it is evident that Mark places the crisis of Christ's victory already in the baptism. That act of victory over self, and humiliation under the baptism of John, had already assured Him the victory over the now impotent assaults of Satan.—**With the wild beasts.**—The older expositors find in this circumstance a counterpart of the serpent in paradise. Starke:—The wilderness was probably the great Arabian desert, and Satan attacked Him also through the beasts. Usteri and others:—Christ as the restorer of paradise, and conqueror of the beasts. De Wette:—This is a mere pictorial embellishment. Meyer:—He is threatened in a twofold manner: Satan tempts Him, and the beasts surround Him. But this is a misleading view. A threefold relation of Jesus is here depicted, 1. to Satan, 2. to the beasts, 3. to the angels; and it is arbitrary to separate the second from the third, and make it the antithesis of the first. There is nothing in the μετά to justify this.—**The angels.**—Not merely fortuitous individual angels. By the individuals which minister to Him, the angel-world is represented. Meyer:—By the ministering we are not to understand a serving with food, but a sustaining support against Satan and the beasts. This is more than fantasy.—The theory concerning the various forms of the history of the temptation, of which Mark is supposed to have used the earliest and simplest, we pass over, as flowing from the well-known scholastic misapprehension of this Evangelist's original view and exhibition of the Gospel.—*Ex ungue leonem!* This holds good of Christ, as He is introduced by Mark; and in another sense it holds good of the beginning of the Gospel itself. Remark the expressions: οἱ Ἱεροσολυμῖται πάντες—κύψας λῦσαι—εἶδε σχιζομένους τοὺς οὐρανούς, etc.

DOCTRINAL AND ETHICAL.

1. The self-denial and self-renunciation with which Christ, the Son of God, had lived in the seclusion of Nazareth, was the condition and source of that strength in which He subjected Himself to the baptism of John in the Jordan. This act of subjection sealed His submission under the law, His historical fellowship of suffering with His people, and His passion. The baptism of Christ was consequently the pledge of His perfect self-sacrifice. Hence it was in principle the decision of His conflict and His victory; and therefore it was crowned with His glorification. In this one act there was a consummation of His consciousness as God, of His consciousness as Redeemer, and His consciousness as Victor.

2. Christ really decided, in His baptism, His victory over Satan. He went into the wilderness and

made it a paradise. The serpent in this paradise assaults Him, but cannot hurt Him; the wild beasts sink peaceably under His majesty; and the angels of heaven surround and serve Him.

3. John is in the wilderness, and Satan tempts him not. Jesus is led up from the wilderness into the wilderness,—that is, into the deepest wildness of the wilderness (this being the residence of the demons, *see* Com. on Matthew iv.),—and Satan comes down to assault Him there. But the Evangelist deems it superfluous to remark that Jesus overcame Satan. After what had just preceded, this was self-understood. Moreover, it is in the casting-out of the devils, that Mark presents to us Christ's concrete victories over Satan. Yet this victory is intimated in the fact that He maintained His abode in the wilderness for forty days in spite of all the assaults of the devil, and that in that very wilderness the angels ministered to Him. The incarnate Son of God could hold His heavenly court in the place which Satan preëminently arrogated for himself. The Lord's relation to His surroundings is threefold. 1. It is a sovereign and inimical one towards Satan, whose temptations appear only as impotent assaults. 2. It is a sovereign and peaceful one towards the beasts: they dare not hurt the Lord of creation, nor do they flee before Him. Jesus takes away the curse also from the irrational creation (Rom. viii.). According to the same Mark, who places this circumstance at the outset of his Gospel, Jesus commanded at its close that His Gospel should be preached to every creature. *See* Daniel in the den of lions. Comp. GŒTHE's *Das Kind und der Löwe*. 3. A sovereign and friendly one towards the angel-world. The world of the angels is subjected to the dominion of Christ: Eph. i. 21; Col. ii. 10; Heb. i.

HOMILETICAL AND PRACTICAL.

The abode of Jesus in Nazareth, or His self-humiliation, the foundation of all the Divine victories in His life, Phil. ii. 6 *seq.*—The greatness of Christ by the side of the greatness of John.—Even in humiliation Christ is above John, in that He *voluntarily* submits to his baptism.—With the submission of Christ to the baptism of John, and what it signified, the whole course of His life, and also His victory over Satan in the wilderness, were decided. Hence His tarrying in the wilderness was the festival before a new career.—The perfected unfolding of the consciousness of Christ at His baptism, in its eternal significance.—With the self-consciousness of Christ was perfected the consciousness of the Son of God and of the Son of man at one and the same time: Thus, 1. the consciousness of His eternity in His Godhead, and 2. of His redeeming vocation in His humanity.—The significance of perfect self-knowledge in self-consciousness: 1. Finding self, 2. gaining self, 3. deciding and dedicating self in God.—The kindredness and difference between the development of the Redeemer's consciousness and that of the sinner: 1. Kindredness: humiliation, exaltation. 2. Difference: *a.* Christ's humiliation under the judgment of His brethren; *b.* the sinner's under his own judgment;—*a.* Christ's exaltation through the contemplation of the communion of the Trinity; *b.* the sinner's exaltation through faith in the fellowship of the Redeemer.—As our consciousness, so our history: This holds good, *a.* of our true consciousness, *b.* of our false.—The abode of the Baptist and of the Lord in th wilderness, a token of the destruction of the satanic kingdom.—The inseparable connection between the divine dignity and the redeeming vocation of Christ: 1. He is Christ, and submits to John's baptism of repentance; 2. He sees the heavens open upon Him, and enters into the depths of the wilderness to contend with Satan.—The connection between the Lord's baptism and His temptation.—The connection between the humiliations and the exaltations of our Lord, an encouraging sign to all who are His.—The connection between the invigorations and the new conflicts of Jesus, an admonitory sign to all who are His.—Christ takes possession again of the wilderness (the world), without asking leave of Satan whose dwelling it is.—Christ in the wilderness Ruler of all: 1. Of the abyss, whose assaults He regards not; 2. of the earth, whose wild beasts and passions sink to rest at His feet; 3. of the heavenly world, whose angels minister to Him.—Wherefore the Lion of Judah, according to Mark, so often goes into the wilderness.—How the Holy Spirit opens, with the manifestation of Christ, the decisive conflict with the spirit of apostasy.—How the Holy Spirit, as the Spirit of might, drives the Lord into the decisive conflict. Even Christ did not go led by self into the contest.—Christ changing the wilderness, despite Satan, into a paradise.—Adam in paradise, and Christ among the beasts in the wilderness.

STARKE:—Humility the best adornment of teachers.—Jesus of Nazareth (despised): So little does the great God make Himself, and thus at the same time constructs a ladder by which we may go up.—Jesus sanctifies through His baptism the laver of regeneration in the word.—Rejoice, O soul, in that God is well pleased with His Son, and with thee also, who through Him art reconciled to God! But thou must in faith be made one with Him, Eph. i. 5, 6.—As soon as we become God's children, the Holy Ghost leads us; but the cross and temptation come forthwith.—What the first Adam lost among and under the beasts, the Second Adam has asserted and regained among the beasts.—A pious man has nothing to fear, among either wild beasts or bestial men.

GERLACH:—How infinitely high does Christ stand above all human teachers, even those inspired by God.—SCHLEIERMACHER:—The legal excitement which John occasioned, and the excitement which Jesus enkindled.—GOSSNER:—Solitude and the wilderness have their temptations equally with the world.—BAUR:—No one is near to celebrate this victory, yet God's angels are there to glorify Him.

PART SECOND.

ROYAL Appearance of Christ *after* the Baptist. His Conflicts and Victories in Galilee, in the Old Jewish Church (CH. I. 14—IX. 50).

FIRST SECTION.

ANNOUNCEMENT OF THE KINGDOM OF HEAVEN.

CHAPTER I. 14, 15.

(Parallels: Luke iv. 14, 15; Matt. iv. 12-17; John iv. 43 *seq.*)

14 Now, after that John was put in prison, Jesus came into Galilee, preaching the
15 Gospel of the kingdom of God, And saying, The time is fulfilled, and the kingdom of
God is at hand: repent ye, and believe [in] the Gospel.

[1] Ver. 14.—Codd. B., L., and several cursive MSS. and versions, leave out τῆς βασιλείας. So Lachmann and Tischendorf. Meyer thinks it an exegetical addition. But what follows might also have caused the omission.

EXEGETICAL AND CRITICAL.

See on *Matthew*, ch. iv. 12-17.

Ver. 14. **Jesus came.**—Ewald: He would not let the Baptist's work fall to the ground. Meyer, on the contrary: that He might be safe; but see our Notes on Matthew in refutation of this. By the Baptist's imprisonment the Baptist community in Israel was broken up; Jesus therefore saw occasion first to receive to Himself the poor people in Gentile Galilee, and that as the representative of John. John was put in prison by the Galilean prince; Jesus summons the people of this prince to repentance, and to faith in the Gospel: this is the true political retaliation, and the sacred way to salvation and the restoration of right.

Ver. 15. **The time,** ὁ καιρός.—Not the period, but the *right* time; the great, fore-ordained, predicted and longed-for time of Messianic expectation; more closely defined by the following "the kingdom of God is at hand." (*See* Gal. iv. 4.) **Repent,** Μετανοεῖτε.—*See* the lexicon for the original meaning and the various significations of the word. [It includes the ideas of reflection, afterthought, and change of mind, *i. e.*, of judgment and of feeling, upon moral subjects, with particular reference to the character and conduct of the penitent himself. ALEXANDER *in loc.*—*Ed.*] **Believe the Gospel,** Πιστεύετε ἐν. Gal. iii. 26; Eph. i. 13.—By this expression faith is more strongly emphasized. Entering into the Gospel, we have decisive faith. The object of faith in this view is the manifestation of the kingdom of God.

DOCTRINAL AND ETHICAL.

1. From the still prayer of the wilderness, or from the new paradise in which Christ had conquered Satan, He has now come forth to endure all the individual conflicts of life for the founding of His eternal kingdom. Adam came from his paradise conquered, to endure in his descendants a constant succession of defeats.

2. As here, so everywhere, the economy of the Gospel takes the place of the economy of the law. The legal economy yields at last to the lawlessness of the world: the economy of faith and salvation triumphs over it even in yielding, and saves with itself also the ideality of the law.

3. An economy of the law which, in its tragical conflict with the spirit of the world, recognizes not the deliverance which is in the coming economy of salvation, like Elias (1 Kings xix. 13), is thereby converted into an economy of carnal precepts, which finally combines with the world against the economy of salvation. But, on the other hand, true evangelical faith knows how to give its due to the precursory office of the law, just as Christ gave honor to His forerunner, John the Baptist.

4. "Almost all the Jews of that time hoped for the kingdom of God; but it was a strange and unrecognized idea, that repentance and faith must be the entrance into it. Jesus begins with the promise, but immediately goes on to the conditions." Gerlach.

5. Mark, like Peter in his first and second Epistle, places the announcement of the kingdom of heaven at the head of his writing. The kingdom is his fundamental thought.

HOMILETICAL AND PRACTICAL.

Jesus, in the silent conflicts of the wilderness, prepares for the open conflicts of life—takes the place of John, delivered to death by the carnal mind. 1. The history: A testimony, *a.* that He honored the Baptist, *b.* that He did not fear the enemy, and *c.* that He was faithful to His people and His vocation. 2. The doctrine: *a.* The witnesses of the kingdom of God cannot be destroyed; *b.* after every seeming triumph of the kingdom of darkness, still stronger heroes of God come forward. 3. Christ is always Himself victorious at last in every scene.—Persecution the primitive furtherance of the kingdom of God.—The blood of the Church, the seed of the Church.—Where the law falls in the letter, it is re-established in the spirit.—The preaching of Christ: 1. It appears as the announcement of salvation in the place of danger and ruin. 2. What it announces: that the time is fulfilled, and that the kingdom of God is come. 3. What it requires: repentance (as change of mind, μετάνοια) and faith. 4. What it signifies: the saving presence of Christ Himself.—Christ and John as preachers: the might of their preaching itself. 1. John preaches in his whole life and manifestation; 2. Christ preaches out of the depth of His own divine life.—The seal of evangelical preaching the full harmony of the person and the word.

On the whole section (ch. i. 14–45).—The first victorious appearance of Christ the prelude of His whole path of victory: 1. In the announcement of His Gospel; 2. in His dominion over the hearts of the chosen; 3. in His victory of the kingdom of Satan; 4. in His miraculous removal of human misery; 5 in His salutary shaking of the world.—The glory of the Lord in its first actual exhibition: 1. A glory of grace (vs. 16–20), 2. of sacred judicial and redeeming power (vs. 21–28), 3. of healing mercy (vs. 29–39), 4. of purifying purity (vs. 40–44).—Christ proceeds from the wilderness of the earth into the wilderness of human life for the restoration of paradise.—Christ confirms His victory over Satan in the solitude of the desert by His victories over satanic powers among all the people.

STARKE:—Satan seeks to bind and to oppress Christ and His Gospel; but God's wisdom and power set at naught all his aggression.

GERLACH:—With the public appearance of Jesus, the end of John's work had come.—GOSSNER:—He who understands repentance to mean that he must first become pious and good, and then come to Jesus, and believe His Gospel, goes out at the door of grace instead of entering in. Repenting and believing the Gospel, or believing in Christ, must go together and be one.

SECOND SECTION.

CONQUEST OF THE FIRST DISCIPLES AT CAPERNAUM, VICTORY OVER THE DEMONS IN THAT CITY, AND WITHDRAWAL INTO THE WILDERNESS.

CHAPTER I. 16–35.

1. *The Authoritative Word of Jesus, which calls the four first and greatest Disciples.* VERS. 16–20.

(Parallels: Matt. iv. 18–22; Luke v. 1–11; comp. John i. 35–42.)

16 Now, as he walked[1] by the sea of Galilee, he saw Simon, and Andrew his brother,
17 casting a net into the sea: for they were fishers. And Jesus said unto them, Come ye
18 after me, and I will make you to become fishers of men. And straightway they forsook
19 their[2] nets, and followed him. And when he had gone a little farther thence,[3] he saw
James the *son* of Zebedee, and John his brother, who also were in the ship mending
20 their nets. And straightway he called them: and they left their father Zebedee in the
ship with the hired servants, and went after him.

[1] Ver. 16.—The expression παράγων is recommended by B., D., L., Lachmann, and Tischendorf. Instead of αὐτοῦ Lachmann and Tischendorf read Σίμωνος.
[2] Ver. 18.—Not "their" nets: αὐτῶν is wanting in B., C., L., Lachmann, Tischendorf.
[3] Ver. 19.—Ἐκεῖθεν is wanting in B., D., L., Tischendorf; bracketed by Lachmann. It accords with Matt. iv. 21.

EXEGETICAL AND CRITICAL.

See on *Matthew*, iv. 18 *seq.*

Ver. 16. **As He walked by.**—The Evangelist would make prominent the apparently fortuitous character of this first vocation.

Ver. 19. **Who also were in the ship.**—Both pairs of brothers were called while in the earnest prosecution of their craft. The first two were throwing their nets into new positions in the water; the two others were mending them for new draughts.

Ver. 20. **With the hired servants.**—Why this addition? Paulus: It was to be made clear, how they could without impiety forsake their father. Meyer (after Grotius): It was only a proof that Zebedee did not follow his craft in a petty way, and that he probably was not without means. In any case, it also shows that Zebedee was not left helpless. That they forsook so thriving a business (Ewald), is indeed of less significance.

DOCTRINAL AND ETHICAL.

1. Christ Himself is the great Fisher of men. He catches the four elect ones as it were at one draught. These are the three (Mark ix. 2) and the four (Mark xiii. 3) confidential Apostles of after-

times. Therefore there were first four fishermen called.

2. The power of Christ's word over these souls here appears direct and immediate. We learn the mediating circumstances of this vocation from John i. At the same time, this calling was something entirely new (*see* on *Matthew*, iv. 19), and their following so wonderful, that they at once forsook their calling, in the very act of pursuing it. The fishing life of these men was a preparation for their higher calling, as being fidelity in that which was least.

HOMILETICAL AND PRACTICAL.

The Lord knoweth His own.—The Lord and His elect quickly know each other.—The great increase of grace swiftly enters into our daily life.—Christ's walking by the sea apparently for relaxation, but at the same time the most noble work.—Christ's mark in this world the heart of man.—The great Fisher of men, and His art of making human fishers.—The calling of Jesus a call to become something new.—The mighty calling of the Lord: 1. Gentler than any human request; 2. mightier than any human command; 3. unique as the victorious wooing of heavenly love.—The calling of Jesus a calling at once to one thing and to many: 1. To one thing: into His discipleship and the fellowship of His Spirit, or to the Father; 2. to many: to discipleship and mastership, to coöperation, to fellowship in suffering, and community in triumph.—The greatness of the following of the four disciples was the effect of the great grace of their calling. They broke off suddenly in the midst of a new career of their labor, as sign of the decision of their following.—The spiritual and the worldly vocation of Christians: 1. Opposition; 2. kindredness; 3. union.—The twofold earthly companionship of the disciples a foundation for the higher: 1. Companions in fishing,—companions in fishing for men; 2. brethren after the flesh,—spiritual brethren.—Leaving all for Christ's sake.—The Christian and ecclesiastical vocations in harmony with the sacred natural obligations of life.

STARKE:—Never be idle.—Pious handicraft acceptable to God.—The calling into Christianity binds us to faith and the following of Christ; how much more the vocation to spiritual office!—A true follower of Christ forgets everything earthly.—He who follows Christ loses nothing, though he may forsake all; for he finds in Him a full sufficiency, Matt. xix. 29.

LISCO:—The forsaking all must be experienced inwardly by every believer; and must be fulfilled outwardly also, in particular circumstances and occasions, Matt. xix. 27.—SCHLEIERMACHER:—The two tendencies in the life of the Redeemer: preaching to the multitude, and the separation of individuals to Himself.—GOSSNER:—The Lord's fishermen actually catch the fish; the world's fishermen swim with the fish.—BAUER:—One glance of the Lord, and He knows the heart under its rough garment.

---

2. *The Word of Authority, which delivers the Demoniacs and attracts the People.* VERS. 21–28.

(Parallel: Luke iv. 31–37.)

21 And they went into Capernaum; and straightway on the Sabbath-day he entered
22 into the synagogue, and taught. And they were astonished at his doctrine: for he
23 taught them as one that had authority, and not as the scribes. And there was in their
24 synagogue a man with an unclean spirit; and he cried out, Saying, Let *us* alone;[1] what
have we to do with thee, thou Jesus of Nazareth? art thou come to destroy us? I
25 know thee who thou art, the Holy One of God. And Jesus rebuked him, saying, Hold
26 thy peace, and come out of him. And when the unclean spirit had torn him, and cried
27 with a loud voice, he came out of him. And they were all amazed, insomuch that they
questioned among themselves, saying, What thing is this? what new doctrine *is* this?[2]
for with authority commandeth he even the unclean spirits, and they do obey him.
28 And immediately his fame spread abroad[3] throughout all the region round about Galilee.

[1] Ver. 24.—Ἔα is wanting, it is true, in B., D., and others; but it is as accordant with Mark as with Luke (ch. iv. 34).
[2] Ver. 27.—Lachmann, following B., L., Δ., &c.: τί ἐστι τοῦτο; διδαχὴ καινή· κατ', &c. Tischendorf connects διδαχὴ καινὴ κατ' ἐξουσίαν. Lachmann's is better. [Meyer accounts for the Received Text, by a comparison with Luke iv. 36.—*Ed.*]
[3] Ver. 28.—Καὶ ἐξῆλθεν: "And the fame," &c.

EXEGETICAL AND CRITICAL.

The Evangelist, in harmony with his main point of view, proceeds at once to the act by which the Lord approved Himself the conqueror of the demons.

Ver. 22. **As one that had authority.**—*See* on Matt. vii. 29.

Ver. 23. **With an unclean spirit,** ἐν πνεύματι ἀκαθάρτῳ.—He was *in* the unclean spirit; that is, in his power, under his influence. Concerning the demoniac possession, *see* on *Matthew* iv. 24.

Ver. 24. **Art thou come to destroy us?**—The demoniac consciousness still predominant on the part of the demon. Hence, "to destroy *us!*" Bengel: "*Communem inter se causam habent dæmonia.*" The word involves also, 1. a testimony of the decided opposition between the demon empire and Christ; 2. a testimony of the perfect supremacy of Christ; 3. and a testimony of the beginning of the subversion of the satanic dominion.—**To destroy us.**—Meyer: By dismissing them to Hades. But even in Hades, Christ does not leave their empire to the demons. Thus it was by the destruction of their empire generally

Certainly it was by dismissing them to the Gehenna of torment (according to which, the expression in Matt. (viii. 29), the Hades of torment, is to be explained).—**I know Thee who Thou art.**—The demoniac consciousness in its involuntary presentiment. See Acts xvi. 16. It feels already the influence of Jesus, who would draw it from the side of the demon to His side. The word is ambiguous, so far as it belongs to the demon and to the man.—**The Holy One of God.**—In the emphatic sense, and thus, according to John vi. 69, Rev. iii. 7 (comp. John x. 36), the concealed designation of the Messiah. ("So Origen:" Meyer.) As the typical Old Testament anointed ones represented the Messiah, so the typical saints, priests, prophets, and kings (Ps. xvi.) represented the Holy One κατ' ἐξοχήν. The unclean spirit, however, describes Him by that opposite to himself which torments him, when he terms Him the Holy One of God.

Ver. 25. **Hold thy peace.**—This refers to the outcry of the demon. The Messiahship of Jesus was not to be prematurely spread abroad, least of all by demons. The kingdom of God and the invisible world scorns such precursors and coöperators. It bears testimony to itself by overcoming all these. Only after the decisive victory are such testimonies supplementarily, and in their own significance, admissible; then, when no intermingling is any longer possible.

Ver. 26. **Torn him.**—The decisive paroxysm with which the healing was declared; at the same time, a phenomenon exhibiting the knavish, spiteful, and degraded nature of the demons (ch. ix. 26; Luke ix. 42).

Ver. 27. **Questioned among themselves.**—The spirits are awake. They do not first ask the priests and Rabbis, but proceed to independent suppositions and conclusions.—**New Doctrine.**—From the appearance of a new power of delivering, they infer the appearance of a new revelation; for revelation and deliverance, miracle and prophecy, always to the Israelites were reciprocal in their influence. For various constructions and interpretations of this passage, *see* Meyer *in loc.*

Ver. 28. **Throughout all the region round about Galilee.**—That is, through all Galilee, and beyond into the neighboring districts everywhere.

DOCTRINAL AND ETHICAL.

1. The first miracle recorded by Matthew is the healing of the leper by a touch; for one main point of view with him was the opposition of Christ to the hierarchical theocracy and their ordinances. The first miracle which John records is the changing of water into wine; for his main point of view is the glorification of the old and darkened world into a world of spirit. The first miracle which Luke and Mark relate is this casting out of demons in the synagogue at Capernaum. But the points of view of the two latter in this matter are as different and characteristic as their respective Gospels. Luke, in harmony with his predominant object (the divine humanity of Christ), has in view preëminently the healed man. The demon threw him down, and departed from him, without hurting him at all. To Mark, on the other hand, the supremacy of Christ over the kingdom of the demons is the grand object, even as it declares and approves His doctrine to be a new one. Hence he makes it emphatic, that Christ commanded even the unclean spirits, and that they obeyed Him. This point of view runs through his whole Gospel, down to its concluding words.

2. To Mark belong the chief records of Christ's victory over the devils, while in the other Evangelists there is only a general reference to them. In John we do not find deliverances of this sort; on the other hand, he gives prominence to moral possession (John vi. 70, viii. 44, xiii. 27),—an idea which is found approximately among the other Evangelists as sevenfold possession. Further, here we must mark the relation of Christ and His kingdom to Satan and his kingdom, according to the New Testament teaching. Dogmatics must, more rigorously than heretofore, distinguish between the devil and this kind of demons, as well as between the children of the devil and these bound ones of Satan.

3. The synagogue cannot hinder a demoniac from entering it, nor that Satan should in it declare the victory of the kingdom of order and light. Christ cleanses the synagogue.

HOMILETICAL AND PRACTICAL.

Christ the Saviour of the synagogue and of the Church.—The adherence of Christ to the sanctuary of His people, legal and yet free.—By the perfect sanctification of the Sabbath and the synagogue, our Lord established the Sunday and the Church.—How the Child of the synagogue became the Prince of the Church.—Sabbath and synagogue; or, the holy time and the holy place in their symbolical meaning: 1. They signify rest from the toil of sin, and the temple; 2. the Christian Sunday and the Church; 3. the heavenly feast and the heavenly Church.—The demoniac in the synagogue; or, the daring incursion of Satan into the legitimate Church of God to be restrained only by the word of Christ.—How Christ always victoriously confronts the satanic power which insinuates itself into the Church.—Heavenly and hellish powers meet in the Church.—The healing of the possessed in the synagogue a decisive token of the redeeming empire of Christ: 1. Of His victory over the kingdom of Satan; 2. of His saving mercy to the wretched; 3. of His miraculous sealing of the Gospel; 4. of His awakening conquest of the world.—The consciousness of Christ a healing power for the consciousness disturbed by Satan.—The spiritually disturbed consciousness a figure of the curse of sin: 1. In its destruction and contradictions; 2. in its restraint; 3. in its despair; 4. but also in its dim feeling of its misery and of the coming of its Saviour.—The characteristics of the wicked: 1. Knowledge without love; 2. hatred to the Lord, and withal flattering acknowledgment; 3. pride even to madness, and yet impotent fear and flight. Or, 1. Darkness in its lie; 2. murder in its hatred; 3. death in its rending.—Christ immovably opposed to the flattery and hypocrisy, as well as to the threatening and pride, of Satan.—The antithesis of heaven and hell in the conflict of Christ with the demon: 1. Peace of soul and passion (the devil assaults first); 2. collectedness and distraction; 3. the spirit of mercy and the spirit of torment; 4. dignity and degradation; 5. victory and prostration.—Christ scorns the testimony of the demons, and obtains the praise of the people.—The glory of Christ, that He came into the world to destroy the works of the devil, 1 John iii. 8.

Starke:—The public service of God not to be

neglected, Heb. x. 25.—Unclean spirits are found even in the Church, Jas. ii. 19.—Christ will have no testimony from the spirit of lies.—OSIANDER:—If the devil must give way, yet he rages fearfully: he must, however, give place to the Holy Spirit.—GOSSNER:— The devil knew Him as the Holy One of God, but not as the Saviour.—BRAUNE:—The possessed trembles before Him who is his Deliverer.

---

8. *Healing among the Disciples; Healings and casting out of Demons in Capernaum; the first Return of Christ after He had thus dealt with the susceptible in that city.* VERS. 29–35.

(Parallels: Matt. viii. 14–17; Luke iv. 38–41.)

29 And forthwith, when they were come out of the synagogue, they entered into the
30 house of Simon and Andrew, with James and John. But Simon's wife's mother lay
31 sick of a fever; and anon they tell him of her. And he came and took her by the
hand, and lifted her up; and immediately the fever left her, and she ministered unto
32 them. And at even, when the sun did set, they brought unto him all that were dis-
33 eased, and them that were possessed with devils. And all the city was gathered to-
34 gether at the door. And he healed many that were sick of divers diseases, and cast
35 out many devils; and suffered not the devils to speak, because they knew him.[1] And
in the morning, rising up a great while before day, he went out, and departed into a
solitary place, and there prayed.

[1] Ver. 34.—Some Codd. add, "that He was Christ."

EXEGETICAL AND CRITICAL.

See on *Matthew*, viii. 14–17.

Ver. 29. **They entered into.**—Jesus, Peter, and Andrew are meant; the two latter as the ordinary occupants of the house, which Peter or both possessed in Capernaum (*see* on *Matthew*). In addition came James and John. Thus the Lord was with the collective four disciples who had been called.

Ver. 30. **And anon they tell him of her.**—Here also we have εὐθέως thrice in rapid succession. Immediately into the house, immediately to the matter in hand, immediately healed. Matthew transfers this miracle to a later period (*see* on *Matthew*). Starke for the sake of harmony: "It may have been that the mother-in-law of Peter twice had the fever, and that Christ healed her twice." (!)

Ver. 32. **At even, when the sun did set.**—The full close of the Sabbath. "*Judæos religio tenebat, quominus ante exitum Sabbati ægrotos suos afferrent.*" Wetstein.

Ver. 34. **Sick of divers diseases, and cast out many devils.**—The physically sick and the demoniacs clearly distinguished (ver. 34; Matt. viii. 16); just as they are in relation to the opposite charisms which were given with respect to them, 1 Cor. xii. 9, 10.—**And He healed many.**—Not as opposed to all who were brought to Him, but to describe the abundance and variety of the healings which took place so late in the evening.

Ver. 35. **Into a solitary place.**—To a secret place in the wilderness. It is to be noted that Jesus, according to Mark, thrice in quick succession, withdrew into the wilderness, vers. 12, 35, 45. Here we can understand only a solitude near Capernaum. That He thus took up His abode time after time in the wilderness, declared his supremacy over the demons of the wilderness. He made the desert place a temple of God by His prayers.

DOCTRINAL AND ETHICAL.

1. The succession of events marks the development of Christ's work: 1. The synagogue at home. 2. The house of Peter, as the hearth of the new community of disciples at its outset. 3. The whole town of Capernaum. 4. The entire land of Galilee.—The progression of the influence of our Lord's preaching: 1. His fame goes out through all Galilee. 2. The whole town of Capernaum presses for help at His door, yea, into His doors. 3. All seek Him after He had withdrawn. 4. Even in the wilderness they come to Him from all parts.

2. In order that they may punctiliously guard their own rest on the Sabbath, the people of Capernaum wait till evening with their sufferers, and rob the Lord of His rest in the night.

HOMILETICAL AND PRACTICAL.

Jesus the Saviour of the new as of the old community (Peter's house, the synagogue).—And they told Him of her: with faith waxes intercession.—Peter, as householder, a type of the ecclesiastic at home: 1. He is not hindered from his calling by domestic trouble (he also went into the synagogue); but, 2. he took his domestic trouble with him into his calling (he prayed the Lord for the sick).—The people at Capernaum seeking help; or, Christ the true Physician: 1. As the revealer of human misery; 2. as the marvellous deliverer from it.—An evening and a morning in the life of Jesus; or, His holy day's work: 1. Closed in the blessing of toil; 2. renewed in devotion.—The rapid diffusion of Christ's work and influence: 1. Through the believing house; 2. through the susceptible town; 3. through the amazed land.—New seclusion for new conflicts.—Private prayer the source of Christ's victories.—The Lord's early hours.—His morning devotion.—The significance of morning in the kingdom of God: 1. A festal time in the life of Jesus; 2. an image of His whole life; 3. a blessed time in the life of Christians; 4. figure of their regeneration and their eternity.—How Christ sanctifies all times and all places.

STARKE:—QUESNEL:—The dwelling of a poor fisherman pleases Christ more than a great palace.—OSIANDER:—God is oftener in little huts than in rich palaces.—Christianity and household life agree well together.—Marriage unfits no man for the ministry.—Compassionate love suffers not the wretched long to wait, but thinks at once of help.—QUESNEL:—The love of Jesus is never weary.—There are always wretched ones in this vale of tears, who stand in need of the help of the Most High.—Christ the most approved Physician.—It does not become the man spiritually possessed of the devil to reveal Christ.—Early hours must be thought much of.—For prayer even sleep must be abridged.

GERLACH:—The gracious love of Christ amidst the household necessities of the poor and neglected.—LISCO:—Jesus connects together prayer and work, solitude and public life, in order to do good.—EUTH ZIG.:—We must shun the praise of men, and thank God in silent secrecy.

THIRD SECTION.

CHAPTER I. 36–45.

1. *The Preaching and Healing of Jesus.* CH. I. 36–39.

(Parallel: Luke iv. 44.)

36, 37 And Simon, and they that were with him, followed after him. And when they had
38 found him, they said unto him, All *men* seek for thee. And he said unto them, Let us
39 go[1] into the next towns, that I may preach there also: for therefore came I forth. And
he preached in their[2] synagogues throughout all Galilee, and cast out devils.

[1] Ver. 38.—The *Rec.* omits ἀλλαχοῦ after ἄγωμεν: it is supported by B., C., L., Copt., Tischendorf.
[2] Ver. 39.—"Into their:" εἰς τὰς in A., B., D., Griesbach, Lachmann, Tischendorf. The *Textus Receptus* reads ἐν ταῖς συναγωγαῖς,—an emendation, says Meyer.

EXEGETICAL AND CRITICAL.

Ver. 36. **And Simon, and they that were with him.**—Simon placed first, not on account of any superiority, but as the head of the house and the guide.

Ver. 38. **Into the next towns.**—The κωμοπόλεις only here in the New Testament. The primary object is to record the travelling through the Galilean hill-country, and its villages and towns.—**For therefore came I forth.**—The question is, whether the meaning be, "I am come from the Father to preach generally" (Bengel); or, "I have left the house (or Capernaum) in order to preach in the neighboring villages" (Meyer). We think that Christ lays stress upon preaching as His great vocation, in opposition to the pressure of individual applicants for help in Capernaum. The former of the two interpretations seems to be the better.

Ver. 39. **In their synagogues** (into).—The accusative, twice occurring, makes it emphatic that he filled the synagogues and all Judea with a might of preaching that formed a contrast to the synagogue style.

DOCTRINAL AND ETHICAL.

1. Jesus prepared himself in the desert for His second great expedition. The spiritual awakening and conquest of the land of Galilee was now in question.

2. Here also Mark (like Luke) gives special emphasis to the casting out of devils, and to the command of silence, by which Jesus hindered the devils from uttering His name.

3. It is observed also that Jesus places preaching expressly above miraculous healings; this is seen in the use of the participle, δαιμόνια ἐκβάλλων. But the preaching has its root in the secret devotion: His public work sprang from His solitary prayer.

HOMILETICAL AND PRACTICAL.

How the Lord equipped himself anew for new labors.—Christ goes with His first four disciples into the land of Galilee: the small beginning of the universal mission.—How the Lord's preaching approves itself as the power of divine life: 1. As the spiritual word of His working; 2. as delivering power for the suffering; 3. as judicial power of victory over the demons.—Christ confronting the increasing pressure of the people: 1. How He restrains it (withdrawal into the wilderness); 2. how He regulates it (preaching on the individual miracles); 3. how He surrenders Himself to it (responding to every demand of help).—Christ does not shut up His activity within the walls of Capernaum, nor within the limits of any one people or any one confession.—The way of Christ among the surrounding villages: 1. Already to as many as possible; 2. one day to all.

STARKE:—We must have village preachers.—The Gospel of Jesus must sound out in all places.—Where Christ's kingdom is to be established, the devils must be abolished. So also in thee.—SCHLEIERMACHER:—The preaching of the kingdom of God was Christ's vocation: 1. Concerning Himself, as He who was come to save men; 2. concerning the true righteousness which avails before God; 3. concerning the worship of God in spirit and truth.—Within these limits it was His vocation to spread that kingdom as far as He could.—GOSSNER:—To this end am I come (He says) to save men.—Christ did not scorn the little towns and villages.

---

2. *The Touching of the Leper, and the Return into the Wilderness.* VERS. 40–45.

(Parallels: Matt. viii. 1–4; Luke v. 12–16.)

40 And there came a leper to him, beseeching him, and kneeling down to him,[1] and
41 saying unto him, If thou wilt, thou canst make me clean. And Jesus,[2] moved with compassion, put forth *his* hand, and touched him, and saith unto him, I will; be thou clean.
42 And as soon as he had spoken, immediately the leprosy departed from him, and he was
43, 44 cleansed. And he straitly charged him, and forthwith sent him away; And saith unto him, See thou say nothing to any man: but go thy way, show thyself to the priest, and offer for thy cleansing those things which Moses commanded, for a testimony
45 unto them. But he went out, and began to publish *it* much, and to blaze abroad the matter, insomuch that Jesus could no more openly enter into the city, but was without in desert places: and they came to him from every quarter.

[1] Ver. 40.—The omission of καὶ γονυπετῶν αὐτόν in B., D., and Lachmann and Tischendorf, is not sufficiently supported.

[2] Ver. 41.—Ὁ δὲ Ἰησοῦς omitted in B., D., &c. So Lachmann, Tischendorf. Meyer explains this omission, as also the dropping out of εἰπόντος αὐτοῦ, ver. 42, from an intention to conform the text with Matthew and Luke. So also with the μηδέν, ver. 44.

EXEGETICAL AND CRITICAL.

Respecting this narrative, and the leper, *see* on *Matthew*, viii. 1–13. The occurrence follows the Sermon on the Mount; and this is here intimated by the return of Jesus to Capernaum, ch. ii. 1.

Ver. 43. **And He straitly charged him.**—The ἐμβριμησάμενος is the opposite of the preceding σπλαγχνισθείς. Probably the leper had overstepped the limits of his discipline (lepers were not suffered to intrude into others' houses) and of the law, and had penetrated to the house where Jesus might have been tarrying in one of the towns. This Meyer reasonably infers from the ἐξέβαλεν—He forthwith sent him away. First of all, Jesus regarded the misery of the case, and, seized with compassion, healed the sick man. But then He proceeded to guard the legal obligation under which the sick man stood, and household rights and general order. Mark gives us a vivid view of the sending away of the healed man, and exhibits the scene in his own lively expressions.

Ver. 44. **To the priest.**—The Vulgate, romanizing, explains: *Principi sacerdotum.* But it only means the priest in general, whose function concerned the man.—**For a testimony unto them.**—The actual cleansing must be confirmed in a Levitically legal manner.

Ver. 45. **To blaze abroad the matter,** τὸν λόγον.—Fritzsche: The word of Jesus. De Wette: The matter. Meyer: The narrative of what had passed. There is implied, perhaps, a distinction between his narrative and the embellished report of the event which was spread abroad, and to which it gave occasion.—**Could no more openly enter.**—The reason of this withdrawal was not merely to obviate the increase of the crowd, but the fact that Jesus had touched the leper, which, according to the law, made a man unclean for a season. *See Leben Jesu*, ii. 2, 639. Moreover, this solitude imported a new withdrawal for a new advance.

DOCTRINAL AND ETHICAL.

See Com. on *Matthew*, *in loc.*

1. Wherefore does Mark close the delineation of Christ's first manifestation in public with the healing of the leper? This narrative is, first, a witness that Christ entered into the fellowship of sinners in order to suffer for them; and so far was a prelude of the end. Secondly, it marked His relation to traditionalism, the offence and assaults of which now follow.

2. The present withdrawal of Jesus took place under the presentiment of His conflicts with traditionalism, and as a preparation to meet them.

HOMILETICAL AND PRACTICAL.

The healing of the leper a testimony of the mightily cleansing purity of Christ.—Christ even in the influence of His purity the Lion of Judah.—Redemption, like creation, an omnipotent *Let there be!* (He speaks, and it is done: "I will, be thou clean.")—The need of deliverance breaking through the law. The leper presses into the house, like the paralytic through the roof, and the sinner into the Pharisee's house.—The leper a pattern of those who seek help, but not of those who give thanks: 1. His perfect trust and humble submission (If Thou wilt, etc.); 2. regardlessness of his friends, lack of docility towards the ceremonial law and of discipline.—Christ's interchange with the leper a symbol of His interchange with the sinner: He makes the leper clean, and contracts Levitical defilement. So Christ was made sin for us, that we might be made righteousness in Him.—The compassion of our Lord the source of our salvation—The miraculous hand of Christ the instrument of all heavenly healing: 1. As delivering, 2. as distributing, 3. as consummating.—The disobedience of the leper; or, lack of ceremonial discipline in the reception of healing: 1. Excusable as far as it was the interchange of illegality and freedom; 2. blamable, because he constrained the Lord (even in His Church) to atone for transitory illegality by the legalities of prudence.—Christ in the wilderness and everywhere the centre of a wretched and needy world.—Christ, through His divine compassion, involved with human traditions.—A new collectedness of the spirit, a new blessing and victory.

STARKE:—The spiritual leper.—QUESNEL:—Prayer, humility, and faith as the source (the organs for the reception) of all righteousness.—We are directed to keep all right ordinances, etc. Abide by the public service of God.—Deliverance from misery demands its right and peculiar offerings of praise.—The more a servant of God withdraws himself from the world, the more highly does the world esteem him.

GERLACH:—The healed leper was like those who, out of thankfulness of heart indeed, but yet inconsiderately, neglect the inward commandment of the Holy Spirit, and make too much talk about the grace of God, to their own and others' hurt.—SCHLEIERMACHER:—The Redeemer by His touch took away the ban which sundered the leper from all human intercourse.—Likeness between leprosy and sin.—The one leper and the ten.—BAUER:—How Jesus respected the ordinances of His people.

FOURTH SECTION.

ATTRACTING AND REPELLING INFLUENCE OF THE LORD. THE ENTHUSIASTIC MULTITUDE AND THE OFFENDED TRADITIONALISTS. MORTAL HATRED OF THE HOSTILE PARTY, AND WITHDRAWAL OF JESUS INTO A SHIP. THE PREACHING IN SYNAGOGUES GIVES PLACE TO PREACHING ON THE SEA-SIDE.

CHAPTER II. 1—III. 12.

First Conflict.—The Paralytic, and the Power to forgive Sins. VERS. 1–12.

(Parallels: Matt. ix. 1–8; Luke v. 17–26.)

1 And again he entered into Capernaum after *some* days; and it was noised that he
2 was in the house.[1] And straightway many were gathered together, insomuch that there
was no room to receive *them*, no, not so much as about the door: and he preached the
3 word unto them. And they come unto him, bringing one sick of the palsy, which was
4 borne of four. And when they could not come nigh unto him for the press, they uncovered the roof where he was: and when they had broken *it* up, they let down the
5 bed wherein the sick of the palsy lay. When Jesus saw their faith, he said unto the
6 sick of the palsy, Son, thy sins[2] be forgiven thee. But there were certain of the scribes
7 sitting there, and reasoning in their hearts, Why doth this *man* thus speak blasphemies?[3]
8 who can forgive sins but God only? And immediately, when Jesus perceived in his
spirit that they[4] so reasoned within themselves, he said unto them, Why reason ye these
9 things in your hearts? Whether is it easier to say to the sick of the palsy, *Thy* sins
10 be forgiven thee; or to say, Arise and take up thy bed, and walk? But that ye may
know that the Son of man hath power on earth to forgive sins,[5] (he saith to the sick of
11 the palsy,) I say unto thee, Arise, and take up thy bed, and go thy way into thine
12 house. And immediately he arose, took up the bed, and went forth before them all;
insomuch that they were all amazed, and glorified God, saying, We never saw it on
this fashion.[6]

[1] Ver. 1.—Lachmann reads ἐν οἴκῳ, after B., D., L.,—a gloss, says Meyer.
[2] Ver. 5.—Elzevir, Scholz, Lachmann read σοι αἱ ἁμαρτίαι; Griesbach, Fritzsche, Tischendorf, B., D., G. read **σου αἱ ἁμαρτίαι**. Lachmann, after B., reads ἀφίενται for ἀφέωνται.
[3] Ver. 7.—Lachmann and Tischendorf read λαλεῖ βλασφημεῖ, after B., D., L., Vulgata.
[4] Ver. 8.—Αὐτοί before διαλογίζονται, after A., C., E., F., Syr. (utr.), Goth., Slav., Bengel, Matth., Griesbach, Fritzsche, Scholz, Tischendorf; οὕτως erased by Lachmann after B.
[5] Ver. 10.—Various order of the words: The ἐπὶ τῆς γῆς ἀφ. ἁμ. is given by Griesbach and Lachmann, after C., D., L., and others.
[6] Ver. 12.—Tischendorf reads οὕτως οὐδέποτε, after B., D., and L., &c.

EXEGETICAL AND CRITICAL.

See the exposition on Matthew, and on Luke. Mark introduces the conflicts of the Lord with traditionalism earlier than Matthew; hence the earlier position of this narrative. Matthew, indeed, represents the chronological order, according to which the paralytic was healed after the journey to Gadara. The conclusion in Mark itself intimates that this must have been one of the later miracles.

Ver. 1. **That He was in the house,** εἰς οἶκόν ἐστι.—This means the house which Jesus occupied with His mother and His brethren, after His settlement there, ch. iii. 31. His adopted sisters probably remained, as married, in Nazareth (*see* ch. vi. 3), when the family of Joseph passed over with Him to Capernaum.

Ver. 3. **Bringing one sick of the palsy.**—*See* on *Matthew*, viii. 6. Κράββατος, a portable bed, used for mid-day sleep, and for the service of the sick.*—**Borne of four.**—Pictorial definiteness. So also the vivid description of the uncovering of the roof, or the breaking of a large opening through it. Luke tells us how they did it: "*through the tiling;*" thus they must have taken away the tilings themselves. MEYER:—We must suppose Jesus to have been in the upper room, ὑπερῷον, where the Rabbis frequently taught: LIGHTFOOT, *in loc.;* VITRINGA, *Syn.* 145. Meyer rightly rejects the view of Faber, Jahn, and others, that Jesus was in the court, and that nothing more is meant than a breaking up of the roof-awning. Certainly it is not improbable that the roof and the upper room were connected by a door; at least, the not improbable supposition of steps leading from the street to the roof suits that view. It is not at variance with the text to assume, with Lightfoot and Olshausen, an extension of the door-opening already there. Uncovering the roof can mean nothing else than actual uncovering, whether or not by means of an already existing opening. Strauss, after Wetstein, remarks, that the proceeding would have been too dangerous for those below. But *see* HUG'S *Gutachten*, ii. p. 21. Moreover, a little danger would better suit the heroism of the act. It takes for granted the Oriental house with a flat roof, to which men might gain access either through the neighboring house, or by the steps on the outside.

Ver. 6. **Certain of the scribes.**—According to Meyer, who cites Mark ii. 16, Luke (ver. 17) introduces the Pharisees too soon at this place. But why may not the scribes have been mainly of the pharisaic party? These were so manifestly.—**The scribes:**—*See* on *Matthew*, ii. 4, and the article in WINER.

Ver. 7. **Why doth this man thus speak blasphemies?**—That is, *such a man* (scornfully), *such things* (such great words as are fit only for God, or for the priests in His name). MEYER rightly: "This man in this wise: emphatic juxtaposition." The idea of blasphemy, as expressed by Mark and Luke, is shown to be direct blasphemy: they cast that upon Him, because He was thought to have wickedly intruded into the rights of the Divine Majesty.

Ver. 8. **And immediately, when Jesus perceived in His spirit.**—The Searcher of hearts. In this lay already the proof that He could forgive sins. Matthew (ix. 4) here takes as it were the place of Mark: † *Jesus seeing* (ἰδὼν) *their thoughts.*

Ver. 10. **The Son of man hath power.**—Dan. vii. 13; comp. LANGE'S *Leben Jesu*, ii. 1, 235. Meyer asserts, without reason, against Ritzschl, that Christ by this expression declared undoubtedly, and even technically, His Messiahship. Certainly Daniel's Son of Man signified Christ; but the correct understanding of this expression does not seem to have been current in the Jewish schools at this time. Hence the choice of the expression here. They should know Him to be the Messiah, not according to their *false* Messiah-notions, but according to His *true* demonstrations of Messiahship; and the expression was meant to lead them to this.

Ver. 12. **We never saw it on this fashion.**—We must assume in εἴδομεν an object seen; and that can be no other than the essential phenomenon which corresponds to essential seeing, viz.: the appearance of the kingdom of God. But it is also included, that the omnipotent working of miracles had never been so manifest in Jesus before.

DOCTRINAL AND ETHICAL.

1. *See* on the parallels in Matthew and Luke. Quickly as the glory of Christ was manifested in His first works, so quickly did the contradiction of the pharisaic worldly mind develop itself. It is most significant that the evangelical forgiveness of sins was the first stumbling-block.

2. The healing of the palsied man gives us, in a certain sense, the key to all the miraculous works of our Lord; inasmuch, that is, as the healing of the members is here definitely based upon the healing of the heart, the forgiveness of sins, awakening and regeneration. Because Christ Himself was the new birth of man from heaven, He was the principle of regeneration to sinful man. That is, in other words, because He Himself was the absolute miracle—the new principle of life breaking into and through the old—therefore the miraculous energies for the renewal of life issued from Him as sudden and great vivifications, which, proceeding from the heart of the renewed, pervaded their whole life. The quickening of the heart was, therefore, always the soul of light in the miracle; the external miracle was its dawning manifestation, though not all such quickenings resulted in permanent bodily healing. Therefore, also, the kernel of the miracle has remained in the Church, and becomes more and more prominent, that is, regeneration. The dawn has retreated and vanished, since this sun of the inner life has come forth. Yet the dynamic unfolding of the heart's renewal in the renewal of the bodily members has in reality remained; only, now that Christianity has been incorporated with human nature, it develops itself only in gradual effect, until its full manifestation in the day of resurrection. The regenerating principle works in the regenerate gradually, and in almost invisible, leaven-like influence and transformation. But, as certainly as the regeneration of the heart is effected, so certainly is the germ of the renewal of the whole life present. Our scholastic notions have too carefully separated the external miracle from the internal, making it almost of itself a higher class of miracle. Luther, however, recognized regeneration as the great and abiding miracle, and had some feeling of its connection with the resurrection, as symbolized in the Supper of the Lord.—The power of Christ over the whole life, a demonstration of His power over the centre of life, the heart.

3. Christ the Searcher of the heart, knowing all things. In His messianic vocation, in His concrete sphere of life, He proved His Divine omniscience, and that too in the personal unity of the God-man. This concrete Divine-human knowledge He Himself distinguished from the universal omniscience of the Father. STARKE:—"Christ knoweth all things even according to His human nature; not, however, through the human, *tanquam per principium quo*, but through the divine." In a certain sense, also, through the human; through human sensibility to hostile dispositions, which assuredly had its source in the Divine nature.

* Oftentimes, however, the bed was a simple mattress or sheepskin.—*Ed.*

† In picturesque descriptiveness, *i. e.*—*Ed.*

HOMILETICAL AND PRACTICAL.

See on the parallels of Matthew and Luke.—How the Lord's redeeming power, breaking in, awakens the daring courage of faith.—Christ the restorer of victorious courage on earth.—Man inventive, above all in his faith.—The inventions of faith.—The boldness of faith, which leaps out of the anguish of a believing spirit.—How the miracle of Christ is appended to the word of Christ.—The miracle not without the previous word.—The return of Christ to His town; or, Christ does not willingly leave the place in which He has once settled.—And it was noised abroad that He was in the house,—when Christ is in a church, or in a house, it cannot be hid.—The courage of faith by which they uncovered the roof, in connection with the Divine courage in which Christ uncovered their hearts.—Great faith discovers and adopts wonderful plans.—Christ the Searcher of hearts: 1. This has a many-sided confirmation, 2. is full of comfort, 3. and full of terror.—The power of the forgiveness of sins a free and legitimate prerogative of Christ's rule: 1. A free exercise of His love; 2. a legitimate administration between free grace and free faith; 3. therefore the free prerogative of Christ.—The Divine love will not be restrained by man's narrow-heartedness.—God's grace is not bound to the ordinances of man.—The Gospel makes the Church, not the Church the Gospel.—The ordinance of absolution no monopoly of absolution.—The glorious and boundless blessings which result from the forgiveness of sins.—The paralytic more troubled about his sins than about his bodily suffering.—Christ the *fundamental* Healer.—As the paralytic had a new power of moving, so the witnesses had a new power of seeing.—Only he who has seen Christ has learned rightly to see.—Christ's miracles of grace always preachers of salvation, which prepare for new miracles.—All awakenings in order to regeneration are miracles of Christ, the subsequent influences of which must be manifest in the bodily life, though, it may be, in a very gradual manner.—The harder and the easier miracle: 1. The internal miracle was, in the Lord's judgment, greater and harder, inasmuch as it was the condition of the external. 2. The external miracle was greater and harder in the judgment of His opponents, as something impossible to the absolving priests. 3. Both were equally hard, in as far as both were impossible to man; and hence the external miracle was Christ's authentication in opposition to His enemies.—The limited blessing of healing a witness for the unlimited blessing of forgiveness of sins.

STARKE:—Moving to the house of God with the crowds.—The sick should come to Christ, the true Physician.—Benevolence, and still more, Christian love, demands that we should serve and help the sick in every possible manner.—He who would be a true Christian must strive to bring to Christ others who are weak and sinful, by prayer and all good offices, Jas. v. 16.—CANSTEIN:—We must somehow come to Christ, whether through the door or through the roof; that is, either in an ordinary or an extraordinary way.—True faith, working by love, breaks through all impediments.—Love makes all things good and decorous, though they may not externally seem so.—Those who are troubled we should not trouble more, but comfort, Ps. xxxii. 1; Isa. lxi. 2.—The ungodly change the best medicines into poison, and pervert the holiest truths.—MAJUS:—The slanderer's manner is, not to try to seek what meaning the speaker has, but to pervert at once and wrest his words.—That which is visible and before the eyes seems to men harder than the invisible; and they prefer what is bodily to what is spiritual.—QUESNEL:—Christ by His visible miracles taught men to understand His invisible miracles.—The priceless benefit of the forgiveness of sins worthy of all praise and thanksgiving.

SCHLEIERMACHER:—We have two things to mark in this whole narrative: first, that which passed between the Redeemer and this sufferer; and then, what referred to the thoughts of the scribes congregated around Him.—As sure as we are that the Redeemer knew what was in man, we must assume that the sufferer thought most of the spiritual gift of Christ, and its importance to himself.—The more powerful the might of love is, as being the energy of faith, the sooner vanish all lesser evils, losing their sting, which is the consciousness of sin.—Thus we see in miniature, in this history, the whole history of the kingdom of God upon earth.—BAUER:—We can thus, by our faith and our intercession, be helpful to the good of others.

Second Conflict.—The Eating with Publicans and Sinners. VERS. 13–17.

(Parallels: Matt. ix. 9–13; Luke v. 27–32.)

13 And he went forth again by the sea-side; and all the multitude resorted unto him,
14 and he taught them. And as he passed by, he saw Levi the *son* of Alpheus sitting at
the receipt of custom, and said unto him, Follow me. And he arose and followed him.
15 And it came to pass, that, as Jesus sat [reclined] at meat in his house, many publicans
and sinners sat [reclined] also together with Jesus and his disciples; for there were
16 many, and they followed him. And when the scribes and Pharisees saw him eat with
publicans and sinners, they said unto his disciples, How is it that he eateth and drinketh
17 with publicans and sinners? When Jesus heard *it*, he saith unto them, They that are
whole have no need of the physician, but they that are sick: I came not to call the
righteous, but sinners to repentance.[1]

[1] Ver. 17.—The addition εἰς μετάνοιαν is found only in cursive MSS., after Luke v. 32.

EXEGETICAL AND CRITICAL.

See on the parallels of Matthew and Luke.—The narrative of Mark has here also its characteristic traits of vividness. A congregation of the people around Christ at the sea-side, and a discourse uttered there, form the introduction to the calling of Matthew. From ver. 15 we learn that many followed the Lord who belonged to the class of publicans and sinners (excommunicated persons). Meanwhile Matthew (ix. 13) alone has our Lord's appeal to the saying of Hosea (ch. vi. 6).

Ver. 13. **Forth** (from the town), **again** (ch. i. 16) **by the sea-side.**—Setting plainly before us the position of Capernaum, connected probably with the sea by a suburb of fishers' huts and custom-houses.

Ver. 14. **Levi** (*see* the explanation in Matthew) **the son of Alpheus.**—Not to be confounded with Alpheus the father of James the Less.

Ver. 15. **In his house.**—Not in his own house, as Meyer thinks. *See* on *Matthew*. The ἠκολούθησαν must be understood of the spiritual following of the disciples, and not merely of outward accompanying.

Ver. 16. **When the Pharisees** (*see* on *Matthew*) **saw Him.**—Not coming into the house, which is improbable; but as observers of the feast, after which they came forward towards the disciples coming out.

DOCTRINAL AND ETHICAL.

1. *See* on the parallels of Matthew and Luke.
2. The offence taken at our Lord's table-fellowship with publicans and sinners has significance, first, in respect to Church principles as against Donatism and Novatianism; and, secondly, in relation to the true idea of communion as against Confessionalism; and, thirdly, in favor of Christian and social intercourse in opposition to the narrowness of Pietism.
3. The holy intercourse of Christ with sinners, the redemption of the world, is here represented in a concentrated image.

HOMILETICAL AND PRACTICAL.

1. *See* on *Matthew*.—The multitude of the needy people gave the Lord occasion to summon helpers to Himself.—Levi (Matthew) better than his reputation: a warning against all premature condemnation of our neighbor.—How different is the glance of our Lord's eyes into the world from that of the Pharisees' eyes!—Christ in the house of publicans and sinners an offence to the Pharisee; Christ in the house of the Pharisee was not strange and repulsive to sinners (the woman, Luke vii. 37): 1. Historical; 2. typical.—The feast in which Christ is a guest.—The feasts in which Christ was a guest all-saving and decisive for souls.—The slavish dread with which our Lord's enemies come to attack His disciples.—The attempt of His enemies to turn away His disciples from the Lord.—The narrative of the gradual boldness of our Lord's opponents: 1. The features of its development; 2. its symbolical character.—The mission of Christ a Gospel for sinners, who are in evil case: 1. For them with full assurance; 2. for them preëminently, and before those who think themselves sound; 3. for them in contradistinction to the others.—Jesus come for all, according to the law that He has come only for the sick.—The feast of Christ an expression of His Gospel.—The feast of a Christian an expression of his Christian vocation.—How this history stands in full harmony with Ps. i. 1.

STARKE, QUESNEL:—Grace draws Matthew from the love of gold, and makes of him an apostle; the love of gold drew Judas away from Christ and his apostleship.—HEDINGER:—As soon as God is revealed in thee, take no long counsel with flesh and blood.—Jesus receiveth sinners.—A converted man should bring all his acquaintance to God, and take care for their salvation.—Those are shameful enemies of the truth, who put on the guise of godliness but deny its power.—QUESNEL:—He who has not love cannot understand what another may do in care for his neighbor's salvation.—Be patient, and slow to judgment, 1 Cor. iv. 3.—That in which the children of God find their joy and blessedness is hateful to the wicked.—The more a man thinks himself righteous, the further does he remove himself from Christ.—Jesus calls to repentance.—We must bring into the pastoral work a heart filled with true sympathy with the wretched, and with Jesus the Physician.

GERLACH:—Every invitation to a feast was for Jesus an occasion for issuing His invitation to the heavenly feast.—LISCO:—Jesus the *one* Physician for *all*.—SCHLEIERMACHER:—The Pharisees a pure counterpart of the publicans.—The calling to repentance (that is, to change of mind) the essence of the work of Christ.—He describes them (the Pharisees) as they described themselves; but in such a manner that they could not but see that He thought quite differently concerning them (irony).—We should always, in our friendly social life, have spiritual things in view.

Third Conflict.—The Fasting of John's Disciples and of the Pharisees. VERS. 18–22.

(Parallels: Matt. ix. 14-17; Luke v. 33-39.)

18 And the disciples of John and [of] the Pharisees[1] used to fast: and they come and
say unto him, Why do the disciples of John and of the Pharisees fast, but thy disciples
19 fast not? And Jesus said unto them, Can the children of the bride-chamber fast while
the bridegroom is with them? as long as they have the bridegroom with them, they
20 cannot fast. But the days will come when the bridegroom shall be taken away from
21 them, and then shall they fast in those days.[2] No man also seweth a piece of new [unfulled] cloth on an old garment; else the new piece that filled it up taketh away from

22 the old,[3] and the rent is made worse. And no man putteth new wine into old [skin]
bottles; else the new wine doth burst[4] the [skin] bottles, and the wine is spilled, and
the [skin] bottles will be marred: but new[5] wine must be put into new [skin] bottles.

[1] Ver. 18.—The reading of the *Rec.*, οἱ τῶν Φαρισαίων, is not supported. Griesbach, Scholz, Lachmann, Tischendorf, Fritzsche read οἱ Φαρισαῖοι.

[2] Ver. 20.—*Rec.*: ἐν ἐκείναις ταῖς ἡμέραις, is an emendation. Griesbach, Lachmann, Scholz, Tischendorf read ἐκείνῃ τῇ ἡμέρᾳ.

[3] Ver. 21.—We follow the reading: αἴρει ἀπ' αὐτοῦ τὸ πλήρωμα τὸ καινὸν τοῦ παλαιοῦ; adopted by Tischendorf and Meyer.

[4] Ver. 22.—The Present is more vivid than Lachmann's Future, ῥήξει, found, also, in B., C., D., Vulgata.

[5] Ver. 22.—The addition "new," ὁ νέος, is from Luke v. 37.

EXEGETICAL AND CRITICAL.

1. *See* on the parallels of Matt. and Luke.—The offence at Christ's meal with Levi, as it might represent similar meals, was twofold: 1. As an eating with publicans and sinners; 2. as the opposite of fasting. In the former view the Pharisees took umbrage; in the latter, the disciples of John,—the Pharisees also joining them. This offence was a point in which the legal Pharisees and the ascetic disciples of John, as spiritually related, might meet.

Ver. 18. **Used to fast:** ἦσαν νηστεύοντες.—Meyer: They were then in the act of fasting. It may be easily supposed that the imprisonment of John would give occasion to his disciples, and with them to many of the Pharisees, for an extraordinary fast (*see* art. "Fasten" in Winer). An ordinary legal season of fasting is not meant; for Christ and His disciples would not have neglected or outraged that. But if an extraordinary fast, occasioned by the Baptist's imprisonment or by any other cause, formed the primary reason of this question, yet we think that the participle is to be taken as emphatic, according to the parallels in Matthew (νηστεύουσι πολλά) and Luke (νηστεύουσι πυκνά).—**And they come.**—Of course only some, as representing the mind of all (Weisse); not necessarily all, as Meyer thinks. The combination of both parties on this point does not exclude the prominence of John's disciples, according to Matthew.

Ver. 20. **In those days.**—Emphatically, in those dark days.

Ver. 21. **Else the new piece that filled it up taketh away from the old, and the rent is made worse.**—The new piece is rent away from the old: the most approved reading is also the most expressive. The inappropriate and disproportionate is again made emphatic by the antithesis.

DOCTRINAL AND ETHICAL.

1. *See* on the parallels.

2. Compare the word concerning fasting, Matt. vi. 16. We may distinguish: 1. Legal-symbolical fasting (Lev. xvi. 29, xxiii. 27); 2. personal, real fasting—Moses (Ex. xxiv. 18), Elias (1 Kings xix. 8), Christ (Matt. iv.); 3. ascetic, penance fasting (the Baptist); 4. hypocritical fasting (Isa. lviii. 3, 4), which may easily combine with 1 and 3. Fasting generally is the ascetic symbolical exercise of real renunciation of the world, in which all true fasting is fulfilled.

3. Application of the two parables concerning old garments and old bottles to the history of Ebionitism, of the Interim * in the Reformation age, and of analogous incongruities in the present day.

4. The meal of Christ everywhere a sacred, spiritual feast.

HOMILETICAL AND PRACTICAL.

How often do sincere legal souls suffer themselves to be led away by traditionalists into an assault upon the freedom of the Gospel!—The greatest danger of the *weak* brethren (Rom. xiv. 1, 15), that they fall under the bondage of *false* brethren (2 Cor. xi. 26; Gal. ii. 4), and thus become separated from the peace of the Gospel.—*Wrong* alliances of Christians in the Church lead to *wrong* alliances of ecclesiastical things, even in opposition to the *right* alliances of both.—Openness a characteristic of John's disciples as of their master: they apply themselves, as later the Baptist did, with their offence to Christ Himself.—Yet they are infected with the policy of the Pharisees; for they ask, Why fast *Thy disciples* not? (*see* on *Matthew*).—Christ at once the Physician and the Bridegroom: 1. The Bridegroom as the Physician; 2. the Physician as the Bridegroom. Or, Christ is the supreme festal end, and the only means of salvation, in the kingdom of God: 1. He is the means of healing, while He calls souls to the participation of His blessedness; 2. He is the Prince of the blessed kingdom in the midst of His redeemed.—We should think, on our feast-day, of our coming fast-day.—Even in the greatness of His fast, Christ with His disciples leaves far behind Him all the severe penitents of the old theocracy.—The secret fasting of Christians; or, the great, silent, and festal renunciation of the world: 1. Its form; 2. its reason, the reconciliation of the world; 3. its goal, the glorification of the world.

STARKE:—It is a pharisaic and very common evil, that men are very much more troubled about setting others right in their living than about directing their own.—QUESNEL:—The busybody begins by talking about others, and comes afterwards to himself, but makes the best of his own case, 1 Tim. iv. 8.—CRAMER:—Fasting is good; but to make a merit of it, or even to burden the conscience with it, is opposed to Christian freedom.—It is spiritual pride when, in matters which God has left to our freedom, people desire that others should regulate their piety by their rules.—The fasting of a penitent does not consist only in abstinence from food, but in abstinence also from all the pleasures and all the occasions of sin, Joel ii. 12.—Where Jesus is the Bridegroom of the soul, there is joy and refreshment; where He is not, there is mourning and grief of heart.—CANSTEIN:—The righ measures of pacification in religion are those in which truth and sincerity are consulted.—MAJUS:—The

* An ordinance of Charles V., "that all his Catholic dominions should, for the future, inviolably observe the customs, statutes, and ordinances of the universal church," etc.; by which he endeavored to reëstablish Popery among the Protestants.—*Ed.*

nakedness of sin cannot be covered with old traditions.

GERLACH:—Jesus terms Himself the Bridegroom of His Church.—Longing for the Bridegroom is the feeling of the Church, when He is away; bridal love and delight, when He is present again.—BRAUNE:—It is a special temptation to good-natured, well-meaning souls, not reconciled to Christ, His doctrine, His discipline, His life, His Church, when evil-minded cavillers fall in with them.—The disciples of Jesus a wedding company.—In all Christians there is more or less interchange of cheerful joy and gloomy sorrow, although the joyous temper when the Lord is near predominates.—New wine, new bottles.—SCHLEIERMACHER:—How Jesus would have us understand and treat the great new period which He came to bring in.—Thus the Redeemer compares Himself with John, Matt. xi. 18 *seq.*—"That day": the interval of uncertainty concerning the further course of the divine economy for man's salvation.—The old garment: He would thereby intimate that it was by no means lawful to cut up and divide the spiritual power with which He was furnished by God that He might communicate it to men, in order to repair and set in order again that which was obsolete and effete.—In our joyous fellowship with the Lord, let us preserve the happiness which He declares to be the prerogative of His people.—GOSSNER:—They have now once more discovered something. Envy looks at and judges only others, without caring about correcting itself. Another failing of the Pharisees was, that they required all pious people to measure according to their standard, and adopt their usages. The third error was, that they began to speak about others, in order that they might come to themselves, and exalt their own reputation at the expense of others.

Fourth Conflict.—The Ears of Corn on the Sabbath; the Son of Man also Lord of the Sabbath.

VERS. 23–28.

(Parallels: Matt. xii. 1–8; Luke vi. 1–5.)

23 And it came to pass, that he went through the corn-fields [sowed-fields] on the
Sabbath-day; and his disciples began, as they went, to pluck the ears of corn [began to
24 make a way, by plucking off the ears: Meyer]. And the Pharisees said unto him, Be-
25 hold, why do they on the Sabbath-day that which is not lawful? And he said unto
them, Have ye never read what David did, when he had need, and was an hungered,
26 he, and they that were with him? How he went into the house of God, in the days
of Abiathar the high-priest,[1] and did eat the shew-bread, which is not lawful to eat but
27 for the priests, and gave also to them which were with him? And he said unto them,
28 The Sabbath was made for man, and not man for the Sabbath: Therefore the Son of
man is Lord also of the Sabbath.

[1] Ver. 26.—"Under Abiathar the high-priest" is wanting in D.; omitted on account of the historical difficulty.

EXEGETICAL AND CRITICAL.

1. *See* on the parallels of Matthew and Luke.—In regard to the time, it is to be observed that this event belongs to a later section of the life of Jesus (after He had returned from the Feast of Purim * in 782), when persecution took a decided form against Him. The same remark holds good of the healing of the man with a withered hand. But the motive of Mark in inserting the matter here was evidently to connect appropriate facts. The first offence and the first conflict referred to the forgiveness of sins, which Christ pronounced, and which was alleged against Him as a blasphemous invasion of the rights of God, meaning especially the rights of the priests; the second offence was the intercourse of Christ with publicans and sinners; the third, the opposition of His festal, social companionship to the ascetic and pharisaic fasts,—on which then follows in our narrative the account of the offence taken at the freer position which He and His disciples assumed towards the Sabbath.

* A festival introduced by Mordecai, to commemorate the deliverance of the Jews from the designs of Haman. It was celebrated on the 14th or 15th day of Adar, or March, and was called Purim, from a Persian word which signifies *lot;* because Haman ascertained by lot the day on which the Jews were to be destroyed. Esther iii. 7; ix. 26.—*Ed.*

Ver. 23. **Went through the corn-fields.**—The παραπορεύεσθαι marks the circumstance that He opened His way right and left through the overhanging ears; whereas the disciples began to make their path by plucking and rubbing these ears. Thus does Meyer explain, and doubtless rightly, the ὁδὸν ποιεῖν τίλλοντες τοὺς στάχυας. It is true that Mark says nothing directly about eating; but that is to be taken for granted in any rational rubbing of the ears, and is further manifest from the Lord's justification of them, appealing to the fact of David having eaten the shew-bread. According to Meyer, the allusion to the history of David aimed only to vindicate the rubbing of the ears as an act of necessity; and he thinks that the unessential circumstance of the shew-bread having been eaten led to the insertion into the other Gospels of the tradition concerning eating the ears. This needs no refutation. It is impossible to make the rubbing corn in their hands, in order to clear the way, into an act of sheer necessity, such as eating the shew-bread was. In fact, Mark takes pleasure in presenting a vivid picture of everything. He here tells us how the disciples attained two objects by one and the same act. The less of the two, making a way, occupied his mind merely as the counterpart of Jesus' πορεύεσθαι in another manner; and the suggestion of plucking the ears was quite enough to denote synecdochically the eating them also.

Ver. 24. **Why do they on the Sabbath-day that which is not lawful?**—Meyer tries to establish this discrepancy between the other Evangelists and Mark, that he makes the Pharisees ask in this passage, Why do they on the Sabbath-day something that is forbidden in itself? * But in that case Jesus would have replied only to the first and less important part of their accusation. But if we regard their words as a question of surprise, abruptly asked, and as it were answered by themselves, the harmony of the accounts is sufficiently established. For the Sabbath traditions of the Rabbins, consult Braune. "It was not a journey, being only a walk through a by-path; 2,800 ells' distance from the town were permitted by the law."—"To pluck and rub with the hand ears from the field of a neighbor, was allowed; Moses forbade only the sickle (Deut. xxiii. 25). But the matter belonged to the thirty-nine chief classes (fathers), each of which had its subdivisions (daughters), in which the works forbidden on the Sabbath were enumerated. This was their hypocritical way, to make of trifling things matters of sin and vexation to the conscience.

Ver. 26. **In the days of Abiathar the high-priest.**—According to 1 Sam. xxi. 1, Ahimelech was the high-priest who gave David the shew-bread (JOSEPH. *Antiq.* vi. 12, 6). His son Abiathar succeeded him, who was David's friend (1 Sam. xxii. 20; 1 Kings i. 7). Moreover, in 2 Sam. viii. 17, Ahimelech is inversely called the son of Abiathar. So also in 1 Chron. xxiv. 6 and 31. Hence it was early supposed that the father and son had both names (Euth. Zig.), or that the son was the *vicarius* of his father (Grotius); while some have proposed to modify the meaning of the ἐπί (under Abiathar).† Later expositors, on the other hand, have assumed that the names have been mistakenly interchanged; but to insist, with Meyer, upon this view, appears to us hypercritical and arbitrary, when we remember that in Ex. ii. 18 the same father-in-law of Moses is once called Raguel and then Jethro, and especially that Jewish tradition was possessed of many supplements of the sacred narrative, as appears from the discourse of Stephen (Acts vii.), and the allusion to the Egyptian magicians, 2 Tim. iii. 8. Here the Old Testament itself gave occasion to supplementary tradition, and the scriptural knowledge of the time incorporated and used it. Moreover, it is to be assumed that the priest's son Abiathar stood in a nearer relation to David, which made the unusual proceeding more explicable. The tabernacle was then at Nob.

Ver. 28. **Therefore the Son of Man is Lord.**—The Son of Man, and not merely as man (Grotius); not, however, the Messiah in the official sense, but the Son of Man in His inviolable holiness, and in His mysterious dignity (intimated in Daniel) as the Holy Child and Head of humanity appearing in the name of God.—*Lord* over the Sabbath; that is, administrating and ruling over it in its New Testament fulfilment and freedom (comp. MEYER).

A clause is found appended to Luke vi. 5 in some Codd.: "The same day Jesus saw one working on the Sabbath, and said unto him, 'Man, if thou knowest what thou doest, thou art happy; if thou knowest not, thou art accursed.'" This historically questionable saying has been placed by some in the same traditional category with the words; "To give is more blessed than to receive," Acts xx. 35. *See* MEYER on *Luke*, and BRAUNE, *Evangelium.*

DOCTRINAL AND ETHICAL.

1. *See* on the parallels.—For the Jewish Sabbath and the Sabbath ordinances, consult the article in WINER. First, the opponents of Jesus thought that He sinned against sound doctrine; then they went further, and urged objections against His free treatment of discipline and pious usages; but now, finally, they would allege that He, in the person of His disciples, sinned against the decalogue, and against one of its most sacred commandments, that concerning the Sabbath. And if, at first, their exasperation against Him was only an internal matter, they now directly attack Him in the persons of His disciples, as appears without any disguise in the history that follows in the text.

2. Christ, even in the silent corn-field, is not safe from the plots of His enemies.—The different manner in which Jesus and His disciples made their respective ways through the field.

3. Abiathar = Ahimelech; or, the freer relation of the New Testament believers to the Old Testament. For the shew-bread, consult the article in WINER, as well as the various writings on Old Testament *Symbolism* of BÆHR, KURTZ, HENGSTENBERG, SARTORIUS, etc.

4. The Sabbath for man, not man for the Sabbath.—The spirit of traditionalism and fanaticism perfectly inverts the ordinances of the kingdom of God; making the means the end, and the end the means.

5. The Son of Man the Lord; or the roots of the supremacy and dignity of Christ which are found in the relation of His sacred human nature to mankind. The Son of Man, the Lord in all aspects and on all sides; therefore Lord of the Sabbath.—But the Lord is a ruler, administrator, and fulfiller of His ordinances; not the abolisher of them.

HOMILETICAL AND PRACTICAL.

The Lord's patience in making His way, and in abstaining, as contrasted with the conduct of His disciples.—Christ in the field among the ears of corn, a noble figure.—The blessing of nature and the blessing of grace in their unity.—The first tokens of the coming freedom of the disciples in its significance; or, Christian freedom a child of need and justification felt in the spirit of Christ.—The peculiar need of the moment pointing to the means of help for ever: 1. The failing way; the lacking bread; the idea that one need might be removed by the other. 2. The significance of this fact for the spiritual relations of the kingdom of God.—To make a way for the Lord the best means of nourishment for His disciples.—The Pharisees everywhere like a shadow of the free

* Meyer would find a discrepancy between Mark and Matthew with Luke, in the fact that the former says nothing about *eating* the grain, but only speaks of "making a path" through it. According to him, the Pharisees objected merely to the travelling on the Sabbath and the labor therein involved, and the story of the eating is an interpolation. But aside from the fact that ὁδὸν ποιεῖν may be rendered as in the English version "to go," it seems improbable that the disciples should have taken pains merely to "make a path" through the yielding grain by pulling it up or plucking it off, when the simple stride would tread it down.—*Ed.*

† Wetstein and Scholz suggest that it stands for *coram*. —*Ed.*

Gospel.—Man himself the oldest Divine institution, and what follows from it: 1. Nothing in favor of the arbitrary treatment of Divine institutions; 2. but much in favor of free dealing with human traditions. —The kingdom of heaven is preëminently a kingdom of personal life or of love.—The Sabbath for man; that is, 1. its law is for the life of the soul, 2. its rest is for devotion, 3. the ordinance for salvation.—The Sabbath for man, and therefore for his eternal Sabbath; and this also was made for man, as man for it.

STARKE:—QUESNEL:—Christ never performed miracles to feed Himself and His disciples in their hunger; in order to teach them that they should never without necessity seek extraordinary ways, and that their neighbors' need should press on their hearts more than their own.—Jesus hungers, while His disciples eat; and thereby shows that a teacher, ruler, and leader should be more perfect than his disciples. —OSIANDER:—We should learn to suffer want with Christ, and to abound with Christ.—QUESNEL:—The pride of the Pharisaic nature drives a man to make himself a judge of others, and to demand of them an account of all they do.—CANSTEIN:—God's will is, that we should diligently read the books of the Old Testament, and set them before the people; that we may derive thence teaching and example.—MAJUS: —All errors must be refuted out of Holy Writ.— QUESNEL:—The usages and ordinances of religion should have for their object the glory of God and the profit of men.—The true Sabbath festival.—Believers are with Christ and through Christ lords of the Sabbath, that they may use it for their own and their neighbors' necessities.

LISCO:—The highest end is man himself. The whole law was only the means for the education of men, whom God keeps thus under external discipline until the law is inwardly and spiritually apprehended and obeyed. But believers adapt themselves, in the spirit of love, to all outward ordinances (although, of course, in the spirit of the Lord),—Gerlach rightly adds: To all outward ordinances that assist the need of the Christian Church.—Every arbitrary violation of legal discipline, without the justification of the spirit of grace and love in Christ, is a heavy sin.— Only the spirit of adoption makes free from the yoke of the law.—BRAUNE:—As David was pitilessly persecuted by Saul, so were the disciples by the Pharisees.—Men are to find rest and refreshment in holy days, but not to suffer hunger and distress.—There is no law given to the righteous; and where the Spirit of the Lord is, there is liberty.—SCHLEIERMACHER:—The Redeemer might have more easily vindicated Himself had He referred to the words of the law, Deut. xxiii. 24, etc.; but He aimed at something higher, to show that all such laws were subjected to a higher spiritual law (the example of David).—The Son of Man Lord of the Sabbath; the Redeemer is the measure of all; the question must be, whether a thing is according to His mind and of advantage to His kingdom.—BAUER:—The Lord of the Sabbath has given to every believing mind a Sabbath-law, for its direction and not for its trouble. Thou shalt worship God in spirit and in truth.

Fifth Conflict.—Healing of the Withered Hand on the Sabbath. The Traditionalists hardened into purposes of Murder. Withdrawal of Jesus to the Sea. CH. III. 1–12.

(Parallels: Matt. xii. 9–21; Luke vi. 6–11; vers. 17–19.)

1 And he entered again into the synagogue; and there was a man there which had a
2 withered hand. And they watched him, whether he would heal him on the Sabbath
3 day; that they might accuse him. And he saith unto the man which had the withered
4 hand, Stand forth [up]. And he saith unto them, Is it lawful to do good on the Sabbath
5 days, or to do evil? to save life, or to kill? But they held their peace. And when
he had looked round about on them with anger, being grieved for the hardness of their
hearts, he said unto the man, Stretch forth thine hand. And he stretched *it* out: and
6 his hand was restored [whole as the other].[1] And the Pharisees went forth, and straight-
7 way took counsel with the Herodians against him, how they might destroy him. But
Jesus withdrew himself with his disciples to [εἰς, unto][2] the sea: and a great multitude
8 from Galilee followed him, and from Judea, And from Jerusalem, and from Idumea,
and *from* beyond Jordan; and they about Tyre and Sidon, a great multitude, when they
9 had heard what great things he did, came unto him. And he spake to his disciples,
that a small ship should wait on him because of the multitude, lest they should throng
10 him. For he had healed many; insomuch that they pressed upon him for to touch
11 him, as many as had plagues. And unclean spirits, when they saw him, fell down be-
12 fore him, and cried, saying, Thou art the Son of God. And he straitly charged them
that they should not make him known.

[1] Ver. 5.—"Whole as the other" wanting in the most important Codd. Probably brought over from Matt. xii. 13.
[2] Ver. 7.—Εἰς, after D., P., Lachmann, Tischendorf; stronger than the πρός.

EXEGETICAL AND CRITICAL.

See on the parallels.—The narrative of Mark is here particularly vivid and pictorial. He places the scene actually before us, giving his relation very much in the present tense. Like Matthew, he regards the incident in the light of an important turning-point. But he omits the parabolic word concerning the sheep fallen into a pit.

Ver. 1. **And He entered again.**—According to Luke, this occurred eight days later, on the Sabbath which immediately followed the Sabbath of the previous narrative. By the side of the reading *εἰς τὴν συναγωγήν*, Cod. D. [which Tischendorf follows] places the reading *εἰς συν.*, into a synagogue: probably an exegetical hint that it was not the same synagogue as before But the expression, "into *the* synagogue," does not designate of itself any definite synagogue. It has, however, this advantage, that it marks the fact of Jesus having gone into the synagogue again, in spite of all the machinations of the Pharisees and scribes.

Ver. 3. **Stand forth.**—Meyer: "Up! into the midst!"

Ver. 4. **To do good.**—The ἀγαθοποιῆσαι and κακοποιῆσαι may be taken generally, *to do good* and *to do evil;* or, more concretely, *to benefit* and *to injure.* Erasmus, De Wette, and others, take it in the latter sense; Meyer, in the former, and Matthew decides us for this. The question of Jesus, that is, was an answer to their question, May a man heal on the Sabbath? This question Jesus answers by an impregnable principle; as appears also from the words, It is lawful to do good, to perform a good act, on the Sabbath-day (*καλῶς ποιεῖν*).—**To save life.**—The antithesis of *doing good* and *doing evil* now receives its concrete force, to *benefit* or to *injure*, and thereby its application to the present case.

Ver. 5. **With anger.**—Mark gives vivid prominence to the indignation of Jesus. With a glance of displeasure and discomposure He looked round upon the assembly of men who were hardening their hearts before His eyes, as they could not refute His vindication of the right of healing, by reference to the design of the Sabbath.—**Grieved,** *συλλυπούμενος.*—The *συν* establishes Meyer's translation, "feeling compassion for."

Ver. 6. **With the Herodians.**—Comp. on *Matthew.* De Wette, without reason, thinks that the Herodians have been by error introduced here from Matt. xxii. 16. Tiberias in Galilee was a place of residence for the Herodians, that is, the Herodian political party; and the time had come when they began to take part in the persecution of the Lord. But it marks a great advance in the enmity of the Pharisees, that they, who had before leagued themselves with the disciples of John for the sake of gathering weight against Christ, now entered into fellowship with the Herodians, whom in reality they hated, in order to destroy Him whom they hated still more, by machinations behind his back.—**How they might destroy Him.**—Thus the Galilean conflicts had in rapid process reached their conclusion.

Ver. 7. **To the sea.**—Not merely to the coast. The life on the sea, in the ship which was now His chief place of instruction in opposition to the synagogue, and which more than once served Him for a transient retreat to the opposite bank, here had its commencement. Matthew also had made this turning-point prominent. But in Mark it is plainly enough characterized as a withdrawal of Christ from His customary work in the synagogue to the ship.—**And a great multitude.**—The great crowds who heard the ship-discourses of Jesus were formed of two main masses, who are distinguished by ἠκολούθησαν and ἦλθον πρὸς αὐτόν. Thus, after the words, "followed Him," we must, with Griesbach, and De Wette, and Meyer, place either a colon or a period. The Jews from Galilee followed Him. The strangers from other parts came to Him. The "following" does not merely indicate external following; it includes a moral element also. In the conflict between Jesus and the Pharisees, they held with Jesus. It was the beginning of a specific discipleship, from which indeed most afterwards receded, but from which the germ of the Galilean believers was afterwards developed. The remaining multitude testifies the extent of the fame of Jesus; but we must also take into account the Jewish traffic, and the commercial route through Capernaum, which attracted multitudes in that direction. The description of the crowd brings them from all parts.

Ver. 8. **They about Tyre and Sidon** are the Jews of that district. We quote the good remark of Meyer: "Observe the different position of πλῆθος in ver. 7 and ver. 8. In the one, the *greatness* of the mass of people is prominent; in the other, the idea of the mass itself is presented;" or rather their coming from all distances. With the followers, the most important thing was, that it was a great multitude; with the crowds coming, it was that they came from all parts, and from all distances. Comp. Luke vi. 17; Matt. xii. 15. Moreover, we must remark that the concourse of people round Jesus stood in a reciprocal relation to His excitement and His breach with the Pharisees. The time had now come when the people began to display an inclination to make a political party in His favor, and to exalt Him into a king. And on this account, also, He was constrained to withdraw from the people, now to this and now to the other side of the lake, in the ship that was provided. Comp. Mark iv. 1 *seq.;* John vi. 15. We must bear in mind the tendency of the vigorous and brave Galilean people to insurrection and uproar.—**And from Idumea.**—John Hyrcanus had brought the Idumeans by violence to embrace the Jewish faith. There were possibly some of that people by this time who voluntarily adhered to it, notwithstanding that unholy violence. But the words may refer to Jews who had been dispersed so far as Idumea and Arabia.—["This is the fullest statement to be found in any of the Gospels as to the extent of our Lord's personal influence and the composition of the multitudes who followed Him." ALEXANDER *in loc.—Ed.*]

Ver. 9. **A small ship should wait on Him.**—The immediate object was that the people should not throng Him. But this does not exclude the ulterior purpose, of having a freer position in the ship, and retreating often to the other shore.

Ver. 10. **Insomuch that they pressed upon Him.**—The cause of the thronging. It was not merely the pressure of a vast listening multitude towards the central speaker; it was rather the intenser earnestness of many who were urged by their desire to touch Him for their cure.

Ver. 11. **Unclean spirits.**—That is, demons, who identified themselves with these.

Ver. 12. **That they should not make Him known.**—That is, as the Messiah.

DOCTRINAL AND ETHICAL.

1. *See* on the parallels.—The Pharisees now seek to involve the Lord Himself in the charge of Sabbath desecration. The present case seemed to differ from the former in this, that the healing of the withered hand was a matter that might have been postponed. And it did not appear to be one of those urgent works of necessity which even the Pharisees permit

ted themselves to do. On the other hand, the Lord declares the work of compassionate love, or doing good generally, to be of itself always urgent; and the thought is further involved, that sickness does not tarry at a stand, but that there is a continual sinking into deeper danger and need.

2. On the previous Sabbath a work of necessity was justified and established; on the present, the Lord justifies and establishes a work of love. The Christian glorification of the Sabbath into the Lord's day assumes two aspects: 1. The *ethical law* of the day of rest is, with the other laws of the decalogue, transformed into an *ethical principle* for the Christian social world, especially the State. 2. The divine law, and the human tradition, of the festival become now the Incarnate Lord's creation and institution of the Sunday. The Sabbath was the end of the old world, —a figure of its rest in death after its labor under the law. The Sunday was the beginning of the new world,—a figure of the rising to a new life, which began with the resurrection of Christ. The former was the close of a week of labor which had passed in restless activity, like the days' works of creation; the latter was the beginning of a festal week, the works of which should be performed in the joyful light of the Spirit and of love. On the historical and general relations of the day, consult Hengstenberg's treatise (Berlin, 1852). Comp. also the writings of Rücker, Liebetrut, Oschwald, Wilhelmi, and others.

3. Christ the personal fulfilment and manifestation of the law in glorified form, and thus also of the Sabbath. The source and the founder of the day; Himself the Sun of the Christian Sunday.

4. The Pharisees and the Herodians. "Hierarchs and despots are necessary to each other." F. v. Bander.

HOMILETICAL AND PRACTICAL.

See the parallels.—The Lord's Sabbath work: saving life and the soul; the traditionalists' Sabbath work: destroying life (that of the Messiah Himself). —The needy and wretched in the synagogue; or, the school of the law cannot save and heal.—The envious glance of the spy in the sanctuary; or, how carnal zeal does not look up to the Lord, but sideways at what others are doing.—Christ performs the glorious work of heaven in the midst of the dark contentions of those who harden themselves in unbelief: standing alone as Saviour with His faithful few.—The Lord's glance in the world is a looking *around* in indignation, or a looking *upon* in love.—The hardening of His enemies under the very eye of Christ.—Christ is to some a savor of life unto life; to others, a savor of death unto death.—As the paralytic, who could not move, took the boldest course through faith (over the roof); so the man with the withered hand learns by faith to come forward and stretch out his hand in spite of the mightiest enemies of faith.—As it was divinely great to work wonders in the midst of this envious circle of enemies, so it was humanly great to maintain faith in such a circle.—The old and new connection between need and the boldness of faith.—The leagues between carnal religious zeal and secular power against Christ (Pharisees and Herodians).—The transference of Christ's preaching from the synagogue to the ship, in its significance; or, God's word is not bound.—The thronging of the people round the Lord, in its various aspects: 1. A confused impulse to seek help, confused by a craving for the miraculous in that help; 2. an act of homage to the Prince of life: at Golgotha a band of deadly enemies, who cast Him out as if He had been the great enemy of man and destroyer of the people.—How men have ever sought to change the pastoral office, and preaching of the Gospel of Christ for the good of souls, into an office of external acts and helps (changing the spiritual Messiah into a worldly one).—Christ must often withdraw Himself, not only from His enemies, but also from His friends, in order to maintain the spirituality and freedom of His vocation.—It is beyond all important that we should accept Christ as the Physician of souls; for the redemption of the soul occurs now, the resurrection of the body at the last day.—The earthly mind would fain invert this order.—The ship* of the Church must save Christianity from intermingling with the politics of the world.—How often did Jesus retreat before the disposition of the people to proclaim Him as a Messiah in the carnal sense!—The crying demons mislead the people.—The infinitely discordant mixture of dispositions and characters in an excited mass of people.—The test of right-coming to Jesus: 1. A coming to Him alone, not only with, but also in spite of, the multitude; 2. a being alone with Him, whether among many or few; 3. a remaining alone with Him, and entering through Him into the fellowship of the saved.—The confession of the demons: how the Lord estimated its ambiguity and recoiled from it.—The demons were first in the confession that Jesus was the Messiah, but their confession was a slavish one.—The Lord had here to do not merely with the words of truth, but with the truth of the words.—The glance of Christ's anger a prelude of the judgment; yet it was qualified by compassion.—Christ, the gentlest friend of men, will one day be a most terrible personage to many.

STARKE:—MAJUS:—The contradiction and slander of enemies should not restrain us from avowing the truth, but make us more courageous and joyful in our confession.—QUESNEL:—A miser, an unfruitful Christian, a negligent ruler, a strong man that will not help, are all mere withered hands.—O avarice, how withered is thy hand!—To suck poison out of what is good, or to slander, is devilish.—Hypocrites are very urgent about ceremonies; but as it regards true discipline, they know nothing about it.—When we do what is right, we need not fear secret slanderers.—True love is not afraid of wicked men when it would do good to others.—CANSTEIN:—The enemies of Christ are not sincere; they have seared consciences, and backbite in secret.—QUESNEL:—There is much silence that proceeds from the Spirit of God, but there is also a devilish silence.—Here anger and love meet together; but the Socinians cannot, and will not, reconcile these.—The passions of Christ are a great mystery.—MAJUS:—Divine zeal against sin must be connected with love, with tender compassion towards the sinner.—QUESNEL:—What a mystery is an envious heart! It poisons everything, and extracts poison from everything.—When Jesus is persecuted or forsaken of all, there is yet a little company of the faithful who follow Him.—OSIANDER:—The more fiercely the Gospel of Christ is persecuted, the more surely and widely it is diffused.—The hearing about Christ is not saving of itself; it must lead the soul to Himself.—QUESNEL:—

* Perhaps there is an allusion here to the "nave" of the church edifice, which is derived from the Latin *navis*, from a supposed resemblance to the hull of a vessel.—*Ed.*

True love makes no difference among men, but does good to all, even to those who come with excitement and at an unseasonable time.—Christ would receive no testimony from lying spirits.

GERLACH:—The Sabbath was to remind us of, and introduce us into, that rest which God enjoyed when He contemplated the creatures happy in Himself after creation was finished, and that into which redeemed men shall again enter at the finishing of the new creation.—This rest is not the rest of death, but the highest life; and to spread abroad life and blessedness in the spirit of love, is the proper business of the Sabbath.—LISCO:—Herod's servants are his servile dependants. (This is true; for the dependants of an absolute despot can only be his servants.)—BRAUNE:—That the Sabbath would not tolerate what might be postponed, was a law to them: he that had the withered hand was not in deadly danger, and his cure might as well take place the next day. Jesus penetrated their thoughts.—Jesus established, that the not doing good was equivalent to the doing of evil; the sin of omission as bad as the sin of commission.—Their mouth was stopped, but their heart was not emptied of envy and malice.—Jesus' glance: the enemy of sin, the friend of the sinner.—The withered hand, 1 Kings xiii. 4.—Instead of joining the tempted Saviour, they made a compact with their deadliest enemies, the dependants of Herod; and instead of sanctifying the Sabbath by doing good and preserving life, they engaged in plans to put to death the Lord of the Sabbath and of life.—The hatred which Jesus encountered was already an earnest of His death; and the multitude of the people coming to Him from Gentile lands was already an earnest of the blessing of His death.—The praise of the Holy One cannot issue from unholy lips and an unclean spirit.—BEDA:—Jesus had victoriously defended His disciples from the charge of violating the Sabbath; but the Pharisees were all the more vehement in involving Him, the Master Himself, in the same condemnation.—CHRYSOSTOM:—Jesus places the unhappy man in the midst of the assembly, that his appearance might excite compassion, and his healing shame the wickedness of the enemies.—SCHLEIERMACHER:—What good thing we have to do, we must set about doing at once.—These Pharisees confederated with the officials of Herod against Him; those Pharisees in Jerusalem brought the affairs of the Redeemer before the Roman governor.—We see how one party stood in need of the other in order to accomplish that which was in each party a foul wrong, though there was something at the bottom like a dependence upon what they thought was the law of God.—How many examples of a similar kind in the history of the Christian Church!—(The withdrawal to the sea.) Here also He remained in the way of His vocation, and retreated from them without neglecting His mission.—(The cry of the demons.) The Redeemer would not that any faith in Him should arise which had not the right foundation.—GOSSNER:—The Saviour can be severe; but He is grieved that He must be angry.—BAUER:—The Pharisees were silent. The eye of the Lord rested upon them, but none of the Pharisees could stand that glance.—They kept angry silence, like that which precedes the storm.

FIFTH SECTION.

CONFLICT OF JESUS WITH THE UNBELIEF OF HIS GALILÆAN COUNTRYMEN, AND WITHDRAWAL INTO THE VILLAGES.

CHAPTERS III. 13—VI. 6.

Beginning of the Conflict. The Lord providing Himself Helpers, in the Calling of the Apostles.

VERS. 13–19.

(Parallels: Matt. x. 1–8; Luke vi. 12–16.)

13 And he goeth up into a [the] mountain, and calleth *unto him* whom he would: and
14 they came unto him. And he ordained twelve, that they should be with him, and that
15 he might send them forth to preach, And to have power to heal sicknesses,[1] and to cast
16, 17 out devils. And Simon he surnamed Peter; And James the *son* of Zebedee, and
John the brother of James; and he surnamed them Boanerges, which is, The sons of
18 thunder; And Andrew, and Philip, and Bartholomew, and Matthew, and Thomas, and
19 James the *son* of Alpheus, and Thaddeus, and Simon the Canaanite,[2] And Judas Iscariot, which also betrayed him: and they went into a house.

[1] Ver 15.—"To heal sicknesses, and" wanting in B., L., Δ., Copt., and others. It is omitted by Tischendorf, and seems a supplement from Matt. x. 1. The omission of this makes all the more prominent the casting out of the demons in Mark the main point.

[2] Ver. 18.—The reading κανανaῖος here, as in Matt. x. 4, is best supported.

EXEGETICAL AND CRITICAL.

Ver. 13. *See* on the parallels.—**Into a mountain.**—Not "up into the mountain of that locality," for the locality was the margin of the sea; but it is used in accordance with the relations of the land in Palestine, and the phraseology concerning it: going up into a mountain, in contradistinction to abiding in the narrow vales or low strips of land. And it is to be observed that the expression is used to signify a withdrawal of the Lord, especially for solitary devotion.—**And calleth unto Him.**—The manner of the call is not defined, whether sending for them, or otherwise. The main point is the free choice of the Twelve out of the rest of the discipleship. Meyer supposes that Jesus made first a larger selection, and then in ver. 14 the narrower choice. But there is nothing to hinder our regarding ver. 14 as expressing the more specific end of the call, that is, the appointment and mission.

Ver. 16. **And Simon He surnamed Peter.**—Some cursive MSS. have πρῶτον Σίμωνα. According to De Wette, Mark passed over the statement of Peter's call, because the change of name was to him of special moment. But we may regard the statement of Peter's call as included in the ἐπέθηκε. Thus Christ added, not merely to his name but rather to his general vocation, the distinguishing name of Peter. On account of these distinguishing names, Andrew follows in the fourth rank, after the two sons of Zebedee. The solemn appendage of the name in this place does not contradict the preliminary naming of Simon, which had taken place before, John i. 42.

Ver. 17. **Boanerges:** בְּנֵי רְגַשׁ; in Aramæan, the sheva being equivalent to *oa*. The רְגַשׁ, in Hebrew meaning a threatening people (Ps. lv. 15), in Syriac meant *thunder*.—That the name refers to the event mentioned in Luke ix. 54 (according to Calmet, Heumann, etc.), is not contradicted by the supposition that it must have been a surname significant of praise, and not of blame. Comp. on this point the notes on Matthew. According to the ancients, the sons of Zebedee were so termed as μεγαλοκήρυκες καὶ θεολογικώτατοι (Theophylact, and others), because thunder is the ordinary symbol of solemn and profound utterances. We understand the expression to refer to the fiery, grand, sublime spirit, which found its utterance in correspondingly high, strong, and pregnant words. That the name was not habitually used, like the name Peter, may be explained by the fact that it was a collective one. It was distributed later, or merged in the several dignities of the first apostolical martyr, and the disciple who lay on the Lord's bosom, the last great Evangelist.

Ver. 18. **Canaanite.**—Though the form of the surname has in it something unusual, yet it is easily explicable by the term ζηλωτής in Luke, and the accompanying reading κανανίτης.

Ver. 19. **And they went into a house.**—For the chronology, Comp. the notes on Matthew. The Evangelist's arrangement here is not according to time, but regulated by a classification of the facts. For the circumstance described does not, as Meyer thinks, fall into the period after the return from the Sermon on the Mount, but into a later period, when Christ's work in Galilee was drawing to its close. According to Ewald, an original form of Mark might have introduced, before this return, the Sermon on the Mount, and the narrative of the nobleman in Capernaum. These, and similar suppositions of Hilgenfeld, we have sufficiently dealt with in our introductory account of this Evangelist. Finally, it does not follow from their coming into a house, that the ensuing discourse took place in that house.—["The true sense is most probably that given in the margin of the English Version, and long before by Wiclif, *they came home, i. e.*, returned to Capernaum again as their headquarters, and the centre of their operations. Comp. εἰς οἶκον in Mark ii. 1." ALEXANDER *in loc.*—*Ed.*]

DOCTRINAL AND ETHICAL.

1. Comp. on the parallels.—It is characteristic of Mark, that he gives prominence here to the sons of thunder. On the fiery zeal of John, comp. Gerlach, p. 118. "The peculiarity of John was pure simplicity, and also glowing, fiery zeal; this having been at first disturbed by impure passion (ch. ix. 38; Luke ix. 54), but sanctified afterwards by inward love to Christ. His epistles contain some of the sternest passages in the New Testament. *See* 1 John. ii. 22, 23; iii. 8; 2 John 7–11. Comp. also the Seven Epistles in the Apocalypse. Church history also records many things concerning his sacred zeal." And then Gerlach introduces the narrative of John's hastily leaving the bath in which the heretic was found.

2. As it respects the calling of the Twelve, it must be observed that it falls into two separate crises, according to Mark, ch. iii. 13–19, and ch. vi. 7 *seq.* Only it is evident that the more precise characterization of the mission in ch. vi. 7 is identical with the mission in Matt. x. 1 *seq.*, and Luke vi. 12 *seq.* Hence, we assume that Mark here describes a selection of the Apostles preliminary to that mission, one that was a continuation and enlargement of the call of the four most select disciples at the Sea of Galilee, and intended primarily as a vocation to more decided discipleship and engagement in helping the Redeemer's work. Yet the more express apostolical vocation is kept in view even here, as is manifest from the very solemn account of Mark, in which he anticipates some features of the later vocation. It would appear, indeed, that the point of time to which Mark here carries us, was even later than the proper historical epoch of the more express vocation. The motive for placing it in this connection was the fact of the commencement of the great conflict of our Lord with the unbelief of the world, as it is exhibited in this section.

3. The names of the Apostles, or their call, introduced with respect to Christ by the appointment of the Father: mediate, and yet immediate.

4. Judas possessed a certain species of endowment; yet observe the doubtfulness of such kind of endowments in the affairs of Church and State, inasmuch as the superficial ability may easily outweigh the central character.

HOMILETICAL AND PRACTICAL.

See on the parallels.—The call of Christ's servants a call from the mountain: 1. Christ stands on the mountain; 2. those called go up the mountain to Him; 3. they come down from the mountain into the world of men. *See* Isa. lii. 7.—The place of Jesus' prayer the birthplace of apostolical and evangelical vocation.—Fellowships and collegiate bodies in the kingdom of God: 1. In their meaning: union of the divine and the human, even here. 2. Their design: mutual supplementing and strengthening, lessening of human one-sidedness, and increase of divine power.—Casting out of devils a main branch of ecclesiastical vocation.—The variety and differences of the disciples of Jesus are an unfolding of the riches of Christ and of His kingdom.—Judas

Iscariot among the Twelve an eternal sign, 1. Of the all-endeavoring love of Christ, 2. of the greatness of human depravity, 3. of the dangers of the spiritual office (or of a mere external connection with the Lord) without perfect fidelity in the spiritual life (an internal union with Him), 4. of the aim and end of the Church (not a community of perfect saints, but of redeemed men).—Degrees in the apostolical circle, notwithstanding their unity and equality.—Even the dark power which was displayed by the last of the Twelve testified of the spiritual abilities of this company, over which Jesus reigned in kindly majesty.—"Who betrayed Him:" the called Apostle a denounced traitor.

STARKE:—The choice of a pastor should be entered upon with prayer, Acts i. 24.—He who would be fit for the work of the Lord must first be much with the Lord.—QUESNEL:—Spiritual pastors make up, with Christ the chief Pastor, only one Priest, His priesthood in the preaching of the Gospel being continued, diffused, and perfected, 1 Pet. ii. 9.—The Lord gives the word along with the great host of the Evangelists. They who take their ease when they are placed in office, often become brethren of Judas.—It is a miserable delusion to repose in a legitimate call, while negligent of fidelity and diligence in discharging its functions.—Not all the names of Christians are written in heaven, though they may stand recorded in the books of the Church below.

GOSSNER:—He who would be a witness for Christ and His Gospel, must be much with Him, and by constant communion have learned to know Him—How will they stand before Him, who learn what they have to say by heart, stand up, and only declaim, or read it off!—BAUER:—The death-roll of the Twelve Apostles itself a sermon.

---

1. *Conflict of Jesus with the* blaspheming *Unbelief of His Enemies, and His Triumph over Human Wisdom.* (CH. III. 20–30.)—2. *His Conflict with the well-meaning Unbelief of His Friends; Triumph over Devilish Malice and Human Policy.* (VERSS. 20, 21, and VERSS. 31–35.)

(Parallels: Matt. xii. 22–50; Luke viii. 19–21; xi. 14–26.)

20 And the multitude cometh together again, so that they could not so much as eat
21 bread. And when his friends heard *of it*, they went out to lay hold on him: for they
22 said, He is beside himself. And the scribes which came down from Jerusalem said,
23 He hath Beelzebub, and by the prince of the devils casteth he out devils. And he
called them *unto him*, and said unto them in parables, How can Satan cast out Satan?
24, 25 And if a kingdom be divided against itself, that kingdom cannot stand. And if a
26 house be divided against itself, that house cannot stand. And if Satan rise up against
27 himself, and be divided, he cannot stand, but hath an end. No man can enter into a
strong man's house, and spoil [plunder] his goods, except he will first bind the strong
28 man; and then he will spoil [plunder] his house. Verily I say unto you, All sins shall
be forgiven unto the sons of men,[1] and blasphemies wherewith soever they shall blas-
29 pheme: But he that shall blaspheme against the Holy Ghost hath never forgiveness,
30 but is in danger of [liable to] eternal damnation:[2] Because they said, He hath an un-
31 clean spirit. There came then his brethren, and his mother, and, standing without,
32 sent unto him, calling him. And the multitude sat about him, and they said unto him,
33 Behold, thy mother and thy brethren[3] without seek for thee. And he answered them,
34 saying, Who is my mother, or my brethren?[4] And he looked round about on them
35 which sat about him, and said, Behold my mother and my brethren! For whosoever
shall do the will of God, the same is my brother, and my sister, and mother.

[1] Ver. 28.—The words τοῖς υἱοῖς τῶν ἀνθρώπων precede τὰ ἁμαρτήματα in the best Codd.; and so they are placed in Griesbach, Lachmann, Tischendorf. B., D., G., Lachmann, and Tischendorf read ὅσα, instead of ὅσας.

[2] Ver. 29.—The reading ἔνοχός ἐστιν αἰωνίου ἁμαρτήματος, according to B., L., Δ., and others, is accepted by Griesbach, Lachmann, and Tischendorf. The readings κρίσεως and κολάσεως seem to have been explanatory paraphrases of this strong and pregnant expression.

[3] Ver. 32.—"His mother and His brethren" is the reading of B., C., D., G., Versions, Griesbach, Scholz, Lachmann; better established than the order in the *Recepta*, "His brethren and His mother," which is also adopted by Fritzsche and Tischendorf. Meyer holds to this last, thinking that the mother was afterwards put first on account of her rank, and in conformity with the parallels in Matthew and Luke. It may have been the purpose to make the mother less prominent, in a case of seeming error. An additional clause, καὶ αἱ ἀδελφαί σου, has A., D., E., &c., for it; B., C., L., and many Versions against it. Griesbach, Lachmann, Tischendorf accept it; so also De Wette and Meyer. We think the omission harder to account for than the insertion would be,—which probably had reference to ch. vi. 3.

[4] Ver. 33.—B., C., L., Versions, Lachmann, and Meyer read καὶ οἱ, instead of ἢ οἱ.

[5] Ver. 35.—The μου after ἀδελφή is omitted by Lachmann and Tischendorf, following preponderating authorities.

EXEGETICAL AND CRITICAL.

See on the parallels.

Ver. 21. **When His (friends).**—This very important feature in the evangelical narrative is peculiar to Mark. According to Baur, Mark here represents the mother of Jesus, with His brethren, as confederate with the Pharisees. Meyer, on the contrary, shows that their opinion, ὅτι ἐξέστι, was honest error (not wickedness), and that their design was to provide for Christ's safety. But if they really had thought Him beside Himself, their care for his safety would have taken the form of an attempt forcibly to seize and detain Him. We regard the step as having been the result of timid policy. At the crisis, when Christ's breach with the powerful party of the Pharisees was decided, they sought by a fiction to remove Him from publicity and a supposed extreme danger. We may regard the adoptive brethren of Jesus as the representatives of this idea; but it is evident that Mary also was drawn into this error of worldly policy (*see* the notes on *Matthew*). It is quite in keeping with the character of such a policy, that these brethren soon afterwards sought to thrust Him forward, John vii. 1 *seq.*—The household of Jesus did not come from Nazareth to Capernaum, as Meyer supposes, but from the house of their abode in Capernaum to the place where the crowds were thronging Him. That the Pharisees would here come against him with a public accusation would very well be known in Capernaum.—**For they said.**—Themselves, of course, the household of Jesus; and not, as Olshausen thinks, "it was said" by the malicious Pharisees, or by others generally (Ewald), or by messengers (Bengel).—**He is beside Himself.**—Not, as Luther says, "He will be beside Himself;" but not, with Meyer, "He is mad." It is designedly ambiguous, inasmuch as the ἐξέστη may mean, in a good sense, the being for a season rapt into ecstasy by religious enthusiasm (2 Cor. v. 13), as well as, in a bad sense, the being permanently insane. In His ecstasy, He is no longer master of Himself. The involuntary, religious μαίνεσθαι is, indeed, not an Old-Testament idea, but a Greek one: it was, however, current in the Jewish popular notion; and the more ambiguous it was, the better it would suit the aim of their policy. It must not be confounded, as Theophylact confounds it, with the allegation of Christ's opponents.* On the contrary, if His opponents should say that He was raging in demoniacal possession, the politic answer was at hand, "He is, indeed, beside Himself, but it is in a good demoniacal ecstasy." According to Meyer, this circumstance cannot be reconciled with the previous history of Mary in Matthew and Luke. The supposition of Olshausen (and Lange), that this was a moment of weakness in her life, he thinks very precarious. And Pius IX. would agree with him, though for a different reason. For the various interpretations of the passage, *see* Meyer. Euthym. Zigab.: "Some envious ones said so." Schöttgen and Wolf: "The disciples said that the people were mad." Grotius: "Report said that he had fainted." Kuinoel: "It was the message to come home to eat, for *maxime defatigatus est*," etc.

Ver. 30. **An unclean spirit.**—Characterization of Beelzebub, in opposition to the Holy Spirit.

Ver. 34. **And He looked round about.**—Mark often gives prominence to the Lord's glance around. Here it is in contrast with the indignant looking around of ch. iii. 5.

DOCTRINAL AND ETHICAL.

1. *See* on the parallels.—Mark omits, among other things, to give us the immediate occasion of the main matter of the section,—the healing of the demoniac. The reason that his friends came out to Him as they did seems to have lain in the thronging of the crowds, and in the fact that there was no room to eat. These facts, however, furnished them with a pretext for rescuing Him from the hands of His enemies, whose designs and power they well knew. John came not eating and drinking, and they said *He hath a devil.* Spirit-like oblivion of the body and of its nourishment, they interpreted as involuntary demoniac enthusiasm. Thus did it seem to be with the Lord at this time; and using this representation, his family went out to gain their object.

2. The choice of the Twelve was soon followed by this erring conduct of His own friends towards Him, several of the Twelve being among them. These, therefore, mistook their vocation, in the same manner as Peter and the sons of Zebedee mistook theirs on another occasion. The new impulse given to the Lord's cause, and the new step it had taken, is followed by a new defeat and counter-stroke. As soon as He takes assistants to Himself, they aim to infuse earthly policy into His plans.

2. The worst manifestation of the kingdom of evil is the blasphemy with which hypocrites, unconsciously standing in the service of darkness, interpret the most glorious manifestations of the kingdom of heaven as works from below. The blasphemy against the Son of God, as approximating to the blasphemy against the Holy Spirit, is the most fearful display of the power of the arch-blasphemer.

4. While the pictorial vividness of the Evangelist is observable throughout the whole of the conflict which he depicts, he, however, omits the sign of Jonas, the statement concerning possession by seven devils, and the like.

5. *And looking round.*—Jesus, in His conflict with His enemies and the dark kingdom which they serve, does not trust to men, but does trust to His own influence on mankind; that is, he does not confide in His own friends, so far as they would dictate to Him with carnal policy as his natural family; but to His friends as they trustingly hang upon His lips as his spiritual family.

6. Christ's defence becomes immediately an attack. Earnest apologetics pass over into polemics.

HOMILETICAL AND PRACTICAL.

See on the parallels.—*No room to eat.* How often did the Lord, in the zeal of His vocation, forget eating and drinking and sleep!—The highest freedom of spirit and self-government are interpreted even by His people as bondage and being beside self.—How much to be reprobated is an ambiguous and feigned adoption of the notions of the enemies of truth, on the part of those who would represent the truth!—The concessions of carnal ecclesiastical policy to the unfriendly world always spring from evil.—The sound concession is the infinite forbearance with which Christ enters into the notions of His opponents to refute their assertions.—Christ exalted equally above the protection of His friends and the attacks of His foes.—Contrast between the Lord's great conflict with His opponents and his disciples' slight assistance: 1. Contrast in temper: heroic reliance in divine truth; petty trust in human cunning. 2. Contrast in the conflict itself: simple defence and simple attack; ambiguous apology and mediation. 3. Contrast in the result: high victory; deep humiliation.—The false and the true family of Jesus: 1. The one would watch over Him and His cause, the other will be watched over by Him; 2. the one would

* Namely, that he was in league with the demons.—*Ed.*

lead Him, the other will be led by Him; 3. the one would save Him, the other will be saved by Him; 4. the one would restrain and bring Him into danger, the other will be restrained and bound by His word and Spirit.—The Lord detects and cuts asunder the bands of perilous fellowship between His friends and His enemies: 1. He detects them: worldliness in religion, fear, cunning, and policy; 2. He cuts them asunder by the word of severance, by warning, and by blessing.—The divine dignity of our Lord in the decisive conflicts of His kingdom: 1. As opposed to His enemies, the instruments of darkness; 2. as opposed to His family, as they are confused by the apparent danger of His cause; 3. as opposed to His Church, which hangs upon His lips with child-like simplicity, not suspecting its danger.—Christ says to His people, in the days of apparent peril to religion: My thoughts are not your thoughts; neither are My ways your ways.—Christ's defence is, in its own nature, also a victorious attack.—Blasphemy against the Spirit is eternal guilt, and therefore exposed to eternal condemnation.—The calm declaration of Christ, that He wrought in the power of the Holy Spirit, in opposition to His blaspheming enemies, who charged him with being possessed by the spirit of darkness and working under his influence.—Maintenance of this opposition: 1. Divine repose against devilish excitement; 2. divine forbearance against devilish hatred; 3. divine illumination against devilish confusion.

STARKE:—CANSTEIN:—If Christ endures, the Christian Church endures.—ZEISIUS:—The devil never gives up the work that his name imports—slandering the good; nor do those who are on his side, John viii. 44.—QUESNEL:—We must strive to preserve our honorable name, so long as it is possible.—It is awful to ascribe to the devil that which comes from God. Thus God is made into Satan.—The Creator endures this blasphemy, in His patience and long-suffering, and men will endure nothing. We should be imitators of God.—Wolf does not eat wolf; nor does Satan drive out Satan.—Satan does not persecute Satan, yet Christians persecute Christians. O fearful wickedness!—Rebellion and insurrection are destructive and ruinous.—When once the devil is master of any heart, none but Jesus Christ can drive him out.—CRAMER:—Children must honor their parents; but in matters that pertain to office, and the things of God and conscience, they should not be overruled by any.—There is no carnal prerogative in the kingdom of God.—QUESNEL:—He who doeth the will of God to the end enters into an eternal alliance with God as his Father, with Jesus Christ as his brother, with the angels and saints as his sisters, and with the heavenly Jerusalem as his mother.—GERLACH: According to Mark, Jesus distinguishes general blasphemy against God from the particular blasphemy against the Holy Spirit; according to Matthew and Luke, He distinguishes from it also the blasphemy against the Son of Man: in both cases there is the contrast between a revelation which has been more external, and one which has seized the inner man with more convincing divine power.—"He that doeth the will of God:" He means thereby faith, which is the fount and beginning of all holy obedience.—BRAUNE: We must watch over zeal, as over fire in a house. But that cold moderation which the world loves so well is most offensive to Christ, who will spue the lukewarm out of His mouth, Rev. iii. 16. This is our Lord's official fidelity.—In the presence of this blaspheming malignity, the Redeemer exhibits a simplicity, a security, a freedom from all bitterness, which must have produced a sacred impression upon all who beheld, even as upon us now.—It is in the Spirit of God that Jesus overcomes Satan.—SCHLEIERMACHER (on the words, *He is beside Himself*):—So those have always been accounted whom God in hard times has chosen for His special instruments: it was in the time of the Church's Reformation, and it will always be so again when times of darkness shall return.—There have never been wanting such enemies of the truth, who have similarly sought to put another character upon that one only institute for human salvation which can never find a substitute. But, as in the text, their efforts are always vain.—How far blind and rash zeal may lead men!—"He that gathereth not with Me, scattereth."—"He that for My sake forsaketh not father and mother is not worthy of Me."—Christ on the cross: "Behold thy son! Behold thy Mother!"—There should be, then, no conflict between our natural and spiritual relationships.—All the household must be members of the one same family.

---

3. *Our Lord's Conflict with the* carnal *Unbelief of the People in the Delivery of His Parables, and His Triumph over Human Narrowness.* (CH. IV. 1–34.)

(Parallels: Matt. xiii. 1–23; vers. 31–35; Luke viii. 4–18.)

1 And he began again to teach by the sea-side: and there was gathered[1] unto him a
great multitude, so that he entered into a [the] ship, and sat in the sea; and the whole
2 multitude was by the sea on the land. And he taught them many things by parables,
3 and said unto them in his doctrine, Hearken: behold, there went out a sower to sow
4 And it came to pass, as he sowed, some fell by the way-side, and the fowls [birds] of
5 the air[2] came and devoured it up. And some[3] fell on stony ground, where it had no
6 much earth; and immediately it sprang up, because it had no depth of earth: But when
7 the sun was up,[4] it was scorched; and, because it had no root, it withered away. And
some fell among thorns, and the thorns grew up and choked it, and it yielded no fruit
8 And other fell on good ground, and did yield fruit that sprang up and increased, and
9 brought forth, some thirty, and some sixty, and some an hundred. And he said unto

10 them, He that hath ears to hear, let him hear. And when he was alone [apart], they
11 that were about him with the twelve asked of him the parable.[5] And he said unto
them, Unto you it is given to know[6] the mystery of the kingdom of God: but unto
12 them that are without, all *these* things are done in parables: That seeing they may see,
and not perceive; and hearing they may hear, and not understand; lest at any time
13 they should be converted, and *their* sins should be forgiven them. And he said unto
14 them, Know ye not this parable? and how then will ye know all parables? The sower
15 soweth the word. And these are they by the way-side, where the word is sown; but
[and] when they have heard, Satan cometh immediately, and taketh away the word
16 that was sown in their hearts. And these[7] are they likewise which are sown on stony
ground; who, when they have heard the word, immediately receive it with gladness;
17 And have no [not] root in themselves, and so endure but for a time [but are transient]:
afterward, when affliction or persecution ariseth for the word's sake, immediately they
18 are offended. And these are they which are sown among thorns; such as hear the
19 word, And the cares of this[8] world, and the deceitfulness of riches, and the lusts of other
20 [remaining] things entering in, choke the word, and it becometh unfruitful. And these[9]
are they which are sown on good ground; such as hear the word, and receive *it*, and
21 bring forth fruit, some thirty-fold, some sixty, and some an hundred. And he said
unto them, Is a candle [the lamp] brought to be put under a bushel [the measure],
22 or under a [the] bed? and not to be set on a candlestick [the lamp-stand]? For
there is nothing hid, which shall not[10] be manifested; neither was anything kept secret,
23 but that it should come abroad. If any man have ears to hear, let him hear.
24 And he saith unto them, Take heed what ye hear: with what measure ye mete, it shall
25 be measured to you; and unto you that hear[11] shall more be given. For he that hath,
to him shall be given; and he that hath not, from him shall be taken even that which
26 he hath. And he said, So is the kingdom of God, as if a man should cast [the] seed
27 into [upon] the ground; And should sleep, and rise night and day, and the seed should
28 spring [sprout] and grow up [elongate], he knoweth not how. For[12] the earth bringeth
forth fruit of herself [automatically]; first the blade, then the ear, after that the full corn
29 in the ear. But when the fruit is brought forth [yields], immediately he putteth in the
30 sickle, because the harvest is [has] come. And he said, Whereunto shall we liken the
31 kingdom of God? or with what comparison shall we compare it?[13] *It is* like a grain of
mustard-seed, which, when it is sown in the earth, is less than all the seeds that be in
32 the earth: But when it is sown, it groweth up, and becometh greater than all herbs, and
shooteth out [makes] great branches; so that the fowls [birds] of the air may lodge
33 under the shadow of it. And with many such parables spake he the word unto them,
34 as they were able to hear *it*. But without a parable spake he not unto them: and
when they were alone, he expounded all things to his disciples.

[1] Ver. 1.—Συνάγεται instead of συνήχθη: Lachmann, Tischendorf, after B., C., L.
[2] Ver. 4.—"Fowls of heaven." Τοῦ οὐρανοῦ has only D. of the uncial MSS. in its favor. Probably added from Luke viii. 5.
[3] Ver. 5.—Καὶ ἄλλο instead of ἄλλο δέ: Lachmann and Tischendorf, after the best MSS.
[4] Ver. 6.—Lachmann and Tischendorf, after B., C., D., L., Δ., Vulgate, read καὶ ὅτε ἀνέτειλεν ὁ ἥλιος, instead of ἡλίου δὲ ἀνατείλαντος.
[5] Ver. 10.—Τὰς παραβολάς instead of τὴν παραβολήν: Tischendorf, after B., C., L., Δ. The parable just delivered gave them occasion to ask about the design of parables generally.
[6] Ver. 11.—The γνῶναι is wanting in A., B., C.* So Lachmann, Tischendorf.
[7] Ver. 18.—Καὶ ἄλλοι εἰσί instead of καὶ οὗτοί εἰσιν: Griesbach, Lachmann, Tischendorf, after B., C.*, D., Vulgate, &c.
[8] Ver. 19.—Τούτου is wanting in the best MSS., and rejected by Griesbach, Fritzsche, Lachmann, and Tischendorf.
[9] Ver. 20.—Ἐκεῖνοι instead of οὗτοι: Tischendorf, after B., C., L., Δ.
[10] Ver. 22.—Ἐὰν μή, the most difficult and best authenticated reading (A., B., C., Tischendorf). [Meyer thinks that the ὃ is an addition, and would explain by comparison with Mark x. 30. He denies the assertion of Fritzsche and De Wette that ἐὰν μή is absurdly used here, and contends that it contains a logical analysis of the thought.—*Ed.*]
[11] Ver. 24.—Τοῖς ἀκούουσιν, omitted in Lachmann and Tischendorf, after B., C., D., G., L.
[12] Ver. 28.—The γὰρ must be given up. Πλήρης σῖτος instead of πλήρη σῖτον: B., Lachmann, Tischendorf.
[13] Ver. 30.—Πῶς instead of τίνι: Tischendorf, after B., C., L., Δ., Versions. Ἐν τίνι αὐτὴν παραβολῇ θῶμεν instead of ἐν ποίᾳ παραβολῇ παραβάλωμεν αὐτήν: Tischendorf, Lachmann, after B., C.*, L., Δ.
[14] Ver. 31.—Κόκκῳ: Elzevir, Fritzsche, Tischendorf, Meyer; κόκκον: Griesbach, Scholz, Lachmann.

EXEGETICAL AND CRITICAL.

See on the parallels.—Matthew gives us a collection of seven parables; Mark, of three. Thus it is a round sacred number in both. Here also the individual parables are combined into one collective view of the kingdom of God. In Matthew, we see the *chronological* development of the kingdom of God in its historical periods; here, we have a picture of its development in space (statistically) according to its immanent principles of gradual expansion. The first parable depicts the kingdom of God in its universally difficult foundation; the second (a procious addition to the treasury of parables, in Mark alone), its certain and natural development; the third, its wonderful and glorious spread and consummation. It is probable that these three parables formed originally one single connected discourse; furnishing the basis of a later historical representation of the kingdom in the seven parables. The beginning of the parabolic discourses, however, had an earlier position than Mark indicates. His purpose is to connect them with the transference of Jesus' teaching to the sea-side; but he has also a motive arising out of the nature of the events for placing these parables here. They form a crisis in the conflict of Christ with unbelief in Galilee, and mark His conflict with the specially sensuous unbelief of the people. Hence, in ver. 12, he has the well-known strong ἵνα (βλέποντες βλέπωσι καὶ μὴ ἴδωσι); while Matthew has the ὅτι. He also quotes in a very suggestive manner, vers. 21–23, the words of Christ which we find in Matthew's Sermon on the Mount, ch. v. 15, and in the instructions to the Apostles, ch. x. 26, and which in Luke, ch. viii. 16, are connected with the parable of the sower. There is nothing improbable in the supposition that our Lord used these figures in various connections. Here the figure of the candle is designed to teach that the parables have it for their positive purpose to enlighten; that is, that the disciples should at the right season discover the spiritual meaning of the parables; and the figure of the measure, that the disciples were to measure out instruction liberally in hope.

Ver. 1. **And He began again to teach by the sea-side.**—Another emphatic reference to the contrast of this with His customary course of teaching; and as an expression of His decided breach with the Pharisees.

Ver. 2. **In His doctrine.**—In His doctrinal instructions. "Of the many things (πολλά), Mark makes some particular things prominent." Meyer.

Ver. 8. **Fruit that sprang up and increased.**—We understand the former, of strong and vigorous upward growth; but the latter, the αὐξανόμενον, of the seed-corn's spreading out into a number of stalks, as is the case with prosperous increase. Meyer also understands the καρπός as meaning the stalks in contradistinction to the grains, these not being mentioned till later: "some," etc. But the idea of the fruit is thus artificially weakened. The actual and excellent growth is described; but under the point of view of its fruit, this and the luxuriant stalk being embraced in one. It is better to understand the springing up and increasing of the fruit as meaning the springing up of the ears of grain with the stems.

Ver. 10. **They that were about Him, with the Twelve.**—The specific company of Christ's disciples, independent of and with the Twelve. Euthym. Zig.: The Seventy. But these were not distinguished from the rest until later.

Ver. 11. **Unto you is given to know the mystery.**—Significant; and to be explained in accordance with Matthew and Luke. The mystery is given through the knowledge of it.—*But unto them that are without*, οἱ ἔξω: in later phraseology, all non-Christians (1 Cor. v. 12); with the Talmudists, all who were not Jews; but also the uninstructed and uninitiated Jews. Here, however, it is doubtless a hint of the germ of the opposition between the old and the new community, which in the word ἐκκλησία Matt. xvi. 18) came somewhat later into full use.

Ver. 12. **They may see.**—The ἵνα is not to be softened, as if *ita ut*, as Rosenmüller and others assert. We must maintain that this hard utterance was based upon Isa. vi. 9 *seq.*, and therefore that it must be interpreted in the meaning of that passage not as an absolute sentence, but as a *deserved, economical*, and *pedagogical* visitation. *See* on *Matthew.*

Ver. 13. **Know ye not this parable?**—The first parable of the kingdom is the basis of all the rest. If they understood not this, they could not understand any that followed. If they had the explanation of this, they had the key for the understanding of all others. According to De Wette, these are rebuking words; according to Meyer, they are a mere recurrence to the question of ver. 10. But it is certainly, at the same time, an intimation of the connection of all the parables in the idea of the kingdom of heaven; so that with the explanation of this one, all were explained.

Ver. 15. **These are they by the way-side, where the word is sown.**—Through the whole parable we must embrace in one view the field with the seed on it. In Luke, the idea of seed predominates; in Mark, the idea of ground sown over; in Matthew, there is an alternation. In the first instance, the view of the ground sown predominates; in the last, the view of the seed scattered.

Ver. 16. **Which are sown.**—Mark the change of tense in Mark: σπειρόμενοι, vers. 16 and 18, and σπαρέντες in ver. 20.

Ver. 18. **Who have heard the word.**—Hearers preëminently. Diligent hearers, but not doers; ἀκούσαντες instead of ἀκούοντες: B., C., D., L., Δ., Tischendorf. Mark gives the most vivid picture of them.

Ver. 21. **Is a candle brought to be put.**—Not an exhortation to virtue, as Theophylact and others thought, but a statement of the end for which He confided to them the mystery of the kingdom in parables. According to Erasmus: "Do not suppose that what I now commit to you in secret, I would have concealed for ever; the light is kindled by Me in you, that by your ministry it may disperse the darkness of the whole world."

Ver. 22. **For there is nothing hid.**—The concealed is in its very nature destined to be revealed in its time. A thing absolutely and forever concealed would not be concealed; it would as such have no meaning. There is this design in all the concealments of the kingdom of God. Thus the clause forms the complement of the ἵνα above, ver. 12.

Ver. 24. **With what measure ye mete.**—De Wette (after Euthym. Zig.): "According to the measure of your ability and diligence (as hearers, *see* the preceding verse), ye will receive instruction." But it seems more obvious, in the process of the thought, to say, According to the measure of your diligence in teaching will your Master add to your knowledge (*docendo discimus*, especially in the kingdom of God). For the mere hearing and receiving cannot well be described as a measuring out.

Ver. 25. **For he that hath.**—The proverb has, here, more reference to zeal in the teaching function. The living treasure of knowledge will always, by its own nature, go on increasing. We may compare the words concerning the spiritual life springing up within, John iv. 14; vii. 38; for living knowledge is never separable from internal spiritual life.

Vers. 26–29 are a continuation of the parabolic instruction addressed to the people. Meyer: Observe the Aorist βάλῃ, and then the following Presents: *has cast*, and then *does sleep*

Ver. 29. **When the fruit is brought forth.**—But the παραδῷ is not intransitive: When the fruit shall have yielded itself. This relative spontaneousness of the fruit is as if it did not suffer premature cutting before its full ripeness.

Ver. 30. **Or with what comparison.**—Meyer: The hearers are now formally addressed in the discourse, as the omission of αὐτοῖς with ἔλεγεν shows.

Ver. 33. **And with many such parables.**—Manifestly, Mark knew of other parables of our Lord, which he passes over. **As they were able.**—This does not refer to their worthiness (Grotius), but to their ability to apprehend (Theophylact, De Wette). It also includes, however, their being able to bear without being offended. Thus it is not a mere literal ἀκούειν in the sense of being able to receive, as Meyer thinks.

DOCTRINAL AND ETHICAL.

1. *See* on the parallels.—On the ἵνα, ver. 12, *see* the notes above.

2. The parable of vers. 26–29 teaches, in the figure of the *relative* independence of nature in the regular development of the seed through an internal energy of growth (αὐτομάτη), the higher *relative* independence and regular development of the growth of the kingdom of God, or the establishment of Christianity and the Church in the world down to its consummation for the final manifestation of the kingdom of God. (The reapers: the angels, Matt. xiii. 39.) The proper point of comparison is the seed's impulse of growth from within outwardly, as if by an internal energy of its own, whence follow the apparent spontaneousness, regularity, gradualness, progressiveness, security, and perfection of the development. Thus the naturalness of nature, so to speak, the "metamorphosis of plants," becomes a symbol of the development of the divine life from the seed of the divine word or regeneration. The germinant energy of growth is here the actual freedom of the new divine-human (not abstractly human, but also not abstractly divine) energy of life in humanity; whether in the regeneration and sanctification of the believing community, or in that of the individual Christian. Here also the development proceeds from within, from the conscious internal being: independent or free (not from God, but in God), naturally and regularly legitimate, gradual, progressive, down to certain and decisive consummation. But it is assumed that human nature in its essence bears the same relation to the word of God, and has as much in common with it, as the earth to the seed-corn. And as the earth only by culture, and tillage, and sowing, overcomes its tendency to wildness, and the bringing forth of thorns and thistles, so also the human heart is set free from its wicked bias, and its thorns and thistles, only by the culture of grace and the seed of the word of God. Meyer: The spontaneousness here set forth does not negate the divine energies of grace; but the end of the parable is not to make the latter prominent, but the former. De Wette: The parable teaches patience, as that of the tares forbearance.—The period of the New Testament Church presents the natural development of the kingdom of God, yet not without the Lord's overruling, and not without the constant energy of His Spirit. The miraculous seed has become a new nature, from which at the Lord's appearance new fruits will grow.

HOMILETICAL AND PRACTICAL.

See on the parallels.—Christ teaching in the ship a parable itself of the kingdom of heaven: 1. A figure of the form of that kingdom: *a.* of the evangelical ministry, *b.* of the church, *c.* of missions; 2. a figure of its condition: *a.* small beginnings, *b.* poverty, *c.* mobility, freedom.—Christ in conflict with the *sensuous* unbelief of the world.—Christ the deliverer of the people from the bonds of ignorance, of carnal notions, and sensuous narrowness.—The teaching wisdom of Christ, as it speaks in parables, a seal of His divine power (of His love as of His wisdom).—He that hath ears to hear, let him hear!—The parables of Jesus as signs of the divine judgments: 1. Figuring the judicial concealments and symbols of truth in the spiritual life of mankind, *a.* in the Gentile world, *b.* in the people of Israel, *c.* in the Christian, specially the medieval Church; 2. figuring their scope and purpose, *a.* to spare, *b.* to instruct, and *c.* to discipline and educate the soul.—The interpretation of the parable of the sower a key to the interpretation of all the rest.—The three parables of our chapter combined, present a figure of the unfolding of the kingdom of heaven, as to its foundation, progress, and completion.—The parable of vers. 26–29. Nature, in its normal development from within, a representation of human freedom, and its development in the kingdom of grace.—The word of life in the figure of a grain of wheat: 1. Its internal energy of life; 2. its growth according to laws; 3. its gradualness; 4. its progressive stages; 5. the certainty of its development.—The work of grace, its normal unfolding, in the Church and in individuals.—In the kingdom of grace we must learn not to misapprehend even the immature forms of development (not counting the green stalk as common grass, etc.).—The seed of divine grace requires patient waiting for its maturity.—The human heart may become one with the word of God (in consequence of its original relation to it) through faith; and then there is unfolded in it a divine energy of new life.—For him who rightly cares for the seed, the fruit gradually ripens, although he himself may not know it.—Even in unconscious life, the divine word goes on maturing. (Narratives of the feeble-minded, in whom it gradually was developed. The action of the mind in going to sleep continues in sleep.)—Influences upon the seed of the kingdom of nature analogous to those of the kingdom of grace: the mysterious operation and movement of the Holy Spirit are the sunshine and rain in the kingdom of grace.—The seed, with all its certainty of development, under the necessary condition of sunshine and rain. Application of this to the work of divine grace in the soul of the believer.

STARKE:—QUESNEL:—An imperfect church, an unworthy pulpit, and poor hearers, may nevertheless form a true church, accepted of God.—CRAMER:—Jesus makes the little ship His pulpit: if we do not diligently hear and obey, He removes Himself with His little ship and pulpit.—CANSTEIN:—Tilling the land is the oldest work of men's hands, and the most pleasing to God; therefore Christ took His parables so willingly from that occupation.—God's word is a living seed, by which the spiritually dead hearts of men are made living and fruitful.—HEDINGER:—Unchanging seed, variable hearts.—OSIANDER:—If men did not harden themselves, they would not fall into the danger of reprobation.—HEDINGER:—We must not look at the mere shell, but at the kernel of Holy Scripture (on ver. 13).—QUESNEL:—The knowl edge of divine mysteries is of God, and not of man.—The wisdom of God has not always remained secret, but at the right season has been made manifest to men, 1 Cor. ii. 7.—All things must come to light, whether after a longer or a shorter time.—Faithful pastors and diligent hearers obtain from day to day a larger measure of light and grace.—A faithful and diligent soul has a great treasure—its riches extend to eternity; but an idle soul becomes every day poorer, until at last it loses all.—Oh, how far should we have advanced in the way of salvation, if we had only always used aright the means of grace!—By the sleeping is signified an expectation of blessing, which leaves all care to God; as one may say, I sleep, but my heart wakes.—MAJUS:—God's servants should not be impatient when they do not at once see the fruits of their labors.—We must do our work sincerely, and commit to God the result; He will make His true servants rejoice in the day of harvest.—God conceals from His ministers some of the fruits of their diligence, to keep them in humility.—Hope in God, who will not neglect his work in thee.—Christians must aim high, and strive after perfection.—Where God's word is rightly sown and received, it is never long without fruits of salvation.—OSIANDER:—We must not expect at once perfect trees of righteousness in the paradise of the Christian Church; time is required for rooting, growing, and bringing forth fruit.

GERLACH:—The longer man retains and studies any one divine truth, the more manifest it becomes, and itself brings all others to light.—BRAUNE:—The unostentatious development of the divine word and the kingdom of God in the heart of man.—As the husbandman hardly distinguishes seeds, so is it with the results of the seed of the word. Learn patience.—SCHLEIERMACHER:—(He observes that Christ was not misled by the flocking of multitudes around Himself, but perfectly penetrated His whole auditory—four kinds of soils; but that at the same time He was not angered by this character of His auditory.) If the divine word is received and retained, it is changed into the life of the man; and then in a natural manner his acts are like his words, and become more and more the expression of thy divine word.—The fruit is that which is to be detached again from the plant, itself to be again sown, and from which new life is to arise.—The Redeemer says truly, that there is no other power be which the kingdom of God prospers than this power of the seed, this power of the divine word; that is, in relation to the office and work of the human sower.—The preparatory work, the tilling of the land, must be distinguished from the sowing.—GOSSNER:—On ver. 23. Him who made the ear, man will not hear.—If we mete out with the measure of Christ, it shall be meted to us again with the same.

---

4. *Conflict of Jesus with the* feeble-minded *Unbelief of the Disciples; the Stilling of the Storm; and His Triumph over Human Seafarers in their vocation.* (VERS. 35–41.)

(Parallels: Matt. viii. 18, 23–27; Luke viii. 22–25.)

35 And the same day, when the even was come, he saith unto them, Let us pass over
36 unto the other side. And when they had sent away the multitude, they took him even
37 as he was in the ship. And there were also with him other little ships. And there
arose a great storm [squall] of wind, and the waves beat into the ship, so that it was
38 now full. And he was in the hinder part of the ship, asleep on a pillow [the boat-
cushion]: and they awake him, and say unto him, Master, carest thou not that we
39 perish? And he arose, and rebuked the wind, and said unto the sea, Peace, be still.
40 And the wind ceased, and there was a great calm. And he said unto them, Why are
41 ye so fearful? how is it that ye have no faith? And they feared exceedingly, and
said one to another, What manner of man is this, that even the wind and the sea obey
him?

[1] Ver. 37.—Lachmann, Tischendorf, following B., C., D., L., &c., read ἤδη γεμίζεσθαι τὸ πλοῖον, instead of αὐτὸ ἤδη γεμίζεσθαι.

[2] Ver. 40.—The οὕτω is rejected by Lachmann, after B., D., L., Δ., Vulgate. Tischendorf defends it by important Codd. The insertion, indeed, is more easily explained than the omission. Griesbach, Lachmann read οὔπω, instead of πῶς οὐκ, in conformity with B., D., L., Vulgate, Itala, &c.

EXEGETICAL AND CRITICAL.

See on the parallels.—Pictorial vividness in the narrative of the voyage: evening, the sudden departure, the convoy of ships, the violence of the storm, the ship all but sinking, the image of Him who slept on the pillow, the reproach of the distressed men that Jesus cared not, the words of rebuke to the wind, the strong reproof of the disciples, their great fear, and its effect.

Ver. 35. Besides the arrangement according to matter, there is here a definite historical sequence to the preceding section.—**And the same day, He saith unto them.**—Thus it was before the stormy voyage that our Lord uttered the first parables concerning the kingdom of heaven.

Ver. 36. **Even as He was in the ship.**—That is, they proceeded at once, before they could make special preparation for the voyage. The evening voyage over the sea to the southeast coast was extended to several hours, and became a night voyage.

Ver. 37. **The waves beat into the ship.**—The ἐπέβαλλεν intransitive, referring to the waves.

Ver. 40. Meyer: The disciples' weakness in knowledge and faith is made more prominent by Mark than by the other Synoptics: comp. ch. vi. 52; vii. 18; viii. 17, 18, 33; ix. 6, 19, 32, 34; x. 24, 32, 35; xiv. 40.

DOCTRINAL AND ETHICAL.

1. *See* on the parallels.

2. Significance of the crisis of deep excitement: mutual reproaches. The disciples allege against the Lord, groundlessly and irreverently, the reproach of not caring for them; He on His side inflicts the well-founded reproof of despondency and lack of faith. They uttered their charge prematurely, before they had waited to see the Lord's manner of action; Christ did not utter his reproof (fully, comp. Matthew), until He had brought relief in the danger. This often recurs in the history of the Church's great tribulations, as well as in the private difficulties of the Christian life.

3. The personification of the wind and sea in Christ's address is most emphatic in the rebuking words of Christ, as found in Mark. But at the base of this personification there is a dogmatic element, to wit, that nature has acquired a character of apparently wild independence and anarchy since man became unfaithful to his destiny: Rule over it, and make it subject to you. But in this seeming anarchy, which is under the power of God, and is used by Him as a means of discipline and judgment, is reflected that real anarchy, that lack of obedience and faith in the human breast, which is at the same time felt as a lack of self-government and rule over the creature. Therefore we see confronting the unbelief of the disciples Jesus' confidence; His peace is opposed to their excitement, His self-possession to their distraction; His majestic supremacy over the winds and waves is opposed to their subjection to natural terrors. And the effect is, that his own disciples experience towards Him the same awe of reverence and fear which they had experienced before towards the frightful sublimity of nature. But now they are the subjects of a fear which passes over into the utterances of a rising and blessed faith.

HOMILETICAL AND PRACTICAL.

See on the parallels.—The voyage of the disciples of Jesus a night-voyage (according to Mark; *see* the notes) in the life of the disciples: 1. The history; 2. its significance.—The victory of the Lord over feeble-minded unbelief: 1. He leads little faith into danger; 2. He lets it wrestle with the peril to the utmost point; 3. He convicts, humbles, and heals it.—The fear of man before the terrors of nature, a sign that he is not consecrated through the terrors of the spirit.—The Lord's supremacy over human vocations (seafaring, fishing, government, learning).—Trial of the disciples in the danger of death.—The pride of the little apostolical crew, and its humiliation; a sign.—Jesus' sleeping and awaking: 1. His sleeping, the repose of His divine power, an exercise and test of the human; 2. His awaking, a new glorification of the saving divinity in humanity needing salvation.—Jesus the star of the sea (the anchor the rudder, the lighthouse, the rescuer of the wrecked).—Danger to life always danger to the soul.—Divine help in our human life should be to us a sign for quickening and salvation.—How all fear of the creature should be changed by the awe of Christ's presence into peace.—To reverence the Son of God, and to obtain kingly power over the creaturely world, are one and the same—Perfect love casts out fear.—The wide wild world glorified by the Spirit of Christ into a blessed house of God.—Jesus Christ, the commander of wind and sea: 1. In nature; 2. in history; 3. in the fates of the Church.—What follows from His being obeyed by the winds and the waves,—as to Himself, as to the world, as to us?—Christ as the Ruler of nature, and Restorer of its paradisaical peace.

STARKE:—The evening may be very different from the early morning.—Faithful servants of God may have some seasons of rest permitted them, lest they sink under their burden.—Going forth with Christ into a sea of tribulation.—If He be with us, we shall not sink and perish.—The little ship of the Church is often so beaten by the storms of tribulation and persecution, that it seems as if it must go down.—Distress teaches man to pray, although faith is never without prayer.—It is the error of men, that they take, at once, danger to be a mark that God takes no heed of them.—CANSTEIN:—A great storm followed by a great calm: so is it ever with God's consolations after trial.—QUESNEL:—God is so gracious and gentle, that He does not despise a slender faith, or reject an imperfect prayer, or cast out a fearful heart.—How profitable would Christians find it, if they would discourse in their social meetings about the wonders of God and the glory of Jesus Christ!

GERLACH:—It is always a blameable unbelief, when we fear to enter the ship with Christ.—BRAUNE:—The difference between Jonah's sleeping in the ship and that of Jesus.—He that is in us is greater than he that is in the world.—SCHLEIERMACHER:—That was their unbelief, He meant, that they thought He could sink at a time when He had not yet given them any commission; that they thought God could take so little care of His work, as that it should sink with them.—There is no one among us who can assure himself that the old man, however entirely he may seem to be buried into the death of Christ, will not rise up with his giant lusts, and involve the soul in storm and tempest.—But if we are members of His body, we should maintain the sure confidence, that in all times of severe trial and temptation, the bond of union between Him and us will not be severed.—As certainly as He could not sink with His disciples on that day, He will not suffer his disciples to sink in this.—GOSSNER:—When the help of man ceases, God's help begins; or, faith in the sure word.—When there is storm in the soul, and when thou art in great peril, thou knowest what it is for, and whither to fly.—What calmness in the soul, when the Lord arises and utters His voice

6. *Conflict of Jesus with the* despairing *Unbelief of the Demoniac, and the* selfish *Unbelief of the Gadarenes; Healing of the Demoniac, and Triumph over Human Devices for Security.* (CH. V. 1–20.)

(Parallels: Matt. viii. 28–34; Luke viii. 26–39.)

1 And they came over unto the other side of the sea, into the country of the Gada
2 renes. And when he was come out of the ship, immediately there met him out of the
3 tombs a man with an unclean spirit, Who had *his* dwelling among the tombs; and no
4 man could bind him, no, not with chains: Because that he had been often bound with
fetters and chains, and the chains had been plucked asunder by him, and the fetters
5 broken in pieces: neither could any *man* tame him. And always, night and day, he
6 was in the mountains, and in the tombs, crying, and cutting himself with stones. But
7 when he saw Jesus afar off, he ran and worshipped him, And cried with a loud voice,
and said, What have I to do with thee, Jesus, *thou* Son of the most high God? I ad-
8 jure thee by God, that thou torment me not. (For he said unto him, Come out of the
9 man, *thou* unclean spirit.) And he asked him, What is thy name? And he answered
10 saying, My name *is* Legion: for we are many. And he besought him much that he
11 would not send them away out of the country. Now there was there, nigh unto the
12 mountains [mountain], a great herd of swine feeding. And all the devils besought
13 him, saying, Send us into the swine, that we may enter into them. And forthwith
Jesus gave them leave. And the unclean spirits went out, and entered into the swine;
and the herd ran violently down a steep place into the sea (they were about two thou-
14 sand), and were choked in the sea. And they that fed the swine fled, and told *it* in
the city, and in the country. And they went out to see what it was that was done.
15 And they come to Jesus, and see him that was possessed with the devil, and had the
16 legion, sitting, and clothed, and in his right mind [sane]; and they were afraid. And
they that saw *it* told them how it befell to him that was possessed with the devil, and
17 *also* concerning the swine. And they began to pray him to depart out of their coasts.
18 And when he was come into the ship, he that had been possessed with the devil prayed
19 him that he might be with him. Howbeit Jesus suffered him not; but saith unto him,
Go home to thy friends, and tell them how great things the Lord hath done for thee,
20 and hath had compassion on thee. And he departed, and began to publish in Deca-
polis how great things Jesus had done for him: and all *men* did marvel.

[1] Ver. 1.—Many Codd. read ἦλθεν instead of ἦλθον. But this is not sufficiently authenticated: "probably from Matt. viii. 28." Lachmann and Tischendorf, after B., D., Vulgate, read Γερασηνῶν; L., Δ., &c., Γεργεσηνῶν; Cod. A., *Recepta*, Scholz, Meyer, Γαδαρηνῶν. Comp. the parallel in Matthew.

[2] Ver. 3.—Ἁλυσει, instead of ἁλύσεσιν, Lachmann, Tischendorf, after B., C., L. Οὐκέτι οὐδείς, Lachmann and Tischendorf, after B., C., D., L., Vulgate: strong negation.

[3] Ver. 5.—"In the tombs and upon the mountains," is the best attested order: Griesbach, Scholz, Lachmann, Tischendorf.

[4] Ver. 9.—Instead of ἀπεκρίθη λέγων (Elzevir), the better reading is λέγει αὐτῷ.

[5] Ver. 12.—Πάντες (Elzevir) is wanting in B., C., D., L., Versions; οἱ δαίμονες is wanting in B., C., L., Griesbach, Tischendorf.

[6] Ver. 13.—The ἦσαν δὲ is wanting in B., C.*, D., Syriac, Vulgate, Griesbach, and Tischendorf.

[7] Ver. 18.—A., B., D., Vulgate, Lachmann, Tischendorf, ἐμβαίνοντος.

[8] Ver. 19.—Καὶ οὐκ, A., B., C.; Elzevir reads ὁ δὲ Ἰησοῦς οὐκ.

EXEGETICAL AND CRITICAL.

Compare on the parallels.—Mark's vividness of realization here again appears in many characteristics: the untameableness of the demon, whom no man could bind, even with chains; his crying in the mountains, and the self-tormenting fury of his cutting himself with stones; his seeing Jesus afar off, running to Him, and crying with a loud voice at the first sight of the Lord; the adjuration of Jesus by God; the vehemence of his anxiety that He should not send him away out of that country (Luke: into the abyss); the number of the swine, two thousand; the contrast of the demoniac who was possessed by the legion, sitting clothed and in his right mind; the observation, that the healed man spread the report of the miracle through all Decapolis; and other similar traits. Luke, in his representation of the event, approximates to Mark. Matthew alone makes mention of two demoniacs, on which we may consult the parallels. As it respects the chronology, Mark goes back in the history, manifestly because his order is that of things and not of time. The voyage to Gadara fell in the first year of Christ's work, and preceded the healing of the paralytic and the controversies touching the Sabbath.

Ver. 4. **Fetters and chains.**—This distinction has been explained by referring the fetters to the hands, which Meyer rejects. Fetters are fetters, to whatever part of the body applied. However, these chains were ordinarily used for the hands.

Ver. 5. **Crying, and cutting himself with stones.**—Fearful picture of a demoniac terror,—having reached the extreme point of madness, down to rending his own flesh.

Ver. 6. **When he saw Jesus afar off.**—Vivid description of the wonderful influence of Christ upon the demoniac. Probably some intelligence concerning Jesus had reached his ears; but that he knew Him at once in this His appearance, can be explained only by an intensified spiritual presentiment. It is not probable that he was a heathen.

Ver. 7. **I adjure Thee by God.**—The daring misuse of the name of God in the mouth of the demoniac has nothing in it inconsistent, as Strauss and others have thought. The intermixture of praying and adjuring is characteristic of the demoniac, as under the influence of Christ.—**That Thou torment me not.**—Meyer: "The possessed man, identifying himself with his demon, dreads the pains and convulsions of the casting out." But if that had been meant, the possessed man would have distinguished himself from his demon, and not identified himself with him. In that identification he felt the nearness and the supremacy of Jesus itself a torment, and still more banishment into the abyss.

Ver. 8. **For He said** (had already said).—Compare Luke: παρήγγειλε γάρ, etc.—"If we rely on the exactitude of the sequence of the particulars in the narrative of Mark and Luke, we find here the remarkable circumstance, that the demoniac was not at once healed when the Lord spoke the decisive word. Christ had said to him, Come out of the man, thou unclean spirit! Now by this the demoniac consciousness in this man was shaken to its depths; but as he then felt himself to be possessed of a legion of evil spirits, the demoniac in him was not reached altogether by an address in the singular. Christ saw at once how the healing was to be perfected, and He asked him his name, etc." *Leben Jesu*, i. 296.

Ver. 9. **Legion.**—"The word occurs also in the rabbinical writings." Description of a psychical victim of all possible demoniac influences and possessions. At the same time, it gives a frightful picture of the unclean country in which so many impure spirits were congregated. At this crisis, however, it was partly a word of resisting pride, which sought by boasting to resist the influence; partly a word of silent complaint, in as far as the suffering consciousness of the possessed man coöperated. He does not give his own name, because he still identified his consciousness with that of the unclean spirits, and spoke through them. But when in this sense one calls himself Legion, he describes himself as their leader: as it were, the head of a whole regiment of demons. But the indistinctness and the error of the reply is characteristic of the condition of the man.

Ver. 10. **Not send them away out of the country,**—where they found themselves so much at home; especially, as Luke adds, into the hateful abyss of hell. The lawless nature of the country (where Jews lived mingled with Gentiles), which pleased the demons well, Mark denotes by the circumstance of the two thousand swine, emphasizing the greatness of the herd. If their owners were only in part Jews, who merely trafficked in these animals, still they were not justified before the law. Certainly we cannot regard this as exclusively a Gentile territory.

Ver. 14. **And in the country.**—In the villages and peasants' huts, where the swine-feeders partly lived. The whole scene derives from this circumstance a coloring in harmony with the country and the then state of things.

Ver. 15. **Him that was possessed, sitting.**—Beautiful and moving contrast.

Ver. 17. **They began to pray Him to depart.**—Gradually, after they had received intelligence of their loss, they took heart to desire Christ's departure, in the conflict of fear and anger, fawning and obstinacy.

Ver. 18. **That He might be with Him.**—According to Euthym. Zig., and others, fear of the demons conspired with other feelings in this request. Meyer thinks this could not have been the case, as the engulphing of the animals had already taken place; as if the man believed that, with the swine, the devils also had perished. But, doubtless, his present fearlessness stood on a surer foundation.

Ver. 19. **Jesus suffered him not.**—Wherefore? The healed man had friends at home. Probably he was now in danger of despising his own people. But Jesus appointed him to be a living memorial of His own saving manifestation for that entire dark district.

Ver. 20. **In Decapolis.**—*See* on *Matthew* iv. 25. "That Jesus did not *forbid*, but *commanded*, the promulgation of the matter, is explained by the locality (Peræa), where He was less known, and where there was not the same danger as in Galilee from uproar concerning His person." (Meyer.) We must also observe that Christ gave him notice of the things that he was to say. He was to announce to his friends how great things the Lord (the covenant God of Israel, the God of revelation) had done for him. This commission was enlarged by the man in two ways: he preached not only to his friends, but to the whole of Decapolis; and not only what the Lord had done to him (perfect), but also what Jesus (as the revelation of the Lord) had done to him, in that He had had mercy upon him (aorist: ἠλέησεν).

DOCTRINAL AND ETHICAL.

1. *See* on the parallels, and also the heading.—Christ the victor over despairing, as also over selfish, unbelief; and his elevation above human policy for safety, and care of the sick.

2. Demoniac faith, or the faith of fear (Jas. ii. 19), in all its characteristics: 1. Exalted presentiment and excited spiritualism, without the true spirit. 2. Contradiction and internal distraction: running, deprecating, confessing, denying, praying, adjuring. 3. Slavery: deliverance described as torment, and abandonment to a state of torment as deliverance. 4. Impure and destructive to the last breath (entering the swine and injuring the people).

3. Christ can change the demoniac faith of fear into a blessed and spiritual faith.

4. The entrance of Christ into the land of the Gadarenes a type of His victorious entrance into the kingdom of the dead: 1 Pet. iii. 20; iv. 6.

5. To a stupid and carnal people, under the power of demons without being fully aware of it, Christ discloses the terrors of the world of spirits, to give them a warning and arousing sign.

HOMILETICAL AND PRACTICAL.

See on *Matthew* and *Luke*.—The majestic entrance of our Lord into the district of Gadara: 1. The terror of the evil spirits in the land; 2. the deliverer of those who were bound by Satan; 3. the avenger of the law without legal tribunal; 4. a living condemnation of the earthly-minded in His going as in His coming; 5. the rejected one, who, after His rejection, leaves behind Him the preaching of the Gospel.—Christ annihilates, by the divine, awe-inspiring presence of His person, the horrors of darkness, even as the gentle light of day disperses the blackness of night.—Christ's stepping over the frontier, and its importance: 1. Over the border of a land, 2. over the threshold of a house, 3. and entrance into the heart.—The land of the Gadarenes a figure, 1. of sunk and darkened Judaism (lawlessness), 2. of degraded Christendom (estranged from the law of the Spirit, externalized), 3. degenerate Protestantism (indifferentism).—Image of a corrupt state of things in Church or State: 1. Perverted morals—swine cared for, men abandoned; 2. perverse policy—trade unlawful, the ways given up to madmen; 3. perverted legislation—demons tolerated legionfold, Christ rejected; 4. perverted religiousness—driving away Christ by prayers.—The true demons in the land mock at fetters and chains, but Christ rules them with a word.—The demons enter gladly into the swine; the devilish nature into the animal nature (the old serpent; half serpent, half swine).—Spiritual rebellion against God passes into the unbridled, animal nature.—To a besotted people the Lord preaches by grievous and terrific signs.—The towns and peasants of the Gadarenes; or, the hindrances which the kingdom of God meets with in the land.—Christ passes a milder judgment upon the common ignorance of spiritual sloth, than upon the false knowledge of the hardened; He leaves a preacher of salvation for the Gadarenes in the person of the healed demoniac.—The compassion of Christ in His final glance upon the land of Gadara.—Christ uttered no word concerning His rejection; His only answer was the appointment of this preacher.—The greatest demoniac of the New Testament narrative becomes a preacher of salvation to ten cities.—In the dark land of Gadara Christ leaves for a while a representative of Himself, since they cannot bear His personal presence.—All things in the kingdom of Christ have their time: He sometimes silences, and He sometimes stimulates, the witnesses of His miracles.—The rejections of Christ in their several and yet single character: 1. From Nazareth (through envy); 2. from Gadara (through selfishness and base fear); 3. from Samaria (through fanaticism); 4. from Galilee (through fanaticism and policy); 5. from Jerusalem (through obduracy).

STARKE:—MAJUS:—Christ, the true light, shines in all places, and sends forth His beams even into the Gentile country.—Unrestrained rebellion.—QUESNEL:—Hell is a tomb out of which the spirit of impurity proceeds, until God's judgment binds him in it for ever.—CRAMER:—As the devil raged mightily at the time of Christ's first coming, so also will he at the time of Christ's second coming, knowing that his time is short, Rev. xii. 12.—HEDINGER:—The delight of worldlings and slaves of sin, corruption, and the grave.—How tyrannically the devil deals with his slaves.—CANSTEIN:—The devil has special delight in tombs.—The devil's love for mischief.—*Bibl. Wirt.*:—The ungodly do not love to consort with the godly.—It is a fiendish spirit to take it as torment when men receive benefits from Christ and His people.—O how many are in a spiritual sense possessed by a devil! so many ruling sins, so many unclean spirits.—That the devil desired to abide in that country, was, doubtless, because there were many Jews there who had fallen from their Judaism. (For, as Josephus tells us, this district was full ἑλληνιζόντων.) Eph. vi. 12; 1 Pet. v. 8.—The devil is in truth a poor spirit; he has nothing of his own, and is driven hither and thither by the glorious power of God.—MAJUS:—The children of God should have no fear of the devil, or of wizards, or of any other creatures of Satan.—If God be for us, who can be against us? Rom. viii. 31.—It is better that earthly creatures should perish, than that a child of God should be kept from salvation.—God's goodness may be discerned not only in manifest kindnesses, but also in misfortunes.—In rude and earthly hearts God's wonders excite only fear and flight.—QUESNEL:—He who loves this world's goods will not have Christ long in his heart.—The converted soul longs to be with Jesus.—CANSTEIN:—God uses every one as His wisdom sees will best subserve the interests of His kingdom.—QUESNEL:—The grace of conversion is a talent which must be put out to interest, partly in spreading abroad God's grace and mercy, partly in edifying others in salvation.—OSIANDER:—God sends preachers for a season even to the unthankful.—Wonder the first step to faith in Jesus.

GERLACH:—The manifold misuse of the name of God among wicked men shows the falseness of the early notion that the devil could not utter it. (Yet this notion contains, in a mythical form, a secret truth, which appears in the declaration that no man can call Jesus Lord but by the Holy Spirit.)—BRAUNE:—We see the same thing now in a certain sense: many there are who reject Christ or repel Him, in the secret consciousness or fear that if they obtain His help they will have to suffer much interruption of their ordinary habits of life, have to submit to many things unpalatable, and endure many severe sacrifices.—When the Christian spirit revives, there are many who would have it shut up only in the minds of others, or who would bind it in a dead letter, because they are concerned to save their unrighteous possessions, or their abused rights, or their licentious wickedness, or their cowardly idleness; not remembering the destruction which came upon those towns forty years after the rejection of Christ, and which always surely comes upon the same sin, and often in a much shorter time.—We must frankly and freely acknowledge the salvation of God and His grace in Christ.—SCHLEIERMACHER:—For all the perverse anxiety of men, who set not before them that goal of union with God which Jesus presents to us,—who indeed live under rule, but not that of the kingdom of God,—there is much of the same recoil from Christ as that of the demoniac; they are not in the way to reach the right end, any more than the miserable man in our Gospel. That which holds us firm to Him and His great design, is the immediate influence of the nearness of Christ the Redeemer, which holds our minds fast in a firm and established order, makes our steps sure in this changeable world, and directs them to that ultimate goal, to guide men to which He came into the world.

GOSSNER:—He (the devil) marked that he was going to be hunted out, and therefore he cried. So is it with all hypocrites.—They saw Jesus, they saw the man, they saw the miracle on the man; but their swine they saw no longer, and that was their grief.—BAUER:—When the Lord comes to demand a sacrifice from them, how many are there in our own day who rather, that being the case, would send Him away altogether!

6. *Conflict of Jesus with* desponding *Unbelief on the Sick-bed and Bed of Death; Healing of the Woman with the Issue of Blood; Restoration of Jairus' Daughter; and Triumph of Jesus over the Healing Art, and the World's Lamentations for the Dead.* VERS. 21–43.

(Parallels: Matt. ix. 1, 18–26; Luke viii. 40–56.)

21 And when Jesus was passed over again by ship unto the other side, much people
22 gathered unto him; and he was nigh unto the sea. And, behold,[1] there cometh one of
the rulers of the synagogue, Jairus by name; and when he saw him, he fell at his feet,
23 And besought[2] him greatly, saying, My little daughter lieth at the point of death: I
pray thee, come and lay thy hands on her, that she may be healed; and she shall live.
24 And *Jesus* went with him; and much people followed him, and thronged him.
25, 26 And a certain woman,[3] which had an issue of blood twelve years, And had suffered
many things of many physicians, and had spent all that she had, and was nothing bet-
27 tered, but rather grew worse, When she had heard of Jesus, came in the press behind,
28 and touched his garment. For she said, If I may touch but his clothes, I shall be whole.
29 And straightway the fountain of her blood was dried up; and she felt in *her* body that
30 she was healed of that plague [scourge]. And Jesus, immediately knowing [having
known] in himself that virtue had gone out of him, turned him about in the press, and
31 said, Who touched my clothes? And his disciples said unto him, Thou seest the multi-
32 tude thronging thee, and sayest thou, Who touched me? And he looked round about
33 to see her that had done this thing. But the woman, fearing and trembling, knowing
what was done in[4] her, came and fell down before him, and told him all the truth.
34 And he said unto her, Daughter, thy faith hath made thee whole; go in peace, and be
35 whole of thy plague [scourge]. While he yet spake, there came from the ruler of the
synagogue's *house certain* which said, Thy daughter is dead; why troublest thou the
36 Master any further? As soon as Jesus heard[5] the word that was spoken, he saith unto
37 the ruler of the synagogue, Be not afraid, only believe. And he suffered no man to
38 follow him, save Peter, and James, and John the brother of James. And he cometh
to the house of the ruler of the synagogue, and seeth the tumult, and them that wept
39 and wailed greatly. And when he was come in, he saith unto them, Why make ye
40 this ado, and weep? the damsel is not dead, but sleepeth. And they laughed him to
scorn [jeered him]. But when he had put them all out, he taketh the father and the
mother of the damsel, and them that were with him, and entereth in where the damsel
41 was lying.[7] And he took the damsel by the hand, and said unto her, Talitha cumi;
42 which is, being interpreted, Damsel, (I say unto thee,) arise. And straightway the
damsel arose, and walked; for she was *of the age of* twelve years. And they were
43 astonished with a great astonishment. And he charged them straitly that no man
should know it; and commanded that something should be given her to eat.

[1] Ver. 22.—The ἰδού not in B., D., L., Vulgate, Versions, Tischendorf; Meyer; bracketed by Lachmann.
[2] Ver. 23.—The Present παρακαλεῖ, Tischendorf, after A., C., L.
[3] Ver. 25.—Τὶς wanting in A., B., C., Vulgate, Versions, Lachmann, Meyer.
[4] Ver. 33.—'Επ' wanting in B., C., D., Syriac, Coptic, Tischendorf; bracketed by Lachmann.
[5] Ver. 36.—Παρακούσας, Tischendorf, after B., L., Δ.
[6] Ver. 38.—The Plural ἔρχονται has most support, viz.: A., B., C., D., F., Versions, Lachmann, Tischendorf.
[7] Ver. 40.—The ἀνακείμενον (Elzevir) is set aside by Tischendorf, after B., D., L., Versions; bracketed by Lachmann.

EXEGETICAL AND CRITICAL.

See on the parallels.—Mark connects the return from Gadara with the narrative of the first raising of the dead, in accordance with his own principle of arrangement. According to the more exact account of Matthew, we must place in the interval the healing of the paralytic, the calling of Matthew, and the offence taken by the Pharisees and John's disciples at Jesus' eating in the house of the publican. In his presentation of the events that now follow, we once more observe the exact delineation of Mark. Concerning his little daughter (θυγάτριον), the father here says ἐσχάτως ἔχει, and in an appeal which announces itself at once by an ὅτι. In the account of the woman with an issue, Mark makes it very prominent that she had suffered much from many physicians, which Luke, the physician, much more gently intimates. And the woman's healing is emphatically expressed: The fountain of her blood was dried up; she felt in her body (in her feeling of bodily vigor) that she was delivered from her plague (scourge). He does not (like Luke) expressly mention Peter as the one who replied to the Lord's question as to who touched Him, "Thou seest the multitude," etc.; but he records once more that Jesus turned and looked round to find out who had done this. We see how the woman comes forward trembling with fear, falls down before the Lord, and confesses all. We see Jesus separating Himself with Jairus and the three elect disciples, from the multitude, in order to go into the house of death. The tumult of the lamentation for the dead is here vividly depicted. He defines accurately the group of those who enter; we hear the original Talitha cumi; we see the damsel at once, after her restoration, arising and walking, as she was able, being twelve years old; and hear how rigorously Jesus charged the people not to make much rumor about the miracle (which in itself could not be concealed); and finally, how He commanded that they should give the maiden food. Here and there Luke, and here and there Matthew, approximate to Mark's description.

Ver. 21. **He was nigh unto the sea.**—Meyer: "Here there is a discrepancy with Matthew's account, according to which Jairus entered the house of Jesus in Capernaum." But it was neither in Jesus' house, nor in that of the publican Matthew; for the transaction with the Pharisees and the disciples of John doubtless took place after the meal in a public place. Hence there is no discrepancy in the narratives.

Ver. 23. **My little daughter.**—(Tender expression of the troubled father).—**That Thou mayest come** (ἵνα ἐλθὼν ἐπιθῇς).—The ὅτι and the ἵνα give vivid reality to his urgent words; they are to be referred to the kneeling and cry for help (παρακαλεῖ). Hence there is nothing to be supplied in the text.

Ver. 26. **Had suffered many things from many physicians.**—"How various were the prescriptions of Jewish physicians for women in that case, and what experiments they were in the habit of making, *see* in LIGHTFOOT, p. 614." Meyer. Comp. also the article *Krankheiten* in WINER. "She probably suffered from a chronic hæmorrhage in the womb, and its long continuance endangered life." *See* also the article *Reinigkeit.* "Such a woman was, according to Lev. xv. 25, through the whole time unclean, and was required, after the evil had passed away, to bring on the eighth day an offering for purification." On the strong Oriental abhorrence of such persons, *see* the same article.

Ver. 28. **For she said,**—thinking in audible words.—**Touch but His clothes.**—That the more precise "hem of His garment," occurring in Matthew and Luke, is wanting in Mark, gives no warrant for conjectural emendation.

Ver. 29. **The fountain of her blood.**—Not euphemistic description of the womb, but vivid description of the cause of the evil; the blood being represented as flowing from a fountain.—**She felt in her body.**—Euth. Zig.: As her body was no longer moistened, etc. But here there is something greater signified: she experienced the healthy feeling of new life.

Ver. 30. **Virtue had gone out of Him.**—Meyer maintains that Jesus perceived the flowing of His virtue after it took place; a simultaneous knowledge of it being thought at variance with the words. But, on the contrary, it must be observed that the simultaneousness of the knowledge is declared in the ἐπιγνούς; first by the ἐπι, and then by the Aorist. The opposite explanation might be made to favor a magical interpretation of the event, and Strauss' criticism upon it. Yet Meyer himself refers with an emphatic note of exclamation to Calovius: "Calovi is quoted the passage against the Calvinists: *vim divinam carni Christi derogantes.*"

Ver. 38. **Them that wept.**—A scene of Jewish ceremonial lamentation over the dead, in which Mark omits the minstrels (*see* Matthew), and lays less stress than Luke upon the weeping and bewailing, but only to give more prominence to the tumult and mechanical liturgical cries (by ἀλαλάζειν). On the Jewish lament for the dead, *see* GROTIUS on *Matthew*, and WINER's article *Trauer*.

Ver. 41. **Talitha cumi,** טְלִיתָא קוּמִי.—Similar original Aramaic words occur in Mark, ch. iii. 17; vii. 11, 34; xiv. 36.

Ver. 42. **She was of the age of twelve years.**—Reason for the statement that she arose and walked at once. Bengel: *Rediit ad statum, œtati congruentem.*

Ver. 43. **That no man should know it.**—That is, should know the occurrence in its precise characteristics, viz., the way and manner of the restoration of the dead. On the motive of this prohibition, *see* Meyer.*—**That something should be given her to eat.**—Theophylact: That the raising might not be regarded as only an appearance. Meyer: In order to show that the child was not merely delivered from death, but from sickness also. Chiefly, however, because she was in need of strengthening by food.

DOCTRINAL AND ETHICAL.

1. *See* on the parallels.—The touching of Christ's garment, and the conscious issuing of a divine virtue from Him as the result, are a testimony to the living unity and reciprocal influence of the divine and human natures in His personal consciousness; in which the human nature was not (as the old dogmatics taught) merely in a passive relation.

2. Two miracles of healing were wrought on diseased women. Otherwise, they are mainly male sufferers who are adduced as examples of His healing acts. Not that other instances were wanting; for the very first healing recorded by the Evangelists took place on a woman, Peter's wife's mother. Luke mentions some women who were dispossessed of devils, ch. viii. 2. But the deliverance of Mary Magdalene from seven devils we regard, after the analogy of Matt. xii. 45, as a symbolical expression of an essentially great conversion.—The woman with an issue of blood, the dead maiden: progression in the manifestation of suffering in the female sex. That the former had been afflicted twelve years and the latter was twelve years old, was a coincidence from which rash criticism has vainly sought to extract ground of suspicion.

3. We term this narrative a history of victory over *despairing* unbelief. This appears in the comfortless wail of the Jewish lament over the dead; in the circumstance that the people around the dead maiden laughed at the Lord, when He declared that she was not dead, but slept; but especially in the message which they sent to the ruler of the synagogue, Why troublest thou the Master any further? wherein there is an evident tone of bitter and almost ironical unbelief. The faith of Jairus itself appears, at first, as only a fruit of distress. Hence it was subjected to a severe test, that period of deep anxiety during Christ's delay while He cured the woman with the issue of blood. The weak germ of Jairus' faith was encompassed by desponding unbelief. Even the faith of the sick woman struggles with the despondency into which a long series of disappointed

* Meyer makes the motive to be, a desire on the part of Christ to repress the tendency to fanatical expectations and tumults concerning the Messiah, among the Jews.—*Ed.*

acts of trust in physicians had thrown her. She does not venture to bring her distress publicly before the Lord's notice; the rather as, being ceremonially unclean, she had in a forbidden manner mingled with the crowd, and as her malady was of such a kind as shame would not allow her to speak of. Hence her faith must be brought to maturity by a public confession, even as that of Jairus by a season of delay.

4. As Christ's work of salvation assumed a specific form in many acts of blessing in favor of the male sex, so also Christianity has wrought immeasurable specific benefits for the female. Here we see, first, a wretched sick woman, lost in the crowd; and Christ delivers her not only from her sickness, but also from the morbid dread and fear of her feminine consciousness. Even shame required redemption and sanctification by the Spirit of truth. And so the female sex has been redeemed from the reproach of inferiority, impurity, the rude contempt of man's prejudice, and the ban of self-depreciation.

5. Reischl: "The woman was afraid; partly ashamed on account of the nature of her malady, partly disturbed by the consciousness of impropriety, as having, while Levitically unclean, mingled with the people, and even touched the great Teacher Himself." In the last point she forms a contrast to the leper, whom the Lord Himself touched. Under the veil of diffidence, however, there was a touch of womanly boldness, which was excused by the faith that the touching of Christ would heal her.

6. "Daughter, be of good courage, thy faith hath saved thee: go in peace." Thus He blessed her in the same manner as He had blessed that palsied man. And in fact we must connect together these two petitioners for help, in order that we may see two characteristic forms of faith in the male and in the female contrasted. Both applicants pressed through with confidence, and seized their deliverance almost by force: the man did it in man's fashion, entering through the roof like a robber; the woman in woman's fashion, as it were, like a female thief. But both were recognised by the Lord, as showing the pure spirit of confidence." (LANGE's *Leben Jesu*, ii. 682.) But the faith of this woman had a superadded conflict to maintain with her timorous natural feeling confronting the fearful power of prejudice.

HOMILETICAL AND PRACTICAL.

See on the parallels.—The miracles of Christ a wonderful connected chain.—New life added to new life in the way of Christ, until the great word is fulfilled, Behold, I make all things new!—Christ at once ready to help the man who comes from the powerful party of His opponents.—The ruler of the synagogue at the feet of Jesus; or, the victory of the Gospel over party spirit.—The triumph of Christ over the whole domain of sickness and death, a sign also of His supremacy over all natural means of help and human skill in healing.—Christ the Physician of physicians (as the Preacher of preachers, the Teacher of teachers, the Judge of judges, the Prince of kings).—Christ's divine power the sign of salvation to all the despondency, little faith, and unbelief of man.—Christ in our history the conqueror of all hindrances to His own work and man's faith. —The woman with the issue, and the dead maiden; or, Christ the Helper in all suffering, whether secret or public.—Christ the Prince of salvation in the domain of secret sorrows and silent sighs.—Hearing and answering all the sighings of faith.—The test to which the faith of the ruler and of the woman was subjected: 1. The element common to both: they were wanting in the full surrender of trust. Both must be set free from fear and despondency. 2. The difference: the spiritual ruler must retire, wait, submit, despair of all signs for hope, and then in his despair learn to believe. He scarcely believed in the invigorator of the sick, and now He must believe in the awakener of the dead. He must, at the same time, in humility yield precedence to a poor unclean woman, and in the case of a seeming religious impropriety.—The woman must come forward and confess.—Even amidst the pressure of thousands the Lord perceives the silent and gentle touch of a single believer.—Internal union with Jesus high above the external.—The hastening and the delaying of Jesus sublime above the haste and delay of the world.—Christ purposed here to effect, not the healing of the sick, but the raising of the dead.—Twice (in the history of Lazarus too) He first yielded the point to death, that He might approve Himself afterwards his conqueror.—With the Lord the spiritual is everything, and the edification of the inner life the great concern.—The gradually progressive manifestation of Christ's power in raising the dead, a sign and symbol of the great and universal resurrection.

STARKE:—QUESNEL:—God has His own times and seasons; He delays and yet helps. Have patience, and walk in the way He marks.—HEDINGER: —Daring wins.—QUESNEL:—Men are slow to do for the healing of the soul what they are ready enough to do for the cure of the body.—CRAMER:—Medicines are not to be despised, Ecclus. xxxviii. 1; but God does not always see fit to prosper them.—To use them is not displeasing to God, but ungodly trusting in them is.—The humility of the woman.—CANSTEIN:—Shame and fear would keep us back from Christ, but faith presses near to Him with a right and laudable shamelessness.—OSIANDER:—In our sickness we should put our trust, not in medicine, but in God.—Faith is stronger than all earthly medicaments.—The Lord is not ignorant what benefits we have received from Him, and He will demand an account of all the good deeds He has done to us.—*Bibl. Wirt.*:—Tempted souls think that God takes no care of them, but He faithfully remembers their case; the deeper they are in misery, the more graciously does His compassionate eye rest upon them.—CANSTEIN:—To acknowledge our own weakness and God's power, is to speak the truth indeed.—What God has done for us in secret we should publicly speak of to His glory.—Go in peace.—HEDINGER:—Reason despairs at sight of death.—In perfect faith there is no fear.—QUESNEL:—Let us learn from Christ to confide only to a few elect ones the works of God which we have to do, that those works may not be thwarted.—To sorrow in secret over our dead is Christian, but to howl and cry is heathenish.—HEDINGER:—God's wonderful works must have devout and attentive witnesses: away with tumult!—*Nova Bibl. Tub.*:—Why do ye mourn, ye parents, over the departure of your children? Jesus will one day lay His mighty hand upon them, raise them, and give them back to you.

LISCO:—The question of our Lord was designed to free the woman from her false fear of man.—The delay of help, and the message, were severe tests of Jairus' faith; but the healing of the woman strengthened his faith again, as did the word of Jesus, ver

36.—BRAUNE:—The urgency and continuance of her malady, the vanity of all human help, the lack of substance, were three steps which brought the sick woman to faith; and the feeblest cries of the believing heart were understood by her Lord.—The Jews received this custom of lamentation from the Romans [Qy.: *see* Jer. ix. 17]. This purchased grief was intended to make the occasion of death important, to distribute the impressions of sorrow over many, and lighten the grief of the friends. Thus it was mere heathenish vanity.—SCHLEIERMACHER:—The more mighty love is in those who can help others, and, on the other hand, the more longing and trust there is in those who need help, the more good will be the result in the particular case, though we may not be able to show how, and the beginnings of cause and effect may be concealed from us.—It is always the case that from those whom God has called to do good, many influences proceed which they themselves do not in the special cases know of. But how much more efficacious would charity be, if those from whom the influences proceed did not think so much about those which they themselves receive!—How important it is for the general order of the community that we should not neglect our own individual personal relations!—Christendom has now still to press through the world violently with its blessings.—Although the power of Christ is continually entering more and more into the order of nature, yet that which Christianity has wrought in the world from its beginning is the greatest miracle that we know; but we must be careful to distinguish from it the internal miracle, which only those see who live in internal fellowship with the Redeemer.—BAUER:—Mark how He does not break the bruised reed, or quench the smoking flax!

---

7. *The Lord's Conflict with the* envious *Unbelief of His own City; His Triumph over Human Prejudice; His Return to the Mountain-Villages.* CH. VI. 1–6.

(Parallels: Matt. xiii. 54–58; Luke iv. 14–30.)

1 And he went out from thence, and came[1] into his own country; and his disciples
2 follow him. And when the sabbath day was come, he began to teach in the synagogue:
and many hearing *him* were astonished, saying, From whence hath this *man* these
things? and what wisdom is this which is given unto him, that even such mighty works
3 are wrought[2] by his hands? Is not this the carpenter, the son of Mary, the brother
of James, and Joses,[3] and of Juda, and Simon? and are not his sisters here with us?
4 And they were offended at him. But Jesus said unto them, A prophet is not without
5 honour, but in his own country, and among his own kin, and in his own house. And
he could there do no mighty work, save that he laid his hands upon a few sick folk,
6 and healed *them*. And he marvelled because of their unbelief. And he went round
about the villages, teaching.

[1] Ver. 1.—Tischendorf, ἔρχεται, after B., C., L., Δ.
[2] Ver. 2.—Codd. C.*, D., K., ἵνα γίνωνται; B., L., γινόμεναι, which Tischendorf adopts.
[3] Ver. 3.—Codd. B., D., L., Versions, Lachmann, Tischendorf, read Ἰωσῆτος; the reading Ἰωσήφ occurs in some cursive MSS.

EXEGETICAL AND CRITICAL.

See the parallels on *Matthew* and *Luke*.—As to Nazareth, consult ROBINSON, iii. 419; WINER, *Real-lex.*; my *Leben Jesu*, ii. 550. Mark's narrative is not only identical with Matt. xiii. 54 *seq.* but also in its leading features with Luke iv. 16, as is manifest from the recurrence of the question, "Is not this Joseph's son?" and the saying, "A prophet," etc. Notwithstanding, the points of time are so diverse, and have such an interval between them, that we must, following Matthew and Mark, assume a second and later appearance in Nazareth; one, however, which was only transitional and brief, inasmuch as the unbelief of the people of Nazareth remained the same. The special features of the narrative seem to belong mainly to the former of the two occasions. But how can a second visit of our Lord to Nazareth be conceivable, after he had been once rejected there? The first rejection had been no better than a tumult. This time He visits His own city in quietness, and for His own repose, after the decree to kill Him had gone forth from the Galilean Pharisees. But, experiencing the same utter lack of sympathy and regard on the part of His former fellow-citizens, He retreated back into the surrounding mountain-villages. It was the time (in the first year of His ministry) when He had accomplished the itineration of the mountains in the first Galilean journey, as also the second Galilean voyage over the sea to the farther bank; and when He was on the point of travelling over the towns of the valley of Southern Galilee, in the direction of Jerusalem. As He would confirm and corroborate this third and last Galilean preaching-journey by sending out the Twelve, a retreat into the mountains, and especially to a particular mountain, was fixed upon to precede. And He most probably took this occasion of visiting the district of Nazareth.

Ver. 1. **And He went out from thence.**—Not merely, that is, "from the house of Jairus." From this time forward, He ceased to have His abiding residence in Capernaum; although He still assembled His disciples around Him there on passing occasions. After the first conflict in Nazareth, He went down to Capernaum; He now designedly abandons again His permanent abode in Capernaum, without formally giving up His residence there.

Ver. 2. **He began to teach.**—This does not

mean His first entrance and its result; it rather refers to the interruption that soon followed.—**That even such mighty works are wrought by His hands.**—The ἵνα is characteristic. They regard the doctrine of Christ merely as a secret doctrine, which was intended to be the medium or instrument for the ultimate end of working miracles. And they enviously assume that this mysterious doctrine must have been entrusted to him by some one in a suspicious manner. Hence the emphasis laid upon the *hands* (laying on of hands, touching, etc.), as the method of performing the miracle. The working hands of the carpenter, they would say; as appears from what comes next.

Ver. 3. **Is not this the carpenter?**—According to the custom of the Jewish people, even the Rabbis learned some handicraft. We have the example of the Apostle Paul: *see* Lightfoot, Schöttgen. But Justin Martyr (contr. Tryph.) has the tradition, that Jesus made ploughs and the like. "Whether with an ideal allusion, so that they became in His hands symbols, as Lange (*Leben Jesu*, ii. p. 154) thinks, may very properly be left to fancy." Meyer. That Jesus regarded with a symbolizing mind and interpretation the toil of the fisherman, the fall of the sparrow from the housetop, the play of the children in the market-place—all this is not matter of mere fancy. But there is a kind of fancy, which men call inductive proof. It is represented, further, as a mere airy and baseless notion, to suppose that the brethren of Jesus would hardly have suffered Him to work much, because they saw in Him the glory of Israel. And yet it is not an airy and baseless notion, that His brethren early sought to deliver Him from the machinations of His enemies. What really deserves to be called fancy in the theological domain, is that aggregation of myth and anecdote which the scholastic learning of the present day so much abounds in.

No dogmatic importance can be attached (with Bauer and others) to the omission of "the carpenter's *son*," which Matthew has; since the expression, "the carpenter," is only a stronger declaration of the same thing. But the former expression would not occur to the people of Nazareth, since they spoke from recent observation or past remembrances. In this way, the position of Jesus was referred back to, or identified with, Joseph's. And it is obvious to suppose that Joseph had long before (between the twelfth year and the thirtieth of the Lord's life) gone off the scene. As τέκτων has primarily a general meaning, and signifies any artisan, some, following Justin, have thought it signified here a maker of carriages, etc.; while others have interpreted into "smith." But smith in the New Testament is ὁ χαλκεύς, and τέκτων is specifically a *faber lignarius*. Whether workmanship in wood was distributed into various kinds of handiwork, is a question not settled.—**The brother of James.**—As to the brethren of the Lord, comp. on Matthew. The apocryphal tradition adds to the four brethren, two sisters of our Lord: Esther and Tamar or Martha. Romanist expositors have, without reason, or for reasons well known, made these the sisters of His mother. These sisters seem to have been married in Nazareth; and therefore did not accompany the migration of Mary's family to Capernaum.

Ver. 4. **Among his own kin.**—Naturally, the immediate dependants and followers of Jesus stood related in manifold ways to the people of Nazareth. Christ does not say that His own house remained unbelieving, in the common sense of the term. But that there were restrictions of faith to be overcome even in this circle, springing from too great familiarity, is proved not only by the history of the Lord's brethren, but also by that of His mother.

DOCTRINAL AND ETHICAL.

1. *See* on *Matthew*.—This narrative exhibits to us the narrow, petty, bigoted, envious unbelief, which was unable to apprehend and understand the Divinely great in its human nearness and familiarity; and this makes the section a most striking example of unbelief, as it confronts and embarrasses the Lord. It is the unconscious self-condemnation and self-contempt of the spirit which, alienated from God, and sunk into the lowest level, cannot appreciate the prophet that has arisen in its own city. In our Lord's experience of this kind of unbelief,—to which a prophet is nowhere less esteemed than in his own country, and among his own kin,—we have fore-written for us a long chapter of the history of the world and of the Church. The history of Monophysitism, on the one hand, and of Nestorianism and Rationalism, on the other, may be referred to this principle. The prejudice of the base nature, that out of Nazareth, in the immediate neighborhood, from our own home, and finally out of humanity itself, nothing good can come, led to all those systems in succession which, on the one hand, *dehumanize* the God-man, and, on the other, *undeify* Him. But when we say that Christ celebrated His triumph over this unbelief of envious prejudice and of human self-depreciation, we do not thereby assert that He removed that unbelief in anything like a magical manner. He triumphed over it rather by leaving it alone, by going on His way, and by performing His miracles in the neighborhood around. He drew round the pestilent prejudice a circle of divine manifestations, like a besieger. The honor paid to the Divine, which from all sides reacts upon this centre of prejudice, and leads back the homeborn, with acclamation and celebrity on all hands, to his home again—that is His final triumph over Nazareth, over Judaism, over humanity.

2. *And He could there.*—This does not express inability in itself; but, as Theophylact rightly observed, it indicates the absence of the ethical conditions on which the miracles of Jesus depended. His miraculous power was not magical; but an ethical influence which required and presupposed faith. It is true that Christ also creates faith; but then that presupposes the felt need of faith. It is true that He excites that feeling also; but then that presupposes susceptibility, and the capacity of reception. And if this likewise is awakened by Him, it further presupposes sincerity, and a certain devotion which could not become hardened through evil motives into the always evil act of the heart of unbelief. The Evangelist further shows us that Jesus wrought miracles, even in this circle, according to the slender measure of faith there was; for he adds the observation, that He laid His hands upon a few sick folk, and healed them. Thus, he distinguishes from these lower miraculous works, the great manifestations of His wonder-working power; these latter could have and should have no demonstration under such circumstances. The condition on which the miraculous power of Christ was suspended was the reflection and copy of the conditions upon which the

divine omnipotence, in love wisdom and righteousness, deals with the freedom of the world of spirits.

3. *And He marvelled.*—Fritzsche: "ἐθαύμαζον (they wondered at Him, on account of their unbelief), following only two cursive MSS.: manifest error of copyist." Meyer: Stress has with great propriety been laid upon the contrast between the wondering of our Lord at the faith of the Gentile centurion, and His wondering at the unbelief of His own countrymen, who had so long been witnesses of His divine life. Jesus does not marvel at other human things generally; but He does marvel, on the one hand, at faith, when it overcomes in its grandeur all human traditional hindrances, and, on the other, at unbelief, when it can, in the face of multitudes of divine manifestations, and under the daily view of the opened heavens, harden itself into the pitiful acceptance of dead traditional prejudices. The former wondering might, humanly speaking, elevate and strengthen Himself; the latter, on the other hand, grieve and restrain His divine Spirit. He hastens away from the sphere of such spiritual evils, that He may in the distance unloose those spiritual breezes that shall dissipate them all. The Accusative (διὰ τὴν), "on account of their unbelief," makes His astonishment all the more emphatic. It was hard for Him to reconcile Himself to this seemingly unconquerable dulness and limitation.

4. The history of Nazareth has been repeated on a large scale in the history of Israel. Israel, as a whole, also made the nearness of Jesus, His external "not being afar off," an occasion of unbelief and fall. This temptation, resulting from the constant beholding of the Holy One with common eyes, was pointed to in Deut. xxx. 14, according to Paul's interpretation of it in Rom. x. 8. It is the temptation which besets the intimates and fellow-citizens of chosen spirits and great geniuses; which besets theologians in the daily study and service of the truths of revelation, ministers in their commerce with the ordinances of grace, and all the lesser officers of the house of God in their habitual contact with the externals of divine things. It is the temptation also of ancient towns and churches, which have enjoyed exalted privileges, and indeed of the whole Church itself. "When the Son of man cometh, shall He find faith on the earth?"

HOMILETICAL AND PRACTICAL.

See on the parallel passages of Matthew and Luke.—Jesus was renounced by His own city, both at the beginning and at the end of His Galilean labors: or, the stiffneckedness of prejudice, which is bound to the lower and earthly sense by a thousand bonds (envy, cowardice, indolence, self-delusion, dissipation, slavish sympathies and antipathies, etc.).—How far was Jesus actually of Nazareth, how far not?—No man is altogether of the place where he was born or brought up: 1. He is so in his derivation, but not in his individuality; 2. he is so in his outward lot, but not in his personal endowments; 3. he is so in his external training, but not in his internal education; 4. he is so in his human relationship and acquaintance, but not in his highest relations; 5. he is so in the petty events of life, but not in his greater fortunes; 6. he is so in his immediate calling, not in his highest vocation and destiny.—Christ an alien, and yet at home, in His own city; both in an infinite measure: every man the same in his own degree.—The error of the men of Nazareth concerning the coming of Christ: 1. They forgot that He was of Bethlehem; 2. they did not know that He was from heaven.—The double origin and the double home of Christ: 1. An original contrast in Him; 2. an analogous contrast in every man's life below.—How Christ victoriously contends with the unbelief of prejudice among His own countrymen: 1. Prejudice everywhere opposes Him; and that, *a.* in an impure and gross apprehension of His dignity, as of a magical secret doctrine and art; *b.* in the reckoning up of all His earthly relationships, in order to urge them to the disparagement of His heavenly dignity; *c.* in a slavish community of envious and low judgment upon His life. 2. How the Lord lays hold of and overcomes this prejudice: *a.* He refers it all to a universal fact, which they might afterwards reflect upon (a prophet is not without honor, etc.); *b.* He does not forget, but heals, the few who needed and were susceptible of help among His scorners; *c.* He gathers up His influences, and withdraws; *d.* and He causes the light of His presence to shine brightly throughout the whole district around.—How the Lord surrounds the places which exhibit a corrupted prejudice against Him with the fiery circles of His divine deeds, in order to subdue them.—The Lord's not being able in Nazareth, an expression of the divine freedom as over against the abuse of human freedom.—The Lord's impotence a testimony to His perfect power and ability: 1. Of the divine power of His love (patience); 2. of the divine skill of His love (wisdom).—The sacred conditionality and free self-limiting power of Christ.—The omnipotence of God is not lessened, but glorified as spiritual power, by the fact that it conditions itself in love, wisdom, and righteousness.—To the man who had lost himself, and become to himself an object of contempt, the Lord brings back again his life.—Christ is both far off and nigh at hand, in order to overcome the stolid, careless minds of those who are bent on this world.—Christ's retirement among the villages; or, the loftiness of the Gospel in its humility.—Christ's own city, the old and the new: 1. Poor Nazareth, which rejects Him; 2. the great city of God in heaven and upon earth, in ten thousand places, which glorifies Him.—Nazareth a symbol of multitudes of streets and places rendered desolate by spiritual guilt.—How the Lord's love with holy tenderness encircles His poor land and people.

STARKE: — MAJUS: — The unreasonableness and wickedness of our countrymen should never restrain us in the performance of our duty, or cause us to forget any of our obligations to them.—*Nov. Bibl. Tub.*:—Birth, lineage, and descent are far from making a man a Christian; they often rather, on account of prejudices, are the greatest hindrances to Christianity.—QUESNEL:—Wicked men often admire and magnify gifted preachers; but they are never without some excuse or other for not obeying their instructions.—It is common enough for those who would defeat the force of a sermon, to exalt themselves above the preacher.—When we entertain ourselves with a thousand strange matters that have no connection with spiritual profit, the power of the divine word is lost.—CANSTEIN:—He who built heaven and earth became, in His humbled condition upon earth, a carpenter.—Christ honored and sanctified all honorable human employments and handiwork.—QUESNEL:—Christ's humiliation has been to many a stone of stumbling and an occasion of falling; while it was most essentially necessary to our external exaltation.—HEDINGER:—What is there that can grieve the Christian teacher beyond contempt and evil fruits?—Christ's example is a most mighty consolation.—*Nova Bibl. Tub.*:—Thou complainest that God saves thee not, and dost not reflect that thou thyself hast bound His hands.—QUESNEL:—The unbelief of a whole people does not hinder the mercy of God from extending to the small number of the righteous who are found amongst them.—BRAUNE:—Faith, which in its nature is *receptive* love, alone makes us partakers of the grace of God, which is *imparting* love.

SCHLEIERMACHER:—We find this (that a prophet is without honor in his own country) true among men, even as we sometimes find the contrary of it true. When any one is distinguished beyond others in any particular, his fellow-townsmen take pride in him, their vanity being flattered. Yet the contrary is not arbitrary, but usually dependent on the earlier or later period, and various spiritual or worldly influences. (The prophets killed, and the sepulchres of the prophets garnished.)—Much impressive truth is lost upon men, because they do not so much regard the matter as the source from which it comes.—Christ has as much cause to marvel at the unbelief of the present time, as He had to marvel in His own time.—GOSSNER, on ver. 4:—A warning to all preachers who do not like to leave their own home, kin, and country.—Nothing more outrages God's goodness than unbelief or rejection of it.

SIXTH SECTION.

CONFLICT OF JESUS WITH HEROD. THE CALL AND MISSION OF THE TWELVE APOSTLES. THE BEHEADING OF JOHN THE BAPTIST. THE WITHDRAWAL OF JESUS INTO THE WILDERNESS, AND THE MIRACULOUS FEEDING OF THE FIVE THOUSAND.

CHAPTER VI. 7-44.

1. *The Calling and Mission of the Twelve.* CH. VI. 7-13.

(Parallels: Matt. x. 1, 7, 9-11, 13; Luke ix. 1-6.)

7 And he called *unto him* the twelve, and began to send them forth by two and two;
8 and gave them power over unclean spirits; And commanded them that they should
take nothing for *their* journey, save a staff only; no scrip, no bread, no money in *their*
9, 10 purse [girdle]: But *be* shod with sandals; and not put on[1] two coats. And he said
unto them, In what place soever ye enter into an house, there abide till ye depart from
11 that place. And whosoever shall not receive you, nor hear you,[2] when ye depart thence,
shake off the dust under your feet for a testimony against them. Verily I say unto
you, It shall be more tolerable for Sodom and Gomorrha in the day of judgment than
12, 13 for that city. And they went out, and preached that men should repent. And
they cast out many devils, and anointed with oil many that were sick, and healed *them*.

[1] Ver. 9.—The best reading is ἐνδυσήσθε (A., C., D., E., &c.), which Griesbach, Lachmann, Tischendorf, and others adopt. The change in the construction, or the direct quotation of this command, makes it more emphatic.

[2] Ver. 11.—Tischendorf, after B., L., Δ., &c.: ὃς ἂν τόπος μὴ δέξηται μηδὲ ἀκούσωσιν ὑμῶν. Preferable in regard to importance of Codd., and is the more difficult reading. "Verily," &c., wanting in B., C., D., L., Δ. Probably taken from Matt. x. 15.

EXEGETICAL AND CRITICAL.

1. Compare on the parallel passages of Matt. x. and Luke ix.—It has been already observed, on Mark iii. 13-19, that he distinguishes the *separation* of the Twelve from their first *mission*: Luke does the same, while Matthew combines their call and mission in one. The two events are indeed one, as Matthew records them, in this respect, that the separation took place with reference to an appointment of duty which then immediately impended. But they are distinguished by this, that the election occurred in the solitude of the mountain-range (hence Mark and Luke place them on a mountain, the latter connecting with the event the Sermon on the Mount; while the mission, on the other hand, occurred at the beginning of the third preaching-journey, on which our Lord passed through the sea-towns of Galilee, as we are told by Matthew. But, since the calling of the Twelve, between the Sermon on the Mount and the passage to Gadara (the second Galilean journey), was only as yet a preparatory vocation, we must make a distinction between a general separation of the narrower circle of disciples and that calling of the Twelve on the mountain which briefly preceded their sending forth in the valley; during the first year of Christ's ministry. Now it is peculiar to Mark that he gives prominence only to the most essential points of the mission; that he records it as the beginning of the apostolical missions (ver. 7), and as a mission in pairs; that he lays emphasis exclusively upon the power given over unclean spirits (not that of healing the sick), in harmony with his fundamental point of view, and that to him this involved at the same time the preaching of the kingdom; that he most precisely gives the Lord's injunctions touching their staff, their shoes, and their clothing; and that he finally makes allusion to the anointing the sick with oil, in its relation to the work of the Apostles—here mentioning

the sick, who had been previously omitted. Mark's more limited account of the instructions given to the Apostles in comparison with that given by Matthew, is to be explained by the fact, that he has this first mission exclusively in view; while Matthew combines it with all subsequent missions, and consequently presents it in its ideal meaning.

Ver. 8. **Save a staff only.**—Meyer insists that there is here a discrepancy between Mark, on the one hand, and Matthew and Luke, on the other—to be explained, as it regards the two latter, by exaggeration. (Comp., on the contrary, EBRARD, p. 382; LANGE, *Leben Jesu*, ii. 2, p. 712.) They were to go forth with their staff, as they had it at the time; but they were not to seek one carefully, or make it a condition of their travelling. And thus it becomes no more in Mark than a rather more precise statement of the meaning of Matthew and Luke. The same may be said of the permission to take sandals, in opposition to the prohibition of the ὑποδήματα, or travelling shoes proper, in Matthew. So the injunction not to put on two coats (in change), is only another form of the injunction not to have two garments. The fundamental idea is this, that they were to go forth with the slightest provision, and in dependence upon being provided for by the way. Gfrörer and Baur see in Mark's expressions only intentional qualifications and softenings. We find in them no other than a more express view of their pilgrim-state, burdened with the least possible incumbrance, and as free as might be from all care.

Ver. 11. **For a testimony against them.**—As a symbolical, but to an Israelite perfectly intelligible, declaration, that they were excommunicated, —"no better than heathen."

Ver. 12. **Preached, that men should repent** (ἵνα).—They not only preached the doctrine of repentance, amongst other articles of doctrine; but their whole preaching had for its end the producing of penitence, and change of mind.

Ver. 13. **And anointed with oil.**—Oil was generally a very important medicament among the Orientals, according to Lightfoot and others. Here it is simply a symbolical medium of the miraculous work; just as the application of the spittle was (ch. viii. 23; John ix. 6), on the part of the Lord Himself. Meyer does well to contend against the supposition that the oil was applied as a natural means of cure (Baur, Weisse), or that it was used as a mere symbol (Theophylact, Beza, etc.),—not to mention other still less tenable notions. He is not right, however, in altogether detaching the symbolical significance from the medium. It is a fact, that the Old Testament anointing with oil preceded, as a symbol, the New Testament bestowment of the Spirit; and that it re-appears in the Catholic church, where the real impartation of the Spirit is wanting. Hence, it may be assumed that for the disciples, who could not like the Lord Himself awaken faith, it was appropriate to appoint such a medium for their miraculous power as would be at the same time a symbolical sign of the impartation of the Spirit, and the energy that awakens faith. Thus the anointing was a symbol of the bestowment of the Spirit as the preliminary condition of healing; consequently, not of the divine mercy (Theophylact), the healing virtue of which was symbolized by balsam, or of the divine regeneration (Euthym. Zigabenus), the symbol of which was water. The anointing with oil, which James prescribed to the elders in their ministry for the sick (ch. v. 14), appears, on the other hand, to have been a blending of the natural means of health with the saving energy of prayer as symbolized by it.

DOCTRINAL AND ETHICAL.

1. *See* on the parallel passages of Matthew and Luke.

2. *The sending of the Apostles by two and two.*—According to Grotius, with allusion to the Old Testament law concerning witnesses *ad plenam testimonii fidem.* But also for mutual complement, and encouragement, and strengthening. We have, accordingly, six special embassages: six was the number of labor and toil. The twelve missions of the individual Apostles were as yet only in the prospect.

3. We need only suggest here, that the New Testament anointing with oil—even that later one which James prescribed to the elders in their care of the sick—forms a perfect contrast to the extreme unction of the Romish Church. To us, this ecclesiastical anointing seems no other than an unconscious admission, on the part of the ceremonial church, that it had yet to bestow on its dying member the real communication of the Holy Spirit, whose type the oil was.

HOMILETICAL AND PRACTICAL.

The first sending of the Apostles abroad into the world may also be likened to the little seed-corn.—He began to send: the end of His sending is the end of the world.—The mission of the Apostles by two and two, in its significance for the Church: 1. As to ecclesiastical office, 2. as to the people.—The blessing of the mutual help of laborers in the kingdom of God.—The embarrassments, dangers, and disgraces which so often follow a too early isolation in office, and in the religious life generally.—Christianity in life and office is a discipline of unenvying brotherly love.—The messengers and pilgrims of Christ not without needs, but without anxious needs.—The world loses, amidst its external equipments and means of resource, the internal end of life: the servants of the Gospel obtain, while they supremely regard the end, all the other equipments and resources.—The destruction of the kingdom of Satan, and the abolition of his power, is the great task of Christ's servants, after the example and in the strength of their Lord.—The shaking the dust from their feet is in its kind a Christian martyrdom to the disciples of Jesus (a testimony in suffering).—The anointing with oil; or, how the miracles of the kingdom of Christ have leaned upon the marvellous powers of the kingdom of nature.—The kingdom of the Son attaches itself to the kingdom of the Father in the great whole as well as in individual things.—Those bound by Satan, and the sick, are everlasting tokens of the need of Christ and His messengers.

STARKE:—This authorization a demonstration of the divinity of Christ.—The ministers of the Gospel should be one and united.—QUESNEL:—Ambition and avarice perilous things to the preacher and his work.—OSIANDER:—Ministers should be satisfied, though they do not at once have all advantages they could desire, and things at their will.—GERLACH:—On account of their weakness, the Lord does not send His disciples alone. Laborers in the Lord's harvest should look round for helpers in their work.—SCHLEIERMACHER:—The Lord's direction in regard to the equipments of the Apostles no literal rule [he refers to the cloak of Paul, 2 Tim. iv. 13], but a rule of wisdom.—If the provision of all these external things is so great as to rob us of a portion of our true strength, they are no real advantage, but tend rather to impair our usefulness and peace.—BAUER: —They were not to act as if they thought they might force men to hear.

---

2. *Beheading of John the Baptist.* VERS. 14–29.

(Parallels: Matt. xiv. 1–12; Luke ix. 7–9.)

14 And king Herod heard *of him;* (for his name was spread abroad;) and he said,
That John the Baptist was risen from the dead, and therefore mighty works do show
15 forth themselves [miraculous powers work] in him. Others said, That it is Elias.
16 And others said, That it is a prophet, or as one of the prophets. But when Herod
17 heard *thereof,* he said, It is John, whom I beheaded:[1] he is risen from the dead. For
Herod himself had sent forth and laid hold upon John, and bound him in prison for
18 Herodias' sake, his brother Philip's wife; for he had married her. For John had said
19 unto Herod, It is not lawful for thee to have thy brother's wife. Therefore Herodias
20 had a quarrel against him, and would have killed him; but she could not: For Herod
feared John, knowing that he was a just man and an holy, and observed [protected]
21 him; and when he heard him, he did many things,[2] and heard him gladly. And when
a convenient [favorable] day was come, that Herod, on his birth-day, made a supper to
22 his lords, high captains, and chief *estates* of Galilee: And when the daughter of the
said Herodias came in, and danced, and pleased Herod,[3] and them that sat with him,
the king said unto the damsel, Ask of me whatsoever thou wilt, and I will give *it* thee.
23 And he sware unto her, Whatsoever thou shalt ask of me, I will give *it* thee, unto the
24 half of my kingdom. And she went forth, and said unto her mother, What shall I
25 ask? And she said, The head of John the Baptist. And she came in straightway
with haste unto the king, and asked, saying, I will that thou give me, by and by [im-
26 mediately] in a charger, the head of John the Baptist. And the king was exceeding
sorry; *yet* for his oath's sake, and for their sakes which sat with him, he would not re-
27 ject her. And immediately the king sent an executioner, and commanded his head to
28 be brought: and he went and beheaded him in the prison, And brought his head in a
29 charger, and gave it to the damsel; and the damsel gave it to her mother. And when
his disciples heard *of it,* they came and took up his corpse, and laid it in a tomb.

[1] Ver. 16.—The reading which drops ἐστιν, αὐτός (B., D., L., Δ., &c.), is strongly authenticated; but the omission is explained here by the similarity of οὗτος and αὐτός.—The omission of ἐκ νεκρῶν (Tischendorf, after B., D., L., Δ.) is not sufficiently supported.

[2] Ver. 20.—The reading πολλὰ ἠπόρει ("was often in doubt") has B., L. in its favor. So Ewald and Meyer. But it is probably a modification of the strong πολλὰ ἐποίει.

[3] Ver. 22.—Instead of the Participle καὶ ἀρεσάσης, the Codd. B., C.*, L., and others read ἤρεσεν, and afterwards εἶπε δὲ ὁ βασ. This construction loses the emphatic preparation of the words: "Then the king said unto the maiden." But the Greek construction of the *Recepta* may seem to be simply a softening of the text.

EXEGETICAL AND CRITICAL.

See on the parallel passages of Matthew and Luke.—The time of this occurrence was the return of Jesus from the Feast of Purim at Jerusalem, in the year 781; that is, in the second year of His ministry. On His return from this feast, the disciples were once more gathered round Him at the Sea of Galilee. It is peculiar to Mark, that he connects the suspicious observation of Herod Antipas (*see* Matthew) with the work of Christ as extended by the twelve Apostles. And this is quite natural; since the fame of Jesus was not only extraordinarily increased by their means, but also invested with the semblance of a political import. With regard to Herod's judgment of Jesus, Mark is more distinct than Luke; in exhibiting the relation in which Jesus stood to the Baptist, he is more distinct than Matthew. He is moreover very circumstantial in detailing the binding of John, the favorable crisis for Herodias, Herod's promise to the dancer, the scheme concerted between mother and daughter, the daring urgency of the latter, and other similar traits. But he omits the circumstance, that the disciples of John carried intelligence of the event to the Lord.

Ver. 14. **King Herod.**—The βασιλεύς in the ancient and wide sense. Matthew and Luke say more precisely, the tetrarch (here equivalent to prince). Starke: "Luke calls him, after the manner of the Romans, a tetrarch; Mark, after the manner of the Jews, a king."—**Heard.**—That is, that the disciples of Jesus preached and performed such miracles (Meyer), and that Jesus sent them forth. Hence what follows: *for His name was spread abroad.* Therefore, not (according to Grotius and others), he heard the name of Jesus.—**John the Baptist.**—Ὁ βαπτίζων, substantively. Yet, perhaps, hinting an avoidance of the acknowledgment of his authority.* According to Luke, others declared that John was risen from the dead, and Herod was troubled at it. But the apparent contradiction is solved by our assuming that the idea was introduced by the courtiers, and that Herod, after slight hesitation, entered into their views with hypocritical superstitious policy (*Leben Jesu*, ii. 2). The expression might then be regarded as blending in itself a secret political meaning and a more popular one. According to the former it says, This new movement proceeds from the execution of John the Baptist; and if John was politically dangerous, the appearance of Jesus with His twelve Apostles is tenfold more so. Yet, at the same time, the expression might have been employed, in order to burden the conscience of the king and the people in reference to the execution of John.—**Therefore mighty works do show forth themselves in him.**—John had wrought no miracle; and the prince seems to have made this his excuse, the high legitimation of a prophet having been wanting to the Baptist. Now, in his new form, said the theologizing king, it is seen that he is actually a prophet; the miraculous powers at length manifest themselves in him.

Ver. 15. **As one of the prophets.**—That is, of the old prophets, even if not so great as Elias. It is manifest, first, that the opinions which then prevailed concerning the Person of Jesus, agreed in a certain acknowledgment of His higher mission; secondly, they differed in regard to the more specific definition of His dignity; thirdly, they presented a descending scale of lessening honor paid to Him, starting from a point below the primary recognition that He was the Messiah. And thus they mark the time when the persecution of Jesus was beginning, although the people generally were, in a narrower sense, entirely absorbed with His works and words. Matthew introduces this index of public opinion in connection with another event, which, however, falls within the same year of persecutions, ch. xvi. 14; and now this wavering judgment has become the popular cry.

Ver. 16. **Whom I beheaded.**—Meyer: "Ἐγώ has the emphasis of a guilty conscience." "Mark the urgent expression of confident assurance which the terrified man utters: This is he; he is risen."

Ver. 20. **For Herod feared John.**—Seeming discrepancy when compared with Matthew, as Meyer here and always urges. Compare, on the contrary, EBRARD, p. 384; LANGE, *Leben Jesu*, ii. 2, p. 783. The θέλειν often indicates, in the New Testament, the natural willing in its weakness, the *fain would*, which, however, does not involve necessarily the full and perfect purpose of the will. Matthew, in his exhibition of the feeble, vacillating Herod, at the same time has in view his position on the side of Herodias as in opposition to the people; while Mark has in view his position on the side of the people in opposition to the thoroughly decided and resolute Herodias (*see* Macbeth).—**And observed him,** or *kept him*.—Not, *esteemed him highly* (as Erasmus and others, with De Wette, contend), but he protected him a long time against the attempts of Herodias (as Grotius and Meyer). And this, at the same time, reveals the vacillation of the man, since, as prince, Herod might have set John free. "Herodias was instigated partly by revenge, but partly by fear that her present husband might, in consequence of the exhortations of the Baptist, repent of his sin, and separate from her." Beda.

Ver. 21. **And when a convenient day was come;** that is, favorable for Herodias.—Grotius: "*Opportuna insidiatrici, quæ vino, amore et adulatorum conspiratione facile sperabat impelli posse nutantem mariti, animum.*"—**Lords, high captains, and chief estates.**—The first two classes are servants of the state, civil and military officials; the third includes the great men of the land generally.

Ver. 22. **The king said unto the damsel.**—The antithesis between "king and damsel" gives emphasis to his wicked folly.—**To the half of my kingdom.**—Starke: "This was a grand imitation of the great Ahasuerus; but in one without the supreme power, it was idle and boastful enough."

Ver. 25. **I will that thou give me, by and by.**—Strong emphasis, in the θέλω ἵνα. "Observe the *boldness* of the malignant girl." Meyer.

Ver. 26. **Would not reject her.**—Ἀθετεῖν, to make anything an ἄθετον, illegal: therefore, to make invalid, or abolish, a decree, ordinance, covenant, or oath; and, in reference to persons, it means to deprive of a legal claim, or declare one unjustified: hence it involves the notion of humiliating, the *repudiare*. But the translation to "suffer her to ask in vain," is much too weak.

Ver. 27. **An executioner,** σπεκουλάτορα: one of his body-guard.—"To them was committed the execution of capital sentences (SENECA, *De Ira*, i. 16, Wetstein)." Meyer.

Ver. 28. **And the damsel gave it to her mother.**—Salome, the dancer, afterwards married her father's brother, the tetrarch Philip.

DOCTRINAL AND ETHICAL.

1. *See* on the parallel passages in *Matthew* and *Luke*.

2. The institution of the apostolate, and the mission of the Apostles, were like a revelation of avenging spirits to worldly policy and despotism, cowardly and superstitious, suspicious and fearful from the beginning.

3. Herod a forerunner and confederate of Pilate in this, that he acknowledged the innocence and dignity of John, and yet had not the courage to set him free. He is also like Pilate in the vacillation of his weak character.

4. The opinions of those who surrounded Herod were like the verdicts of the great world concerning Christianity.

5. Herodias a typical character: woman in the demoniac grandeur of wickedness—the opposite of Mary. The New Testament Jezebel, as Herod is the New Testament Ahab. Herodias, the murderess of the greatest prophet, with whom the old covenant ended; Mary, the mother of the Lord, in whom the new covenant is sealed.

6. The intriguing woman, the courtezan in the royal court, an historical symbol. So also the dancer, and the vain festivity, and the sympathies of pride and presumption.

7. One sample of the influences of Grecian habits, as introduced into Palestine and spread there by the Herodians. Doubtless this influence could not but serve to efface the limits between Judaism and heathenism; but the true reconciliation between Greece and the theocracy could be effected only by Christianity.

* He whom men call John the Baptist, *i. e.*—*Ed.*

8. The oath, and the word of honor, and the honorable deeds of the worldly-minded great, as they often clash with the eternal laws of God. In the godless oath there is a real and essential nullity; for God cannot be the avenger of a broken vow which was in itself impious. "But the breach of an ungodly oath demands an open confession." Gerlach. "Herod should have said, *Thou askest of me more than my kingdom, for what shall it profit a man?*" etc.

9. Fearful contrasts, in which are reflected the satanic powers of wickedness: the head of the greatest preacher of repentance in the ancient world made a fee by an Israelite prince to a little Greek dancer at the court (a Jewess, who dances after the Greek fashion at the Israelite court); Christ, the Messiah of the Jews, betrayed by the kiss of a disciple to the hierarchy, condemned and given over to the Gentiles by the high-priests and the priesthood in Zion.

HOMILETICAL AND PRACTICAL.

See on the parallel passages in Matthew and Luke, and also the Reflections above.—Christ, with His twelve Apostles, described as John the Baptist risen from the dead: 1. How far this was a gross error, composed of a mixture of guilty conscience, superstition, policy, cunning, ignorance, and blindness; 2. how far, in another sense, a great truth, in which the living law of the kingdom of God found expression (ineffaceableness, growth, progress, consummation, "the blood of the martyrs, the seed of the Church"). —The internal conflict of Herod and Pilate: 1. Similarities: impotent striving, long delay, critical suspense, shameful surrender. 2. Differences: a Jew, a Gentile; Herodias in the one case, the warning devout woman in the other; the people against the evil deed, the people in favor of it.—John the Baptist dignified and self-consistent as the great, heroic preacher of repentance: 1. Confronting the prince of the land, Herod; 2. in prison, and with the fear of death before his eyes.—The good impressions, which Herod had lost: therefore, 1. He continued in the sin; 2. in vacillation between the right and wrong; 3. in self-deception; 4. under the power of temptation. —The conflict between good living and living good. —The convenient season; or, the feasts and banquets of the world, and those of the kingdom of God.—The world's estimate of the value of things: the head of a prophet of less importance than a dance; a blasphemous, drunken oath more sacred than the eternal law of God.—How the weak and wavering characters, whilst they delay, are overcome by the bold and daring conduct of those who are resolute in their wickedness.—The judgment which followed the beheading of the Baptist: pierced conscience, further guilt touching Jesus, a death of misery.—The frightful abandonment by the Spirit, which, in the great world, may cloak itself under the disguise of brilliance and vigor of spirit.—The fidelity and troubles of the disciples of John figurative of the troubles of faith as held bound in legality: 1. The heroic courage with which they buried their master; 2. the lack of believing courage to attach themselves to Jesus.

STARKE:—Even the great of this world have always been excited and moved by the Gospel of Christ.—QUESNEL:—The sinner has no peace when he would seek it; because he rejected it when it was offered him by God.—HEDINGER:—The judgments of this world are always out of square when they deal with spiritual things; therefore, dear fellow-Christian, inquire not about them.—Public teachers should without fear rebuke the sins and blasphemies even of the great; they may rely, in doing so, on the Divine help.—LANGE:—O ye court-preachers, learn of John what your duty is: he was no court-preacher, and yet he bore fearless testimony to the truth.—HEDINGER:—Devotion is always honorable, even in the eyes of the most frenzied children of the world.—Carnality befouls the best thoughts.—QUESNEL:—The festivities of the world are the best appointed tables of sin.—ZEISIUS:—The poor have to give the rich their sweat and blood, and they riot in the proceeds, etc.—Vain swearing.—Promises made over the wine-cup.—OSIANDER:—At the court there are often heavy payments for ridiculous trifles.—A foolish promise brings repentance after it.—QUESNEL: —The oath is sinful, and therefore null, when it cannot be carried out but with sin and injustice.— LANGE:—No servant or official should let himself be made an instrument of injustice; rather should he let everything go.—Christians pay honor to the pious on their death, and carry them reverently to their tombs.—GERLACH:—Close connection between debauchery and cruelty.—GOSSNER:—Thus does the world deal with God's ambassadors.—BAUER:—See, what a marriage this was!

---

3. *Withdrawal of Jesus into the Wilderness on the other side of the Sea of Galilee, and the miraculous Feeding of the Five Thousand.* VERS. 30–44.

30 And the apostles gathered themselves together unto Jesus, and told him all things,
31 both[1] what they had done, and what they had taught. And he said unto them, Come
ye yourselves apart into a desert place, and rest a while: for there were many coming
32 and going, and they had no leisure so much as to eat. And they departed into a desert
33 place by ship privately. And the people[2] saw them departing, and many knew him,
and ran a-foot thither out of all cities, and outwent them, and came together unto him.
34 And Jesus, when he came out, saw much people, and was moved with compassion toward them, because they were as sheep not having a shepherd: and he began to teach
35 them many things. And when the day was now far spent, his disciples came unto him,

36 and said, This is a desert place, and now the time *is* far passed; Send them away, that
they may go into the country round about, and into the villages, and buy themselves
37 bread: for they have nothing to eat. He answered and said unto them, Give ye them
to eat. And they say unto him, Shall we go and buy two hundred pennyworth of bread,
38 and give them to eat? He saith unto them, How many loaves have ye? go and[4] see.
39 And when they knew, they say, Five, and two fishes. And he commanded them to
40 make all sit down by companies upon the green grass. And they sat down in ranks,
41 by hundreds, and by fifties. And when he had taken the five loaves and the two fishes,
he looked up to heaven, and blessed, and brake the loaves, and gave *them* to his disci-
42 ples to set before them; and the two fishes divided he among them all. And they did
43 all eat, and were filled. And they took up twelve baskets[5] full of the fragments, and
44 of the fishes. And they that did eat of the loaves were about five thousand men.

[1] Ver. 30.—The καὶ (ὅσα) of the *Recepta* has the weight of the Codd. against it.

[2] Ver. 33.—The οἱ ὄχλοι is an addition (from Matthew), and is wanting in A., B., D., Griesbach, Scholz, Lachmann. Lachmann and Tischendorf have συνέδραμον ἐκεῖ καὶ προῆλθον αὐτούς. The many variations are essentially the same in meaning.

[3] Ver. 36.—'Αγοράσωσιν ἑαυτοῖς, τί φάγωσι—Tischendorf, after B., L., Δ., &c.

[4] Ver. 38.—Καί before ἴδετε wanting in B., D., L., Versions, Tischendorf.

[5] Ver. 43.—Tischendorf and Meyer, following B. and cursive MSS., read κοφίνων πληρώματα.

EXEGETICAL AND CRITICAL.

See on the parallel passages of *Matthew*, *Luke*, and *John*.—The time is designated most clearly by John. Jesus has returned from the Feast of Purim (in the second year of His ministry) to Galilee; and the journey begins probably from the district of Tiberias. The time is evidently just before the Passover; as it is manifest, from Mark's mention of the green grass, that the spring was just beginning. According to Luke, it was, also, the time when the Apostles once more assembled around their Master, and when Herod began to take an interest in Him and in His doings. According to Matthew, finally, this miracle coincided with the time immediately after the execution of the Baptist, and the report brought concerning it. The peculiarities of Mark in this section are as follows: The disciples tell the Lord also what they had taught. They were to take a little rest in the desert place. As elsewhere there was no time for either the Lord or His disciples to eat, on account of the press of the people, so it was here. The fact also is mentioned, that the Lord's departure was made known to many, and that the crowds hastened to anticipate Him. We must add the allusion to these as sheep without a shepherd, and the vivid description of the people's dejected state.

Ver. 34. **When He came out.**—The crowds of people might seem to have rendered abortive the design of Jesus to withdraw for a season with His disciples; for, according to the most obvious connection, we should suppose that ἐξελθών must mean: "When He came forth from the ship." But as the Evangelist has mentioned the fixed purpose of Jesus to go into a desert place apart, we must retain the connection with this, and assume that the "coming out" refers to His leaving the wilderness again.—**And He began to teach them many things.**—This likewise confirms the previous explanation. Since a large portion of the day was gone, the time must have been drawing too near to the decline of day; and hence His discourse was interrupted by the suggestion of the disciples.

Ver. 37. **Two hundred pennyworth.**—*See* for the details in John,—"through whom this part of the scene, not recorded by Matthew and Luke, obtains the confirmation of authenticity." Grotius: "The amount that happened to be in the chest was two hundred denarii." Meyer: "This does not follow; it was the estimate made by the disciples of what the provision would cost." But they would doubtless make their estimate according to the condition of their treasury. The denarius, δηνάριον, was a Roman silver coin; it was used also at a later period among the Jews; somewhat lighter than the Attic drachma, but current at about the same value, being the customary hire of a day's labor, about sevenpence halfpenny. *See* particulars in WINER.

Ver. 39. **By companies,** συμπόσια συμπόσια.—A Hebraism, like the subsequent πρασιαὶ πρασιαί. Starke: "So that there were on each side 50, and 100 always together. Fifty such tables full made them just 5,000. Or, there were 50 seats in breadth, and 100 in length." But, why not simply companies of 100 and of 50, through which they might freely pass? A living town in the wilderness. Gerlach: "Two longer rows of 100, a shorter one of 50 persons. The fourth side remained, after the manner of the ancients' tables, empty and open."

Ver. 43. **And of the fishes.**—Reckoned among the relics which filled the twelve baskets. According to the account, these relics are distinguished from the κλάσματα, or broken pieces of bread.

DOCTRINAL AND ETHICAL.

See on the parallel passages in *Matthew*, *Luke*, and *John*.

HOMILETICAL AND PRACTICAL.

See on the parallel passage of *Matthew*.—The return of the Apostles, and the first resting-place provided for them by their Lord.—Come into a desert place apart, and rest a while: Christ's call to His overwrought, excited, and restless laborers.—This word of Christ perverted by many of His servants into a toleration of idleness: He says, *a while!*—Christ's rest, and His disciples' solemn prayer, in solitude.—The refreshments of the world, and the refreshments of Christ's disciples.—Into solitude, but with Christ.—How the Lord sacrificed for men both His solitude and His refreshment.—How He turned the seeming failure of His plan (touching solitude) into a higher realization of the same object.—How we should fashion the web of our life—our plans and the conjunctures of circumstances—into higher unity of godly action and suffering.—The miraculous festival which our Lord prepared for His disciples after their labors and journeys in the world.—How He continually comes forth in His mercy: 1. From the bosom of heaven; 2. from the darkness of Nazareth; 3. from the solemn season of prayer in the wilderness; 4. from the glory of the new life in the resurrection; 5. from the throne of heaven.—The school of Christ a free school in the highest sense.—With Christ, all that we have we have freely.—Christ was already King when they wanted to make Him king; but King: 1. In the kingdom of the Spirit; 2. in the kingdom of love; 3. and in the kingdom of divine blessing.—His earthly exaltation would have been the translation of His throne from the realm of the infinite into the realm of the finite and transitory.—Christ was constrained to repel the people with as much earnestness as that with which the mercy of His Shepherd-heart sought them.—Christ the breaker of bread, because He Himself is the Bread of life.—The riches of His kingdom.—Sufficiency with Christ is lavish abundance.

STARKE:—OSIANDER:—We should in such manner wait on our ministering as preachers of the Gospel, that we may be able to give in our account to the supreme Shepherd with joy.—It is good to rest after labor.—When we can separate ourselves from the tumult of the world, and send our spirits upwards to God, rest both of body and of soul is the result.—HEDINGER:—He who is in earnest to go to Christ, will let no trouble, labor, or expense hinder him.—OSIANDER:—Although we may have a certain amount of rest in this world, yet that is soon disturbed again by business. Here all is unrest; yonder is perfect repose.—The Church of God has indeed many shepherds; but since many of them are shamefully given to negligence, and many are busy with vain labor, it is reasonable to lament that the poor sheep have, after all, but few true shepherds.—QUESNEL:—The love of devout souls is indeed wise, but God's love is better in this than all.—Poor people cannot do better than hang upon God, &c.—HEDINGER:—Piety and faith never die of hunger.—What in men's eyes is impossible, may become possible through God's power.—As to the fragments, order and economy are in all things well-pleasing to God.—God is a God of order.—Take your food with prayer and thanksgiving, 1 Tim. iv. 4.—SCHLEIERMACHER:—Thus they came back with minds excited, and perhaps disturbed, by all these various opinions concerning Christ; and, therefore it was very important that they should become composed, and readjust all their views in their original relation to the truth.—We should never find a contradiction between that which is our duty and the internal bias of our hearts.—Christ found between this will (to be alone with His disciples) and the great pressure of the people no contradiction: He knew how to reconcile one with the other, and by the other.—There is nothing more essential in the kingdom of God than what is incumbent upon us as duty, and what is the object of our wishes, should coalesce and coincide, the one upholding and preserving the other.—There is one entirely and purely simple wisdom.—To this nothing is so absolutely essential as simplicity of spirit.—The disciples were to be convinced (by the miraculous feeding), that if they applied themselves to the duties and obligations of the spiritual kingdom, their outward life would take no harm; whilst, on the other hand, everything would be interrupted if the Master should always act as they might think best.

SEVENTH SECTION.

CONTEST OF JESUS WITH THE ENMITY OF THE PHARISEES AND SCRIBES FROM JERUSALEM; HIS WITHDRAWAL INTO THE GENTILE BORDERS OF TYRE AND SIDON, AND INTO THE DISTRICT OF DECAPOLIS.

CHAPTER VI. 45—VIII. 9.

1. *The Return to Gennesaret; the Contrary Wind; Christ's Walking on the Sea; New Miracles on the Western Coast.* CH. VI. 45-56.

(Parallels: Matt. xiv. 22-36; John vi. 15-21.)

45 And straightway he constrained his disciples to get into the ship, and to go to the
46 other side before unto Bethsaida, while he sent away[1] the people. And when he had
47 sent them away, he departed into a [the] mountain to pray. And when even was
48 come, the ship was in the midst of the sea, and he alone on the land. And he saw[2]
them toiling in rowing; for the wind was contrary unto them: and about the fourth
watch of the night he cometh unto them, walking upon the sea, and would have passed
49 by them. But when they saw him walking upon the sea, they supposed it had been a
50 spirit [spectre], and cried out: For they all saw him, and were troubled. And immediately he talked with them, and saith unto them, Be of good cheer: it is I; be not
51 afraid. And he went up unto them into the ship; and the wind ceased: and they were

52 sore amazed in themselves beyond measure, and wondered.[3] For they considered not *the*
53 *miracle* of the loaves: for their heart was hardened. And when they had passed over,
54 they came into the land of Gennesaret, and drew to the shore. And when they were
55 come out of the ship, straightway they knew him,[4] And ran through that whole region
round about, and began to carry about in beds those that were sick, where they heard
56 he was. And whithersoever he entered, into villages, or cities, or country, they laid
the sick in the streets, and besought him that they might touch if it were but the border of his garment: and as many as touched him were made whole.

[1] Ver. 45.—Ἀπολύει, after B., D., L., Δ. Tischendorf, Lachmann, Meyer.

[[2] Ver. 48.—B., D., L., Vulgate, Lachmann, Tischendorf, Meyer, read ἰδών instead of εἶδεν, and omit the following καὶ (B., L.), making a parenthesis of ἦν γὰρ ὁ, &c.—*Ed.*]

[[3] Ver. 52.—B., L., Δ., Coptic, Vulgate, Tischendorf omit καὶ ἐθαύμαζον; rejected by Griesbach, bracketed by Lachmann, retained by Meyer.—*Ed.*]

[[4] Ver. 54.—After αὐτόν Lachmann inserts in brackets οἱ ἄνδρες τοῦ τόπου ἐκείνου, following A., G., Versions. Meyer rightly regards it as a gloss.—*Ed.*]

EXEGETICAL AND CRITICAL.

See on the parallel passages of *Matthew* and *John*.—We owe to Mark the very important record, which sheds light upon the whole narrative, that the disciples were sent forward before the Lord in the direction of Bethsaida—that Bethsaida, namely, which lay on the eastern side of the sea. (*See* on *Matthew*.) Thus it was a passage across. Then his expression, ἀποταξάμενος, is an important parallel to the ἀνεχώρησε in John: it gave Him trouble to release Himself from the excited and enthusiastic people. Also, in the expression, ἤθελε παρελθεῖν, he coincides, in the meaning at least, with John, ver. 21, ἤθελον οὖν λαβεῖν αὐτὸν, κ.τ.λ. But while Mark omits the intervening incident connected with Peter —which that Apostle, whose Evangelist he was, would modestly pass over, as making himself prominent—he lays stress upon the fact that the disciples had not been brought to a true and living faith, even by the miracle of the feeding. But he has painted most copiously and vividly the tumultuous excitement of the people, as it was occasioned by the Lord's landing, and how they immediately knew Him and followed Him with their sick from place to place.

Ver. 45. **Unto Bethsaida.**—Meyer's notion, that this was the western Bethsaida, and not the eastern, appears entirely groundless. [Wieseler understands by it the eastern Bethesda. Alexander remarks that it was "not the city of Gaulonitis, at the north-eastern end of the lake and eastward of the place where the Jordan enters it, in the desert tract south-east of which the miracle had just been wrought (Luke ix. 10), but Bethsaida of Galilee, the birth-place of Simon, Andrew, and Philip (John i. 45), elsewhere mentioned with Capernaum (Matt. xi. 21; Luke x. 13), and therefore probably not far from it, but at all events upon the lake-shore, as Eusebius expressly mentions."—*Ed.*]

Ver. 46. **Sent them away,** ἀποταξάμενος.—Not merely, "bade them farewell," for which there would have been no necessity to send the disciples away first.

Ver. 48. **Would have passed by them.**—They were to follow Him in a westerly direction: no longer fruitlessly rowing eastwards against the wind (*see* on *Matthew*). He went before them, as it were, to show the way. They had wished to take Him up on the eastern coast (John); He would go before them to the western coast (Mark): an intermediate course was the result in the end.

Ver. 51. **Were sore amazed in themselves beyond measure, and wondered.**—The latter feeling found expression in exclamations; the whole strength of their internal amazement they did not express.

Ver. 52. **They considered not.**—They had not yet come to an understanding, οὐ συνῆκαν. They had not attained that living, self-developing apprehension of spirit, which would know how to draw the right consequences. Bengel: *debuerant a pane ad mare concludere.*

Ver. 53. **The land of Gennesaret.**—*See* on *Matthew*.

Ver. 55 **Began to carry about.**—Not merely in general, but some hither and others thither. It is also meant that they went with a sick man after Jesus from one place to another, when He had left the former.

DOCTRINAL AND ETHICAL.

1. *See* on the parallel passages of *Matthew* and *John*.

2. The first miraculous feeding marks precisely the moment when our Lord had most expressly to contend with the people's design to challenge Him as the Messiah, and make Him a king. In contrast with this design of the people, we must here take notice of the expression of Jesus' pity for the wretched multitude: so little can the attempt of a people to exalt Him prematurely, and in a worldly sense, exert any influence upon Him. In that very circumstance the misery of the people presented itself to His view most plainly. But even this earnest effort of our Lord to withdraw Himself from the people was successful only for a short period. Very soon afterwards He was obliged, in the synagogue at Capernaum (according to John vi.), to declare Himself most emphatically; and from that time onwards, that enthusiastic fanaticism among the people, which had before been prepared to take side with Him, even against Pharisaism the hierarchy and Herod, declined. From this time treachery began to germinate in the soul of Judas.

3. The miracle of Christ's walking upon the sea was a manifestation of His divine power, not only over external objective nature, but also over His subjective nature, in the medium of His human equanimity. The mystery of this equanimity is the manifestation of the paradisaical, holy man in the midst of the nature subjected by the fall to vanity. (Meyer does not understand this: *see* Note on *Mark*.)

4. It is observable that the Evangelist Mark most expressly, and in the plainest manner, describes the state of the Apostles, down to the revelation of the

risen Lord among them, as a state of dulness, hardness, and unbelief. He does not thereby deny their fidelity as disciples. But the true and perfect faith did not, in his conception, exist until the new evangelical Spirit of life was given, that life which could approve itself in a personal spontaneous development. And the disciple of Peter approaches John in this, as in many other traits of his evangelical representation.

HOMILETICAL AND PRACTICAL.

See on the parallel passages in Matthew and John. —The temptability of the disciples of Jesus as over against the fanatical excitement of the people.—How Christ constrained them to take ship and go over the sea, in order to separate them from the people; and what significance this has for the Church and the ministers of Christ.—Christ (and Christianity) the guide on the sea.—The walking of Christ upon the waters.—How the phantoms and scarecrows of vain fear vanish before the glory of Christ, in sacred reverence of His divine power.—The climax of the enthusiasm of the Galilean people on behalf of Christ was also a turning-point.

STARKE:—QUESNEL:—Man is in the world like a little ship upon the stormy sea in the night; since he can neither counsel nor save himself. He who does not know danger, and does not pray, may soon perish.—Jesus sometimes leaves us alone, that we may know ourselves and our own weakness, and feel how deeply we are in need of Him; but He never leaves us out of His sight.—The wind of persecution is a useful wind; for it brings Christ to us, and us to land.—Christ is Lord also over all nature.—LUTHER:—By such an example (the feeding) they should have been made so strong in faith as not to have been terrified at an apparition.—SCHLEIERMACHER:—Thus, as the living consciousness of the Redeemer is awakened within us, our temper must be calmed into the true equanimity; and this will smooth and regulate all things external.—All the powers which God has given us we should put in motion to glorify the kingdom of God.—GOSSNER:—We are all still upon the sea of life.—But He never loses us out of His sight.—BAUER:—When they have rightly heard the Master's word, phantoms and night and storm are all forgotten.

---

2. *Contest with the Pharisees and Scribes from Jerusalem concerning Traditions respecting Eating.* CH. VII. 1–23.

(Parallel: Matt. xv. 1–20.)

1 Then came together unto him the Pharisees, and certain of the scribes, which came
2 from Jerusalem. And when they saw some of his disciples eat bread with defiled [com-
3 mon], that is to say, with unwashen hands, they found fault.[1] For the Pharisees, and
all the Jews, except they wash *their* hands oft, eat not, holding the tradition of the
4 elders. And *when they come* from the market, except they wash, they eat not. And
many other things there be, which they have received to hold, *as* the washing of cups,
5 and pots, brasen vessels, and of tables. Then[2] the Pharisees and scribes asked him,
Why walk not thy disciples according to the tradition of the elders, but eat bread with
6 unwashen hands? He answered and said unto them, Well hath Esaias prophesied of
you hypocrites, as it is written, This people honoureth me with *their* lips, but their heart
7 is far from me. Howbeit, in vain do they worship me, teaching *for* doctrines the com-
8 mandments of men. For, laying aside the commandment of God, ye hold the tradi-
tion of men, *as* the washing of pots and cups: and many other such like things ye do.[3]
9 And he said unto them, Full well ye reject the commandment of God, that ye may
10 keep your own tradition. For Moses said, Honour thy father and thy mother; and,
11 Whoso curseth [revileth] father or mother, let him die the death: But ye say, If a man
shall say to his father or mother, *It is* Corban, that is to say, a gift, by whatsoever thou
12 mightest be profited by me; *he shall be free.* And[4] ye suffer him no more to do aught
13 for his father or his mother; Making the word of God of none effect through your tra-
14 dition, which ye have delivered: and many such like things do ye. And when he had
called all the people *unto him*, he said unto them [again[5]], Hearken unto me every one
15 *of you*, and understand: There is nothing from without a man, that entering into him,
can defile him: but the things which come out of him,[6] those are they that defile the
16, 17 man. If any man have ears to hear, let him hear.[7] And when he was entered into
18 the house from the people, his disciples asked him concerning the parable. And he
saith unto them, Are ye so without understanding also? Do ye not perceive, that
19 whatsoever thing from without entereth into the man, it cannot defile him; Because it
entereth not into his heart, but into the belly, and goeth out into the draught, purging[8]
20 all meats? And he said, That which cometh out of the man, that defileth the man.
21 For from within, out of the heart of men, proceed evil thoughts, adulteries, fornications,

22 murders, Thefts, covetousness, wickedness, deceit, lasciviousness an evil eye, blasphemy
23 pride, foolishness: All these evil things come from within, and defile the man.

[1] Ver. 2.—The addition ἐμέμψαντο (after ἄρτους) has slight support; and the κατέγνωσαν (after ἄρτους) of Cod. D. is equally weak. The former arose from undervaluing the emphatic συνάγονται, which itself suggests an act of the synagogue. Hence we cannot, with Tischendorf, take vers. 3 and 4 as a parenthesis, and ver. 5 as the conclusion.

[2] Ver. 5.—The ἔπειτα is a continuation of the former misunderstanding: Codd. B., D., L., Lachmann, Tischendorf, Meyer, &c., read καί.—The κοιναῖς, instead of ἀνίπτοις, is sanctioned by B., D., Versions.

[3] Ver. 8.—Βαπτισμοὺς to ποιεῖτε is wanting in B., L., Δ., &c. It is bracketed by Lachmann, struck out by Tischendorf. Meyer defends it.

[4] Ver. 12.—The καί is omitted by Lachmann and Meyer, after B., D. It disturbs the connection of thought.

[5] Ver. 14.—The reading πάλιν, recommended by Griesbach and adopted by Lachmann, Tischendorf, and Meyer, following B., D., L., Δ., is important. It shows, that is, that the previous incident must be regarded as an examination by the synagogue, in which Christ was separated from the people.

[6] Ver. 15.—Τὰ ἐκ τοῦ ἀνθρώπου ἐκπορευόμενα, according to B., D., L., Δ., Lachmann, Tischendorf.

[7] Ver. 16.—This verse is wanting in B., L. Omitted by Tischendorf, it is retained by Lachmann and Meyer. An interpolation here is not probable. The connection requires this point.

[8] Ver. 19.—A., B., E., F., G., Δ., Chrysostom, Lachmann, Meyer, read καθαρίζων, not καθαρίζον; D. reads καθαρίζει.

EXEGETICAL AND CRITICAL.

Comp. the parallel place in Matthew. The occurrence before us took place in the summer of the year 782: in the midst of the year of persecutions. The combination of the Pharisees of Galilee and the Pharisees of Judea in their opposition to Jesus had already been concerted and entered upon. They had begun to institute against Him ecclesiastical proceedings in Galilee, and to watch His every step. The basis of the conspiracy consists of the preceding Galilean crisis, ch. ii. and iii., and the confederacy against Jesus at the Feast of Purim in Jerusalem, 782 (John v.). The progress and the conclusion of the scheme appear in ch. viii. 11. From the time of the Feast of Purim a common action and combination of the Sanhedrim in Jerusalem and the Galilean synagogue was inaugurated. The Sanhedrim were in constant connection and correspondence with the synagogues of the provinces, and even with those of foreign lands (*see* Acts ix. 2). Some, therefore, appointed by them, diligently visited the provinces; and watched especially those teachers whose doctrines declined from the principles of Pharisaism, at the head of which stood that of tradition (AMMON, *Leben Jesu*, ii. 264). There were two official transactions or interferences. And there were two retreats on the part of Jesus: the first time, as far as the borders of the Gentile territory; the second time, into the solitude of the mountain beyond the sea, and even to the borders of the other world (transfiguration);—and all for the preparation of the new Church. (*See* my *Leben Jesu*, ii. 2, 858.)—Between the narrative of the first feeding, the walking of Christ upon the sea, and our present narrative, there are many things to be interposed, which Mark has already communicated. Among these are the heretication of Jesus in the cornfield; the healing the man with a withered hand; the allegation of the Galilean Pharisees, that the works of Christ were done in the power of Beelzebub, etc. (*See* the Table of Contents, *Leben Jesu*, ii. 2, 14.)—Peculiar to Mark is the expression, συνάγονται πρὸς αὐτόν, in which we cannot fail to see reference to an official interference of the Sanhedrim with our Lord. Also the exact account of the religious washings of the Jews; the detailed characterization of the conflict between the Pharisaic traditions and the commandment of God, including the Corban; the striking and profound sentence concerning the purging all meats; and the perfect description of those evil things which proceed out of the heart. Also, in the following section, which may be glanced at here, the design of Christ to remain concealed in a house (belonging to a friend) on the borders of Phœnicia, during the time of His sojourn there; and the Lord's return to the Sea of Galilee through the Sidonian territory and that of Decapolis. It is observable that Peter must have communicated the account of these remarkable travels, having faithfully preserved the individual details. On the other hand, this Evangelist omits the intercession of the disciples on behalf of the woman of Canaan, and the declaration of Christ that He was sent only to the lost sheep of the house of Israel.

Ver. 2. **And when they saw.**—Probably on the appearance of the disciples in Jerusalem at the Passover, which He did not attend in the year 782. The spiritual impulse of freedom which actuated the disciples might at that time have led them into the commission of certain acts of thoughtlessness.—**With common, that is to say, with unwashen hands.**—So Mark explains for Roman readers. We must particularly define the idea of unwashen hands by that of unwashen in the sense of a religious ceremony prescribed by tradition; and the idea of common by that of ecclesiastically profane, unclean, and defiling. Those who persisted in this uncleanness, which had for its result excommunication, must at last draw down upon themselves the decisive ban.

Ver. 3. **With the fist; oft.** [Margin of Eng. Ver. *diligently.*] Πυγμῇ.—Among the many explanatory translations which have missed the meaning of the difficult expression are these: Vulgate, *crebro*; Gothic, *ufta* (oft); Syriac, *diligenter*. *See* in De Wette and Meyer the various exegetical methods adopted. "Probably it was part of the rite, that the washing hand was shut; because it might have been thought that the open hand engaged in washing might make the other unclean, or be made unclean by it, after having itself been washed" (*Leben Jesu*, ii. 2, 858). The expression might mean a vigorous and thorough washing.

Ver. 4. **And from the market.**—Codex D. has the addition, ἐὰν ἔλθωσιν, *when they come;* which Meyer, De Wette, and others regard as a sound interpretation. According to this view the progression would be this: 1. Before every meal the washing of hands; 2. but, after the return from market, where there was so much danger of coming into contact with unclean men, the bath was used as a washing of the whole body; hence ἐὰν μὴ βαπτ. But that which follows—the βαπτισμοὶ ποτηρίων—requires still another degree in the progression, and proves that βαπτισμός here must be understood in a wider sense. Therefore we interpret it, with Paulus, Kuinoel, and Olshausen, of that which came from the market. De Wette, on the contrary, observes that this was everywhere customary. But it was not cus tomary as a *religious* ceremony of washing, or as a kind of baptism, like that of the pots and cups, or the Romish baptism of bells. And, moreover, the same held good of the washing of hands; for the washing of hands before eating was generally customary amongst the Persians, Greeks, and Romans. Thus, in our view, there was a triple washing at meals: 1. That of the persons; 2. that of the victuals; 3. that of the vessels. — **Cups and pots.**— Made of wood, in contrast with those of brass, which follow; or, it may be, considered as earthen. ["Pots," ξεστῶν, perhaps from ξέω, to polish; or else from the Latin *sextus* or *sextarius*, denoting the sixth part of a larger measure.—*Ed.*] Meyer says, indeed, "Earthen vessels, when they were Levitically unclean, were broken to pieces, according to Lev. xv. 12." But the case supposed there was that of positive desecrations; and it is not to be supposed that the Jews, after or before every meal, broke all the earthen vessels which they used. [*Tables* (in the margin *beds*), *i. e.*, couches, anything on which men recline, whether for sleep, or, according to the later use of the ancients, to partake of food,—which accounts for the word used in the text of our Bible. That these couches were immersed in every instance of ceremonial washing, can be thought probable, or even possible, only by those who are under the necessity of holding that this Greek word not only means to dip or plunge, originally, but, unlike every other word transferred to a religious use, is always used in that exclusive and invariable sense, without modification or exception; to those who have no purpose to attain by such a paradox, the place before us will afford, if not conclusive evidence, at least a strong presumption, that beds (to say no more) might be baptized without immersion. ALEXANDER, *in loco.*—*Ed.*]

Ver. 9. **Full well,** καλῶς.—Ironically, as among ourselves. — **Your own tradition,** ἵνα. — Very strong and deep. At the bottom of all rigorous enforcement of traditional observances there is an unconscious or half-conscious repugnance to submit perfectly to the law of God. Bengel: *Vere accusantur, hanc suam esse intentionem.* "Not only unconsciously, but with the fullest purpose, the Rabbis exalted their precepts above the law of Moses." In the Talmud we read: "The words of the scribes are more noble than the words of the law; for the words of the law are both hard and easy, but the words of the scribes are all easy (to be understood)." —"He who deals with Scripture, it is said in the Bava Mezia, does a thing indifferent; he who reads the Mishna has a reward; but he who devotes himself to the Gemara is most meritorious of all." SEPP, *Leben Jesu*, ii. p. 345.

Ver. 11. **Corban.** — Comp. on Matthew xiv. 5; as also, for the ellipsis in ver. 11, Luther's marginal note: "Corban means an offering, and it was as much as to say, Dear father, I would willingly give it to thee, but it is Corban: I count it better to give it to God than to thee, and it will help thee better."

Ver. 14. **He said again.**—The significant πάλιν —the reading we adopt—throws light upon the whole preceding occurrence; and, together with the συνάγονται at the beginning, gives it the appearance of a judicial process of the synagogue.

Ver. 17. **His disciples asked Him.**— Comp. Matthew, where Peter is marked out as the questioner; and observe here, as elsewhere, his modest suppression of himself in the Gospel which sprang from himself. And here, again, there is emphatic prominence given to the disciples' want of developed spiritual vigor and insight of faith, and their slow advancement in knowledge.

Ver. 19. **Purging all meats.**—Meyer: καθαρίζον might be connected with the ἐκπορεύεται as an appositional expression. The apposition, however, would not be connected with the ἐκπορεύεται, but with its subject, that is, meat; and that could not be tolerated. Καθαρίζον is rather the substantival definition of ἀφεδρῶν, as being a general means of purification for all the external impurities of meats: the better supported reading καθαρίζων, on the other hand, expressed the same thought adjectivally.—The ἀφεδρῶν makes all meats clean, not because it simply takes away all impurities, but because the uncleanness or impurity of the object consists in its being out of its place, and therefore defiling something else. It is therefore a place of filth for all the house; a place of cleansing, on the contrary, for the great household of nature. Not without irony does Christ make prominent this ideal significance of the external means of cleansing for meats, addressing as He did the men of traditions, who strove to ensure a *prophylactic external* purity to their food.

Ver. 21. **Evil thoughts.** — In relation to the distribution here, we must notice the change between the plural and the singular forms; or, 1. predominant actions, and 2. dispositions. The acts in the plural are arranged under three categories: *a.* lust; *b.* hatred; *c.* covetousness. They then combine into wickednesses (πονηρίαι), by which the forms of evil dispositions are then introduced: *deceit* and *lasciviousness* indicate, in two contrasts, the concealed and the open wickedness of self-gratification; whilst the *evil eye* and *blasphemy* indicate concealed and open enmity (blasphemy against God and man). Pride or self-exaltation, and foolishness (נְבָלָה), are the internal and the external side of the one ungodly and wicked nature. "*The evil eye*" is notorious in the East; here it is the description of an envious look.

DOCTRINAL AND ETHICAL.

1. *See* the parallel passage in Matthew.

2. The Jews have fallen through their Sabbath or Rest-day traditions into eternal unrest, through their law of purification into moral defilement, through their many baptisms into an abiding lack of baptism, through their service of the letter into Talmudist fables, through their separation into dispersion all over the world, through their millenarian Messiahship into enmity to Christ, through their trifling with the blessing into the power of the curse. The irony of the Spirit, that He punishes extremes by extremes.

3. The prophecy of Isaiah (ch. xxix. 13) pronounces a condemnation, always in force, upon all dead and fanatical zeal, and upon all mere ceremonial worship and work.

4. Zeal for traditional observances in its abiding conflict with the eternal commandments of God and laws of humanity. The conflict between false ecclesiasticism and morality. The contradiction of fanaticism has for its foundation an evil bias towards externalizing the inner life. The worm of superstition is unbelief; the worm of fanaticism is religious death or atheism; the worm of hypocritical outside religion is impiety. For the conflict between human fanatical ecclesiasticism and the divine fundamental commandments of morality, *see* the history of Byzantism and Romanism.

5. Tradition and human ordinances identical. Tradition needs continual reform through the law of God; and human ordinances, through the living development of this law.

6. Contrast between external and internal fellowship; *i. e.*, between being excommunicated, and being out of the Church.

HOMILETICAL AND PRACTICAL.

See on Matthew.—Christ in judgment upon human tradition.—Christ the Deliverer of His disciples: 1. The Originator, 2. the Defender, 3. the Guardian, 4. the Director and Consummator, of their freedom.—Christ and Christianity a hundred times exposed to spiritual censure: 1. The censure of school-learning (theology); 2. of the tradition of the elders (clerical office); 3. of the synagogue (popular assembly).—Christ and tradition: 1. He is the foundation or kernel of all true internal tradition; 2. therefore He unites in one and renews all external tradition; 3. and He is the Judge of all externalized and impious tradition.—The conflict between the law and human ordinances, or between ecclesiasticism and morality. It is, 1. an unnatural conflict, for true ecclesiasticism and true morality can never come into collision. 2. It is a light conflict, when false morality contends with true ecclesiasticism. 3. It is a critical conflict, when false ecclesiasticism fights against true morality. 4. There is a frightful doom upon both, when false ecclesiasticism and false morality struggle with each other.—The old conflict between fanaticism and humanity. Ecclesiastical systems which bury piety (household relations, filial obligations, etc.) condemn themselves.—The indivisible unity of faith and love, of piety and duty.—The fearful perversion of the conflict between divine revelation and human sin into a contradiction between the divine and the human nature.—The triumph of human ordinance is always upon the ruins of the law of faith.—To enjoy with thankfulness, is the sanctification of enjoyment, 1 Tim. iv. 4.—In the place of the washing of hands before meat, has come in the folding of hands. Therefore we must mind the reality of the symbol, even in this latter case.—Isaiah, Christ, and the Reformation, agreeing in their judgment upon what is true and what is false worship of God.— The right process of a true reformation: 1. It distinguishes between spirit and flesh, between the internal and the external. 2. It fights against the false intermixtures of the two, in which the spirit is made subservient to the flesh, and the internal to the external. 3. It seeks to connect the two aright, so that the spirit may make the flesh its own and glorify it. 4. It therefore contends also against a false and unnatural separation between the two.—The purity and the purifying power of the great divine economy of nature.—Christianity has consecrated even natural infirmity; or, a beam of the glorification which shines upon the dark natural ways of men.—The decisive objection against human ordinances, that they vainly attempt to effect symbolically a purity which actual life better provides for: 1. Holy water, God's streams; 2. arbitrary penances, divine burdens; 3. ecclesiastical purgatory fires, God's salting fires.—The evil things which proceed from the heart and defile the man. *See Critical Notes* on ver. 21.

Starke:—Majus:—As Christ and His disciples were not without their slanderers, so the devout are never without their accusers and rebukers, 1 Pet. ii. 12.—*Nova Bibl. Tub.*:—From Jerusalem hypocrisy went forth into all the land.—Hedinger:—What is the dross to the pure gold? what the inventions of men to the truth of God? what superstition to faith?—Quesnel:—As man may dishonor God by overmuch caring for beauty and external purity, Isa. iii. 16, so God is honored by the neglect of these things, when that neglect springs from humiliation of self and true mortification, Jonah iii. 6–10.—We must wash the heart after having been defiled by the world; that is, we must test ourselves and cleanse ourselves of sin, Job i. 5.—Majus:—With hypocrites, regard to man and human ordinances has more weight than the commandments of God.—The hypocrisy of hypocrites must be revealed.—Cramer:—The enemies of the truth must be confounded by the word of God.—Canstein:—The true worship of God is the union of the heart with Him.—Men commonly do willingly and cheerfully all things that do not set them about changing their own hearts.—Self-love, or the selfish mind, is so mad, that it prefers expending its care upon pots and cups rather than upon itself.—Many external ceremonies and human ordinances are not good in the Church of God; for, those who are bent upon rigidly observing them easily come to forget, or postpone to them, the true commandments of God.—Quesnel:—The openly impious do not dishonor the truth of the divine law so much by their evil life, as those do who give themselves out to be lovers of the law of God, and yet falsely interpret it.—After God, our parents are most important; and them their children should honor as the channel of the first gifts of God—nature, life, nourishment, and education.—*Bibl. Wirt.*:—Christian children should learn well the fourth and fifth commandments.—Quesnel:—Man may disguise his godlessness under the fairest show of piety, but God sees it nevertheless; and, as He condemns it now, He will hereafter make it manifest to all the world.—Majus:—Vows against the honor of God are sinful, and must not be paid.—*Bibl. Wirt.*:—He who departs from God's word in one point, and in that point prefers the ordinances of men, may become so thoroughly entangled as not again to escape, Tit. i. 15.—In the New Testament, the making distinctions of meats is classed among the works of the devil, 1 Tim. iv. 1–3.—Canstein:—All depends upon the state of the heart: as that is, we are.—As the heart is the source of all evil, we should carefully watch its issues, Jer. xvii. 9.

Schleiermacher:—This was the sense in which the Lord Himself said that His yoke was easy and His burden light; for He contrasted Himself, and the fellowship which He would found upon His own name, with the yoke and the manifold external burdens which the elders were never weary of imposing upon the Jews.—Those who rest wholly on external things have always the same vain labor as the Pharisees; and this has its ground in a lack of confidence. It springs from the fact that man can never have so much firm assurance concerning that which is not the truth as he can concerning that which is the truth; and this unrest manifests itself in looking anxiously at the letter, and in seeking after external uniformity. The greater the number, the greater their hope of internal confidence: of that which is *strictly* internal they have nothing.—This also He would say, that whosoever contributes to confirm such notions in the minds of men, and make their notions of God's service purely external, leads them thereby away from the true worship of God in spirit and in truth, and seeks to give their ideas of God such a direction and such a form, that they no longer represent to themselves *that* God who will be worshipped in spirit and in truth, but an imaginary Being, such as the Gentiles frame in their imaginations.—The same feeling which leads to the honor of father and mother leads to the honor of our Father in heaven.—GOSSNER:—Manifestly, wicked human ordinances do not injure the divine doctrine so much as specious and seemingly holy superstitious inventions and false interpretations, which are received with confidence by the weak devout, and held fast with stubborn pertinacity.

---

3. *The Withdrawal of Jesus to the Gentile Borders of Tyre and Sidon, and to the District of Decapolis. The Woman of Canaan.* VERS. 24–31.

(Parallel: Matt. xv. 21–29.)

24 And from thence he arose, and went into the borders of Tyre and Sidon,[1] and en-
tered into an house, and would have no man know *it:* but [and] he could not be hid.
25 For a *certain* woman, whose young daughter had an unclean spirit, heard of him,[2] and
26 came and fell at his feet; (The woman was a Greek, a Syrophenician by nation,) and
27 she besought him that he would cast forth the devil out of her daughter. But Jesus
said[3] unto her, Let the children first be filled: for it is not meet to take the children's
28 bread, and to cast *it* unto the [little] dogs. And she answered and said unto him, Yes,
29 Lord: yet the [little] dogs under the table eat of the children's crumbs. And he said
30 unto her, For this saying go thy way; the devil is gone out of thy daughter. And
when she was come to her house, she found the devil gone out, and her daughter laid
31 upon the bed.[4] And again, departing from the coasts of Tyre and Sidon, he came unto[5]
the Sea of Galilee, through the midst of the coasts of Decapolis.

[1] Ver. 24.—Ὅρια: Lachmann, after B., D., L., Δ. Καὶ Σιδῶνος is wanting in B., L., Δ., &c. Tischendorf and Meyer omit it; taken from Matt. xv. 21.

[2] Ver. 25.—Tischendorf, after B., L., Δ., Versions: ἀλλ' εὐθὺς ἀκούσασα γυνή.

[3] Ver. 27.—Lachmann and Tischendorf: καὶ ἔλεγεν, after B., L., Δ., &c. (D.: καὶ λέγει; Vulgate: *que dixit*). And this is more in keeping; for it is not a definitive utterance, like the ὁ δὲ Ἰησοῦς εἶπεν.

[4] Ver. 30.—*See* Meyer, concerning the inversions of this clause. [Lachmann and Tischendorf, after B., D., L., Δ., Versions, have adopted the transposition: τὸ παιδίον βεβλημένον ἐπὶ κλίνην καὶ τὸ δαιμόνιον ἐξεληλυθός. The Received Text is to be retained; the reading of Lachmann is accounted for from the fact, that the copyist passed immediately from the καί following ἐξεληλυθός to the καί in ver. 31, so that the clause, καὶ τὴν θυγατ. to κλίνης, was left out, and was afterwards inserted in the wrong, but what seemed to be the more fitting, place. Hence the clause, θυγατ. to κλίνης, and not the clause, τὸ δαιμόν. ἐξεληλ., is the omitted and restored one; so that all the variations in the readings are found in the former and not the latter. Meyer, *in loco.*—*Ed.*]

[5] Ver. 31.—Griesbach, Lachmann, Tischendorf, after weighty authorities, read εἰς instead of πρός (as in Mark iii. 7). Lachmann and Tischendorf, after B., D., L., Δ., Coptic, Ethiopian, Syriac, Vulgate, Saxon, Itala, read ἦλθε διὰ Σιδῶνος instead of καὶ Σιδῶνος ἦλθε.

EXEGETICAL AND CRITICAL.

See the parallel passage in Matthew, and the preliminary summary of the foregoing section, *Critical Notes*, p. 282.

Ver. 24. **And from thence He arose, and went.**—That His departure was at the same time a breaking away from the Pharisaic party, is emphatically shown both by Matthew and Mark. His travelling towards the borders of Tyre and Sidon was the prophetic and symbolic representation of the future progress of Christianity from the Jews to the Gentiles. So in ancient times Elijah travelled out of his own land into Phœnicia. Elijah was driven away by the ascendency of idolatry in Israel; Christ was driven away by ascendency of a hierarchy and of a traditionalism which in his eyes was apostasy from the law of God, and therefore idolatry. Yet Jesus did not yet separate from His unbelieving people; He did not actually go into Phœnicia, but only into the adjoining borders of Galilee (εἰς τὰ μεθόρια), that is, into the district of the tribe of Asher. But afterwards, during His travels among the mountains and on His return to the Galilean sea, He actually passed through the Sidonian region. On those travels, *see* on *Matthew*, xv. 21, *Critical Note*, p. 281.—**And entered into an house.**—Here also He had friends and dependants, as He had in the opposite direction, on the borders of Perea.

Ver. 26. **A Gentile, or Greek.**—Ἑλληνίς, according to the Jewish phraseology of the time, indicating a Gentile woman generally. This was not merely the result of the intercourse of the Jews with the Greeks specially; but it sprang from the fact that in the Greeks and in Greece they saw the most finished and predominant exhibition of this world's culture and glory. *Syrophenician*, as distinguished from the Λιβυφοίνικες, the Phœnicians of Africa, that is, Carthage (Strabo). The *Tex. Rec.* has Συροφοίνισσα; but the true reading wavers between Συροφοινίκισσα (Codd. A., K., &c., Lachmann) and Συραφοινίκισσα (Tischendorf, after Codd. E., F., &c.). Thus she was a Phœnician-Syrian woman: most generally viewed, a Gentile; more specially, a Syrian; and still more specifically, a Phœnician. Phœnicia belonged to the province of Syria. But the word may also, more precisely still, describe the Syrian of Phœnicia, the Canaanite woman (Matthew).

Ver. 30. **And her daughter laid upon the bed.**—A sign of her perfectly tranquil condition:

the demon had previously driven her hither and thither. But there is also an intimation of her exhaustion after the last paroxysm; and this is one more instance of that gradual restoration which Mark loves to describe. The arrival of her mother, who was the subject of healing faith, perfected then her new life and vigor.

Ver. 31. **Through Sidon.**—Meyer thinks that the analogy of Τύρου requires us to understand the town of Sidon. But the coasts of Tyre do not refer to Tyre as a city, but to Tyre as a country. Thus we agree with Ewald, that only the travelling through the district of Sidon is settled. The direction of the journey was first northward towards Lebanon; thence from the foot of Lebanon northeasterly, and back through the district of Decapolis, that is, back through the region which lay to the east, or the farther side, of the sources of the Jordan, to the eastern bank of the Sea of Galilee. On Decapolis, comp. WINER, and the *Critical Notes* on Matthew xv. 21.

DOCTRINAL AND ETHICAL.

1. *See* on the parallel passage in *Matthew*.

2. The circumstance that Mark passes over the mediation of the disciples on behalf of the Gentile woman, is explained by the critics in various ways, after their favorite fashion of *external* comparison. Meyer thinks Matthew's the original account. But if we look at *internal* motives, this whole intervening occurrence, which would be very easily understood by the Jewish-Christian readers of Matthew, would not, without some commentary, be at all intelligible to the Gentile-Christian readers of Mark. Matthew gave prominence to the points which proved to the Jewish-Christian how strictly Christ remained, during His work in the flesh, within the limits of His calling; and that He received the Gentile woman into communion and fellowship of His healing works, only on account of her strong faith, attested by the Israelite witness of the disciples themselves. This motive had no force in Mark's account. Hence he might, in harmony with his own design, paraphrase the repelling word of the Lord, modifying it according to its inner meaning; and we need not, with Meyer, attribute it to the "softening down of later tradition."

3. As Christ, in the former narrative, let a ray of His transfiguring glory fall upon the low region of meats and the "draught," so here He casts one upon the poor dog. Under the light of the kingdom of heaven, everything common and natural obtains a higher meaning; it obtains a value in the economy of God, and as a figure of the relations of His kingdom. The place of daily corruption is a figure of the purifying grave and kingdom of the dead; the dog a figure of the Gentile world. Sin remains more than ever condemned, but only that it may be made subservient to the judgments and honor of God.

4. As the earnest coming of the Syrophenician woman evinced a strong susceptibility among the Phœnicians, humbled by many severe judgments, it was needful that Christ should for the present leave this country, in order that His Jewish people might not be alienated by his premature labors among the Gentiles. But He left the region with the glad anticipation that the prophecy of Ps. ii. 8 would one day be fulfilled.

HOMILETICAL AND PRACTICAL.

See on *Matthew*.—A solemn sign, when Jesus only seems to go forth.—The travels of Jesus towards west, north, east, south: also a sign.—Jesus has everywhere His hidden friends.—He could not remain hidden: that is, 1. He hid from Himself, in His humility, the consciousness of the great influence of His majesty; 2. He sacrificed His rest to the restlessness of passionate men; 3. He ever submitted His human will to the ruling will of His Father.—The work of the Son, under His Father's government, though free, yet conditioned: 1. In Nazareth, His own city, He could not reveal Himself; 2. in the dark boundary of heathenism, He could not be hidden.—The Gentile longing everywhere feels from afar and seeks after salvation, whilst the Jews reject it before their very eyes. (The nobleman at Capernaum; Cornelius, Acts x.; the Canaanitish woman the symbolical man of Macedonia, Acts xvi. 9.)—The Gentiles likened to the dogs (house-dogs, not wild ones), not to awaken, but to humble a fanatical party spirit: 1. Unclean indeed, and without the natural gift to distinguish the pure from the impure; 2. but modest, tractable, docile, thankful table-companions of unthankful children.—Christ present with His fulness of help, wherever there is the slightest germ of faith.—"For this saying." Faith manifest in new and wonderful words: 1. Its source. words unspeakable (Rom. viii. 26); 2. its expression, new words of the Spirit, clear and joyful in confession, preaching, and prayer; 3. its glory, the speaking with new tongues.—The regeneration, sanctification, and glorification of speech.—Christ, the terror of evil spirits far beyond His own personal manifestation.—The great sign which the Lord gave His disciples, that the door of the Gentile world was open.—Even among a people of Moloch-worshippers, maternal love was not extinct.—Humility the test of faith.—Humility the deep ground into which all the streams of heavenly blessing are poured.—The Lord is high, and yet hath respect unto the lowly, Ps. cxiii. 5–7.—As Mary prophesied in her song of praise, such was Christ's rule.—The tarrying of Jesus in the mountain-range of Lebanon, a silent anticipation of His entrance into the heathen world; as the tarrying in the wilderness was an anticipation of His entrance into Israel.

STARKE:—CANSTEIN:—Christ's travels from one place to another.—QUESNEL:—A servant of Christ in the Gospel may indeed remain hidden, but it must be so as not to incur the shame of neglecting any duty owing to his neighbor.—CRAMER:—When we pursue honor in an unreasonable manner, it flies from us; when we fly from it, it pursues us.—QUESNEL:—Every sin is an unclean spirit which possesses the sinner; from Jesus we must in all humility, every man for himself, seek the only remedy.—Sufferings urge men to seek God: happy those who use them to that end.—Christ is still, and for ever, the Saviour of the Gentiles, Rom. iii. 29.—Parents should feel the utmost anxiety on account of their children, that they be delivered from the power of Satan and led back to God.—LANGE:—The sharper the test, the more blessing does it bring when believingly endured. —*Bibl. Wirt.*:—Faith in the heart permits no displacence against God's rule to arise in the soul. However God disposes, and whatever He says, must be best, 1 Pet. v. 5, 6.—HEDINGER:—Perseverance presses through, and a good warfare obtains the prize.—QUESNEL:—It is a great consolation to a Christian mother when God converts, in answer to her prayer, a daughter possessed by a worldly spirit. But how little prayer is urged for that blessing!—RIEGER:—A very little word, falling into a softened, broken, and humbled heart, works great things.—Faith derives greater advantage and strength from humble submission and willing acknowledgment of its unworthiness than from anything else.—BRAUNE:—Let every one limit himself to the field of labor which God has appointed to him: he will soon see whether or not God gives him a commission to go beyond it.—Let no one be offended if he is hemmed in by a narrow limit, according to God's will. Holy charity and heroic love are all in all.—SCHLEIERMACHER:—*For this word, go thy way:* It was not merely a word of faith, but such an answer, too, as fell in with our Saviour's design. Without abolishing the distinction between those who belonged to the people of the old covenant and those who were idolaters, it yet threw such a veil over the distinction that many demonstrations of love might seem proper to pass from the one to the other.—GOSSNER, on ver. 24:—Many might remain hidden enough, but they will not.—A seemingly great severity is often a preparation for great benefactions.—BAUER:—The first act of salvation in the Gentile world.—AHLFELD:—Persevering faith is sure to win its object. When a heavy cross weighs thee down, seek the light of Christ's countenance; hold on in faith, and doubt not; He will give at last all that thou needest.—THOMASIUS:—How the Lord awakens faith in the hearts of men.—GREILING:—The time of suffering is a time of test.—HARTOG:—The three stages of victorious faith: 1. It looks with longing at the divine Saviour; 2. it waits with all humility for help; 3. it holds fast its hope with firm confidence.—BÖDECKER:—Wherefore doth God delay His help?—C. G. HOFFMANN:—The mighty word of faith: I will not let Thee go.—DITTMAR:—Great faith in its three stages: 1. Its stage of distress; 2. its stage of sifting; 3. its stage of confirmation.

---

4. *The Healing of the Deaf and Dumb Man.* VERS. 32-37.

(Parallel: Matt. xv. 29-31.)

32 And they bring unto him one that was deaf,[1] and had an impediment in his speech
33 [a stammerer]; and they beseech him to put his hand upon him. And he took him
aside from the multitude, and put his fingers into his ears, and he spit, and touched his
34 tongue: And, looking up to heaven, he sighed, and saith unto him, Ephphatha, that is,
35 Be opened. And straightway[2] his ears were opened, and the string of his tongue was
36 loosed, and he spake plain. And he charged them that they should tell no man: but
37 the more he[3] charged them, so much the more a great deal they published *it;* And
were beyond measure astonished, saying, He hath done all things well: he maketh
both the deaf to hear, and the dumb to speak.

[[1] Ver. 32.—After *κωφόν*, Lachmann and Tischendorf, after B., D., Δ., Versions, have *καί*.—*Ed.*]
[2] Ver. 35.—*Εὐθέως* is wanting here in B., D., L., Δ., Versions, Lachmann, Tischendorf. Instead of *διηνοίχθησαν*, Lachmann and Tischendorf, after B., D., Δ., read *ἠνοίγησαν*.
[[3] Ver. 36.—*Αὐτός* is wanting in A., B., L., Δ., Vulgate, Lachmann, Tischendorf.—*Ed.*]

EXEGETICAL AND CRITICAL.

See on *Matthew*.—The healing of the deaf and dumb man on the east side of the Jordan is a narrative peculiar to Mark. In regard to time it is closely connected with the two foregoing events: occurring at the termination of the Lord's travels towards Phœnicia and through Decapolis back to the eastern border of the Sea of Galilee (Gaulonitis). Mark shows, in his account of the miracles, a preference for those healings in which the gradual process of the cure, as connected with the instrument and the development of it, is vividly presented. Thus, in his account, the daughter of the Syrophenician woman lies exhausted upon her bed after her deliverance. Thus, he represents Jesus as commanding them to give the daughter of Jairus something to eat. And he alone records the healing of the blind man at Bethsaida—a process which was gradual, and performed in two stages. And here he alone communicates a narrative in which the miraculous act of the Lord is closely connected with the application of the saliva.

Ver. 32. **A deaf man, who could not well speak.**—Meyer opposes this translation: "*κωφὸν μογιλάλον* is wrongly translated, a deaf man difficult of speech (*see* Beza, Maldonatus, De Wette).—*Μογιλάλος*, although it seems in its formation to be *hard of speech*, corresponds in the Septuagint to the Hebrew אִלֵּם, dumb. *See* Isa. xxxv. 5, &c. Hence it is a deaf and dumb man (Vulgate, Luther, Calovius, Ewald), which is also confirmed by *ἀλάλους*." Since *μογιλάλος* does literally mean one who speaks with difficulty,—and it is said of this one, that after his cure he spoke *ὀρθῶς* (not simply *he spoke*),—the meaning of the words is sufficiently established. With deafness there is connected a disturbance of the organs of speech, or a general perversion of speech.

Ver. 33. **Aside from the multitude.**—Wherefore? 1. He would make no display (Theophylact); He would not nourish superstition (Reinhard); He would have an undisturbed relation between Himself and the sick man (Meyer). This last is the weakest reason; for we might for the same reason except the same thing elsewhere. Rather we may assume that the district of Decapolis was something like the region of Tyre and Sidon: it was not a purely Jewish land. Here it was necessary, especially in this time of crisis, that He should avoid a publicity which might bring together the Gentiles in crowds, excite superstition as much as faith, and create in the minds of the Jews a prejudice against Him. In an analogous manner the Lord acted in the case of the blind man of eastern Bethsaida: He led him altogether out of the village. In both cases, however, we must remember that it was a susceptibility of faith which was to be gradually awakened. *See* the *Doctrinal Reflections*.—**And put His fingers.**—A similar circumstantial procedure we have in the healing of the blind man, ch. viii. "But we are not to assume that Jesus desired in any sense to conceal the miraculous element in the cures (LANGE, *Leben Jesu*, ii. 1, p. 282), which would amount to untruth." Meyer. But, upon this principle, the disguise thrown over the evangelical truths of the Gospel through the employment of parables, would amount to untruthfulness.

And He spit.—Spitting, He touched His tongue. Meyer thinks that the touching was the direct spitting upon the tongue. But as the touching (ἅπτεσθαι) is elsewhere an application of the hand, it may be assumed that He moistened His finger and touched therewith the man's tongue. Saliva used in healing: here; ch. viii. 23; John ix. 6. De Wette: Saliva was in antiquity a remedy for the eyes (Plin. *H. N.* 28, 7; Tacit. *Hist.* 4, 21; Sueton. *Vesp.* Cp. 7; Tanchuma, f. 10, 2; Sanhed., f. 101, 1; Hieros. Sotah, f. 16, 4; Vajikra Rabba, f. 175, 2. Comp. WETSTEIN and LIGHTFOOT, *ad Joh.* ix. 6). Meyer: "The saliva is, like the oil (ch. vi. 13), to be regarded as a conductor of the miraculous power." Yet it was not applied in the cure of the ear, but only in the healing of the tongue here, as ch. viii. in the healing of the eyes. Wherefore then was this distinction? Probably because the saliva was better suited to be a symbolical medium for the awakening of faith, and it was never wont to be applied to the ear.

Ver. 34. **Looking up to heaven, He sighed.**—Manifestly the sighing of prayer. How much more easily He seemed to accomplish His healing on other occasions! Or was deafness, in its spiritual significance, much worse than blindness and possession; and did the Lord intend to signify that? We assume, 1. that in this half-heathen district, more imperfect and disturbed forms of faith presented themselves to Him, which made the healing on His part more of a conflict; and 2. that in this half-heathen district, where they generally believed in demigods and magic, He desired to make more definitely prominent His own dependence on God the Father. For the like reason—that is, because the Pharisees had blasphemed the source of His miraculous power—He accomplished the raising of Lazarus before the Jews from Jerusalem in connection with a loud prayer to the Father; and in healing the man born blind, John ix., He joined with Himself in the work the temple-fountain Siloam, the holy spring of the priests. 3. Since the Lord could not influence the deaf man by word, it was necessary that He should influence Him by a strongly speaking sign.—Mark everywhere sets a special mark on the sighing of the Lord, as also upon His manner of looking: comp. ch. viii. 12. Meyer remarks, and rightly, that this sigh was at the same time a sigh of painful sympathy.—**Ephphatha.**—An Aramæan word, in the Imperative: Be thou opened. Related, though not identical, is the Hebrew הִפָּתַח, in the Imper. Niphal.

Ver. 35. **And the string of His tongue was loosed.**—Thus he did not merely speak with difficulty on account of his being dumb, as Olshausen supposes.

Ver. 36. **But the more He charged them.**—The stronger His prohibition was, the more it enkindled a desire to spread the report of the miracle.

Ver. 37. **He hath done all things well; that** is, in the healing.—Thence they draw the conclusion: As well the deaf, He hath, &c.

DOCTRINAL AND ETHICAL.

1. Nothing is more instructive and full of significance than the prudence of our Lord in respect to the publication of His miracles, as soon as He had entered the borders of the land where there were closer relations with heathenism, and the people were more infected by heathen views:—the history of the woman of Canaan, the present narrative, and the healing of the blind man in eastern Bethsaida, all illustrate this. The reason was, that Christ would have a monotheistic faith, which traces all up to God the Father as the final source, and that He would not suffer His divine power of healing to be mingled and debased with superstitious and magical notions. This holy prudence will explain many and great restraints upon the full influence of Christianity in the heathen or heathen-Christian world, down to the present day.

2. We may compare the doxology of this people, ver. 37, with the doxologies of ch. i. 27; ii. 12; iii. 11, &c. Matthew explains: They glorified the God of Israel.

3. It must be particularly observed here also, that Jesus could affect this deaf and dumb man only through His glance, His immediate revelation, His signs, and manner of action. So far this instance stands alone; for the youth who was deaf and dumb through possession, ch. ix. 25, suffered not through the sealing up of his organs, but through the perversion and violence done to his soul. So also the possessed who was dumb, Matt. ix. 32; and the demoniac who was blind and dumb, Matt. xii. 22.

4. Our Christian institutions for the deaf and dumb are an abiding monument of that miraculous healing in the mountains: the natural development of the miraculous act of our Lord. The healing of the deaf and dumb by signs, was a type of the instruction of the deaf and dumb.

5. The Romish rite of baptism relies especially on this miraculous history, because it exhibits the use of several symbolical elements: 1. Separation from the multitude: dedication of Christ in baptism. 2. The baptizing priest touches, with an Ephphatha, the ears of the infant; 3. moistens its nostrils with saliva; 4. lays salt in its mouth. The Christian Church should do all this in a *real* manner, and not in a symbolical. As the symbol for it, and at the same time the reality of it, Christ instituted simple baptism.

HOMILETICAL AND PRACTICAL.

Sufferers to be brought to Jesus.—The healing of the deaf and dumb; or, the double disease and the double cure in their reciprocal connection. 1. The connection between deafness and the inability to speak: *a.* in physical things; *b.* in spiritual. 2. Right speaking conditioned by right hearing: in natural life, in spiritual things.—He who does not persevere to the end in hearing aright will surely cease by degrees to speak aright.—The true obedience is of eminently quick and sure hearing.—The education of the deaf and dumb man in faith: 1. He must yield himself up to be led by the strange Wonder-worker, who can only speak to him by looks, into the wilderness; 2. he must *see* His signs, especially the signs of His prayer and His sighing; 3. he must hear his word of power, that he may have his hearing and be able also to speak.—The holy care of the Lord in all His wonderful works, aiming ever at the glory of God's name.—How the wonder-working majesty of Jesus is concealed in His humility.—Christ, as He went on His way, opposed and avoided with the same decided earnestness the heathenism which deified men and the world, and the Judaism which deified the letter and ceremonial observances.—Christ had to struggle as well with superstition as with unbelief, to exalt both into faith.—All Christ's miracles were to the honor of God: 1. All His miracles were miracles of prayer, dependence on God, and strict union with His Father; 2. all His miracles were distinguished, not only in their reason and their end, but also in their form and manner, from the magical works of the heathen world.—Christ ever conceals the thousands of His miracles by the disguise of an unpretending medium.—Christ in His whole being full of saving power.—The sighing of Christ and of His Spirit (Rom. viii. 26) over the sin and the misery of humanity and the creature.—The sympathy of Christ.—Guilt and innocence in the popular proclamation of Christ's works.—The words of His astonished people: He hath done all things well: 1. In its human limitation; 2. in its higher significance.—Concerning redemption as concerning the creation, the word holds good, The Lord hath done all things well (Gen. i. 31): 1. in the whole, 2. in the details.

STARKE:—Where Jesus goes in and out, there is nought but blessing.—CANSTEIN:—When we look at the deaf and dumb, it should make us reverence all the more the glorious gifts of hearing and speech, and determine to use both prudently to the glory of God.—ZEISIUS:—Most people can both hear and speak; but how great and how common is spiritual deafness and dumbness!—LUTHER:—Christ begins His cure with the ears, and acts in accordance with nature; since from hearing speaking comes: ἀκοή begets ὑπακοήν.—LANGE:—Let us seek silence.—A Christian should often sigh over spiritual and bodily misery.—The ears should be open for God, but shut to the devil and the world.—It is a sign that the tongue has been loosened by Christ, when the words become holy, and the new song is sung to His glory out of a new heart.—QUESNEL:—The humility of the benefactor, and the thankfulness of him who has received the benefit, may contend without damaging peace in the heart.—Wondering at God's works is well; but it should never end there.—*Nova Bibl. Tub.*:—God doeth all things well, not only in healing and binding up, but also in smiting and wounding.—ZEISIUS:—As Satan damages and ruins everything, so, on the contrary, Christ repairs all things.—BRAUNE:—The Lord guides all His own in various ways, every one in his own; but the goal for all is the great salvation longed for.—Jesus speaks the right language of signs to the deaf and dumb.—GERLACH:—The words, "He hath done all things well," seem to express an anticipation of the new creation.—Jesus finds His glory in the deaf ears of hardened sinners, and in the speechless or restrained tongues of unthankful, earthly-minded unbelievers. Even from among them He takes many into solitude with Him: His creating hand touches the sealed ear and the idle tongue, His high priestly intercession groans to the Father for them, and often His Ephphatha opens the ear and looses the bonds of their tongue, so that they may speak plainly.—LISCO:—The turning of the eyes of Jesus towards heaven should teach us to expect our help from thence, and thither to direct our thanksgivings.—SCHLEIERMACHER:—That love which could manifest itself so mightily in the Redeemer is among us in our benevolent institutions. But if we ask what has driven men to think upon this, we can say no more than that it is the selfsame Spirit of love who is for ever striving to meet and overcome all the woes and sufferings of humanity.—What a great and wonderful word is this "Be opened," which the Redeemer was ever speaking throughout His whole manifestation, and the influences of which have never ceased, but will go on until the whole race of mankind have come to the hearing and knowledge of His salvation, and their tongues shall be loosed to the praise of the Most High!—HEUBNER:—The significance of the healing of the deaf and dumb (in its spiritual application): 1. The person of the wretched one; 2. the leading him to Jesus; 3. the action of our Lord; 4. His looking up to heaven and sighing; 5. His work; 6. His prohibition (the conversion of a sinner should not be boastfully trumpeted to the world; it should exert its influence silently).—Christ the only Physician who can repair the mischiefs in God's creation.—How much knowledge of God may come through the senses.—BAUER:—How many are still deaf and dumb towards the kingdom of God!

KLEFEKER:—Even in the sufferings of His creature man, God finds His glory.—REINHARD:—How we, as Christians, should sanctify to our own good the defects, infirmities, and sicknesses of our bodies.—HUFFELL:—The Christian's look to heaven.—REINHARD:—The quiet unostentatious zeal with which Christians should do good.—THIESS:—The deaf and dumb man is a type of us.—COUARD:—He took him out of the crowd apart.—BOMHARD:—The Ephphatha of our Redeemer: 1. A word of omnipotence and grace; 2. great and glorious in its effect; 3. it is uttered to all of us; 4. it is vain for many; 5. it proves its virtue on believers, ever more beautifully and abundantly; 6. it will one day abolish for ever all our fetters.—RAUTENBERG:—He hath done all things well: 1. Praise of His perfection—wonder; 2. praise of His benevolence—thanksgiving; 3. praise of His glory—adoration.

5. *The Miraculous Feeding of Four Thousand.* CH. VIII. 1–9.

(Parallel: Matt. xv. 32–39.)

1 In those days the multitude being very great,[1] and having nothing to eat, Jesus
2 called his disciples *unto him*, and saith unto them, I have compassion on the multitude
3 because they have now been with me[2] three days, and have nothing to eat; And if I
send them away fasting to their own houses, they will faint by the way: for divers of
4 them came from far. And his disciples answered him, From whence can a man satisfy
5 these *men* with bread here in the wilderness? And he asked them, How many loaves
6 have ye? And they said, Seven. And he commanded[3] the people to sit down on the
ground: and he took the seven loaves, and gave thanks, and brake, and gave to his
7 disciples to set before *them;* and they did set *them* before the people. And they had
8 a few small fishes: and he blessed, and commanded to set them also before *them.*[4] So
they did eat, and were filled: and they took up of the broken *meat* that was left, seven
9 baskets. And they that had eaten[5] were about four thousand: and he sent them away.

[1] Ver. 1.—Instead of παμπόλλου, B., D., G., L., M., Δ., [Vulgate, Coptic, Gothic, Lachmann, Tischendorf,] read πάλιν πολλοῦ.—The ὁ Ἰησοῦς is probably an explanatory interpolation.
[2] Ver. 2.—Μοι is wanting in B., D., [Lachmann, Tischendorf, Meyer.]
[3] Ver. 6.—B., D., L., Δ., [Lachmann, Tischendorf, Meyer:] παραγγέλλει.
[4] Ver. 7.—Καὶ εὐλογήσας αὐτὰ εἶπεν καὶ ταῦτα παρατιθέναι. B., L., Δ., [Meyer.]
[5] Ver. 9.—The οἱ φαγόντες wanting in B., L., Δ., [Tischendorf, Meyer;] following ch. vi. 44.

EXEGETICAL AND CRITICAL.

See on the parallels in *Matthew.*—Mark's second miraculous feeding, with the following events, stands in the same connection as Matthew's with the mountain travels of our Lord. There is not in the slightest particular a difference between Matthew and Mark. The representations of the second feeding are more than ordinarily alike in both: the beginning and the end, especially, are essentially the same.

Ver. 7. **And he blessed and commanded to set them also.**—The Evangelist distinguishes the thanksgiving over the fish as a particular act, with the word εὐλογήσας, while concerning the bread he used εὐχαριστήσας. Both acts of devotion are to be regarded as benedictions of the food. But the prayer of praise (εὐλογεῖν) is related to the prayer of thanksgiving, as praise is related to thanks: it is the same thing carried to its higher pitch. That the thanksgiving becomes here blessing, characterizes the second act of the feeding, the festival anticipatory of the great feast; and it is all the more sublime as being pronounced over the ἰχθύδια ὀλίγα. The following Romanist distinction (Reischl) is without foundation: "Thanksgiving (eucharist) Jesus presents as man (and High-Priest) to the Father; but He Himself, as Lord and God, distributes the blessing of omnipotence."

Ver. 8. **Seven baskets.**—Comp. the explanations on *Matthew.*

Ver. 9. **About four thousand men.**—Matthew adds: *besides women and children.*

DOCTRINAL AND ETHICAL.

1. *See* on the parallel passage in *Matthew.*—The divine side of the second miraculous feeding is presented all the more expressly and clearly by the circumstance, that in the present instance the multitudes of the people were more alien, the scene of it was a place more desolate and remote from human habitation, the excitement of the people more intense; not to mention that Christ had just returned from an extended and fatiguing journey. As it respects the human side of the miracle, and its relation to the measure of faith, we cannot fail to observe the circumstance that a more abundant provision of food is made for a smaller number of the fed. As it regards the difference between the fragments gathered up in the two miracles respectively, we have to notice the distinction between σπυρίδες and κόφινοι: the former seem to have been vessels of larger capacity.

2. STARKE:—Σπλαγχνίζεσθαι means such a feeling of compassion as not only moves the mind, but causes a physical emotion—the rush of blood, yearning of the bowels, &c.—likewise. The word is used several times concerning our Saviour by the three Evangelists. The greater the love of Jesus was, the more susceptible was His sacred humanity of sympathy.

3. The first miraculous feeding took place when the malignity of Herod occasioned the Lord's departure from Galilee; the second, after He had retired from Galilee before the hierarchical and pharisaic party. Both times, as driven away, and as a refugee, He took upon Himself, forgetting His own sorrow, the needs of all the people.

HOMILETICAL AND PRACTICAL.

See on *Matthew.*—Christ's compassion towards the people was a compassion for their want of bread.—The Lord's resting-place after long travelling.—Christ does not let His people depart without food.—Where Christ is in the midst, the multitude never go away unfed.—The rebuke contained in the example of the people, who waited on Christ three days, though they had nothing given them to eat.—The impotence of the disciples, and the Lord's provident care.—Christ's thanksgiving becomes blessing, whilst the provision is diminishing.—Christ's royal law for the table.—The second miraculous feeding seemingly less, but in fact more, wonderful than the first. 1. Seemingly less; there was more provision, and a smaller number. 2. Really greater: *a.* in regard to the Lord (returning from long journey and much labor); *b.* in regard to the despondency of the disciples; *c.* in regard to the foreign elements of which the mass of this mountain-people was made up (probably in part Gentiles).—Wells are made, as by the Lord, so by the pilgrims of Zion, passing through the valley of banishment, Ps. lxxxiv.—The Lord's heavenly peace in His earthly need: He is Himself as a refugee in great straits, and yet feeds with compassion a host of thousands. 1. The peace of God in the forgetfulness of His own distress. 2. The self-renouncing love of others in this forgetfulness. —To-day He gives the people a feast; to-morrow all sorrows await Him.

STARKE:—True brotherly love does not look so much at the worthiness of the person as at his need and misery.—Believers may sometimes fall, even though Jesus be near, into temporal difficulties and need; but they do not and cannot come to harm or perish, Rom. viii. 35–39.—The Lord knows our need earlier and better than our complaints can tell Him. —OSIANDER:—How different from these people are some Christians amongst us, who can scarcely tarry one hour with Christ's servants, hearing the divine word!—Preachers should care not only for the souls, but also for the bodies, of their hearers.—*Nova Bibl. Tub.*:—When we truly love Jesus, we think little of the length or hardship of the way; we care nothing for want and weariness; but wait with Him, and prefer the kingdom of God to all other things.—Our unbelieving heart hangs on the means, and will believe nothing that it does not see, Matt. vi. 25–30. —We should thank God for everything, even for our scanty provision; He is bound to us for nothing.—(The breaking of bread.) When God puts anything into our hands, we should not keep it unbroken for ourselves alone, but break and dispense abundantly to others.—CANSTEIN:—Preachers should dispense the food of God's word among the people; but they should give to the multitude nothing which God has not first put in their mouth and in their heart.—The meek shall eat and be satisfied, Ps. xxii. 26.—The gifts of God satisfy the *heart*.—In every fragment there is God's blessing: therefore it is right to gather up the fragments.—With God it is all the same whether there be little or much.—SCHLEIERMACHER: —He kept them near Him, and distributed spiritual gifts; nor did He remember their earthly need until He had found that they were filled with desires that extended much further. And this is the divine order, in this connection, between the spiritual and the temporal. All earthly things, so far as they go beyond necessity; have value only so far as they are connected with the spiritual.

HEUBNER:—Perseverance in hearing the word of God.—The design of Providence in letting us encounter earthly need.—Have we sought diligently, and first of all, heavenly things?—Trust in God when the season of scarcity comes.—The prevenient providence of God, and His anticipating care.—The Christian's attention to his neighbor's need.—God can bring help by small means.—Giving is better than receiving.—Christ's miracle as a figure of the miracle of divine sustentation.—Jesus as Householder.—The Christian householder after the pattern of Jesus: 1. Watchfulness, and attention to all needs; 2. love and sympathy for the distress of each; 3. trust in God when the question is, Whence shall we get? (Do the best: God will do the rest in His own way); 4. spiritual care of all who belong to Him.—How our partaking of food may be sanctified. —RAMBACH:—How may the Christian give God His honor in the enjoyment of his daily food?—MARHEINEKE:—The Christian should always see a higher significance in the means of his daily sustentation.—HARMS:—Instruction concerning table-worship.—DIETSCH:—The miracle in our nourishment.—HUFFELL:—The divine blessing on our food.—MEHLISS: —The glorifying of God in the care of His creatures. —REINHARD:—The connection between the necessity of nourishment in order to the sustentation of our bodies, and the growth and nourishment of our souls. —VALERIUS HERBERGER:—How should the guests at God's table comport themselves?—HEUBNER:—Jesus the people's holy Friend.—BURK:—Jesus Christ supplies all our need out of His riches in glory.—STIER:—The miraculous blessing of God's power, as shown, 1. in the domain of nature, and 2. in the kingdom of grace.—ULBER:—The meal blessed by prayer.—The compassionate heart of Jesus moaning over all our misery.—COUARD:—Reproof of the prevalent complaint over hard times.—REINHARD:—Christian benevolence at a time of general need.—BAUER:—When Christ's blessing rests on anything, it becomes infinitely more than it was in the hands of men.

EIGHTH SECTION.

THE DECISIVE CONFLICT OF JESUS WITH THE PHARISEES IN GALILEE, AND HIS RETURN TO THE EASTERN SIDE OF THE SEA. PREPARATIONS FOR THE NEW CHURCH.

CHAPTERS VIII. 10—IX. 29.

1. *Return to the Galilean Shore. Conflict; Return; the Leaven of the Pharisees and the Leaven of Herod.* CH. VIII. 10-21.

(Parallel: Matt. xvi. 1-12.)

10 And straightway he entered into a [the] ship with his disciples, and came into the
11 parts of Dalmanutha. And the Pharisees came forth, and began to question with him,
12 seeking of him a sign from heaven, tempting him. And he sighed deeply in his spirit,

and saith, Why doth this generation seek after a sign? Verily I say unto you, There
13 shall no sign be given unto this generation. And he left them, and entering into the
14 ship again,[1] departed to the other side. Now [And] *the disciples* had forgotten to take
15 bread, neither had they in the ship with them more than one loaf. And he charged
them, saying, Take heed, beware of the leaven of the Pharisees, and *of* the leaven of
16 Herod. And they reasoned among themselves, saying,[2] *It is* because we have no bread.
17 And when Jesus knew *it*, he saith unto them, Why reason ye because ye have no
bread? perceive ye not, neither understand? have ye your heart yet[3] hardened?
18 Having eyes, see ye not? and having ears, hear ye not? and do ye not remember,
19 When I brake the five loaves among five thousand, how many baskets full of fragments
20 took ye up? They say unto him, Twelve. And when the seven among four thousand,
21 how many baskets full of fragments took ye up? And they said, Seven. And he said
unto them, How[4] is it that ye do not understand?

[1] Ver. 13.—The πάλιν precedes ἐμβάς, according to B., C., D., L., Δ. Εἰς τὸ πλοῖον (*Recepta*), or εἰς πλοῖον (Lachmann, after A., E., F.), wanting in B., C., L., D., and omitted by Tischendorf [and Meyer].

[2] Ver. 16.—The λέγοντες wanting in B., D., and Itala; and B., Itala read ἔχουσιν for ἔχομεν. So Lachmann and Tischendorf.

[3] Ver. 17.—Ἔτι not in B., C., D., L., Δ., [Lachmann, Tischendorf, Meyer.]

[4] Ver. 21.—Lachmann: πῶς οὔπω, according to A., D., M. Tischendorf merely οὔπω, according to C., L., D. So Meyer.

EXEGETICAL AND CRITICAL.

See on *Matthew*.—What follows is here closely and certainly connected with the preceding; and in this Matthew and Mark concur, as also in the essentials of the whole. Mark passes over the rebuke of Christ in relation to the Pharisees' knowledge of the weather, and also the sign of Jonas. On the other hand, he mentions the Lord's deep sighing. He notices the circumstance that the disciples had with them in the ship one loaf. Instead of the leaven of the Sadducees, he has the leaven of Herod; and he gives most keenly the Lord's rebuke of the unbelief of the disciples.

Ver. 10. **Dalmanutha** was a small place, not otherwise known; it lay probably in the district of Magdala, where, according to Matthew, Jesus landed. Robinson (iii. 514) leaves it undecided whether or not the present village of Delhemija is its modern representative. The specifications of locality by the two Evangelists, respectively, are not to be referred to any hypothesis of *earlier* and *later* accounts: Matthew's narrative has a more general cast, and Mark's a more special, in these respects. The landing was manifestly in a desert and unfrequented place; and the reason of this was, that the Galilean party of Pharisees were on the alert to seize Jesus, in order to bring Him under a judicical process; for this purpose having many spies abroad. The first illustration of this is found in Mark ii. 6; the second, ch. iii. 22; the third (in connection with ch. vi. 29–31), ch. vii. 1. That allegation touching neglect of purifyings, which the Pharisees, in connection with the scribes from Jerusalem, made against Him, is carried out here into its last issues.

Ver. 11. **And the Pharisees came forth.**—Meyer: "Out of their dwellings in that country." People generally come out of their dwellings; but these men came forth as spies out of a hiding-place; and their coming was proof that the most extreme care as to the circumstances of the landing of Jesus, in a quiet place and in the dead of night, could no longer protect the Lord from their eyes (*see* on *Matthew* and *Leben Jesu*, ii. 875). On the western side of the sea there might be, here and there, rich mansions, belonging to Herodian courtiers, which were well adapted to be loopholes of observance for the political and hierarchical party. According to Matt. xvi. 1, 2, the Sadducees were leagued with them. The act, therefore, was not merely an act of the Pharisaic school, but the act of the priests and politicians. Mark merges the Sadducees in the Pharisees; for they hypocritically played the Pharisee, inasmuch as they demanded a sign from heaven, although they believed in no such thing.—**And began.**—They had made their arrangements for a decisive contest, which began with the demand of the sign from heaven. For this sign, *see* on *Matthew*, p. 287.

Sighed deeply in His spirit.—Comp. ch. vii. 34. He sighed so deeply, not merely in general sorrow for the hardened unbelief of these men, but also in the feeling that the decisive crisis of severance from the predominant party had come. For the demand of a sign from heaven was a demand that He should, as the Messiah of their expectation, accredit Himself by a great miracle; thus it was fundamentally similar to the temptation in the wilderness, which He had repelled and overcome. But His deep sigh also signifies here the holding in of His judicial power, the silent resolution to enter upon the path of tribulation. Hence the refusal of the sign is immediate, and in the form of an affirmation most strongly uttered. It is to be observed that, the article being wanting, the nature of the sign from heaven is left free to Him: He was to perform *a* sign from heaven, which should be acknowledged as *the* sign from heaven.

Ver. 15. **And the leaven of Herod.**—*See* on *Matthew*; and for the combination of Pharisees and Herodians, compare the notes on Mark iii. 6. The one passage depends on the other; and it is observable how Mark both times gives marked prominence to this hypocritical and malignant combination of extreme parties. Meyer concludes from Matt. xiv. 2 that Herod was no Sadducee. But that passage must not be pressed too far. Herod certainly coincided with the anti-scriptural, anti-Messianic, Hellenizing universalism of the Sadducees, although he did not adhere to their party in its dogmatic views and coloring. Thus we have here only two aspects of the same idea. The Jewish dependence upon traditions and human ordinances, and the Jewish freethinking, form in their respective principles the two kinds of leaven which the disciples were to guard against. Compare on *Matthew*.

DOCTRINAL AND ETHICAL.

1. *See* on the parallel in *Matthew*.—The debasing effects of party spirit. The Sadducees must here submit to the Pharisees, and be merged in them.

2. As it regards the desired sign from heaven, it is to be observed further: 1. As they asked for *a* sign from heaven, they demanded the decisively attesting sign expected from heaven. 2. The conseuence of this authentication would have been, that Christ must have come forward as a Messiah in their sense. Hence it is said that they tempted Him. The demand of a sign from heaven was like the temptation in the wilderness. The Lord had hitherto, since that time, escaped any such demand. If He now refused it, His death was certain. 3. The demand was so far not absolutely hostile, as they were still disposed to accept Christ, if He would adapt Himself to their views, and become a party instrument for their purposes. (*See* on *Matthew*.) 4. The sign from heaven which Christ denied to the Pharisees, stood in close relation with the sign of Jonas. The denial of the one was the announcement of the other. 5. What He denied to the Pharisees, He provided soon afterwards for the three chosen disciples on the Mount: the heavenly sign of His transfiguration.

3. The sighs of Jesus.—The Lord's sigh (ch. vii. 34) was the sigh of self-devoting mercy to the world; His deep sigh (ch. viii. 12) was the restraint and holding back of His judicial power over the world, under the holy resolution to suffer for it. The sigh of the Lion of Judah over the hardening of His enemies: the prophecy of His path of suffering, but also the prophecy of the world's judgment. The groaning of His spirit was, 1. a sighing from the depths of His being, 2. in the all-embracing glance of His consciousness over the path of His own suffering, and the path of the world's wretchedness.

4. *The return of Jesus.*—Not without a plan, but as the result of His last experience, Jesus now returns back to the eastern bank. It is clear to His consciousness that He must now go up to confront His death. He therefore needed solitude, that He might regulate the process of His departure. And to this there was necessary, 1. the confirmation of the disciples in faith for the establishment of the new Church, and 2. the provision that His death should take place at the right time and in the right way.

HOMILETICAL AND PRACTICAL.

See on *Matthew*.—The Pharisees perfect spies on all our Lord's ways.—The Lord cannot escape the Pharisees, and therefore the Pharisees cannot escape the Lord.—The demand of a sign from heaven: the tempting crisis that our Lord foresaw in the wilderness.—The confusion of the disciples, occasioned by this decisive conflict (and shown in the forgetting of bread, and anxiety about it), as opposed to the divine repose of the Lord: a prelude of their confusion on the eve of the Passion.—The great decisive No of the Lord.—The Lord's deep sigh in its great significance: 1. A silent and yet decisive sign of His conflict and of His victory; 2. an unuttered word, which contains a world of divine words; 3. a fulfilment of the primitive prophecy concerning the breach between the external and the spiritual Israel; 4. a prophecy which stretches forward to the cross and the final judgment.—The infinite meaning of this sigh of Christ: 1. As a breathing forth of the divine patience over the visible world (Omnipotence restraining itself in love and wisdom, when dealing with the enmity of the free will of the world); 2. a collective expression of all the sufferings and of all the patience of Christ; 3. a declaration of all the incarnate sorrow and endurance of the Lord in His Church.—The significance of sighs: 1. In the creature (Rom. viii. 22); 2. in humanity, and in the kingdom of God (Rom. viii. 23; 2 Cor. v. 2; Rev. vi. 10).—The return of Christ to the other bank: a sign of His return back to the other world.—How little the disciples understood that crisis.—The last loaf in the ship, the last loaf in the house (the last meal, the last piece of money, the last sheet-anchor).—In this matter, mark, 1. the disciples' spirit: they misinterpret the most sublime and the most spiritual things through their own over-anxiety; 2. the Lord's spirit: He makes provision for the testing of His disciples, especially now.—The displeasure of Christ at the lack of spiritual development among His own disciples.—True remembering, in its full import: 1. Christian wakefulness; 2. Christian life; 3. Christian progress.—The influence of the Holy Spirit, and life in the Spirit: bringing to remembrance (John xiv. 26; xvi. 13).—The retreat of Jesus in order to arrange His death.

STARKE:—Many desire new wonders; and when they have thought they have seen them, have not yet turned to God.—It is not becoming to prescribe to God the means by which we are to arrive at divine knowledge and blessedness.—HEDINGER:—Ingratitude drives Christ away.—QUESNEL:—It is a fearful judgment when the truth altogether forsakes men, and they are left to themselves.—Forgetfulness gives an opportunity for new instruction; and therefore even their failings should be turned to account by believers.—CRAMER:—Faithful teachers should, after the example of the Great Shepherd, diligently warn their sheep against false doctrine and false teachers (against every evil leaven to the right or left).—Out of one error many others gradually arise, so that the whole system of religion may become perverted. —QUESNEL:—Concerning the tendency to Sadduceism among courtiers.—The weaker our faith is, the more anxious and troubled we are about bodily need, and the more likely to make spiritual possessions of less account.—OSIANDER:—Ministers must be always ready to exhort their hearers with severity, and to rouse them out of the sleep of security.

BRAUNE:—When, after a joyful event, or the attainment of a great success, one is suddenly opposed by an obstinate contradiction, the result is often great disquietude or blank despondency. The Lord, whose case this was on the present occasion, knew very well what He would do, and did it without any restraint. Let all men learn this. They need the lesson in their family circles, and in their civil and political relations, whether more or less exalted.—Scarcely had Jesus ended with His enemies, when He must begin again with His friends.—Before His spirit rose the whole wickedness of His enemies' spirit, so perverse in itself, pervading with evil the whole of the people, and invading even His disciples. It had already seized and possessed the mind of Judas, 1 Cor. v. 7, 8.

SCHLEIERMACHER:—The Redeemer often uses the idea of leaven, as something of which only a little is needed in order to make the whole like itself.—In truth, He was the leaven, in the form of a servant indeed, destined to penetrate the whole mass of mankind and all human life by the divine power dwelling in Him.—If ye use only a little of the leaven of the Pharisees, ye will very soon be pervaded throughout with its influence.—The leaven of Herod: the family of Herod was a foreign one; they held to the law, and affected much devotion to ceremonial ordinances, in order to attach the people more firmly to themselves. The disciples must not use Christianity as something that might exert a good influence upon their external condition.—We must be pure disciples of the Master, and desire nothing but the pure kingdom of God.—GOSSNER (on ver. 19):—This is a test. They had the whole history in their head and memory, but they did not understand how to apply it.

---

2. *The Blind Man in Eastern Bethsaida.* VERS. 22–26.

22 And he cometh[1] to Bethsaida; and they bring a blind man unto him, and besought
23 him to touch him. And he took the blind man by the hand, and led him out of the
town; and when he had spit on his eyes, and put his hands upon him, he asked him if
24 he saw aught. And he looked up, and said, I see [the] men as trees, walking.[2]
25 After that he put *his* hands again upon his eyes, and made him look up: and he was
26 restored, and saw[3] every man clearly. And he sent him away to his house [home],
saying, Neither go into the town, nor tell *it* to any in the town.[4]

[1] Ver. 22.—The Plural, ἔρχονται, after B., C., D. Lachmann, Tischendorf, [Meyer.]

[2] Ver. 24.—The beautiful reading: βλέπω τοὺς ἀνθρώπους, ὅτι ὡς δένδρα ὁρῶ περιπατοῦντας is adopted by Meyer, Lachmann, Tischendorf, following [A., B., C.*, E., F., G., K., L., M., Δ., Gothic, Theophylact, Euthymius. (D. and most of the Versions have the Received Text).]

[3] Ver. 25.—Tischendorf, [Meyer,] διέβλεψεν, after B., C.*, L., Δ., &c.

[4] Ver. 26.—The Received Text and Lachmann follow Cod. A. Tischendorf, following B., L., Coptic, omits the clause μηδὲ εἰς . . . κώμῃ.

EXEGETICAL AND CRITICAL.

Mark alone records this history of Christ's healing miracles during the time of His final mountain-travels along the Gaulonite range, on the eastern side of the Jordan and the Sea of Galilee. The remembrances of Peter preserved for us these special treasures, belonging to a time so preëminently memorable to him and his spiritual development. But we have too often observed the peculiar feeling of Mark for the gradual, natural, progressive development of the kingdom of God (*see* his record of the parables, and the final miracles), not to perceive that this period of the ministry and work of Jesus would strongly rivet his attention.

Ver. 22. **To Bethsaida.**—It is evident that the Bethsaida of the western coast, in Galilee (John xii. 21), is not here meant, as Theophylact and others have supposed; but, as Grotius rightly perceived, it was Bethsaida Julias, which lay upon the north-eastern coast of the Sea of Tiberias. Reland was the first to indicate that there were two Bethsaidas. Josephus tells us (*Antiq.* 18, 2, 1), that the tetrarch Philip, who ruled only in the eastern part of Galilee, made the village of Bethsaida into a town, and named it Julias, after the daughter of Augustus. (*See* also *De Bell. Jud.* 11, 9, 1; and JEROME on Matthew xvi.) According to Pliny (*Hist. Nat.* v. 15), Julias was situated on the farther coast of the Sea of Galilee; according to Josephus, on the Jordan, 120 stadia above its junction with the sea. Pococke thought the ruins of Taluy, on the east side of the Jordan, marked the ancient Julias; Seetzen thought the same of a little village, Tellanihje; and Robinson, the ruins of Et-Tell. According to Luke ix. 10, the first miraculous feeding also took place in a desert place near this same Bethsaida. *See* VON RAUMER, *Palæstina*, p. 109. Bethsaida lay in the way from the sea towards Cæsarea Philippi, in the higher mountain-range, a district to which Jesus subsequently returned.—**A blind man.**—What follows shows that he was not born blind, but had become so. He had evidently seen men and trees aforetime.

Ver. 23. **And led him out of the town.**—Here the separation from all others is still more effectual than in the case of the healing of the deaf and dumb man, ch. vii. 33. In addition to the motive already mentioned for performing His works as much as possible in retirement, viz., that He might insure His own decease in Jerusalem, we may assume that there was also a pædagogic element that influenced Him on the present occasion. The deaf and dumb man could not hear His voice, but only see His signs; this blind man could not see Him, he could only hear Him speak and feel His hand. Thus it was a test and a discipline of his faith, when he was led into solitude: a test and exercise which probably was still much needed by him.—**And when He had spit on his eyes.**—*See* the notes on ch. vii. 33 and John ix.

Ver. 24. **I see men.**—Expression of joy.—**As trees**; that is, I see men walking, large and unformed as trees. A distinct figure of an indistinct, twilight beholding. It was the first stage of healing. According to Euthymius Zigabenus, He healed the man by degrees, because his faith was weak, and the gradual experience of recovered sight would lead him to a higher degree of faith. In relation to this, we may observe the strikingly passive bearing of this blind man, as of the deaf and dumb man before: with this we may compare the passiveness of the impotent man at Bethesda, John v. According to Olshausen, a too rapid process of recovery might have been injurious, and the gradual cure had regard to the eyes themselves. But this and the preceding notion we leave to the reader's consideration; they may have a certain degree of force. But if we combine all the traits of this and the foregoing history, we see that Jesus designedly repressed the fame of

His miraculous works in a district where He was seeking an asylum of perfect retirement, in order to settle everything with His disciples; at a time, too, when, for their sake and His own, absolute solitude was essentially necessary with reference to the decision of the future. But the symbolical significance of these miraculous dealings—as bringing the divine power into gradual contact and contest with human nature—was more expressly brought out for the instruction of His disciples than in most of His miracles of healing.—The persons who appeared to the half-seeing man were probably his companions, and other sympathizing people, who looked on in restless motion.

Ver. 26. **To his house.**—He did not belong to Bethsaida, and he must go immediately from the place to his own home—not even to the village to which he had already come. Indeed, he was not to mention it to any one belonging to that village, and whom he might meet in the way. This explanation of the last expression ["any *in* the town"] is not, as Meyer terms it, an invention, to meet the difficulty; it is the obvious and only natural meaning of the expression. Even the man's companions should find him recovered and seeing, only when they reached home; that is, if they were not permitted to be present at the healing.

DOCTRINAL AND ETHICAL.

1. Christ sought with His disciples the deepest solitude among the mountains. His feeling was that of an anticipation of His death, and all things in the signs of the times said, Set Thine house, Thy Church, in order! In this journey the people who brought the blind man interrupted Him, and there seemed danger of His way being embarrassed. It is true that this did not hinder His healing the man, but He healed him in the most undemonstrative and hidden manner. The secrecy of the performance was paralleled by the extraordinary care with which He sent the blind man to his own house, under a prohibition to speak to any man in the neighborhood concerning the miracle. The blind man, however, was not merely a means to an end; his own spiritual edification was in question also. Since his faith was weak, his spiritual state required the protection of solitude: only in the profoundest silence could the blessing of his experience ripen into perfection. But, thirdly, we must not forget the Lord's reference to those who surrounded the blind man. They asked that He would *touch* him. To this demand for an instant act, followed by an instant influence, the Lord opposed His own slow and circumstantial method of procedure. So also in the case of the deaf and dumb man of the same country: they asked Him that He would lay His hand upon the man. And if in this district of indistinct, half-heathen notions there was any idea arising of a magical influence on the part of Christ, His wisdom dispersed these foolish imaginations. He made prominent, 1. the religious aspect of the act; and 2. the struggle in His own spirit connected with its performance.

2. This present narrative illustrates how Christ performed His miracles in the most absolute self-renunciation (at the most unseasonable time); with the most profound humility (without any desire for honor among men); and with the most supreme wisdom and confidence.

3. The healing of the blind man at Bethsaida, like some other similar miracles, was especially fitted and intended to exhibit the harmony of miracle with nature, the natural elements in the miracle, the gradual entrance of the divine power into the old nature, and its issues in the new nature.

HOMILETICAL AND PRACTICAL.

The Lord, deeply occupied with thoughts of His cross and of His death, does not repel as an interruption the cry of the wretched.—The festal season of the Prophet's miracles is passing away, because the season of the high-priestly miraculous sufferings is drawing near.—The healing of the blind man at Bethsaida a testimony of the heavenly wisdom of the Lord: 1. In respect to Himself; 2. in respect to the blind man: he should not first see the multitudes of starers in the street, but the Lord in His solitary glory, and thus would he be taught more fully the lesson of faith; 3. in respect to the people around; 4. in respect to the disciples.—Abundant as was the inward life of Christ, His acts are equally abundant in their forms.—Christ, in performing His miracles, avoided a fixed and uniform manner, in order to obviate all the idle, superstitious notions of a magical influence.—How the mind, contemplating the same unchanging fundamental forms, has a tendency to become mechanical in its views.—As the wonder-working power of Christ's hand wrought in many fleeting forms of action, so also the fundamental forms of the ministerial work of the Church, in teaching, worship, and life, should be moulded, moved, and inspired by the life of the Divine Spirit.—The education of the blind man into faith.—The gradual return of the blind man's sight, a type of the gradual illumination of the soul.—Even the spiritually awakened see at first men as trees, unformed, without definite distinction.—I see men as trees. This represents, as it may be viewed, different conditions of the spiritual life: 1. It is a happy state, if it is the first stage towards clearly seeing in perfect knowledge; 2. it is a gloomy and uncertain state, if the Christian should remain in it; 3. worst of all, if through his own guilt he should return to this stage, falling into the new blindness of despair.—The blessed experience of the first believing look: a strengthening of faith, which becomes the transition to perfect sight.—Go not into the town: a solemn word concerning Bethsaida.—Bethsaida the modern city of the world, with an imperial name, and Bethsaida the town of the fishermen: the bright and the dark side.—How Jesus avoids the fame of His works, in order that He may seek in the shame of His sufferings His highest honor and glory.

Starke:—Christ's gifts within us change with times.—Canstein:—A weak and slight beginning is yet a beginning; and in God's methods a little is intended to become gradually greater.—Quesnel:—The cure of spiritual blindness is only begun on earth; it will be fully accomplished only in heaven.—Osiander:—God often turns away our misfortune, and mends our unhappiness, by slow degrees: have patience!—Solitude and silence after conversion is much safer than much talk and running about.—We should let the truth take firm root in us, before we speak much about it.—The converted man must take care not to turn round again to the world.—Canstein:—Fearful judgment, when God reckons a man, or a city, or a land, no longer worthy of the knowledge of His word and works.

GERLACH:—The gradualness of the operation is often our first inward assurance of the certainty of the change.—RIEGER:—Do not despise slight means [referring to the application of spittle].—BRAUNE:—Men must be ever known, not as trees, as perishable plants, but as rational creatures, called to eternal glory.—First of all, however, the blind man came to know Jesus aright; to know Him clearly is eternal life.

SCHLEIERMACHER:—The cure of the blind man in its resemblance to the next section: 1. The withdrawing to a place apart (special reasons for this in both cases respectively); 2. the gradual work (men as trees; obscure views concerning Christ); 3. the Redeemer's care as to what men say of Him; 4. the sight restored, and the confession of Peter.

---

3. *The Opinions of the People, and Peter's Confession. Pre-announcement of His Sufferings. The Presumption of Peter. Christ's Teaching concerning Cross-bearing.* CH. VIII. 27—IX. 1.

(Parallels: Matt. xvi. 13–28; Luke ix. 18–27.)

27 And Jesus went out and his disciples into the towns of Cæsarea Philippi: and by
the way he asked his disciples, saying unto them, Whom do men say that I am?
28 And they answered,[1] John the Baptist: but some *say*, Elias; and others, One of the
29 prophets. And he said unto them,[2] But whom say ye that I am? And Peter answer-
30 eth and saith unto him, Thou art the Christ. And he charged them that they should
31 tell no man of [respecting] him. And he began to teach them, that the Son of man
must suffer many things, and be rejected of [by] the elders, and *of* the chief priests, and
32 scribes, and be killed, and after three days rise again. And he spake that saying
33 openly. And Peter took him, and began to rebuke him. But when he had turned
about, and looked on his disciples, he rebuked Peter, saying, Get thee behind me,
Satan: for thou savourest [mindest] not the things that be of God, but the things that
34 be of men. And when he had called the people *unto him* with his disciples also, he
said unto them, Whosoever[3] will come after me, let him deny himself, and take up his
35 cross, and follow me. For whosoever will save his life[4] shall lose it; but whosoever
36 shall lose his life for my sake and the Gospel's, the same shall save it. For what shall
37 it profit a man, if he shall gain the whole world, and lose his own soul? Or what[5] shall
38 a man give in exchange [as a ransom] for his soul? Whosoever therefore shall be
ashamed of me, and of my words, in this adulterous and sinful generation, of him also
shall the Son of man be ashamed, when he cometh in the glory of his Father, with the
holy angels.

1 And he said unto them, Verily I say unto you, That there be some of them that stand here, which shall not taste of death, till they have seen the kingdom of God come with power.

[1] Ver. 28.—According to B., C.*, D., L., Δ., [Vulgate, Itala,] Lachmann, and Tischendorf add αὐτῷ λέγοντες. [Superfluous, and therefore more likely to be omitted than added. (Meyer.)]

[2] Ver. 29.—Ἐπηρώτα αὐτούς, instead of λέγει αὐτοῖς, after B., C., D., is the reading of Lachmann, Tischendorf, [and Meyer.]

[3] Ver. 34.—B., C.*, D., L., Δ., [Vulgate, Itala, Lachmann, Tischendorf,] read εἴ τις instead of ὅστις. A., B., Lachmann, Tischendorf have ἐλθεῖν instead of ἀκολουθεῖν.

[4] Ver. 35.—Τὴν ψυχὴν αὐτοῦ, Codd. A., D., Lachmann. (Τὴν ἑαυτοῦ ψυχήν, Griesbach, Scholz, Tischendorf.)

[5] Ver. 37.—Tischendorf, τί γάρ, instead of ἢ τί, after B., L., Δ.; he also omits δώσει ἄνθρωπος.

EXEGETICAL AND CRITICAL.

See on *Matthew* and *Luke*.—In respect to time, this is another section which stands in strict internal connection with the preceding crises. There are some important peculiarities in Mark. Matthew mentions the district of Cæsarea Philippi, Mark the villages which surrounded it, as the first goal at which our Lord aimed; and the latter transfers the question to the way thither. Among the people's thoughts and verdicts concerning Jesus, he omits the mention of Jeremiah. It is observable that he leaves out the benediction of Peter, and the special prerogative assigned to him after his confession. Luke also omits these, while Matthew details them all in full. Here, as elsewhere, Peter, Mark's informant and voucher, omitted or kept in reserve points which tended to his own honor. On the other hand, Mark states prominently that the Lord's prediction of His passion was part of the instruction which He openly gave; he also quotes the Saviour's rebuking word to Peter, "Satan," without any of the definite explanatory particulars which Matthew gives, and without Christ's "Thou art to Me a σκάνδαλον." Mark speaks of the people as also called by Jesus to hear the statement of the universal law of suffering in the kingdom of God. He alone has the emphatic word, that he who is ashamed of the Lord is ashamed of Him (in a disgraceful manner) in an adulterous and sinful generation. In conclusion, Mark represents the coming of Christ more expressly than the other two Evangelists as a coming in power (majesty); while Luke speaks of His kingdom, and Matthew of His appearing in that kingdom.

Ver. 31. **After three days.**—General and popular way of speaking, instead of "on the third day," which afterwards is used as the more definite statement.

Ver. 34. **And when He had called the people unto Him.**—This scarcely requires us to understand great multitudes. But Christ makes the people who were present sharers in this part of His instruction, in order to impress it the more upon His disciples that the way of suffering was absolutely imperative, and in order to lay down the fundamental laws of self-denial and holy suffering in all their universality of application.

Ver. 37. **In exchange for:** ransom-price.—The ἀντάλλαγμα is the counter-price antithetic to the price, ἄλλαγμα. The price which the earthly-minded gives for the world, the ἄλλαγμα, is his soul. But, after having laid that down as the price, what has he for an ἀντάλλαγμα, to buy the soul back again?

Ch. ix. ver. 1. **There be some of them that stand here.**—*See* on *Matthew*.

DOCTRINAL AND ETHICAL.

1. *See* on the parallels of *Matthew* and *Luke*.

2. According to Mark, Jesus first called and collected the Twelve in the villages outside of Nazareth (ch. vi. 6, 7); then, in the villages of Cæsarea Philippi, again gathering them together and confirming them. Solitude and sequestered probation, a condition of establishment and confirmation in the spiritual office.

3. It is of great significance that Peter does not, in his own Gospel, once mention the word of Christ concerning *his* own personal priority among the Apostles, least of all as the institution of an official primacy.

4. So it is to be observed how strictly, according to Mark, the confession of Christ is conjoined with the announcement of His passion, and with the requirement of following Him in the way of the Cross.

5. *Let him take up his cross.*—An obscure intimation of His own approaching suffering upon the cross, which, even in its general terms, gave a definite meaning. Let him hold himself ready to follow Me, regarded as the vilest malefactor, and exposed to the deepest shame and the most cruel death. The cross of Christ, as such, is not a kind of suffering which is the natural consequence of sin, but which crosses the views of an ideal or newly awakened higher life.

HOMILETICAL AND PRACTICAL.

See on *Matthew*; and compare *Luke's* parallel.—The question of Christ: "Whom say the people that I am?" a means of exciting a definite Christian consciousness, in opposition to the uncertain notions of the world.—The answer of the disciples in all its significance: 1. No man says, and no man could say without madness, that Christ was nothing, or a person of no importance. 2. The scorners and slanderers of Christ are not regarded or alluded to. 3. The testimonies or opinions: *a.* John the Baptist (according to Herod, returned from the dead): thus Christianity was something ghostly and preternatural. *b.* Elias (in the sense of Malachi): thus they were not able to distinguish Elias from Christ. Christianity seemed to them as a power exerted after the manner of Elias; thus in a spiritual sense as something legal. *c.* One of the prophets: something indefinite, a spiritual power, which none could clearly understand.—The question was not, what the people said concerning Christ, but what the Apostles said concerning Him.—Christ could be preached as the Christ of all the world, only after the fulfilment of His passion as the Crucified and the Risen. The confession of His people was to the Lord no sign that He would escape from suffering, but a certain sign that He would suffer.—What it means, that the Lord announces His sufferings to the disciples without any restraint: 1. In reference to Himself, 2. to the disciples, 3. to the world.—Only after we have known the person of our Lord in His word and work, can we understand and bear the knowledge of Christ's work in His passion.—The true confession of Christ must be confirmed by a readiness to follow Him.—The suffering of Christ is a divine sympathy: 1. As suffering through and for the world, it sprang from His sympathy with the world; 2. it establishes a divine sympathy in the world, as suffering on its own account and with Christ.—Self-renunciation of the believer is the soul of the confession of Christ.—The fundamentals of the Christian fellowship: I. Its fundamental laws: 1. The true denier (of himself) is the true confessor; 2. the true cross-bearer is the true knight of the cross; 3. the true follower (after Christ in obedience) is the true conqueror. II. Its grounds: 1. He who will save his life in self-seeking, shall lose it; he who loses it in devotion to Christ, shall gain it. 2. He who lays down his soul to win the world, loses with his soul the world also; he who has gained his soul, has with his soul gained the world also. 3. To seek honor in the world while ashamed of Christ, leads to infamy before the throne of Christ; but shame in the world leads to honor with Him. 4. Readiness to die with Christ leads through death to the day of eternal glory.—It is in self-denial that we first find our true selves, recovering our personality again.—True self-denial is the raising of our buried personality out of the grave of self-deceptions.—The false and the true self.—How shameful to be ashamed of Christ in an adulterous and sinful generation: 1. As the deification of a vanishing honor, which is eternal shame; 2. as the refusal of a vanishing shame, which is eternal honor.—How Christ detects the thoughts of men in His communion.

STARKE:—CANSTEIN:—We may lawfully ask what others hold us for, if the question does not spring from pride, but from a desire to do ourselves or others good.—HEDINGER:—It is not wrong to be jealous of one's public repute. But Christ remains ever what He is, despite all the various opinions concerning Him.—QUESNEL:—The true knowledge of the secret mysteries of Christ is attained only by scholars of truth and light.—Here is a catechetical lesson given by Christ Himself.—All truths have a set time for their full revelation: we should be always careful that we do not prematurely speak, or anticipate that time, Eccles. iii. 7; we must suffer with willing heart, be rejected of the world, and be crucified with Christ, if we would be raised with Him, Rom. vi. 6–8.—The ungodly can do nothing against us but what the wise decree of God has already determined.—*Bibl. Wirt.*:—Flesh and blood always look rather at external danger and damage, than at the solemnity and claims of the call (Rom. viii. 6–8

1 John ii. 15-17; 1 Pet. ii. 11, 20, 21; Gal. v. 21.)—You must not watch Christ, but follow Him; you must not boast about Him, but act like Him.—*Nova Bibl. Tub.:*—World gained, nothing gained; soul lost, all lost.—The greatest good is not to be met with in the transitory world, nor in the debauchery of the flesh: he whose soul is united with God has found it.—If thou art ashamed of Christ in His humble and lowly state, thou wilt have no part in His exalted and glorified state.—To die before one has seen the kingdom of God, is a wretched end.

BRAUNE:—The kingdom of God is, in a certain sense, near at all times: there is no season when its beginnings are not manifest.—GERLACH:—(Peter), rash and impetuous, spoke only, as he was wont to do, in the name of all the rest.

GOSSNER:—He who opposes himself to the cross of Christ and its doctrine, is a Satan, even though his name were Peter.—In the kingdom of God, all the world is inverted.—Losing is there called gaining, and gaining is there called losing.—BAUER, on ver. 35:—The beginning towards eternal life.

---

4. *The Transfiguration.* VERS. 2–13.

(Parallels: Matt. xvii. 1-13; Luke ix. 28-36.)

2 And after six days Jesus taketh *with him* Peter, and James, and John, and leadeth
them up into an high mountain apart by themselves; and he was transfigured before
3 them. And his raiment became shining, exceeding white as snow;[1] so as no fuller on
4 earth can white them. And there appeared unto them Elias with Moses: and they
5 were talking with Jesus. And Peter answered and said to Jesus, Master, it is good
for us to be here: and let us make three tabernacles [tents]; one for thee, and one for
6 Moses, and one for Elias. For he wist not what to say:[2] for they were sore afraid.
7 And there was a cloud that overshadowed them: and a voice came out of the cloud,
8 saying, This is my beloved Son: hear him. And suddenly, when they had looked
9 round about, they saw no man any more, save[3] Jesus only with themselves. And as
they came down from the mountain, he charged them that they should tell no man
10 what things they had seen, till the Son of man were risen from the dead. And they
kept that saying with themselves, questioning one with another what the rising from
11 the dead should mean. And they asked him, saying, Why say the scribes that Elias
12 must first come? And he answered[4] and told them, Elias verily cometh first, and restoreth all things [in the baptism of the people for the Messiah, and of the Messiah for
the people]; and how it is written of the Son of man, that he must suffer many things,
13 and be set at nought.* But I say unto you, That Elias is indeed come, and they have
done unto him whatsoever they listed, as it is written of him.

[1] Ver. 3.—The ὡς χιών is omitted by B., C., L., Δ., Tischendorf, probably on account of the strange comparison. [Meyer retains it, remarking that if it were an interpolation, it would be ὡς τὸ φῶς, in conformity with Matt. xvii. 2.]

[2] Ver. 6.—Most Codd. (A., D., E., F., G., H., K., Euthymius, Theophylact, Meyer) λαλήσει; other readings, λαλήσῃ (Elzevir, Fritzsche, Scholz, Lachmann), ἀποκριθῇ (B., C.*, L., Δ., Tischendorf).—B., C., D., L., Δ. have ἐγένοντο instead of ἦσαν.—B., C., L., Δ., Lachmann, Tischendorf, Meyer read ἐγένετο, with Luke ix. 35.

[3] Ver. 8.—B., D., Lachmann read εἰ μή instead of ἀλλά, with Matt. xvii. 8.

[4] Ver. 12.—Tischendorf and Meyer: ὁ δὲ ἔφη instead of ἀποκριθεὶς εἶπεν, after B., C., L., Δ., and Syriac, Coptic, Persian versions.

* [There are different modes of punctuation. According to Lachmann and Meyer the version would be: "And how is it written of the Son of man? that he must suffer," &c. According to another punctuation, followed by Hahn, the rendering would be: "And how is it written concerning the Son of man, that he must suffer many things, and be set at nought."—*Ed.*]

EXEGETICAL AND CRITICAL.

See on the parallel passages of *Matthew* and *Luke.*—This narrative stands in a definite historical connection with what precedes (ver. 1); as it does also in the accounts of Matthew and Luke. In regard to the locality, we may refer to our notes upon the scene in *Matthew.* The Tabor tradition is sufficiently accounted for by the manifestation of Christ upon the mountain in Galilee, Matt. xxviii. In describing the effect of the transfiguration, Mark uses the strongest illustrations ("white as snow," etc., "as no fuller," etc.). He, in common with Luke, records that Peter knew not what he was saying, or what he wanted to say. But he alone has the sudden vanishing of the heavenly visitors, and the inquiring look around on the part of the disciples. He joins Matthew in communicating the Lord's dealing with the disciples on coming down from the mountain. But he alone observes that the disciples questioned among themselves what the rising from the dead should mean. On the other hand, he omits, what Luke mentions, that Moses and Elias (ὀφθέντες ἐν δόξῃ) conversed with Jesus concerning His decease in Jerusalem. So only Luke has the delicate notices of the slumbrous and yet wakeful condition of the beholding disciples; while Matthew, on his part, alone applies the Lord's word concerning the Elias who had already appeared, to John the Baptist. Mark narrates the history of the transfiguration in his own characteristic manner, exhibiting its main traits in vivid and living touches.

Ver. 2. **After six days.**—*See* on *Matthew.*

Ver. 3. **No fuller on earth.**—The white glitter was supernatural. Gerlach: "In ancient times they wore but few colored garments. The fuller's business was to wash what was soiled, and to make it clean and glistening." Starke: "They used in the East to make linen garments so beautiful that they glittered with whiteness; but such as these the Lord's garments now outshone. The white color was that which the Romans called *candorem*, and which was so clear and so deep as to glisten splendidly. Materials prepared of such linen or other materials were, among the Jews, appropriated to priests and kings. Such garments also were in high estimation among other people, especially among the Romans. They were worn only by the highest personages, who were by such garments distinguished from those below them; hence, when they were seeking high offices of state, they distinguished themselves by such clothing, and were called *candidati*. And since among the Romans the glittering white upon their garments was refined to the highest lustre by art, and the Jews had been long in the habit of endeavoring to imitate it, we can understand the phrase, *That no fuller on earth could so whiten them.* That Solomon's magnificence was white, has been gathered from the fact that his array was likened to the lilies of the field (Matt. vi. 28, 29). What kind of glory was that of Herod's royal apparel, spoken of in Acts xii. 21, is shown in JOSEPHUS, *Antiq.* xix. 7.

Ver. 6. **For he wist not what to say** (or, **he would say**).—His words were an utterance of immediate feeling, expressing a state of perfect complacency, after the manner of dreams, ecstasies, and visions, in figure,—in figurative language which came to him he knew not whence.—**They were sore afraid.**—Matthew observes that *after* the sound was heard, they fell on their faces and were sore afraid. But there is no real difference. For their trepidation began naturally at the beginning, and continued increasing throughout. Matthew describes its climax; whilst Mark mentions the disciples' fear only for the sake of explaining the words of Peter.

Ver. 10. **And they kept that saying with themselves.** — Luke ix. 36. They concealed the fact which they had witnessed, after that command. Fritzsche: They obeyed the prohibition of Jesus. Meyer, on the contrary: They kept the words concerning the resurrection, and pondered them. The second, indeed, followed from the first. While they religiously kept their silence down to the day of His resurrection, they must have often asked when and how the bond of secrecy would be relaxed. Starke: "It requires much effort to overcome the tendency in beginners to prate. The word κρατεῖν shows it was not without trouble, and putting much restraint upon themselves, that the disciples kept this secret so long. The other disciples probably put questions," &c.—**The rising from the dead.**—That is, this express and particular resurrection from the dead which the Lord had predicted for Himself.

Ver. 12. **And restoreth all things.**—The way and manner in which Elias should do this (the idea is still indefinite, in the Present) is explained by what follows: *And how is it written of the Son of Man?* — What holds good of Him, that He must suffer many things, holds good also of His forerunner. This introduces the subsequent thought: Elias is come already. The punctuation given above, according to which the note of interrogation stands after "Son of Man" (Lachmann, Meyer), gives a clearer and more emphatic idea than the customary position of the note of interrogation after "be rejected." Instead of καί, one would in the latter case expect a particle of opposition; and the construction of ver. 13 should then have been different. Another construction is this: Elias cometh and restoreth all things. And how? It is written, &c.—**How it is written of the Son of Man.**—That is, his restoring all things proceeds, like the work of the Son of Man, through sufferings and death.—**That He must suffer many things.**— The ἵνα is here especially striking. Meyer says, that it sets before us the design of the γέγραπται. We take the sentence as a breviloquence, referring to what precedes — "Elias cometh first." And how is it written of the Son of Man, sc. that He cometh? In order that (ἵνα) He may suffer, &c.

Ver. 13. **As it is written of Him.**—That is, in regard to the persecution of the real Elias. *See* 1 Kings i. 19. (Grotius, Meyer.) That the unworthy treatment of the prophets accords (Kuinoel), is proved by the previous verse, where from the impending sufferings of the Messiah the conclusion is drawn that Elias-John must also suffer.

DOCTRINAL AND ETHICAL.

1. *See* on *Matthew.*

2. The transitory transformation of Christ a prelude of His abiding transformation. The transfiguration, as a transition into the second higher condition of human nature, was like the glorification. The transfiguration has the glorification for its result: the glorification is conditioned by the transfiguration. Into this condition the glorified Christ will raise His people also, 1 Cor. xv. But the glorification is the consummated, internal, spiritual power and glory, exalted above the changed, creaturely life, and manifested as the perfected light of life.

3. According to the privately communicated opinion of a respected Romanist theologian—personally unknown to me—the transfiguration upon the mountain was a night-scene. This was Schleiermacher's opinion also (*see* his *Sermons on the Gospel of Mark*). In favor of this supposition we may observe, 1. that the transfiguration of Jesus followed a solemn season of prayer; and we know that He commonly held these solemn seasons of prayer in the night; 2. that Luke mentioned their having gone down from the mountain on the day after that event. The transfiguration, by being considered as a night-scene, evidently has a peculiarly mysterious light thrown upon it.

4. As on the baptism of Christ His personal divine-human consciousness came to full maturity, so was here consummated the consciousness of His perfected prophetic work of word and deed. The goal of His prophetic work, in the narrower sense, was already reached. As Jesus, regarded in Himself, apart from His connection with sinful humanity, as the *personally* perfected God-man, might at His baptism have ascended into heaven, if He had willed to sever His destiny from that of mankind, so He might, as Prophet of the New Testament word of revelation, with the consummated consciousness of having done His prophetic work, have made the Mount of Transfiguration the Mount of Ascension. [But if Christ had ascended to heaven from the Mount of Transfiguration, He would have falsified the very prophecies alluded to; for these included His Passion and Crucifixion. — *Ed.*] The authority al-

ready referred to brings this out very excellently; and we also have alluded to it, in the *Leben Jesu*, ii. 908. "In fact, this was the moment (when the cloud received Jesus, and separated Him from the disciples) to teach them that He had power to retain His life, and that it was only free love that made Him leave the fellowship of the heavenly beings, and go down with His disciples into the valley of death."

5. Moses and Elias conversed with the Lord, according to Luke, concerning His departure in Jerusalem. The unknown Romanist expositor just alluded to thinks that these men appeared to the Lord as representatives from the kingdom of the dead, that they might add their argument to ensure His voluntary determination to encounter the sufferings of death, and thus redeem those who were held in the realm of death, or generally complete His work of redemption. The gratuitous and unwarranted idea of the intercession of the saints for the dead will not prevent our doing justice to the penetration of this view. But there are two things to be noticed: 1. According to Luke, Moses and Elias appear to the Lord in glory (ver. 31), not as supplicating intercessors; 2. Christ had already much earlier preannounced His passion: His baptism itself was, in this relation, decisive in its force as a preintimation. But that the kingdom of the dead had some interest in the voluntary determination of Christ to go on His way of suffering, Ebrard has well shown, and remarks: "In the transfiguration, Jesus had given the fathers of the ancient covenant the blessed intelligence of His perfect readiness to redeem them by His own death." Comp. my *Leben Jesu*, ii. 909.

6. *Let us make three tabernacles.*—A significant Future is added: for he knew not what he would say (λαλήσει). The man in ecstasy (as in a dream) brings the feeling or the thought; but the figure or form of the thought is imparted to him according to the secret laws that rule the figurative perception and language of the visionary condition. Thus came the figure to Peter: "build three tabernacles, one for Thee," etc., as an expression for his blessed feelings which he would utter.

HOMILETICAL AND PRACTICAL.

See on *Matthew*. So also *Luke*.—Between the confession and the transfiguration lies the week of temporal trials.—The mountain of prayer is the mountain of transfiguration.—The revelation of the life of Christ in His glorification here, a promise and sign for His people, 2 Cor. v.—The Lord's heavenly beauty.—Christ at the turning-point of His deeds and sufferings; by festal remembrance and sacrificial consecration glorified.—Consecration to the Lord changes man: 1. Internally: he is elevated into the spiritual world, and surrounded by blessed spirits. 2. Externally: he is renewed, adorned, transfigured.—The only true adornment of men: divine life of the Spirit.—Man upon the mountain: the first Sunday festival of the youthful Church of the Confession.—The transfiguration a sign and symbol 1. of the Sunday, 2. of the Ascension, 3. of the new Paradise.—The wish of Peter; or, the ideals of young Christians and the Lord's training: 1. Ideals of young Christians: that of retaining their early experiences, that of entire separation from the world, life of contemplation. 2. The Lord's guidance; further onward, deeper, higher.—All else comes and goes: Jesus alone abides.—Moses and Elias vanish from the disciples before His glory, and in the end they see Him alone.—The law and the prophets are merged in the glory of the Gospel.—The transfiguration of Christ upon the mountain: for Him, as for the three blest disciples, a preparation for Gethsemane.—The transfiguration of Jesus: 1. As a single central point in His life; 2. in its earlier types and symbols (Enoch, Abraham, Moses, Elijah, earlier crises in the life of Jesus Himself); 3. in its significance for the future, pointing to the resurrection, the ascension, the great manifestation of Christ, the glorification of believers.—The transfiguration of Christ the sure pledge of the renewing of the world, Rev. xx. 21, and of that new state of glory wherein the word is fulfilled, Behold, I make all things new!—The prophetic history of Christ's life and suffering, the history of the life and suffering of His people.—The Lord gives unasked to His disciples that sign from heaven which He had denied to the asking world.

STARKE:—OSIANDER:—God strengthens the faith of His people before trials come, that they may be able to endure them.—*Bibl. Wirt.*:—He who would be conversant with heavenly things must tear away his soul from earth, and soar towards God.—The heavenly glory is incomparable; greater and more excellent than all beauty and grace upon earth.—*Nova Bibl. Tub.*:—Moses and Elias still live: witnesses of eternity.—*Bibl. Wirt.*:—In Christ the law and the prophets attained their goal and fulfilment. Jesus is Lord of the dead and living; He has the keys of hell and of death, Rev. iii. 7; Ps. lxxxiv. 2, 3, 5.—LANGE:—God lets His people have, even in this world, extraordinary glances and views; but they are only of short duration, because their longer enjoyment would not be tolerable and profitable.—OSIANDER:—Human nature cannot bear the glory of eternal life; therefore our bodies will be glorified.—We must depend only and absolutely upon Jesus Christ.—QUESNEL:—Jesus Christ had His Elias who announced Him in the world; He will have more of them yet in times to come and before His last appearance.—One place of Scripture must not be opposed to another, but Scripture must be compared with Scripture.—The ungodly accomplish, against their own will, the holy will of God: they by their persecution not only create happiness for the saints, but make their own misery.—Marvel not that faithful ministers of Christ are cast out as evil, for it was clearly enough predicted in the Scripture.—RIEGER: Probably the disciples would desire, on going down, that they might communicate this vision to others; but the prohibition of Jesus forbade. The same holds good of us in many instances now.—SCHLEIERMACHER:—And that also was a spiritual glorification of the Lord when the disciples were taught that they had nothing more to do either with the one or the other (Moses and Elias), neither with the letter of the law nor with revolutionizing zeal. (Yet Moses and Elias were not set aside by Christ; but they were lifted up and lost in Him as their fulfilment.)—This spirit, which can only from within outwards renew our holy relation to God, and will spread abroad only through the energies of love the living knowledge of God among the children of men, will be to the end of time His glorification.

BRIEGER:—To glorify and transfigure, means to make perfectly clear and transparent (but of men, and especially of Christ, it means to exhibit the creaturely life in its spiritual glory). The eternal destiny of man was glorification.—Christ went on now to meet His sufferings. In order to obtain strength for the endurance of the extremest sorrows, He must have a foretaste of the glory which awaited Him.—But on account of His disciples too, it was needful that Christ should be glorified.—BAUER:—Peter would build tabernacles: for the heavenly beings who dwell above, skins and huts.

---

5. *The Healing of the Possessed Child after the Transfiguration.* VERS. 14–29.

(Parallels: Matt. xvii. 14–21; Luke ix. 37–43.)

14 And when he came to *his* disciples, he saw a great multitude about them, and the
15 scribes questioning with them. And straightway all the people, when they beheld him,
16 were greatly amazed, and, running to *him*, saluted him. And he asked the scribes
17 [them[1]], What question ye with them? And one[2] of the multitude answered and said,
18 Master, I have brought unto thee my son, which hath a dumb spirit; And wheresoever
he taketh him, he teareth him; and he foameth, and gnasheth with his teeth, and pineth
away; and I spake to thy disciples that they should cast him out, and they could not.
19 He answereth him,[3] and saith, O faithless generation, how long shall I be with you? how
20 long shall I suffer you? Bring him unto me. And they brought him unto him: and
when he saw him, straightway the spirit tare [convulsed] him; and he fell on the
21 ground, and wallowed [rolled] foaming. And he asked his father, How long is it ago
22 since this came unto him? And he said, Of a child. And oft-times it hath cast him
into the fire, and into the waters, to destroy him: but if thou canst[4] do anything, have
23 compassion on us, and help us. Jesus said unto him,[5] If thou canst believe, all things
24 *are* possible to him that believeth. And straightway the father of the child cried out,
25 and said with tears,[6] Lord, I believe; help thou mine unbelief. When Jesus saw that
the people came running together, he rebuked the foul spirit, saying unto him, Thou
dumb and deaf spirit, I charge [command] thee, come out of him, and enter no more
26 into him. And *the spirit* cried, and rent him sore [convulsed greatly], and came out of
27 him: and he was as one dead; insomuch that many said, He is dead. But Jesus took
28 him by the hand,[7] and lifted him up; and he arose. And when he was come into the
29 house, his disciples asked him privately, Why could not we cast him out? And he
said unto them, This kind can come forth by nothing, but by prayer and fasting.[8]

[1] Ver. 16.—Αὐτούς, B., D., L., Δ., Vulgate, Coptic, Æth., instead of τοὺς γραμματεῖς (Elzevir, Scholz, Lachmann in margin).

[2] Ver. 17.—Αὐτῷ must be inserted after ἀπεκρίθη, according to B., C., D., L., Δ., Lachmann, Tischendorf, Meyer.

[3] Ver. 19.—Instead of αὐτῷ, it is preferable to read αὐτοῖς (A., B., D., L., Δ., Versions).

[4] Ver. 22.—Instead of δύνασαι here and ver. 23, Tischendorf and Lachmann read δύνῃ, according to B., D., L., Δ., Meyer. This form, in itself the Conjunctive, was used later even in the Indicative, instead of δύνασαι; but it lays stronger stress upon the question.

[5] Ver. 23.—The τὸ was omitted by many Codd. (D., K., M., U., Syriac, Persian) on account of its difficulty. Tischendorf omits the πιστεῦσαι, following B., C.*, L., D., and many Versions; Meyer says, it was an exegetical addition to the mere εἰ δυνῇ, not understood. But the clause, "If thou canst believe," may have been found still harder; and therefore corrected into "as it regards, If thou canst? All things are possible," &c.

[6] Ver. 24.—The μετὰ δακρύων is wanting in A.*, B., C.*, L., Δ., Versions, [Lachmann, Tischendorf, Meyer.] The κύριε is very doubtful; Meyer rejects it.

[7] Ver. 27.—Lachmann reads τῆς χειρὸς αὐτοῦ, after B., D., L., Δ., Vulgate; Meyer cites in comparison, Mark i. 31; v. 41; viii. 23.

[8] Ver. 29.—The omission of νηστείᾳ by B. (which Tischendorf follows) is not decisive.

EXEGETICAL AND CRITICAL.

See on the parallels of *Matthew* and *Luke*.—The immediate connection between this event and the transfiguration is affirmed by all three Evangelists. The time and the place are established, therefore, by the narrative of that event. In the communication of the incidents here before us, Mark is rich in individual traits, which place the scene in a much more vivid light. Jesus finds His nine other disciples at the foot of the mountain, not only surrounded by a multitude of people, but involved in controversy with the scribes, who have surprised them in a condition of entire impotence. The people are amazed, or are very much excited, when they see Jesus coming. They were probably in a profane and mocking state of mind, in consequence of the disciples' failure to work the miracle, and of the attack of the scribes; and were disposed to indulge this inclination, when the sudden and overpowering appearance of Christ smote their consciences. To this may have concurred better motives, which induced the multitude to run to Jesus as the real arbiter and the only helper in this strange case. Thus we find that our Saviour at the very outset reduced the scribes to silence by His question, Wherefore do ye contend with them? While Mark passes over Matthew's notice, that the demoniac youth was lunatic, and that of Luke, that he was the only son of his father, he gives the most vivid representation of his state of wretchedness; his dumb behaviour (he had a speechless spirit), his frightful sufferings (in his paroxysms foaming and grinding his teeth, and swooning away). In the Lord's rebuke he is content with the description, γενεὰ ἄπιστος: the explanatory διεστραμμένη he omits; on the other hand, he paints more vividly than Luke the scene in which the youth at once, on seeing Jesus, was overcome by the demoniac influence, fell down to the ground, and wallowed, foaming. But of priceless value is the passage between Jesus and the father of the youth, from ver. 21 to ver. 25. We see how the Lord, by His question as to how long the youth had thus suffered, pacified the excited feelings of all, especially of the father, and encouraged their faith. We hear the never-to-be-forgotten words, "If thou canst believe," and the cry, "Lord, I believe; help Thou mine unbelief." The words which expelled the demon, Mark recites in all their solemn emphasis; and in them the addition is remarkable, Enter no more into him. Mark alone describes the paroxysm under which the demon departed, and the important circumstance that the youth lay as one dead; that Jesus took him by the hand, and raised him to conscious life. Moreover, he makes prominent (as he often does the like) the entrance of Christ into the house, where the disciples put their confidential question to Him as to the reason why they could not cast out the demon. And he gives the answer of Jesus without Matthew's additional clause concerning the unbelief of the disciples, and without the words that liken faith to the grain of mustard-seed. Nor does he mention the circumstance, recorded by Luke, of the people's renewed astonishment and increasing excitement.

Ver. 15. **All the people were amazed.**—At what? Euth. Zigabenus: "Either on account of the singularly seasonable and sudden coming of Jesus, or at His glorious appearance." Of this latter we read nothing, and Meyer therefore thinks the former the sounder view: it was an astonishment of joyful surprise. But θάμβος betokens an astonishment which is related to fear, which sometimes passes over into amazement, and is sometimes called terror. Hence we explain the astonishment as the amazement of a crowd somewhat profanely disposed at the sudden interposition of a punitive event like this (*see Leben Jesu*, ii. 2, 317). "They sought to repair their error by running to Him with eager denials." And it is obvious to connect with that the supposition, that the reflection of the transfiguration glory still lingered on the Lord's countenance. *See* Ex. xxxiv. 29, 30.

Ver. 16. **And he asked them.**—Bengel refers this to the disciples; Griesbach, to the disciples and scribes; Fritzsche, with most others, to the scribes alone; Meyer, to the people, because the people were just before spoken of. But the context points simply to the scribes as the contending party; not excluding, however, the people, so far as they sympathized. — **What question ye with them?** — Concerning what? The scribes were dumb. But the father of the possessed child gave the answer as to what they were contending about, ver. 17. Evidently they had impugned the power of the disciples to work miracles, and the authority of Christ; therefore they were now silent, because they suspected that the Lord would by a miraculous act convict them.

Ver. 17. **Brought unto Thee my son.**—That was his purpose. He was seeking the Lord in the place where the disciples were. But as Jesus was absent, His disciples and the man became engaged together.

Ver. 18. **Wheresoever he taketh him.**—This does not hint at an intermitting possession, in favor of which Meyer, without reason, adduces Matt. xii. 44, but to the antithesis between a latent action (in which, however, the youth by his dumbness betrayed his possession) and frenzied paroxysms, in which the spirit seized the youth, in order, as it appeared, to destroy him; and, according to Matthew, these crises had a connection with the changes of the moon. The following μηκέτι εἰσέλθῃς, Meyer himself acknowledges, implies that the demon had continuous possession.— **He teareth him.**— Probably this manifested itself in convulsions, St. Vitus' dance, or the like. The fundamental form was epilepsy, or something of the kind. These circumstances depended partly on the change of the moon, partly on demoniac influences.

Ver. 22. **To destroy him.** — The father regarded the demon as a malicious enemy, who was bent upon the murder of his only son.—**If Thou canst do anything.**— Expression of doubt or infirm faith, which, having been at the beginning too weak, had become more and more weak in consequence of the failure of the disciples' attempt.

Ver. 23. **If thou canst believe.** — The difficulty in the reading of the *Text. Rec.*, together with the critical authorities in its favor, constrain us to retain it. The easiest solution explains the τό as a sign of quotation preceding the direct address (De Wette). For other explanations, *see* Meyer.* We take the sentence as a breviloquence: "the *if thou canst* means, *if thou canst believe.*" Τὸ εἰ δύνασαι = εἰ δύνασαι πιστεῦσαι. *To be able*, and *to be able to believe*, are with the Lord one and the same,—especially throughout Mark's Gospel. Hence the clause, "All things are possible to him that believeth," is an illustration of this fundamental law, this mathematical formula, so to speak, of the kingdom of God. The explanation of the passage on the other reading is indeed simpler: "As it respects *if thou canst*, all things are possible," etc. (Meyer); or, the first clause is a question: Dost thou ask, *If thou canst?* all things, etc. (Ewald).

Ver. 24. **Help Thou mine unbelief.**—Bengel: Help away mine unbelief. Meyer thinks to improve it: Do not deny me on account of my unbelief. Certainly the βοήθει, ver. 24, refers to the help of healing itself; but the man knew very well by this time that his son would be healed, if his unbelief was healed. And the faith which now sprang up in the man was the more spiritual, in that it was a belief that Jesus could strengthen the deficient faith into the ability perfectly to believe, and so by this means remove also his external distress.

Ver. 25. **When Jesus saw that the people came running together.**—His desire to preserve the secrecy of His journey tended now to hasten the

* ["After omitting πιστεῦσαι, the clause τὸ εἰ δύνῃ (δύνασαι) is to be regarded as Nominative Absolute: *The 'if thou canst,'—all things are possible to him that believeth, i. e.*, so far as concerns the words, '*if thou canst*,' which thou hast just spoken, everything depends upon *faith*; the believer can obtain *anything*. The article τὸ, belonging to εἰ δύνῃ as its substantive, takes up the words of the father, and with lively emphasis isolates them in the grammatical structure, in order to put them into relation to the faith that is required on his part. Griesbach, Tischendorf, and Ewald regard τὸ εἰ δύνῃ as a question, and παντα δυν. τ. πιστ. as its answer: '*Tune dubitans* SI POTES *aiebas? Nihil non in ejus, qui confidat, gratiam fieri potest.*' But in case of a question we should expect τί τὸ εἰ δύνῃ." MEYER, *in loc.—Ed.*]

performance of the miracle.—**I charge (command) thee.**—"Emphatically, as in contrast with the disciples." Meyer.

Ver. 26. **The spirit cried.**—The crying out of the demoniac youth, seeming to be a work of the demon, though a shriek in inarticulate tones, was the first sign of cure: the youth had previously been dumb, whilst foaming and gnashing his teeth. *See* ver. 18.

DOCTRINAL AND ETHICAL.

1. *See* on the parallels in *Matthew* and *Luke*.

2. We have here not only the grand contrast between the heavenly glorification upon the mountain, and the demoniac degradation reminding of hell at the foot of it, but also the contrast between the sound spiritual ecstasy of the disciples, and the diseased physical possession of the youth. So also a contrast between the supreme festival and the severe toil of the Lord.

3. As the contemplation of the disciples upon the mountain had to contend with infirmity and sleep, so the premature activity of the disciples in the valley had to contend with impotence and vain endeavors. Christ is the Master upon the mountain and in the valley, in contemplation and in activity.

4. The heaviest burden which oppressed the Lord in His career upon earth, even amongst His disciples, was the burden of unbelief.

5. The colloquy of Jesus with the father of the child a school of faith.

6. Christ in this narrative may be compared to a general, who retrieves by his own presence a battle well-nigh lost by his army.

7. Through the faith of the father the son is healed (as in the history of the nobleman, and of the Canaanitish woman). These facts tell against the Baptists. Even the blessing upon the faith of sponsors is represented by the history of the centurion.

8. Reischle: "Over the life of the child the demon, despite his malignity, had no power. Later examples also show that possessed persons, falling from great heights, or into fire or water, are not easily killed or grievously hurt, while in their condition of unnatural paroxysms."

HOMILETICAL AND PRACTICAL.

See on the parallels of *Matthew* and *Luke*.—How the entrance of the living Christ into the community of the disciples changes its whole character: 1. The profane disposition of the people gives place to reverence; 2. the supremacy of the divine word takes the place of school controversy; 3. excitement is allayed by the spirit of His peace; 4. faith conquers unbelief; 5. His miraculous help and salvation follow their impotence and bewilderment.—The Lord comes at the right time for the help of His people.—Not only the demon of the abyss, but also the scribes, embarrass the company of the disciples not firmly standing in the power of faith.—The poor demoniac youth, and the world of poor, afflicted children (deaf and dumb, cretins, possessed, orphans, etc.).—The anguish of the father's heart could lead to faith, even as the anguish of the mother's heart (of the Canaanitish woman: but the mother's heart was the more brave).—The colloquy of the Lord with the father of the youth, a type of the way in which He guides the soul to faith. 1. The preparation: allaying of excitement, and clear view of the affliction. 2. Help reference to the power of faith. 3. Support and consummation of faith.—The communication between Christ and the needy soul: 1. What is thy grief? 2. If Thou canst, help. 3. Thou canst, if thou canst believe. 4. I believe; help, etc.—Thou canst; that is, if thou canst believe.—The measure of faith, the measure of our ability.—Weak faith must, with the prayer, "Lord, help mine unbelief," stretch forward to its perfection.—The faith of parents is to the advantage of their children.—Prayer and tears the element of faith: 1. The expression of its ground, humility (prayer, the spiritual expression; tears, the bodily expression); 2. the voice of its need; 3. the nourishment of its strength.—The father's concurrence with the Lord in faith, severs the connection of the child with the evil spirit.—What are we taught by the final throes of the hostile spirit? 1. Redemption is attained by a decisive conflict, in which all the powers of evil are excited; 2. we must distinguish between the external manifestation and the internal strength of the evil one; 3. when the distress is greatest, the help is nearest.—The miracle of the Lord twofold: 1. Casting out demons with peril of life; 2. restoration of life, seemingly gone.—Unclean spirits must be cast out, even though life seems endangered.—If the soul is freed, the life is saved.—Many kinds of impotence, and the one divine power: 1. Inability: *a.* of the child—a miserable possession; *b.* of the people—a stupid prejudice; *c.* of the scribes—impotence of malice, disguised under wise phrases; *d.* of the disciples—occasioned by want of self-government and collectedness of spirit; *e.* of those who sought help—enabled to believe. 2. The almighty power of the Lord: punishing all the impotence of malignity, and confirming all the impotence of sincere infirmity.—The power of demons having its root in the weakness of men (like the vampire sucking the blood of the living, and nourished thereby), but sinking into nothing before the awaking power of faith, under the omnipotence of the grace of Christ.—The unclean spirit a murderer of man, and Christ the Saviour of man's life, here as everywhere.—Jesus puts compulsion upon the wicked spirit of envious, dumb, and murmuring misery.—He constrains him to cry out in his loudest utterance, and so expels him.

Starke: — When a man has refreshed and strengthened himself in God, through prayer in secret, he must up and betake himself again to his calling.— Canstein: — When the world thinks that Christ has departed from His people, it deems that a good opportunity for tempting them, and misleading them into evil.— Quesnel: — The Lord Jesus sometimes suffers His people to be driven into a corner, that they may know how needful He is to them.—In their presence, the world shows itself respectful enough towards God's servants; but what passes behind their backs, He knows best who knows all things. — Hedinger: — Children a precious gift of God.—Children may be a great joy, and also a great bitterness, to their parents.—Quesnel:—The devil is as angry as ever when he sees that Christ will rob him of a soul.—We must not hold ourselves safe when we are disinclined to any particular sin. Satan knows how to vary his temptations; and to turn our thoughts now in one, and now in another, direction of evil.—Cramer:—Unbelief is the greatest sin, hinders the greatest works of God, and plunges the soul in condemnation.—Hedinger:—Faith is omnipotent (able for everything).—CANSTEIN:—He who implores faith with tears, has it already in his heart.—MAJUS:—Weak faith is nevertheless faith.—Amidst tears and prayers, we shall be delivered from unbelief, and attain unto true faith.—The humble Christian prays incessantly for the increase of his faith.—The devil must be rebuked, which he cannot bear; but he who would do it, must be armed with the power of the Holy Spirit.—QUESNEL:—Those who do not like to speak of God, or hear God spoken of, are possessed by a dumb spirit, from which Christ alone can free them.—OSIANDER:—Let those who are once delivered from Satan's power, take good heed that they be not entangled again in his snares.—Even if Satan, by God's permission, could inflict bodily death upon men, he cannot put their souls to death.—CANSTEIN:—When the Gospel has little fruit, its ministers should examine themselves how far they are the cause.—HEDINGER:—A submissive prayer.—OSIANDER:—Preachers should, beyond all others, be moderate and watchful.—RIEGER:—The future coming of Christ will inspire such terror as this into very many.—Men are not very willing to join cause with the poor disciples when they are in conflict, and at disadvantages. But when they see the Lord approaching, and have reason to think that He will utter His favorable and victorious voice concerning them, there is a great reaction in their favor.—BRAUNE:—The sharp rebuke of Jesus is general; but it touches the disciples most keenly.—Thou sayest to Me, "Canst Thou do anything?" but I must say unto thee, "Canst *thou* do anything, that is, canst thou believe? for then thou canst do all: faith can do everything."—There exists certainly between parents and children a deep, internal relation and sympathy.—This passage is most important in relation to the nature of faith.—It does not depend so much upon the theoretical consciousness of a truth as upon the existence of a real and actual fellowship with God.—It was noble in the disciples so frankly and openly to test themselves in their Master's presence.—We should always act as they acted, when we fail of attaining what is the due of our office, and what our hearts are set upon.—REISCHLE:—Here also we find representative faith, as in Matt. viii. 5. (But connected with profound, living affinity between parent and child.)—LISCO:—(The people were amazed, and ran to greet Jesus.) Have you never found that, on occasion of special and mysterious interpositions of God, your neighbor's heart was more than ordinarily inclined towards you?—SCHLEIERMACHER:—(The disciples excited by disputation with the Jews.) There are only a few men who are able to contend peacefully, and without losing their calm and peaceful temper, even about such matters as do not affect their external prerogatives,—matters, for instance, of faith, which engender difference of opinion.—There can be no doubt that they were the scribes who, in consequence of the estimation in which they were held, moved and swayed the minds of the people on the present occasion; and these scribes were mainly and primarily the persons whom the Lord described as an unbelieving generation.—Ye were not able, because your minds were in so excited a state: ye could have accomplished it only in a tranquil, collected temper, in which alone can reside such spiritual power.—The kingdom of God is never advanced in a passionate temper of mind, even if the zeal is a zeal for good.—They must return into silence, and stillness, and rest (this, however, being attainable only on the condition of prayer and fasting; that is, devotion towards God, and self-denial towards the world).—GOSSNER:—If we do not abide in faith, we can do nothing.

NINTH SECTION.

THE RETIREMENT OF JESUS IN GALILEE PREPARATORY TO HIS JOURNEY TO PERÆA AND JERUSALEM. FURTHER PREPARATION FOR THE NEW CHURCH.

CHAPTER IX. 30–50.

1. *Christ's Prediction among His Galilæan Disciples of His Death.* VERS. 30–32.

(Parallels: Matt. xvii. 22, 23; Luke ix. 43–45.)

30 And they departed thence, and passed [passed by by-ways[1]] through Galilee; and
31 he would not that any man should know *it*. For he taught his disciples, and said unto
them, The Son of man is delivered into the hands of men, and they shall kill him; and
32 after that he is killed, he shall rise the third day.[2] But they understood not that saying,
and were afraid to ask him.

[1] Ver. 30.—Lachmann, ἐπορεύοντο, after B.*, D. Meyer: "The compound was given up as misunderstood."

[2] Ver. 31.—Lachmann and Tischendorf read, following B., C., D., L., Δ., Versions, μετὰ τρεῖς ἡμέρας, as in ch. viii. 31. But it is quite natural that the more definite expression should occur here.

EXEGETICAL AND CRITICAL.

See on *Matthew* and *Luke*.—It is plain that the return of Jesus to Galilee from Cæsarea Philippi is here described. As it regards the chronological relation to what follows, it is questionable whether this was the last residence of Jesus in Galilee before His departure to Jerusalem in the year of His death, or the last but one. The former is the opinion of

Lücke, Wieseler, Hofmann, and Ebrard. But on the other side is the fact, that Jesus now went through Galilee quite in secret; while His last journey from Galilee, through Samaria, was a very public one. (*See* Luke x. 52; xv. 1.) This secret abode of Christ in Galilee coincides with the Lord's refusal, on the occasion of His brethren's challenge to Him to go up with them to the Feast of Tabernacles in Jerusalem, John vii. 1; and this took place before the penultimate and certainly concealed journey of Jesus to Jerusalem (*see Leben Jesu*, ii. 2, p. 28).—The Feast of Tabernacles fell in the autumn (on the fifteenth day of the seventh Jewish month, called Tisri). It began this year—the year of persecutions before the year of His death, 782 A.U.C—according to Wieseler, on the twelfth of October. The present history, therefore, places us in the autumn of that year. (*See* on *Matthew*.) The proper and special characteristics of the present journey of Jesus through Galilee are found in the παρεπορεύοντο, ver. 30 (on which below), in the words, "He would not that any man should know," and in the particulars of the prediction concerning the Passion. Mark is here distinguished from Matthew by being more precise in his characterization. On the other hand, Luke gives prominence to a specific trait, Luke ix. 44—the Lord's reference to the contrast furnished by the praises which He received after the healing of the demoniac youth at Cæsarea Philippi. He also gives special emphasis, ver. 45, to the expression οἱ δὲ ἠγνόουν τὸ ῥῆμα.

Ver. 30. **And passed through Galilee.**—The παραπορεύομαι means a going aside or passing by. Meyer explains, "They were required to go rapidly through Galilee; that is, they so travelled as nowhere to tarry long." In Deut. ii. 4 the passing through the territory of the Edomites was a passing through their borders (not touching their central places). In Mark ii. 23 it means a passing through the cornfields, leaving the overhanging ears of corn. Hence Grotius (*Annott. in Marc.* p. 638: compare *Leben Jesu*, ii. 924; Sepp. ii. 418): they journeyed in by-ways and field-roads. But of a voyage by sea we read nothing. They travelled round the sea, through desert mountain-ways and woody paths; for Jesus desired uninterruptedly to prepare His disciples in Galilee for His approaching sufferings.

Ver. 31. **For He taught His disciples.**—We must understand by these only His disciples dispersed through Galilee; that discipleship out of which He at a later period, before His last journey, selected the Seventy, and from among whom a nucleus of more than five hundred brethren outlived the trial of the cross: 1 Cor. xv. 6; Matt. xxviii. 16. For the Lord had previously led the twelve Apostles to Gaulonitis, over the sea, in order to make them acquainted with the same great mystery. *See* ch. viii. 31.—**Is delivered,** παραδίδοται.—The future vividly exhibited as present.

Ver. 32. **But they understood not that saying.**—Compare especially the parallel passage in Luke. According to Matthew, they were exceedingly troubled. The saying concerning His violent death so contradicted their expectations, that they could not and would not think of it. Hence they would not ask for fuller explanation.

DOCTRINAL AND ETHICAL.

1. *See* on *Matthew* and *Luke*.

2. The whole passage is a psychological example that teaches us how difficult it is to enter into views which are opposed to our former views, and the tendency of our wills; how hard it is for the world, with its view of Christianity, and for Christians themselves, with their worldly views, to take a self-renouncing view of the mystery and doctrine of the cross. So every individual man of the world, and even the individual disciple of Christ, finds it ever.

3. Schleiermacher: "We see that the disciples had then as yet no conviction of the necessity of the death of Christ for the accomplishment of the work of redemption. They thought all was to be done without the intervention of the death of their Lord and Master, although not without many conflicts to befall both Him and them." We see, however, that for that stage their faith satisfied the Lord; but we see also how often He had again to rebuke their unbelief, until, after His crucifixion, resurrection, and ascension, they came to a perfect faith through the anointing of the Holy Spirit.

HOMILETICAL AND PRACTICAL.

See on *Matthew* and *Luke*.—The departure of Jesus from His asylum in the mountains on the other side of the sea.—The silent paths of the Lord in the dreary time of persecution (the ancient Christians in the Catacombs, the Waldenses, the Huguenots, Luther in the Wartburg, &c.).—The by-paths of Christ in contrast with the by-paths of the world.—The Lord's calm autumnal travelling: 1. It was autumn in the year; 2. autumn in His life; 3. autumn in the ancient world.—The Son of Man delivered into the hands of men; or, the heaven-wide difference and contrast between the Man and men: 1. Between the Son of Man and the hands of men; 2. between the new humanity and the old humanity.—The betrayal into the hands of men, the bitterest sting in the anticipation of His sufferings.—The displacency with which man hears the first solemn and fearful words concerning the cross.—Lack of the insight of faith, and lack of the obedience of faith, in their reciprocal influence.—The pains taken by our Lord with His people, before He brought them to believe in the great salvation wrought out in the great judgment.—We learn the meaning of Christ's death by the light of His life and suffering.

STARKE: — HEDINGER: — Christ's suffering was certain and prearranged, but to the natural reason incomprehensible: the flesh for ever hears of it with displacency.—MAJUS:—When the Church is in a prosperous condition, that is the time to remember what has been predicted in Holy Writ concerning the cross and sufferings of the faithful.

2. *The Greatest among the Disciples and the Little Child. Zeal of John. Offences.* VERS. 33–50.

(Parallels: Matt. xviii. 1–9; Luke ix. 46–50.)

33 And he came[1] to Capernaum: and, being in the house, he asked them, What was it
34 that ye disputed among yourselves by [on] the way? But they held their peace: for
35 by [on] the way[2] they had disputed among themselves who *should be* the greatest. And
he sat down, and called the twelve, and saith unto them, If any man desire to be first,
36 *the same* shall be last of all, and servant of all. And he took a child, and set him in
37 the midst of them: and when he had taken him in his arms, he said unto them, Whosoever shall receive one of such children in my name, receiveth me; and whosoever
38 shall receive me, receiveth not me, but him that sent me. And [But] John answered
him,[3] saying, Master, we saw one casting out devils in thy name, and he followeth not
39 us; and we forbade him, because he followeth not us. But Jesus said, Forbid him not:
for there is no man which shall do a miracle in my name, that can lightly [readily]
40, 41 speak evil of me. For he that is not against us[4] is on our part. For whosoever
shall give you a cup of water to drink in my name,[5] because ye belong to Christ, verily
42 I say unto you, he shall not lose his reward. And whosoever shall offend one of *these*
little ones that believe in me, it is better for him that a millstone were hanged about
43 his neck, and he were cast into the sea. And if thy hand offend thee, cut it off: it is
better for thee[7] to enter into life maimed, than having [the] two hands to go into hell,
44 into the fire that never shall be quenched: Where their worm dieth not, and the fire is
45 not quenched. And if thy foot offend thee, cut it off: it is better for thee to enter halt
into life, than having [the] two feet to be cast into hell, into the fire that never shall
46, 47 be quenched: Where their worm dieth not, and the fire is not quenched.[8] And if
thine eye offend thee, pluck it out: it is better for thee to enter into the kingdom of
48 God with one eye [one-eyed], than having two eyes to be cast into hell-fire[9]: Where
49 their worm dieth not, and the fire is not quenched. For every one shall be salted with
50 fire, and every sacrifice shall be salted with salt. Salt *is* good: but if the salt have
lost his [its] saltness [have become saltless], wherewith will ye season it? Have salt
in yourselves, and have peace one with another.

[1] Ver. 33.—Lachmann, Tischendorf, [after B., D., Vulgate]: ἦλθον Πρὸς ἑαυτούς is wanting in [B., C., D., Versions, Lachmann, Tischendorf, Meyer.]

[2] Ver. 34.—The omission of ἐν τῇ ὁδῷ in some Codd. [A., D.] is not important.

[3] Ver. 38.—Tischendorf [and Meyer] read ἔφη αὐτῷ, [with the omission of λέγων,] after B., L., Δ., and Versions. Perhaps an explanation of the more difficult "John answered."—A. and others omit ἐν; B., D. retain it. The former seems more unusual and more correct.—*See* Meyer on the omissions of ὃς οὐκ and ὅτι οὐκ. [Ὃς οὐκ ἀκολουθεῖ ἡμῖν is wanting in B., C., L., Δ., while, on the contrary, this is found in D., X., Versions, Vulgate, Fritzsche, Tischendorf, but ὅτι οὐκ ἀκολ. ἡμῖν is wanting. Meyer retains both.]

[4] Ver. 40.—A., D., E., F., Versions, read ὑμῶν.

[5] Ver. 41.—Τῷ and μοῦ are omitted in A., B., C.

[6] Ver. 42.—Τούτων is added by Tischendorf and Lachmann, after A., B., C.**; Meyer derives it from Matt. xviii. 6.—Lachmann: μύλος ὀνικός, after B., C., D. Meyer derives this also from Matthew.

[7] Ver. 43.—Lachmann, Tischendorf, [Meyer]: καλόν ἐστίν σε, after B., C., L.

[8] Ver. 45.—The omission of εἰς τὸ πῦρ ἄσβεστον [in B., C., L., Tischendorf, Meyer,] is to be explained by the fact of the repetition of the words concerning the worm; which only in ver. 48 is found in all the Codd. [In vers. 44, 46 it is wanting in B., C., L., Δ., and Tischendorf.]

[9] Ver. 47.—Τοῦ πυρός is wanting in many Codd.

EXEGETICAL AND CRITICAL.

See on the parallel passages of *Matthew* and *Luke.*—As it respects the chronology, this residence of Jesus in Capernaum does not immediately follow the former section; but His appearance in Jerusalem at the Feast of Tabernacles must be interposed. According to John, our Lord went up to Jerusalem not only at the Feast of Tabernacles, but also at the Feast of Dedication. The former feast fell in the middle of the month of October; that of the Dedication in the second half of December (the 27th). The question arises, whether Jesus remained in Judæa during the interval between these two feasts, and then returned to Galilee and Capernaum for the last time; or whether this last journey homewards and the departure from Galilee fell within the interval of the two feasts. We assume that the latter is the true hypothesis, and for the following reasons:—1. The last journey of Jesus to Jerusalem led, according to the Synoptists, over Peræa. 2. According to John x. 40, Jesus went back, after the Feast of Dedication, to Peræa. Thus He must already have been once in Peræa; and this could have occurred only between the Feast of Tabernacles and the Feast of Dedication, that is, between October and December 782. Into this season falls His last abode in Capernaum, and His departure from Galilee (*see Notes* on *Matthew*). That between the secret travels of Jesus in the former section, and the position of things in the present, much must have intervened, is proved by the discussion going on among the disciples, which issued now in words, as to who should be the greatest among them. The glorious demonstration of Jesus at the Feast of Tabernacles, the healing of the blind man, the favourable feelings of the many, must have again enkindled within them the hopes of His speedy manifestation of the glory of His kingdom. This made them ever more desirous to give His prophecy of His death a figurative meaning as referring to the sufferings of Messiah, the temporary obscuration of His name and of His cause. Thus they might come to the question as to who would have a fair prospect of the highest place under Him in His kingdom. Mark is more precise in his narrative here than either Matthew or Luke: first, in regard to the occasion of the act and the special circumstances; secondly, in the scene with the little child. The Lord had already spoken the decisive word, before He placed the child in the midst. Mark records that Jesus embraced the child. In the words of application that follow he is more copious than Matthew, somewhat less copious than Luke. Mark, on the contrary, communicates in the fullest manner the transaction between Jesus and John, which Luke has in brief; and, in the discourse touching the offending hand, &c., he is more solemnly detailed than the other Evangelists. The narrative about the stater, Mark seems to have passed over, as being a narrative which Peter omitted because it made himself prominent.

Ver. 33. **By the way.**—The fleeting journey through Galilee cannot here be meant, but the last return of Jesus from Jerusalem, when the disciples had recovered their tone of mind and their hopes.

Ver. 34. **Who should be the greatest.**—Obviously, only with reference to the Messiah's kingdom,—their hopes of the speedy establishment of which being now rekindled.

Ver. 35. **If any man desire to be first.**—Comp. Matt. xxiii. 12; xx. 27; xviii. 4. Our clause seems in one formula to include two rules: whosoever exalteth himself shall be abased; whosoever humbleth himself shall be exalted. Despotism makes man a slave; spiritual despotism makes him the lowest and most abject of all slaves, who must serve the most external and legal behests of a police for the internal kingdom of God. But voluntary service in the kingdom of love, and under the impulse of humility and self-denial, makes a man a spiritual power, and gives him an unconscious and blessed greatness in the kingdom of God, which does not complacently look at its own reflection. In this sense Christ came to minister unto all (symbol, the feet-washing), and has become Lord over all, Phil. ii. 5-11. But the emphasis falls here obviously upon the second rule.

Ver. 36. **When He had taken him in His arms.**—Peculiar to the vivid and pathetic style of Mark. Comp. ch. x. 16.

Ver. 37. **Whosoever shall receive one of such children.**—The natural child in the arms of Jesus is not only a symbol, but also identical in its susceptibility with the spiritual child; and it signifies, not a Christian ripe in humility, but a beginner in faith. The child baptized or blessed is in the catechumen state, like the thirty years' proselyte before baptism, or the beginner in faith. *See* on *Matthew*, p. 323.—**Not Me, but Him that.**—Meyer: "Not *non tamquam*, but with rhetorical emphasis the ἐμὲ δέχεται is absolutely denied." At the same time the rhetorical element must be strongly emphasized. It signifies a "much more," or "infinitely more;" with the child we receive Christ, with Christ we receive God, if the receiving is of the right kind.

Ver. 38. **And John answered Him.**—The ἀποκρίνεσθαι here, as often, in the wider sense: on a special occasion to begin the conversation. John had a fact in his mind which he must bring into the light of this act of Jesus. Meyer, following Schleiermacher: "The disciples had, to one who uttered the name of Jesus, done the opposite of receive." Or, rather, they had hindered one who in the name of Jesus was receiving the miserable, and doing works of mercy. John now hears that precisely to such an one the greatest promises are given.—**In Thy name.**—The τῷ ὀνόματί σου says less than ἐν τῷ, κ.τ.λ. Comp. Matt. vii. 22; Acts ix. 13. By means of uttering the name of Jesus. Meyer: "But our exorcist was not an impostor, he was a believer; yet not one belonging to the permanent company of Jesus." Had he been a deceiver, he would not have been able to cast out demons by the name of Jesus; for the name of Jesus wrought no magical effects: *see* Acts xix. 13. But if he had been a decided believer, John would have known him as such; for the ἀκολουθεῖν must be understood of actual and real following, and not necessarily of merely external discipleship. The passage therefore means, that there was in him a measure of trust in the name of Jesus a germ of true faith. But we must not forget that the words are, "he followeth not with *us*," not, "he followeth not *Thee*:" this is certainly the utterance of an excited human party feeling. Gerlach and others suppose that the exorcist might have been a disciple of John the Baptist; but it is to be remembered that John himself did no miracle. All were indeed disciples of John, in the wider sense, who were hoping for the approaching kingdom, and had been baptized of John.—**We forbade him, because.**—We must regard John as the main agent in all this matter, though in perfect understanding and concert with the rest of the disciples. The "*because* he followeth not with us," &c., signifies that they desired of the man a decided following with them, or an abandonment of all working in the name of Jesus. Thus they did not deny that even an unregenerate man might do something by means of the name of Jesus; but they regarded him as not justified in so doing. Their watchword was: first a full conversion, and then the right and ability to work. It is strictly, "We interdicted him from that," or "hindered him." Easily might the prohibition of the disciples disturb his miracle-working confidence.

Ver. 39. **Forbid him not, for.**—Augustin: "*Distinguit inter neutralitatem epicuream et neutralitatem ex infirmitate.*" Such a man, the Lord tells them, would not immediately dishonor His name. His experience would prevent him from so soon turning round and going over to His enemies. And in this there was expressed, at the same time, the hope that he would earlier or later become an actual follower. Jesus, therefore, would impress it upon His disciples that they must honor and protect the isolated beginnings or germs of faith to be found in the world, without the circle of actual believers. We are not violently to constrain the men in whom such beginnings are seen, to adopt prematurely the party of faith: such a course might have a tendency to repel them, and drive them into the camp of th enemy. Moreover, it is contrary to the demands of a germ, and of gradual development; it is contrary to the rights of conscience, and the nature of the kingdom of God, whose kindled sparks of life fall far beyond the central hearth of the Church. But we must carefully distinguish here between forbidding and commanding. It is not permitted the dis ciples to forbid; they should pay all respect to the unrestrained influence of Christ, and its results, even beyond the fold of the disciples. But it does not follow from this, that the Lord commands, outside the circle of discipleship also, a premature activity of the beginners in faith. It is wholesome and natural that every energy of faith, in every young Christian, should act and move, according to the measure of its development, under the condition of truth, sincerity, and supreme regard for its own internal growth and well-being. Meyer: "We gather, moreover, from this passage, how mightily the words and influence of Christ had wrought outside the sphere of His permanent dependants, exciting in individuals a degree of spiritual energy that performed miracles on others."

Ver. 40. **For he that is not against you.**—The reading ὑμῶν is better supported than the reading ἡμῶν, which the *Text. Rec.*, Fritzsche, and Tischendorf follow; and thus the clause constitutes a formal antithesis to the word in Matt. xi. 42. (*See* the *Critical Notes* on that passage.) "And in order that they might not, in this sacred domain of tender beginnings, hurt any the least sapling, He converts His royal word, *He who is not for Me is against Me*, into a disciple-word for them to use, *He who is not against us is on our part.*" (*Leben Jesu*, ii. 10–12; comp. Stier on the passage.)

Ver. 41. **Whosoever shall give you a cup of water** (*see* Matt. x. 42.) The third γάρ, *for:* a threefold significant establishment of the rule laid down by our Lord, *not to hinder beginnings.* First reason: Such a man will not soon become mine enemy. Second reason: If any one were against you, he would give assurance of the fact; if he is not against you, it is to be assumed at the outset that he is for you. Third reason: The respect and love which is even outwardly shown you in the very slightest degree by men in the world, for Christ's sake, or in His name, proves that they stand in a certain spiritual connection with Him, which under His blessing may increase and become more strict. The smallest token of friendship you receive as disciples of Christ, is a token of friendship to your Master, which is rewarded by Him with the blessing of greater friendship. Thus: 1. The beginning of friendly feeling excludes the thought of a speedy enmity; 2. so much so, that the cessation of enmity, in any instance, is to be regarded as friendship; 3. because the slightest token of friendliness, which is understood by that cessation of enmity, is blessed and furthered until it has become decided love and friendship. From the external friendship which is manifested in external proofs of love, men go on to internal friendship: from the disciples of Christ, whom they acknowledge as such, they come to Christ Himself. Thus we must esteem holy all the roots, relations, and tendencies of good which Christianity finds in the world,—yet that Christianity which does not deny itself and the Lord (ἐν τῷ ὀνόματί μου). We assume that the three *fors* all directly refer to the "forbid him not," without disparaging the connection in which they stand to each other.

Ver. 42. **And whosoever shall offend one of these little ones.**—What follows is, down to the close, a strong utterance of our Lord against that fanatical ecclesiastical zealotry which is so much disposed to throw stumbling-blocks in the way of beginners in the faith, by imposing traditional dogmatic articles of faith. Saunier, De Wette, and others have lost the connection here. But it is evident enough when we bear in mind that the words of Christ, vers. 43–47, have here a reference altogether different from that which the related words of Matt v. 29, 30 have. (Comp. *Leben Jesu*, ii. 2.)—Our passage forms a parallel with Matt. xviii. 6 *seq.* Matthew, however, did not adhere strictly to the place where the words were spoken; Mark places the locality and circumstances very clearly before us. The sons of thunder had a series of their own particula crises to pass through, just as Peter had; a series of crises for their fanatical and enthusiastic party zeal. The first is found here; the second soon follows, on their departure from Galilee (Luke ix. 54); the third falls into a later period, before the final going up to Jerusalem, ch. x. 35.

Ver. 43. **And if thy hand offend thee.**—For the meaning of these words in this connection, *see* the notes on the parallel in *Matthew.* Offences of the hand, of the eye, and of the foot; or, stumbling-blocks of fanatical hierarchism, of heretical Gnosticism, and of political proselytism. In the formal shape which the word of our Lord assumes in Mark, "it may be regarded as an ideal formulary, which is designed to suggest to His Church the pious gentleness of the hand, the sacred spiritual clearness of the eye, and the peaceful and amiable apostolical movement of the feet." (*Leben Jesu*, ii. 2, 1016.)

Ver. 44. **Where their worm.**—Three times solemnly repeated. The reference to Isa. lxvi. 24 is manifest. It is a concrete expression for suffering in the fire of hell, Gehenna.

Ver. 45. **It is better for thee.**—Comp. on *Matthew.*

Ver. 49. **For every one shall be salted with fire.**—On this clause, which has no parallel (and which De Wette, Baur, and others, have so much doubted about), *see* Meyer, and the treatises referred to by him. Meyer, however, is wrong in interpreting this of the fire of hell mentioned previously. He explains: "πᾶς cannot mean every one generally; but must, in harmony with the context, be restricted to those who in ver. 48 are described by αὐτῶν; since afterwards another class is distinguished by πᾶσα θυσία from that which is meant by πᾶς, and its predicate is opposed to the predicate of the latter: πυρί and ἁλί are antitheses." They are indeed distinct points, but yet related to each other; for otherwise we should not read "Every one must be salted with fire." We therefore thus understand the passage: Every (sinful) man must, according to the typical meaning of the burnt-offering, enter into the suffering of fire: either into the fire of Gehenna, which then in his case represents the salt which was wanting to him; or as the burnt-offering of God into the fiery suffering of tribulation, those renunciations, namely and especially, which had just been mentioned—the sacrifice of the eye, the hand, and the foot—after he had been previously consecrated with the salt of the Spirit. This rule holds irreversibly good: those offending members which were not, as God's sacrifices, previously salted with salt, pass immediately into the fiery sufferings of punishment, which then represent and take the place of the salting. The καί in the clause, "*and* every sacrifice," does not therefore mean ὡς, καθώς; but it marks the specific case in which the being salted precedes the suffering of fire, and in which it may perhaps (as in John's own later history) more or less supply the place of, and involve the fiery suffering of, *external* tribulations (1 Cor. iii. 13). Meyer's separation of the salt and fire, and his antithesis between them, with his exclusive reference of the fire to the punishment of the ungodly, are found in Grotius, Lightfoot, and others. On the other hand, both are referred to the good by Euthym. Zigabenus ("the fire of faith in God, the salt of love to man"), by Luther (the Gospel is a fire and a salt: the old man is crucified, renewed, salted), Calovius, Kuinoel, Schott.—Olshausen thus agrees with our interpretation: "On account of the universal sinfulness of the race, every one must be salted with fire; whether by his voluntarily entering upon a course of self-denial and earnest renunciation of his sins, or by his being involuntarily cast into the place of punishment." Similarly Ewald. The γάρ gives the reason of the exhortation which preceded. Sacrifice the hand, the foot, &c., in the self-renunciation of godliness, rather than fall with your whole being into the fire of judgment as a sacrifice of death. For this is a fundamental law for sinful humanity: all must enter the fire. But if the fire becomes to man a sacrificial fire, his sacrifice must be voluntarily prepared and seasoned with salt (made savory, like food); otherwise, the fire of Gehenna *supplies* the place of the salt and the sacrifice.

Ver. 50. **Salt is good.**—The καλόν is not exhausted by the word *good.* Something preëminently good in its kind and effect is intended. The better any product of nature is in itself, the worse it is in its corruption. Therein the salt is an image of man. Saltless salt is not to be saved; and so with the spiritless disciple, or Christian, or minister (without chrisma: without salt). *See* on Matt. v. 13.—**Have salt in yourselves, and have peace.**—The salt is figurative, not merely signifying wisdom, but the Spirit as *the Spirit of discipline;* and on that account it is the symbol of the covenant,—a blessing the preservation and assurance of which has peace for its result. The "have peace one with another" is therefore a consecutive exhortation. Have peace amongst yourselves, such peace as you must have if you have that salt. From this last application it follows that the Lord regarded the contention of the disciples, and their zeal against a beginner in faith not walking in their circle, under the same point of view. All undevout and unholy zealotry, whether towards those within or those without, He explains as resulting from one fundamental offence and fault,—the lack of salt and self-resignation, the want of the Spirit's discipline and of consecration to God.—Here, again, it is Mark who has given most prominence to words of the Lord which most strongly corrected and admonished His disciples.

DOCTRINAL AND ETHICAL.

1. *See* on the parallel places in *Matthew* and *Luke.*

2. Between a hierarchy and the true catechumen's nurture of the little ones in the Church, there is an essential repugnance. The latter seeks to train up the babes in faith to the full maturity of faith; the former would not only keep the babes in infancy, but would train up the adult to be dumb babes. The extreme adherents of hierarchy and the Baptist principle agree, in that the former ascribe no prerogative to baptism, but make the baptized laity a subordinate class of imperfect Christians; and the latter, with hierarchical exclusiveness, deal like a clerus with the little ones in faith.—The sign which Jesus gave to the Church by His repeated embracing (according to Mark) of the children, was directed the first time rather against the fanatical church spirit of the hierarchy, and the last time (ch. x. 16) rather against the theological school-spirit of the Baptists. *Whosoever of you:* compare the history of the Papacy. Gregory the Great called himself the *servus servorum,* that he might be the first. The hierarchy has taken the ironical word of Christ's Spirit with unthinking and unintelligent literality like the word of our Lord, on another occasion, concerning the two swords, Luke xxii. 38 (*see Leben Jesu,* ii. 3, 1345), and other similar expressions.

3. *But John answered Him.*—This history teaches us, in connection with ch. x. 35 and Luke ix. 54, how Christ dealt with and purified the zeal, noble but not yet free from fanatical excitement, of the disciples, and especially what may be called the idealistic fanatical zeal of the sons of thunder, as it formed a contrast to the realistic fanatical zeal of Peter. With every development of true faith there is interwoven, especially in its first stages, a certain measure of that other quality which stains its purity, and requires to be eliminated. But when its heart is sound, the flame is soon cleared of its bedimming smoke; the life of faith becomes ever more christianly human, wise, and gentle (*see* Jas. iii. 17, 18). But where the heart is evil, or becomes so through the influence of external things, the life of faith declines into fanaticism and perishes, as the history of Pharisaism and Judaism everywhere proves. Such a fanaticism lived indeed in the soul of Judas; he went on through enthusiasm and excitement to apostasy. The answer of John was a frank avowal, and revelation of himself or confession, before the Lord (*see Leben Jesu,* ii. 2).

4. *The connection of the beginnings of faith:*—pious work, ver. 38; its root in the devout mind, ver. 39; its nourishment in devout habits, humanity, ver. 41. Hence loving care for the disciples, leading to quiet recognition of their interests, and thence to active usefulness in the name of Jesus.

5. *The bigoted conduct of the disciples towards these beginnings of faith.*—In its issue and result an offence or injury to the little ones, and in a twofold sense: either as they are dishonored and wronged, or as they are offended and tempted to resistance and enmity. In its origin, it is an internal offence; offending self through the hand, or the foot, or the eye (*see Crit. Notes,* ver. 43, and on *Matthew*). In the Church, and for the Church, or in relation to the bride of Christ, that law of self-renunciation and self-sacrifice holds good which is the basis of the relations of marriage, Matt. v. 27 *seq.* We must be subject to the church, if we would edify it, Rom. xii. 3 *seq.*

6. That a millstone were hanged.—*See* on *Matthew.*

7. *Into hell, where the fire is not quenched.*—Concerning the difference between hell and Gehenna, and the kingdom of the dead or Sheol, *see* on *Matthew.* The additional clause, "where their worm dieth not," etc., points back, as it has been remarked, to the passage Isa. lxvi. 24, where the valley of Hinnom is expressly made a symbol of the punishment of the reprobate, and the Old Testament germ of the doctrine of future eternal punishment distinctly appears, as also it does in the earlier Cherem or death-sentence of the law, and in later passages, such as Ezek. xx. 47; Dan. xii. 2, and others. According to the passage in Isaiah, the bodies of those who were apostate from Jehovah lay without before the holy city, an abomination to all

flesh. The worm of corruption, which devoured them from within, died not; and the fire of judgment, which destroyed them from without, was not extinguished. And this manifestly presented a symbolical idea of eternal suffering; for, literally taken, the fire would be extinguished and consumed with the bodies and the worms. Eternal destruction within, eternal judgment without, and these in eternal reciprocal influence. On the doctrine of hell, compare dogmatic treatises.

8. *For every one must be salted with fire, and every sacrifice.*—Fire is the symbol of life in its renewing power, and especially of the judicial power and working of God, renewing by a divine energy: thus it is the presence and action of God in the full energy of His holy, penetrating nature: Gen. xv. 17; Ex. iii. 2; Mal. iii. 3; iv. 1. Hence it is for the sinful man generally a judicial visitation of God, the mercifully rebuking and correcting manifestation of His nature (Mal. iii. 3; iv. 1); for the penitent, believing man, it is the saving judgment of grace, the purifying fire, the fire of new quickening, transforming, glorification (Acts ii. 3); for the reprobate it is a fire of condemning judgment, Heb. x. 27; xii. 29.

9. This gives us the true meaning and significance of the sacrificial fire, of the fire of the altar. It forms a counterpart and contrast to the fire of hell. It is the fire of God, into which man voluntarily enters with his offering, in order that he may escape falling into the terror of the eternal fire. Thus, if we strictly judge ourselves, we shall not be judged. This absolute and inviolable law of the fire-alternative was symbolically exhibited by the Old Testament sacrifice: the Christian must have the reality of it accomplished in himself, whilst he makes himself, as it respects those members and their actions (hand, foot, eye) which might hurt his Christian life, a sacrifice upon the altar. This self-sacrifice is a burnt-offering, inasmuch as the Christian places himself daily at the Lord's disposal in pure self-dedication (Rom. xii.); it is a sin-offering, inasmuch as he actually renounces and rids himself of all those impulses and acts which are a hindrance. This applies, however, not only to sensual tendencies (Matt. v.), but also to those spiritual and ecclesiastical impulses of the self which are colored and disguised by religion (as it respects place and prerogative). Yet the sacrifice must not proceed from fear, but from loving obedience; it must not be an act of constrained dread, but voluntarily, an act of the spirit, of self-discipline. And that is signified by the salt (*see* the article *Salz* in WINER, BUCHNER, and the *Stuttgart Bibelwörterbuch*). The salt is the symbol of the Spirit, as the spirit of purifying and conserving discipline; even as oil is the symbol of the Spirit, as the Spirit of religious life and the living flame of devotion. Salt is the preserving, cleansing virtue of life: the Spirit who checks and kills sin germinating within. Fire is the transforming power of life: the Spirit who punishes the sin that is present, separating the sinner from sin as the judgment of grace, or destroying the sinner with his sin as the judgment of condemnation. Salt is discipline and conservation; fire is punishment, judgment, purification. Out of the fiery condemnation of Sodom a sea of salt flowed forth. The punishment of the doomed is a source of discipline and healing for those who still live. As fire and light are related to each other, and yet form a direct contrast, so it is with salt and light, Matt. v. 13, 14. Because the salt signified the spirit of discipline, it was needful (according to Ezek. xliii. 24; the testimony of this passage, and Jewish tradition) to every offering, and not only to the meat-offering (Lev. ii. 13); hence it was the proper symbol of the establishment and renewal of the covenant in the sacrifice. Hence, on the one hand, the salt is salt of the covenant (Lev. ii. 13), and, on the other, the covenant with Jehovah is a covenant of salt (Num. xviii. 19; 2 Chron. xiii. 5); while, in the common life of the Orientals, it was a sign of sacred covenant engagements and obligations. (*See* WINER, and BAHR, *Symbolik.*) To eat salt together, meant to make peace, and enter into covenant with each other (ROSENMULLER, *Morgenland*, ii. 150.) But as salt, or the spirit of discipline, was the fundamental condition of peace with God, so it was also the fundamental condition of peace in the Church, of the mutual peace of Christian people. Hence the word of our Lord: Have salt in yourselves, and peace one with another. The disciples were amongst themselves to *have* salt, but for the earth to *be* salt. In reference to the symbolism of the sacrifices, *see* the works on the subject by Bähr, Kurtz, and Hengstenberg.

10. In connection with the contrast, wide as heaven, between the salt and sacrificial fire on the one hand, and the unquenchable fire of Gehenna on the other, there must also be observed a certain relation, so far as, first, the salt is regarded as a symbol of the sacrificial fire; and, secondly, as the fire is regarded as a kind of salt: the Lord says that all must be salted with fire. The contrast between the two is this: the salt sustains and conserves; the fire, on the contrary, destroys and annihilates. But there is something more than a contrast; there is a strict relation. The salt preserves and sustains by an influence resembling that of fire: it is keen, biting, and pervasive; like a subtle flame, it penetrates all that is corruptible, separates that which is most corruptible and foul, whilst it fixes and quickens that which is sound. Thus it effects a kind of transformation or metamorphosis. So, on the other hand, the fire is a salt of higher potency: it destroys that which is perishable, and thereby establishes the imperishable in its purest perfection; it leads to new and more beautiful forms of being. Salt seems to petrify the object, fire seems to volatilize it; but the salt fixes it in its healthy normal condition, whilst the fire bears it upwards in its pure constituent elements to heaven. Thus the believer is first purified by the salt; but then by the fire of internal and external tribulation he is carried up to God. So it is with the whole world of mankind and the earth itself. First, it is purified and preserved by the salt of the apostolical Church (Matt. v. 13); then by the final fire at the end of the world it will be delivered from its condition of curse, and glorified: 2 Thess. i. 8; 2 Pet. iii. 10.

HOMILETICAL AND PRACTICAL.

See on the parallel passages in *Matthew* and *Luke*.—Despotism over fellow-disciples, and proselytizing those not disciples, spring from the same source from the self-exaltation of a proud and unpurified zeal. —Spiritual pride is the common source of all hierarchical and fanatical movements.—The silence of the other disciples compared with John's answering: 1. In reference to the persons:—the more noble the disciple, the more free he is to make honest and open confession. 2. In reference to the matter:—

fanatical zeal in the Church is more readily confessed than the impulses of proud ambition and the lust of ecclesiastical dominion, because it is in its first motives much more noble and less guilty.—The question concerning the greater in the Church, is a question in the way to the judgment-seat of Christ. 1. It will not be resolved before: the primacy waits till then. 2. It will be resolved in the end by the Lord, as He resolved it at the beginning (the first, the last). —The simple image of the pure Church of Christ: 1. Christ sits upon His throne; 2. the preaching sounds out, Whosoever will be first, etc.; 3. the only image in the Church is a little child; 4. the prospect: revelation of the great God through the humble care of the little ones.—The Church of apostolical humility. It marks Christ's word, "Whosoever will be first," etc., 1. in its literal significance, a threatening word against all despotism in the external, legal Church; 2. in its spiritual meaning, a word of promise for humble, ministering love in the congregation of His Spirit.—The child and the Apostles: 1. The child their master; 2. the child their scholar; 3. the child their fellow.—How we may receive with the little child the highest life in the name of Jesus: 1. The Lord Christ himself; 2. God himself.—How we may receive with the little child the great God: 1. If the child is received in the name of Jesus; 2. if Jesus is received in the name of God.—The beautiful confession of John.—Christ the holy Master of all the sons of thunder in His Church: 1. How He represses the sons of thunder (or reduces to silence the thunder of carnal zeal); 2. how He arouses the sons of thunder (or lets the thunder of the Spirit resound, Rev. x. 4).—The prohibition of John, and the commandment of the Lord, in relation to free labor in the Church, and for the cause of Christ.—The law of fanatical zeal, and the law of the spirit of freedom in the Church.—Ecclesiastical party zeal in the light of the word and Spirit of Christ.—Christ the defender and guardian of all beginnings of faith, and of all germs of spiritual life: 1. Through His Scripture-word; 2. through His apostolical infant baptism; 3. through the evangelical rights of personal conscience. —The water-cups of mild, human customs, in their connection with the sacramental cup of the God-man. —The connection between false fire of zeal in the Church and the fire of hell.—The three great dangers of ecclesiastical zeal: 1. Dangers of the hand; 2. dangers of the foot; 3. dangers of the eye.—The law of sacred gentleness in the service of Christ.—The true sacrificial fire of self-denial and self-mortification, in relation to the fiery flame of hell: 1. The relation: all must be salted with fire. 2. The contrast: to be prepared for the fire by salt, or to be salted with fire.—We cannot escape the fire; but we have the choice between the fire of life and the fire of death.—Discipline of the Spirit: the fundamental condition of healthy life in the Church: 1. Of the right warfare, 2. of the right peace.—The zeal of Christ the purifying fire for the zeal of His people. —The thundering of men, and the Lord's thunder; or, the exaggeration of little strength, and the mildness of great strength: 1. In their origin: *a.* want of love, want of self-government; *b.* the zeal of love and divine moderation. 2. In their manifestation: *a.* thundering of the cannons, of the bulls, of the curses, scattering sudden and swift destruction; *b.* trumpet-calls to penitence, words of correcting love, alarming and yet not destroying. 3. In their effects: *a.* lost and ended in time; *b.* dispensing blessings for a time, and bringing salvation for eternity.—How Christ, with the anticipating grief of holy love, was inflamed with zeal against all covetous and party frenzy of zeal in His Church.—The alternative of the two fires of history: indifference must be burnt away, either, 1. in the fires of salvation, or, 2. in the fires of judgment.

STARKE:—Doubtless it is our duty to wrest from others their hurtful errors; but we are also bound to bear with them for a while, and give them time to come to a better apprehension.—QUESNEL:—Pride reigns in almost all conditions. Few are content to be placed beneath others; most people are intent only upon getting above their fellows, and mount aloft.—*Nova. Bibl. Tub.*:—Alas, how many will stand before Him with shame and fear, when Christ shall demand an account of all the useless and sinful contentions which they have mutually indulged in!—HEDINGER:—Pride, conceit, ambition, are all utterly out of harmony with the spirit of true Christianity.—LUTHER:—That man has a true nobility who is profoundly humble in heart.—True greatness consists in perfect lowliness.—QUESNEL:—Blessed is it to rest in the arms of the love of Jesus. —It is an honor to receive the great into our house; greater still to receive those who are lacking in all things but the spirit of Christ.—It is a holy work to do good to children, especially to poor and orphan children.—OSIANDER:—The most pious, devoted, and faithful ministers in the Church have their failings.—HEDINGER:—God has a marvellous method in the dispensation of His graces and gifts, and we must not be too ready to reject what is not as yet perfectly pure and flawless, Phil. i. 16.—QUESNEL:—We too often blend our own selves, our prejudices and notions, with the things of God; and our pride uses the honor of His name as a mere cloak.—OSIANDER: —Instead of envying and grudging, we should praise God for the wonderful variety of gifts which He bestows for the common good.—*Bibl. Wirt.*:—God's gifts are not bound to any particular person, or to any particular condition; but He distributes them Himself freely, if He will, to whom He will, and when He will.—CRAMER:—To deal with little children is a delicate matter; we may soon plant either what is good or what is evil in them.—That young people have offences so often thrown in their way is one reason why there is so much wickedness among the adult.—*Bibl. Wirt.*:—To give offence is, in those who hold the office of correction, a threefold sin: 1. They sin themselves; 2. they make others sin; 3. they cannot use their office.—To enter into life halt or lame: his fleshly lusts are as dear to man as one of his members.—CRAMER:—Who can doubt about hell, and the damnation of hell, when Christ has so often repeated and confirmed the truth?—Our foot offends us in two ways: 1. If it goes in evil ways; 2. if it stands still.—QUESNEL:—To be salted with the fire of hell, as an offering to the divine righteousness.—*Bibl. Wirt.*:—If God's word is falsified, or not with all solemnity and earnestness dealt with, there is no other salt for the sinful flesh: it breeds all kinds of corruption, and all kinds of sins have dominion.—CANSTEIN:—Faithful teachers must give all diligence to maintain the integrity of the sound doctrine of the gospel; yet they must avoid all contention, and approve themselves not only true, but also full of love and peace.

LISCO:—In earthly empires power rules; in the kingdom of heaven rules the power of devoted, self-sacrificing, and self-humbling love (ver. 38).—Secret pride was the reason why the disciples so acted

But Jesus is displeased with their conduct; for He would have a love in them that should be ready to love heartily everything in others, wherever seen, that presented anything spiritually congenial.—Jesus rejects and condemns all casting off, shutting out, and repulsion, as unchildlike. The gnawing worm of the evil conscience, and the burning smart of divine wrath, are figures of the eternal destruction which will befall the seducers.—All things, that is, the whole of humanity, must be salted with fire.—GERLACH:—He who is not against you, is with you. Only in things merely external does Jesus include Himself with the disciples in the *we: We* go up to Jerusalem.—But, when internal relations are in question, He does not say *we* and *us*, any more than He says *Our* Father. And for this reason: 1. Because He distinguishes himself from them as sinners; 2. because He identifies himself with them as believers,—the branches united with the vine, John xv. 1.—He who is not with Me, etc. Both words must always be united; so that Christ's disciples must take equal care to instruct the ignorant and to bear with the weak, 1 Thess. v. 14.—BRAUNE:—They had indeed the feeling that this thought was not right in the sight of Christ. Therefore He asks them about it; He gives them opportunity to utter it aloud. And thus their Master makes them sensible how exceedingly improper that thought was.—Earthly, temporal relations, they carried over into their notions of the eternal kingdom of God.—There are indeed distinctions even in the kingdom of God (Peter, John, James); but that He termed Peter the Rock could not at that time have been misunderstood by the Apostles, as He was misunderstood by Catholic Christendom, especially by the whole of the Middle Ages.—At first they kept silence; and when they spoke, it was only through shame. And so it was right. It is not well to be put to shame at death; better is it to come forward and be exposed before God, and the Saviour and His people.—With the unpretending act of receiving a little child, He connects the greatest of all, the receiving God.—With perfect right the disciples of Jesus held their vocation high and precious. But that they supposed their vocation the only channel through which God could reveal His Son in men's hearts, was a great error.—We should be willing to trace and follow out all the threads in others which lead to Christ.—There is such a thing as an internal, though it may be weak, inclination towards Christ, without any external and full fellowship.—The Redeemer undoubtedly had in view those offences which are connected with the teaching office in the Church, when contentions arise, and love, humility, and regard for the little ones are discountenanced. We do not always perceive, or at least sufficiently consider, what great offence and damage may ensue from the neglect of heartfelt humility of poverty of heart and lowliness of spirit.—All that gives offence, and all that takes offence, must alike in the end be abolished and vanish away.—Jesus took no offence, and gave no offence; for God was in Him.—Happy are we if His spirit dwelleth in us.

SCHLEIERMACHER:—(With reference to Matt. xx. 28, and the ministering of Christ.)—He must in spirit descend into the unsaved depths of the human heart: it was needful that He should see how, and in what variety of ways, the most various tempers and spirits might be aided and saved—brought to sink into their own absolute nothingness, in order that they might attain to the new birth in Him.—That was His ministering; and in this sense He says that He—who is the first in the kingdom of heaven, who is all in all, He who is the One supreme over all and in all, He in whom all have all things—is at the same time the servant of all.—The greater the power of Christ in the disciple, and the more that power works through him for the well-being of others, the greater he is in the kingdom of heaven.—To receive God—what greater thing can be conceived!—(The transaction with John.) There is a condition under which the gradual influences of the Spirit best effect their work, and that is undisturbed self-concentration. The more men are excited in reference to external things, the more are their minds closed against higher influences; but when they are in perfect repose, the gentle inspirations of the Divine Spirit have their better effect.

BRIEGER:—Are we to understand the words to mean, that he who burns with desire to be the first should be the last, in order to compass that end? Would any such humility as that possess a value? The Lord could not possibly have intended to say that the being little was a means to becoming great. The "If any man will" is intended rather to show the way in which a man becomes great in the kingdom of God, without willing to be so.—This way is that of self-denial.—Because the Lord from heaven entered into the condition, or assumed the form, of a servant, His Church also must take the same form.—To receive is here indeed a high thing: to take up to Himself.—In reference to ourselves, we have to observe the word "He who is not with Me," etc. In reference to others, we have to observe the word "He that is not against you," etc., that we may judge them in the spirit of Jesus.

GOSSNER:—In the kingdom of humility there is no contention.—The more humble and simple we are, the nearer we are to the Saviour.—The holiest words, without anointing and salt, are good for nothing.—BAUER:—By their ruling we know the great ones of this world; by their serving we know the great ones of the kingdom of heaven.—Where love, the sacred regard for faith however little, is wounded, the retribution of the kingdom of heaven is severe.

PART THIRD

THE Lord's Conflicts and Victories in Peræa. Transit on from the Old Church to the New. The Disciples gathered together for the Passion.

FIRST SECTION.

CARNAL MARRIAGE LEGISLATION OF THE PHARISEES, AND THE SPIRITUAL MARRIAGE LEGISLATION OF THE LORD.

CHAPTER X. 1–12.

(Parallel: Matt. xix. 1-12.)

1 And he arose from thence, and cometh into the coasts of Judea, by [through] the
farther side of Jordan: and the people resort unto him again; and, as he was wont, he
2 taught them again. And the Pharisees came to him, and asked him, Is it lawful for a
3 man to put away *his* wife? tempting him. And he answered and said unto them,
4 What did Moses command you? And they said, Moses suffered to write a bill of di-
5 vorcement, and to put *her* away. And Jesus answered and said unto them, For the
6 hardness of your heart he wrote you this precept: But from the beginning of the crea-
7 tion God made them male and female. For this cause shall a man leave his father and
8 mother, and cleave to his wife; And they twain shall be one flesh: so then they are no
9 more twain, but one flesh. What therefore God hath joined together, let not man put
10 asunder. And in the house his disciples asked him again of the same *matter*
11 And he saith unto them, Whosoever shall put away his wife, and marry another, com-
12 mitteth adultery against her. And if a woman shall put away her husband, and be
married to another, she committeth adultery.

[1] Ver. 1.—The reading of Cod. A. (διὰ τοῦ πέραν, &c.) must not be given up, with Lachmann and Tischendorf (who read καὶ πέραν), on account of B., C.*, L.

[2] Ver. 2.—Elzevir reads οἱ Φαρισαῖοι; but the article is not supported.

[3] Ver. 6.—The ὁ Θεός is wanting in B., C., L., Δ., &c., and omitted by Tischendorf [and Meyer, and bracketed by Lachmann].

[4] Ver. 10.—Περὶ τούτου. Lachmann, Tischendorf, Meyer, following A., B., C.

[5] Ver. 12.—Lachmann and Tischendorf read γαμήσῃ ἄλλον instead of γαμηθῇ ἄλλῳ, following B., C., D., L., Δ.

EXEGETICAL AND CRITICAL.

See the notes on the parallel in *Matthew*, xix.—Christ's abode in Peræa embraces three occurrences: the treatment of the subject of divorce, the bringing of the little children to Jesus, and the rich young man. These transactions all belong, doubtless, to the second abode of Christ in Peræa. We must, according to the connection of the evangelical narratives, assume two residences in Peræa; for we know that Jesus, after the Feast of Tabernacles in the year of persecution 782, returning into Galilee, assembled His disciples there; that with them He journeyed through the boundaries of Galilee and Samaria to Peræa (*see* Luke ix. 51–52, xvii. 11–19; comp. *Leben Jesu*, ii. 2, 1053), appeared then in Jerusalem at the Feast of the dedication, and afterwards returned back to Peræa, John x. 42. That the circumstances related by the Evangelists Matthew and Mark belong to the close of the second abode in Peræa, is manifest from the intimation that the rich young man came to Him as He was on the point of journeying; and the same applies to Matthew's account of the mothers bringing their children. But with this last transaction that concerning divorce was closely connected.—Concerning Peræa, *see* the *Critical Notes* on *Matthew*, as also concerning the *double* residence in Peræa, and the significance of the Peræan narrative in relation to the founding and preparation of the new congregation, the Christian Church.—Christian ecclesiastical regulations begin with regulations for the house: with the Christian legislation, 1. for marriage; 2. for children; 3. for property.

As to the relation of Mark to the Synoptists in the Peræan sections, he and Matthew alone record the matter concerning divorce. Mark states more precisely than Matthew that Jesus penetrated through Peræa to the borders of the land, ver. 1. In Matthew, on the other hand, there is a more definite account given of the first journey of Jesus to Peræa, accompanied by a great train. Matthew says that great multitudes followed Him, and He healed them there. Mark says that the people resorted to Him again (πάλιν, again in Peræa), and that, as He was wont, He taught them again. In the Lord's answer to the tempting question concerning divorce, Mark places first the reference to the Mosaic law of mar riage, and brings in the paradisaical law afterwards: Matthew inverts that order. But it is in harmony with the character of Mark, that he introduces all by the piercing word of decision. The rebuke of the Pharisees is, moreover, made more keen by the fact that he assigns the saying concerning the Christian marriage law (vers. 10–12, compare Matthew ver. 9, ch. v. 32) *to the house* in which Jesus continued His discourse with the disciples on this question. Here also, as often elsewhere, Mark shows that the Lord, after His intercourse with the people, retreated to the house, that is, the inn, where He had been received, for the sake of confidentially continuing His words to the disciples. These are the lesser images of the Lord's greater retreats.—The words that follow were not for the Pharisees. Mark gives the addition, "If a woman shall put away her husband;" but then he omits the conversation between the disciples and the Lord concerning the difficulty of true marriage, "If the case of the man," etc. (Matt. xix. 10–12). In the section about the children (which Luke also has), Mark alone makes it prominent that Jesus was displeased with the disciples. He records, in common with Luke, the saying about not receiving the kingdom of God as a little child. That Jesus here again took the children in His arms and embraced them, as He had done the child in Capernaum, Mark alone mentions. He also makes it more distinctly prominent than Mathew does, ver. 15, that the rich young man came to the Lord on the occasion of His leaving Peræa. Luke alone tells us that the young man was a ruler, probably a ruler of the synagogue. But Mark alone records that, after the declaration "All these have I kept from my youth up," Jesus looked upon him and loved him; as he also later inserts the Lord's approbation of the questioning scribe, ch. xii. 28 *seq*. To him also we owe the striking and vivid trait, that the rich young man put on a gloomy and fallen countenance (στυγνάσας) after the Lord's answer. The amazement of the disciples at the word, "How hardly shall the rich," etc., Mark exhibits as continued and increased, even after the Lord's explanation, "How hard is it for them that trust in riches." In the transaction that followed, between Peter and the Lord, Mark is more express than Luke in recording that Peter only *began* in his confusion to inquire about the reward, and that he did not give full expression to his words. He omits the clause, "What shall we have therefore?" which Matthew inserts. It is very remarkable that Mark omits here again the saying of Jesus concerning the twelve thrones of the Apostles (Matt. ver. 28), even as he had omitted the special prerogatives of Peter. It is obvious to suggest on this point, that the saying about "judging the twelve tribes of Israel" was not so easily intelligible to Gentile Christians (although Luke also has it, ch. xxii. 30). On the other hand, Mark gives the broad and comprehensive promise of the Lord to the disciples who renounce all, and in the most full detail: ver. 30, there is the hundred-fold compensation, houses, and brethren, etc., already in the present life, although amidst persecutions.

Ver. 1. **And He arose from thence.**—In the wider sense, from Galilee; in the narrower sense, from Capernaum, where He gathered together His disciples. — **By the farther side of Jordan.**— That Jesus did not merely come to Peræa, but travelled through Peræa to the borders of Judæa, that is, to the most eastern limits of Peræa, is plain even from the words of Matthew; but is still more plainly declared in the expression here used by Mark. For the whole of Peræa could hardly be described as the borders of Judæa in the wider sense. A whole province of a land can never be merely regarded as its border. On the immediate occasion of this journey to Peræa, *see* on *Matthew, Critical Notes*.— **Again.**—The repeated πάλιν seems to have been employed in consequence of the distinct remembrance of a double abode of Jesus in Peræa. At any rate, the events that follow belong to the second residence.

Ver. 2. **Asked Him.** — Meyer: "Mark omits what Matthew gives, the properly tempting element in the question, κατὰ πᾶσαν αἰτίαν." But, according to the explanation of Ewald (*see Critical Notes* on *Matthew*), the question was a critical and tempting one, even without that addition, because it was dangerous in the territory of Herod Antipas to say any thing against divorce. De Wette supposes that the Pharisees may have been aware of the Saviour's earlier declaration concerning divorce. That may be true; in any case they might very well guess that, on this question, His utterance would perfectly coincide with that of the Baptist. Either, thought they, He must in His answer touch Herod too closely, or the Baptist; that is, He must fall under the condemnation either of worldly power, or of the pious.

Ver. 3. **What did Moses command you?** —The order of the main points is not the same in Mark as in Matthew. Matthew comes down from the paradisaical institute to the Mosaic; Mark, on the contrary, rises from the latter to the former, and moreover makes Jesus Himself put the question concerning the law of Moses, and the tempter give the reply. This seems to have been the natural order. Elsewhere we have it as the first counter-question of Jesus: What is written in the law? (*See* ver. 19, and Luke x. 26.)

Ver. 4. **Moses suffered to write** (*see* Deut. xxiv. 1).—In Matthew we read, Why then did Moses *command* to give a writing of divorcement, and to put her away? and the answer of Jesus: Moses, *because of the hardness of your hearts, suffered* you to put away your wives. And in Mark's account of the Pharisees' words, they give, as in Matthew, a distorted view of the Mosaic law. Moses had *suffered* to divorce, and *restrictingly commanded* that a letter of divorce be given in addition. In Matthew, it is true, the opposition between the design of the Pharisees and the mind of Moses is made more expressly prominent. But in Mark, the opposition is found in the emphatic statement, that Moses wrote this commandment on account of the hardness of their hearts; that is, not in order to divorce, but, with the divorce, to give a *bill* of divorce therewith. The two accounts, in fact, are, as to their results, one and the same. The bill of divorce found divorce existing; it was intended to limit and restrain it, and make it more moral. The man who put away his wife, required the services of a learned scribe in order to construct the bill of divorce; it was necessary that he should give the grounds of the separation, and the ordinance of the lawgiver required those grounds never to be light or trivial. Moreover, there were two cases in which the marriage was indissoluble,— viz., when a man dishonored a virgin, and when he slanderously denied the virginity of his young wife (Deut. xxii. 19, 29). In Mark, also, more weight is attached to the other point of opposition which our Lord brings out: His appealing to the paradisaical ordinance. We must also notice the expression, *wrote this precept*. It refers to a written, restricting law for hardness of heart, in contradistinction to the everlasting and original commandments of paradise: hence the written word is to be interpreted in harmony with these last.

Ver. 7. **For this cause shall a man.**—The words of Adam (Gen. ii. 24) are in Matthew words of God; in Mark, words of Christ. It is all the same; for Adam uttered those words prophetically as a paradisaical, divine, fundamental ordinance. They are words of God, as being eternally valid; and words of Christ, as rules for life to be reëstablished and sanctified. The Futures indicate the necessary realization of the original relation and condition of the sexes in marriage. As it *is* in reality and principle, it must *be* in development. *See Critical Notes* on *Matthew*.

Ver. 10. **And in the house His disciples asked Him.**—Here, as often elsewhere, our Lord, according to Mark's account, retreated, after a public transaction with the people, into the house, where He followed up His public teaching by more confidential instruction. Meyer: "The two Evangelists here differ, as it respects the place, the persons to whom our Lord speaks, and the substance of what He says." He then gives the account of Matthew the preference. But the thought of ver. 11 is already found in the words of ver. 9: What therefore God hath joined together, let not man put asunder. Divorce was by that word forbidden. It is an error to speak of any difference here; all we can say is, that Mark gave a more specific account. And this is strictly in harmony with the circumstances of the case; it was fit that Christ should give His fullest utterance concerning the New Testament law of marriage within the more confidential circle of His disciples.

Ver. 11. **Committeth adultery.**—The marriage contracted with the one is adultery towards the other. Meyer supposes that ἐπ' αὐτήν must mean, "in reference to her," that is, the forsaken woman. But, literally, ἐπ' αὐτήν refers back to the last mentioned. The great point is, that the adultery against the first woman is consummated by marriage with the second, and thus the second marriage is made into adultery. "The μὴ ἐπὶ πορνείᾳ (Matthew) is omitted by Mark. But it makes no difference, as this reason for divorce is self-understood." (Meyer.)

Ver. 12. **And if a woman.**—Meyer denies the genuineness of this added clause. Among the Greeks and Romans it certainly was customary for the woman to be the abandoned party; but not among the Jews, since the examples they furnish—Michal (1 Sam. xxv. 44), Herodias (Matt. xiv. 4), Salome (JOSEPH. *Antiq.* 15, 7, 10)—were preëminent enormities. But he overlooks the fact, that Jesus, according to Mark, here gives His disciples a confidential decree for His new Church, and appoints a new custom which, as did the primitive paradisaical ordinance, goes far beyond the good and ill customs of the Greeks and Romans. It is to be observed that the Herodians introduced amongst the Jewish people laxer customs as it respects woman.

DOCTRINAL AND ETHICAL.

1. *See* on *Matthew*.

2. *For the hardness of your heart.*—This word is in sharp contrast with the sentimental excuses made for breaches of the marriage-vow—such as rest upon the *softness* of the heart, the overpowering emotions of love, etc.

3. *And in the house.*—Confidential household words of Jesus to His disciples, according to Mark: concerning the power of casting out demons, ch. ix. 28; the great in the kingdom of heaven, ch. ix. 33; and here concerning New Testament marriage. In other passages it is solitude generally, or solitude on a mountain, in which Jesus imparts to His disciples the confidential utterances that belong to the future of His new Church, ch. iv. 10, etc. On the other hand, the house of Jesus is often the centre of great assemblages of the people, ch. ii. 1, iii. 20; even the house which Jesus chose for His rest and retirement cannot continue hidden, ch. vii. 24. In the most important crises of His conflict, Jesus turns from official encounters with His opponents to a free exposition of His doctrine to the whole people. So in ch. vii. 14, xii. 36 *seq.* Thus the house of the Redeemer is, on the one hand, the most private, and on the other, the most public, place; always, however, in its most hidden privacy opened and known. And as the Lord, in His method of teaching, passes over from the general announcement of the word into confidential communications to His chosen disciples, so also we perceive that He passes over from dealing with the priests and the officials to a freer application of His words to all the people. In the former case He regulates His teaching according to their *being able to hear* His words; in the latter, according to their *being willing*. The doctrine of Christ is the most secret and the most public: the great and utterable mystery.

4. Not only does monogamy generally lie at the foundation of this passage, but also the idea of the true ideal monogamy, which is constituted not so much by the union of two human "exemplars" as rather by the blending of two human personalities (ἄρσεν καὶ θῆλυ), which are to each other similar to what (we do not say the same that) Adam and Eve were created to be to each other.

5. 1 Cor. vii.: The Pauline development of the Christian marriage-law with reference to mixed marriages.

HOMILETICAL AND PRACTICAL.

See on *Matthew*.—Jesus pressed on all sides to the limits of His land; or, Jesus within the limitations of His earthly vocation: 1. Sacredly observing the legal restrictions; 2. extending to them, touching them; 3. going beyond them in His spiritual life and work (endlessly towards north, east, south, west).—The Lord in Peræa provides beforehand for His Church: 1. He confirms and establishes that which is the fundamental condition of its establishment (the Christian household); 2. in this place He prepares a refuge and hiding-place for the future of His persecuted people.—Peræa the last refuge of the Redeemer; the first refuge of His Church.—The pilgrimages of Christians to Christ: 1. As they spring from impulse of heart, not human traditions; 2. the life of the Spirit, and not spiritual chains; 3. movements towards the true rest, and the true rest in movement (that is, on the one hand, not the running without an object, and, on the other hand, not frigid form).—How the Lord for ever refers the tempters to the word of God.—How He glorifies Moses: 1. As an expositor of the creation; 2. as a prophet of redemption.—How Christ confirms the unison between the old and the new covenants.—Moses wrote his law for sinners; or, the finite side of the written law of God in its changeableness, explained by the finite nature of the fallen child of God.—God, even in the external changeableness of His revelations, confirms His own unchangeable character. — The dignity of marriage measured by the dignity of filial piety (of the relation to father and mother).—In order to true marriage according to the mind of Christ, more than a man and a woman is wanting.—From the right of the husband follows necessarily the right of the wife; as from the obligation of the one follows the obligation of the other.—Concerning the contrast and the reconciliation between the laws of the State and the eternal, fundamental laws of the Church of Christ.— The reciprocal influence of the punishment of death and the divorce appointed in the Jewish law: 1. Ecclesiastically: an actual adultery is spiritual death, and death as to moral fellowship; 2. an inexorable prohibition of all divorce, on civil or ecclesiastical grounds, leads to death in many ways, even to the death of the higher moral family life (*see* the South American and other Catholic states); 3. the reference to spiritual death in adulterous sin must remove and heal the deadly influences of both lax and over-severe marriage ordinances.

The three sections together.—The Christian household 1. in relation to marriage, 2. the children, 3. the property, 4. the vocation of the members to walk according to God's will, and to deny themselves.

STARKE:—*Nova Bibl. Tub.*:—Envy is soon found in the track of a teacher who has a large body of dependants.—QUESNEL:—A true preacher is not soon weary.—Every age has its Pharisees, whom the devil often uses for the temptation of pastors, and whom God permits to test His people.—OSIANDER:—We must take care what answers we make when questions are put to us on doubtful matters; for many ask questions, not that they may learn, but that they may have something to blaspheme or except against.—QUESNEL:—The bond of marriage is a figure of the union of Christ with His bride, the Church; which He will never renounce, even as she will never be separated from Christ, Eph. v. 32.

SCHLEIERMACHER:—And thus we have here an example of the manner in which the Lord administered discipline in relation to the high and mighty ones of the earth. He was not moved by the fact that Herod was an example of the sin; nor did He present the matter in the slightest degree otherwise than it was, because a person was affected in whose land and in whose power He Himself then stood.—It was of the essence of the old covenant, if we go back to the legislation and lawgiver of the Jewish Church, that the divine law and the civil law were one and the same. The civil and political ordinances must be regulated by the condition of men at the time.—The civil law in relation to the actions of men, and the divine law, which utters the laws of conscience (in Christendom), distinguished. — The levity and impure motives which too often enter into marriage contracts.—Therefore we should regard it as a public evil, that such marriages are often contracted as should never be contracted.—Marriages are matters of public concernment.

BRIEGER:—Man must take his right place in the sight of God before he can take his right place in respect to his fellow-men, whether as husband, father, etc.— GOSSNER:— Alas! when we look round upon the condition of Christendom, and observe all the laws, usages, and customs which prevail, touching how many things must we say, *In the beginning it was not so!*—BAUER:—We may here again see how surely the man who stands firm to God's word shall escape the most cunning snares that his most cunning enemies may lay for him.

SECOND SECTION.

THE RABBINICAL (BAPTIST) HOUSEHOLD DISCIPLINE OF THE DISCIPLES; AND THE THEOCRATIC AND NEW TESTAMENT HOUSEHOLD DISCIPLINE OF THE LORD.

CHAPTER X. 13–16.

(Parallels: Matt. xix. 13–15; Luke xviii. 15–17.)

13 And they brought young children to him, that he should touch them; and *his* dis-
14 ciples rebuked those that brought *them*. But when Jesus saw *it*, he was much dis-
pleased, and said unto them, Suffer the little children to come unto me, and[1] forbid them
15 not: for of such is the kingdom of God. Verily I say unto you, Whosoever shall not
16 receive the kingdom of God as a little child, he shall not enter therein. And he took
them up in his arms, and put *his* hands upon them, and blessed[2] them.

[1] Ver. 14.—*And* forbid them not. The καί is wanting in many documents.
[2] Ver. 16.—Κατευλόγει. Tischendorf, after B., C., L., Δ., and before τιθείς.

EXEGETICAL AND CRITICAL.

See on the parallels of *Matthew* and *Luke*.

Ver. 13. **That He should touch them.**—The modest form of request, as in Luke, not necessarily the expression of a superstitious notion of magical influence resulting from it. Matthew tells us that imposition of hands was what was meant.

Ver. 14. **He was displeased.**—This feature is peculiar to Mark. Displeasure against displeasure: the displeasure of the Master against the displeasure of the disciples; or, indeed, the displeasure of the Church, which believes in the blessing of children in Abraham and in Christ, against Separatism.

Ver. 15. **Whosoever shall not receive the kingdom of God.**—The same rebuking sentence in Luke: comp. Matt. xviii. 3. A man must first have received the kingdom of God into his heart if he would gain admission into the kingdom of God. *See* Matt. v. 3, 10; John iii. 3.—The kingdom of God, which a man may receive, is Christ as the personal kingdom of God, with His salvation in His word (hence Theophylact is right, in a certain qualified sense, when he explains it of the preaching of the Gospel); the kingdom of God, into which a man is received, is the heavenly society and Church of Christ's kingdom. The kingdom, as a principle in the heart, is unfolded and developed into the fellowship of the kingdom of Christ's manifestation.—**As a little child.**—In that spiritual condition which the child, in unconscious symbolism, represents by its disposition. And yet the Lord welcomes the little children not as mere figures of the poor in spirit and of simple believers. The symbol is inseparably connected with the reality: the child and the believer are one. In the childlikeness there is present the typical precondition of faith; that is, a germ of susceptibility which the word of God will fructify.

Ver. 16. **He took them up in his arms.**—Abundant answer to the prayers of pious mothers. He was expected only to touch them; He took them up in His arms, laid His hands upon them, and blessed them. Moreover, He made them a type to the disciples and adults.

DOCTRINAL AND ETHICAL.

1. *See* on the parallel passages of *Matthew* and *Luke*, as also the previous notes.

2. The blessings which Christ has brought into the world of little children. Jesus Himself is the proper Protector (patron and saint) of children: not the archangel Michael, not St. Nicolas, not St. Martin; although, as under the Lord, all angels and saints are appointed to love, guard, and minister to children.—We read twice of our Lord's taking to His arms or embracing: in both instances children were the objects.

3. The disciples, infected with the rabbinical zeal for inquiry concerning the laws of marriage, would not have the Lord interrupted by their coming. Jesus, on the other hand, regards the children themselves as the final word concerning the question of marriage.

4. We have no definite account of any ordination of the Apostles by the laying on of Christ's hands; but we do read of a laying on of hands upon children, and consequently of their ordination to the kingdom of heaven.

HOMILETICAL AND PRACTICAL.

See on *Matthew*.—How pious women here understood the Lord better than His apostolical disciples did; and why? 1. The fact. Similar examples: Mary in Bethany; the believing announcers of the Risen Lord. 2. Why? Because themselves nearer to children, and better acquainted with childhood and the childlike nature.—The disciples on the byeway of rabbinical ostentation called back by the Lord to true simplicity.—The sign of rising pedantry: offence at sound life in its most innocent and beautiful forms and expressions.—How often the high school in its pride has oppressed the true schools of life; especially, 1. the school of children, and 2. the school of childlikeness, or of simple faith.—What it signifies, that the Lord demanded childlikeness almost as often as repentance and faith, in order to entrance into the kingdom of heaven: 1. Repentance and faith must have the stamp of childlikeness; 2. true childlikeness is penitent and full of faith.—The cry of the Lord through all ages, Suffer the children to come unto Me, etc.— Jesus the Friend of children.—The great Friend of the little ones: the Founder of infant baptism, infant schools, infant catechising, and of all good institutions that care for children.—The Son of Man among the children of men: 1. As the heavenly new and fresh related to the earthly new and fresh; 2. as the humble One to the artless; 3. as the Prince of faith to the confiding ones; 4. as the great Warrior to the strivers; 5. as the great Hope to the hoping; 6. as the Blessed with the happy.—Christ embraced the children: 1. The fact: *a.* an act of God, *b.* an act of Christ, *c.* an act of holy humanity. 2. A sign of judgment: *a.* for the childhood-hating kingdom of darkness, *b.* for the children-despising proud world, *c.* for Christendom still too little childlike.

STARKE:—*Nova Bibl. Tub.*:—Alas! how many Christians are there who bring their children, not to Christ, but to the devil! who hinder them from entering the kingdom of heaven by their bad example, etc.!—QUESNEL:—Nothing is so precious to God as true simplicity.—All blessings come from the hand of the Lord Jesus.

BRAUNE:—The Lord, who is so gracious to the fruits (the children), is not less so to the tree (marriage).—Klopstock, in the "Messiah," brings many souls of children, before they are conducted by angels into human bodies, to the cross of Christ, in order that they may receive a deep impression of it, such as will fit them afterwards to receive the doctrine of the Crucified.—The source of our life lies beyond any investigation of ours.—Be only a child, that thou mayest be able to become a child of God.—Christ's embracing and laying on of His hands, and blessing, is a gracious figure of the love of God, which works upon us and for us long before we know anything about it.—GERLACH:—Children, to whom the feeling of helplessness and simplicity is rendered easier by their natural weakness and inexperience, enter most easily into the kingdom of God.—LISCO:—To us all, a regeneration for the kingdom of God is necessary.

SCHLEIERMACHER:—We should know that a future is coming after us, when the light of the Gospel will shine more clearly.—It is the proper nature of a child to live altogether and absolutely in the present. What the present moment brings, it receives with simplicity and joy; the past vanishes from its vision, of the future it knows nothing, and every passing instant suffices for the happiness of its innocent nature.—(Here simplicity merely is painted.)—GOSSNER:—The greatest condescends to the least. Oh, how dear to Christ is man!

THIRD SECTION.

THE WORLD'S RICHES, AND THE HOLY POVERTY OF BELIEVERS.

CHAPTER X. 17–31.

(Parallels: Matt. xix. 16—xx. 16; Luke xviii. 18–30.)

17 And when he was gone forth into the way [to Judea, *i. e.*], there came one running,
and kneeled to him, and asked him, Good Master, what shall I do that I may inherit
18 eternal life? And Jesus said unto him, Why callest thou me good? *there is* none good
19 but one, *that is*, God. Thou knowest the commandments, Do not commit adultery, Do
not kill, Do not steal, Do not bear false witness, Defraud not, Honour thy father and
20 mother. And he answered and said unto him, Master, all these have I observed from
21 my youth. Then Jesus, beholding him, loved him, and said unto him, One thing thou
lackest: go thy way, sell whatsoever thou hast; and give to the poor, and thou shalt
22 have treasure in heaven; and come, and take up the cross,[1] and follow me. And he
23 was sad at that saying, and went away grieved: for he had great possessions. And
Jesus looked round about, and saith unto his disciples, How hardly shall they that have
24 riches enter into the kingdom of God! And the disciples were astonished at his words.
But Jesus answereth again, and saith unto them, Children, how hard is it for them that
25 trust in riches to enter into the kingdom of God! It is easier for a camel to go through
26 the eye of a needle, than for a rich man to enter into the kingdom of God. And they
were astonished out of measure, saying among themselves, Who then can be saved?
27 And Jesus, looking upon them, saith, With men *it is* impossible, but not with God:
28 for with God all things are possible. Then Peter began to say unto him, Lo, we have
29 left all, and have followed thee. And Jesus answered and said, Verily I say unto you,
There is no man that hath left house, or brethren, or sisters, or father, or mother,[2] or
30 wife, or children, or lands, for my sake, and the gospel's, But he shall receive an hun-
dred-fold now in this time, houses, and brethren, and sisters, and mothers,[3] and children,
31 and lands, with persecutions; and in the world to come eternal life. But many *that are*
first shall be last; and the last first.

[1] Ver. 21.—The omission of the words *ἄρας τὸν σταυρόν* in B., C., D., Δ., [Vulgate,] is not decisive.
[2] Ver. 29.—According to B., C., Δ., [Lachmann, Tischendorf,] the mother comes first. The transposition is explained by the fact of the more usual order. *See* Meyer.
[3] Ver. 30.—The Sing. *μητέρα* [Lachmann] is a correction. Fritzsche places first *καὶ πατέρα*, which is not sufficiently supported, and, like the *καὶ γυναῖκα* afterwards, came from ver. 23.

EXEGETICAL AND CRITICAL.

See the parallels on *Matthew* and *Luke*.

Ver. 17. **And when He was gone forth into the way.**—This can mean no other than the final departure from Peræa to Jerusalem; and therefore, primarily, the journey to Bethany for the raising of Lazarus. It was the time between the last Feast of Dedication in the winter, when the Jews would have stoned Jesus, and the Passover in the spring (783). *See* John xi.—**There came one running, and kneeled to Him.**—The two words are the more emphatic, inasmuch as he who thus hastened and knelt was a distinguished man, and a head of the synagogue. These clear and realizing traits are peculiar to Mark.

Ver. 18. **Why callest thou Me good?**—As to the various acceptations of this expression, *see* on *Matthew* xix. 16, 17. According to the strongly supported reading of Matthew, Jesus leads the young man up to God, the source of all good, from the question, "What good thing shall I do?" but, according to Mark and Luke, from the appeal, "Good Master!" Both agree very well together. "Good Master, what good thing must I do?" runs the question; the answer is, "How divided and isolated seems to thee what is good! One is the good *Being*, and in this One is *good*." Jesus does not decline the appellation "good;" He repels it only in the superficial sense of the questioner. The young man deals with good in its relative meaning; and in this sense he says "Good," that is, "Excellent" Master. Jesus teaches him to apprehend good in its absoluteness; and to that end he must understand the being good, which he ascribes to Christ, as being founded in God. Thus the answer is not to be explained deistically, but christologically: If thou wouldst call Me good, thou must apprehend My unity with God, and My divine nature. Meyer insists that it is the contrast between the divine perfection, and the human development in Jesus (which he confounds with limitation), that is meant, and he terms the explanation that has been current since Augustine, a dogmatic misinterpretation. That term may better be applied to his own notion of Christ's *relative* sinlessness, and his own confusion between development and limitation.

Ver. 19. **Defraud not,** *μὴ ἀποστερήσῃς*.—The *ἀποστερεῖν* may mean rob or defraud, and also withhold. De Wette translates it as the former, Meyer as the latter; but in both cases half the meaning is lost. We have only to choose between several expressions: take advantage, withhold, defraud, do wrong. We prefer the last, because of its comprehensive and strong meaning; and hold that the ἀποστερεῖν comprises or comprehends all the preceding ten commandments (Beza), and at the same time explains the tenth (Bengel, Wetstein, Olshausen). Meyer thinks, on the contrary, that the specific commandment of Deut. xxiv. 14, οὐκ ἀποστερήσεις μισθὸν πένητος, is meant. But it is impossible that the Lord's summing up of the precepts should have issued in such a speciality, which moreover falls under the commandment, Thou shalt not steal. When taken in its comprehensive meaning, the words present a more concrete expression of the final sentence of Matthew, "Thou shalt love thy neighbor as thyself." Or, in other words, it signifies, Thou shalt not feel and act selfishly or egoistically (giving is better than receiving). In this case, the entire quotation of the commandments concurs with that of Matthew, only that in Mark the words, "Honor thy father and mother," are placed at the end. The last expression in Mark is keen, and comes at the end, because its pungent point was best adapted to touch the conscience of a rich man. Luke has omitted the parallel sayings—"Defraud not," and "Thou shalt love thy neighbor as thyself"—probably on account of the uncertainty of the tradition.

Ver. 20. **Master.**—This time not "Good Master."

Ver. 21. **Beholding him, loved him**; for He penetrated his inmost being and nature: exhibiting an honest striving, notwithstanding the self-righteousness in which he is involved. The ἠγάπησεν does not refer to His speaking to the young man in an affectionate manner, as Grotius and others thought.—**One thing thou lackest,** ἕν σοι ὑστερεῖ.—It is observable that in Matthew we find the word in a question of the man himself: τί ἔτι ὑστερῶ;—evidence that the Apostles drew freely from an abundant and never-ceasing fountain of objective original remembrances of their own, and traditions handed down to them.

Ver. 22. **And he was sad.**—Rather, he stood confounded, ὁ δὲ στυγνάσας. The verb occurs again only in the Septuagint of Ezekiel. In Ezek. xxvii. 35, it is the translation of שָׁמֵם, to be astonished and confounded: properly, to stand in silent, amazed confusion. The expression at the same time denotes the being or appearing to be bewildered. It likewise denotes a sad and downcast state; and this is contained in the word στυγνάζειν.

Ver. 23. **And Jesus looked round about.**—The "looking upon" of Jesus, vers. 21 and 27, and His "looking round," ver. 23—both observable. Comp. ch. iii. 5; ver. 34; ch. viii. 33; Luke vi. 10; xxii. 61.—**They that have riches:** οἱ τὰ χρήματα ἔχοντες.

Ver. 24. **Children, how hard is it for them that trust in riches.**—Tranquillizing and explanatory. The whole discourse is of trusting in riches. But a severer word follows: *It is easier for a camel*, etc.; meaning, that it is infinitely hard to separate the trusting in riches from the possession of riches. The decisive explanation of the whole hard doctrine is found in ver. 27. A miracle of the grace of God can alone solve this dread mystery.

Ver. 28. **Then Peter began.**—It is evident that the "beginning" signifies a venturesome interruption, or taking up the word (comp. ch. viii. 31, 32), followed by embarrassment. According to Mark, Peter himself seems here to have broken off in inward confusion, or at the suggestion of modesty.

Ver. 29. **There is no man that hath left.—Hath forsaken,** ἀφῆκεν. Meyer, correctly: "In case he shall not have received; that is, if the latter is not found the case, it is through the absence of the former. The hundredfold compensation is so certain, that its not having been received presupposes the not having forsaken. Precisely similar is the force and connection of the thought in Luke iv. 22." But it is at the same time positively declared that the ideal receiving of the new possessions in the kingdom of heaven is simultaneous with the renunciation of the old possessions; or even that it is the preparatory condition on which that forsaking depends.

Ver. 30. **Now in this time, and in the world to come.**—The compensating retribution in this world and the other definitely distinguished. So also in Luke. The number in hundredfold is manifestly symbolical, as the expression of an immeasurable advantage. The spiritual nature of the new connections is evident from this, that they do not include the father or the wife. The hospitable houses of friends, Christian brethren and sisters, spiritual mothers, spiritual children, lands, and fields, and ecclesiastical possessions.—**With persecutions.**—That is, not merely in the midst of persecutions and in spite of them: the persecutions are rather part of our best possessions. *See* Matt. v. 12; Rom. v. 3; Jas. i. 2, 4; 1 Pet. i. 6; Heb. xii. 6.—**Eternal life.**—The everlasting, all-embracing unity, consummation, fulness, and depth of all-compensating retribution.

DOCTRINAL AND ETHICAL.

1. *See* on the parallel of *Matthew*.

2. *Jesus looked upon him, and loved him.*—Even after so self-righteous a declaration. Evidently our Lord sees through the features of the self-righteous his inmost nature; and distinguishes that which is a mistaken effort of the soul from that which is a corrupt self-deception, that which is based upon ignorance from that which is based upon hypocrisy. But this man was not thoroughly self-righteous; for he had a lively conviction that something important was wanting to him; and he did not hesitate, disdaining all Jewish conventional notions of propriety and dignity, to cast himself at the Lord's feet, and utter the anxious question of his heart.

3. *Those who trust in riches.*—The explanatory word is peculiar to Mark. Because it is so hard to have riches without coming to regard them as the one thing; to possess much without being altogether possessed by the possession: therefore, with man it is, generally speaking, a thing impossible that the rich should be saved; but the grace of God makes it possible through the miracle of the new birth. Clemens Alexandrinus: τίς ὁ σωζόμενος πλούσιος;

4. It is very observable that Mark, and therefore also Peter, in quoting the words concerning spiritual compensation, speaks indeed of the substitution of spiritual mothers for an earthly mother, but does not set a spiritual father or spiritual fathers over against the earthly father. The reading which places the word *father* here before the word *mother*, has but little support, and is manifestly exegetical. The Singular *mother*, in opposition to the Plural *mothers* is strongly authenticated, and should be preferred.

HOMILETICAL AND PRACTICAL.

See on *Matthew*.—The unsatisfactory encounter of the rich young man in its contrasts: 1. He runs to Jesus enthusiastically, he leaves Him in sorrow; 2. without reflecting, he throws himself at the Lord's feet, but he scorns reflectingly His advice; 3. he comes with the consciousness of his lack, but goes away with the consciousness of slavery and guilt.—How much depends upon the right use of words!—Christ sanctifies our greetings.—Truth is the salt of courtesy, which makes the difference between it and false compliment.—All commandments converge to the one saying: Thou shalt not covet (that is, thou shalt not deal selfishly or egotistically).—How the Lord entered into the legal notion of the rich young man, in order to lead him in the way of perfect knowledge of the law over into the way of evangelical repentance.—Jesus looked upon him and loved him: 1. A somewhat surprising fact (after he had made such a revelation of himself); 2. a very significant one (Jesus looks through the error and the confusion into the secret better impulse, the drawing of the Spirit); 3. a warning fact also (that we should not regard as the final judgment those humbling tests which the Lord applies to beginners).—The poverty of the rich, and the riches of the poor.—Trust in perishable possessions, the fundamental evil of the carnally-minded: 1. The vain image of a false blessedness; 2. the decisive hindrance to the attainment of true blessedness.—Only by a miracle of God can man be saved.—The hundredfold gain of a man who renounces for the sake of God this world's gain.—The persecution of a believer one of his best possessions in this life.—The simple gain of eternal life is infinitely greater than the hundredfold gain of the blessings of this life.—Persecutions are among the possessions of the kingdom of heaven: 1. A lessening of them; 2. an increase of them; 3. a consummating of them.—Christ the perfect example of the promise which He gave to the disciples: His people sacrificed, hundreds of peoples won; His life sacrificed, infinite life won; earth, etc., renounced, heaven with all its worlds won.—Paul also a very illustrious example.

Starke:—Quesnel:—Christ alone can show us the way to heaven, because He Himself is the way.—Osiander:—Men do not thoroughly know their own wicked and perverted nature; hence they fall into the folly of seeking to be saved by their works.—Quesnel:—If we would pray aright, we must be perfectly convinced of our misery, and know that, because God is the perfect fulness of all that is good, we can only by Him be made good ourselves.—The law of God is the rule of our conduct.—Hedinger:—The external in the law is the least matter: an honest heathen may make his boast on that point.—Osiander:—There are few to be found who really prefer heavenly to earthly treasures.—Quesnel:—That we possess with undue satisfaction, which we cannot without smarting renounce. Let every one apply to himself this test.—Who can regard riches as an advantage, when they stand in the way of salvation?—To how many are these riches their greatest misfortune!—Canstein:—Riches may be possessed without the possessor's trusting in them; and then they are neither sinful nor hurtful. Rich men, who rightly use their riches, may become very rich towards God.—The rules of Christianity make many things superfluous, but we must not qualify or alter them.—Salvation we must not regard as a matter so very simple and easy. Strive to enter in at the strait gate, etc.—To a sinner who experiences all his impotence, there is nothing more comforting than to know that God is greater than his heart, 1 John iii. 20.—Thou forsakest much, when thou not only forsakest all things in thy mind and spirit, but also forsakest the thought of any merit, and the hope of any reward.—Quesnel:—It is a small thing to leave earthly possessions; for they are another's, and, strictly speaking, not our own. But we must forsake our own will and our own flesh, and sacrifice them unto God by crucifixion or mortification, Gal. v. 24.—Cramer:—Hast thou at once done much and suffered much? Then do not exalt thyself, on that account, above others; for thou art bound to do and to suffer all this and more.—What they lost in Judaism as friends, they would find again among the converted Gentiles.—Canstein:—Let go for Christ's sake what is taken from thee in persecution; and be fully assured that all will be abundantly given back to thee again. And at length thou hast the treasure of all treasures for thine own—eternal life.—Cramer:—It is among true Christians as among racers for a prize: where one now goes in advance, then falls back, and then again goes forward. Let every one so run as to obtain, 1 Cor. ix. 24.

Gerlach:—The perpetual recurrence of wavering in the carnally-minded between the kingdom of heaven and the world. He feels himself, *a.* attracted by both, *b.* by both repelled.—He thinks, in his folly, that there must be some profound utterance beyond the commandments of God, which shall reconcile God and the world without. (Does not this last idea hold good, in a sacred sense, of the Gospel?) Nothing can be done without decision.—Braune:—"What is good? That which makes itself common, communicates itself (or devotes itself to the life of others). Him we call a good man, who is common and useful. God is the most common and self-communicating of all: He gives himself to all things. Nothing created gives itself. The sun gives only its rays, but keeps back itself; but God gives himself in all His gifts. His Godhead hangs upon this, that He communicates himself to all things that are capable of receiving His goodness."—Master Eckhart:—In Christ, who is entirely for the use and benefit of all, God's Spirit is without measure.—Why does not Jesus suggest to the questioner the commandments of the first table? These all were contained in the words, God is good. And the duties to our neighbor were best fitted to aid the blinded mind in looking into his heart and life, Luke xii. 33; xiv. 33.—(Trusting in riches):—There are poor people also, who with difficulty enter into the kingdom of heaven, because they put too much trust in money. Thus it is the spirit and temper—relying too much upon this world's goods for happiness, whether possessing or not possessing much, whether rich or poor—that makes that entrance hard, Rom. viii. 17.—For Christ's sake, and the Gospel's, that must be given up which is given up; else it is not seed, and the promised harvest can therefore never be reaped.

Schleiermacher:—When thou askest what is really good, and what thou must do as being good, thou shouldst reflect that thou canst do absolutely nothing of thyself (and knowest nothing of thyself), and that God alone can give the power to do or think anything good.—Why did the Redeemer love the young man? On account of unprejudiced and simple words, his earnest aim, and the fidelity with which he followed his conviction and views, albeit these were limited.—And if at this crisis he did not sustain the test, yet we see that the sympathy which the Lord manifested was so entirely without displeasure, that the young man must have been filled with hope, etc.—The heart should never hang upon worldly possessions, as sufficing to impart earthly satisfaction; but we should always regard them as one part of those gifts, for the use of which we must give a strict account.—It was a laudable purpose of the Apostle to clear up for himself and for others, by an express declaration of the Redeemer, the important matter of a reward for the good, and punishment for the evil:—it was not therefore the common desire for reward.—The nature of Christian love consists in this, that the spiritual bond assumes altogether the form of the natural (brothers, sisters).—So long as we find ourselves entangled in the endeavor to prove that there is any value in ourselves, we are liable to be put to the shame of experiencing that those who would be first become the last; and inversely we shall find that the Spirit of God often prepares for Himself His instruments in profound secrecy.—BRIEGER:—All the impediments must be removed, but following was the great thing.—GOSSNER:—When self-love breathes upon the mirror of the law, that mirror becomes obscured or falsified: instead of detecting his own ugliness there, a man finds himself beautiful.—The answer of Jesus was designed to reveal to him the depths of his own heart.—BAUER:—A man must give up, not only his riches, but also himself.

FOURTH SECTION.

THE ASSEMBLING OF THE DISCIPLES ON THE WAY TO THE CROSS.

CHAPTER X. 32–34.

(Parallels: Matt. xx. 17-19; Luke xviii. 31-34; John xi. 53-57.)

32 And they were in the way going up to Jerusalem; and Jesus went before them:
and they were amazed; and as they followed,[1] they were afraid. And he took again
33 the twelve, and began to tell them what things should happen unto him, *Saying*, Behold, we go up to Jerusalem; and the Son of man shall be delivered unto the chief
priests, and unto the scribes; and they shall condemn him to death, and shall deliver
34 him to the Gentiles: And they shall mock him, and shall scourge him, and shall spit
upon him,[2] and shall kill him; and the third day he shall rise again.

[1] Ver. 32.—Meyer adopts the reading οἱ δὲ ἀκολοθοῦντες, after B. and others. So Ewald. Cod. C. reads καὶ οἱ, which dentifies those "following" as the disciples.

[2] Ver. 34.—The spitting connected with the mocking in B., C., L., Δ., [Lachmann, Tischendorf,] may be explained by exegetical motives. B., C., L., Δ. read μετὰ τρεῖς ἡμέρας, Lachmann, Tischendorf. Probably this was introduced to conform it with ch. viii. 31, ix. 31.

EXEGETICAL AND CRITICAL.

See on the parallels of *Matthew* and *Luke*. Comp. also the observations in the Introduction to Mark.—Our Evangelist here brings into clear prominence a critical period in the history of our Lord, concerning which John has given us the most exact account. For there can be no doubt that the narrative has to do with the last retreat of the Redeemer into the town and desert of Ephraim, where He prepared Himself, and collected His disciples for the last journey to Jerusalem (*see* John xi. 53; *Leben Jesu*, ii. 2). We hear their tone of mind expressed on the occasion of the departure of Jesus from Peræa in order to raise Lazarus. In the spring of the year 783 (P. U. C.), Jesus went from Peræa to Bethany, and raised Lazarus from the dead; He then, because the Sanhedrim had laid Him under excommunication, and decreed that He should die, retreated back into the desert of Ephraim. That desert, eastwards from Bethel, extends towards the desert of Quarantania, between Jerusalem and Jericho. (*See* for particulars, ROBINSON, ii. 353.) The last abode of Jesus in the wilderness, His last retreat in this world, forms a counterpart and contrast to His abode in the wilderness after His baptism. In the former, it was necessary for Him to decide on going amongst the people as it were without a name, in order that He might avoid the *Messiahship*, as it had become an idea grossly perverted into a mere watchword of deception; but now He must decide to yield Himself up to the people, according to the true and purified idea of the Messiah, which He had in the whole tenor of His holy life re-established amongst them. This was the great task that He now contemplated; and Matthew himself points to it also. He took His disciples κατ' ἰδίαν ἐν τῷ ὁδῷ, and gave them the last and most express preannouncement of His passion. Luke gives the faintest record of the crisis: παραλαβὼν—ἰδοὺ, ἀναβαίνομεν. But Mark describes, first, the great confusion and terror with which the disciples regarded the final catastrophe, and how they followed their Master not without much fear. This expression, ἀκολουθοῦντες ἐφοβοῦντο, is stronger, in consequence of the seeming inversion of the participle and the Past tense. It indicates a wavering, and a danger of being scattered abroad, which Jesus prevented by the παραλαβὼν πάλιν. We therefore understand it thus, that this morbid depression, which the Lord contended against, was followed by a new and more mighty impulse of excitement, that found its expression in the immediately following appeal of the two sons of Zebedee. Mark is most copious in the prediction of the passion, and presents it to us in simple active propositions in the Future. Matthew lays the main stress on Jesus' being delivered over to the Gentiles: He is delivered up, betrayed to mockery, to scourging, and to crucifixion. Luke makes Christ's person the central-point, and records what He would suffer and encounter. Mark depicts the double betrayal in its vividly apprehended consequences; and the word of Matthew respecting the crucifixion he divides into two parts: they will spit upon Him, and they will kill Him. Luke gives prominence, moreover, to the fact, that Jesus declared at the beginning that the Scriptures must be fulfilled; and lays stress at the end on the circumstance, that the disciples could not and would not understand His prediction.

Ver. 32. **And as they followed, they were afraid.**—Meyer prefers the reading, *οἱ δὲ ἀκολ. ἐφοβοῦντο*, which would give this meaning: The greater number of the disciples held back in astonishment and confusion; those who followed Jesus, who advanced before them, followed Him only with great fear. We agree with Meyer so far as this, that the crisis was a very special one; but his reading makes it too emphatic. It is a reading not sufficiently supported; and, moreover, we have no sign in John that at that time many of the disciples left the Lord. If any are disposed to think that about this time the thought of betraying the Lord entered the soul of Judas as a germ, yet it must be remembered that there was no development of it until the subsequent feast in Bethany, and that it was not a fixed decision until the Passover. An express contrast between those who now left the Lord, and those who followed Him in fear, would have been expressed in stronger terms: as, for instance, at that earlier crisis, after the declaration of Jesus in the synagogue of Capernaum, John vi. 66. The fact that the sentence of death was now uttered against our Lord (John xi. 45), might indeed make some of those who reverenced Jesus waver and apostatize. But how decidedly His genuine disciples still put faith in Him and His cause, is proved by the subsequent palm-entry into Jerusalem, as well as by the circumstance, which Luke prominently mentions, that the disciples did not thoroughly lay to heart and believe the announcement which Jesus had made concerning His own death.—**And He took again the Twelve.**—*See* John's statement, ch. xi. 7 *seq.*, and ver. 54.—**And began.**—The expression intimates that a series of new and decisive explanations took place (comp. ch. viii. 31, ix. 22). These consisted in, 1. The decision of the time. He had first declared that He must suffer death generally (*ὅτι δεῖ*), and that it was near at hand (*μέλλει* in Matthew and Luke; in Mark expressed by the Present *παραδίδοται*): He now declares more expressly that all this would take place at the coming journey to the feast (*ἀναβαίνομεν*, etc., *καὶ ὁ υἱός*). 2. In the more precise statement of the form of suffering: *a.* the being rejected generally (ch. viii. 31); *b.* the betrayal, and the delivering up by the Jews to the Gentiles (ch. ix. 12, 31); *c.* the great double betrayal,—the first betrayal, or the delivering up to the high priests, coming in our passage into marked prominence. 3. In the more precise definition of the critical elements of the passion, especially His execution by the hands of the Gentiles, Matthew expressly mentions the crucifixion, while in Mark and Luke it is plainly hinted at. Compare the *Critical Notes* on the parallel place in *Matthew*.

Ver. 34. **And they shall mock Him.**—The text does not require us, with Meyer, to limit this verb and that which follows to the Gentiles. Why should they be omitted who were the original movers of the whole, and who gave it their continual aid? Compare Matthew and Luke.

DOCTRINAL AND ETHICAL.

1. *See* on the parallel of *Matthew*.

2. Here again, as in many other passages, Mark goes beyond the other Synoptists, and decidedly approximates to John; and the account of the last Evangelist concerning the final abode of Jesus in the wilderness of Ephraim is made more plain by the circumstances given here by Mark. The amazement and hesitation of the Lord's disciples was occasioned especially by His heroic and decisive bearing as He went before them. They saw in His majestic, resolute, solemn, and fixed deportment, that a most important crisis was impending. Since the astonishment and wavering of His disciples precedes the definite prediction of Christ concerning His *now* approaching passion and death, it can only refer to the obscure and anxious foreboding with which the thought of something unknown, but critical and decisive and fearful, filled their minds (De Wette). For all this they were as yet but little prepared; hence the Lord collected them together, and strengthened them in solitude. He foretold to them His whole passion, so far as He could do so (that is, without a premature disclosure of the traitor, who had not yet decided on his treachery); He repeated to them all the comforting promises of His resurrection, and thus prepared them for all, while waiting for the Galilæan-Peræan festival companies.

3. The abode of Jesus in the wilderness of Ephraim, in its connection with His abode in the wilderness of Quarantania, and in its contrast with that abode.

HOMILETICAL AND PRACTICAL.

See on *Matthew*.—Jesus as going before His disciples in the way of sufferings: 1. His heroic spirit; 2. their despondency; 3. their invigoration in His strength.—Follow Me, saith Christ our Leader and Champion.—Jesus, go before us!—Christ, the Captain of our salvation, Heb. ii. 10.—The Lord in the midst of His disciples, before the coming of the hours (or days) of great and solemn crisis and decision.—The shuddering presentiment of the disciples, contemplating the unknown future; excited by, 1. beholding the holy and joyful solemnity of the Lord; 2. the journey to Jerusalem; 3. the consideration of the people's disposition; 4. the consideration of their own frame of mind.—How the Lord seeks to deliver the disciples from an indefinite fear, by setting before them the clear idea of a fearful, but salutary and saving, certainty.—The trembling and wavering discipleship.—We must not tremble and be amazed in the uncertainty of the way of suffering, but be bold and dare in the certainty of it.—Morbid feelings must become cheerful; and feebleness must be invigorated by the thought of the glorious and final end.—The Lord's assembly in solitude for His great and decisive encounter with the world. (*See* running title.)—The importance of stillness for the kingdom of God: 1. Into stillness; 2. in stillness; 3. out of stillness.—How the Lord collects His disciples for the conflict of suffering: 1. Every one to Him (with Christ); 2. every one into himself (in the inner life); 3. every one singly (to his companions).—

The source of the suffering of Christ; or, the enmity of the world against Him.—The ever-recurring cry from heaven, in the prospect of all Christ's sufferings and His people's: and [the cry] on the third day.—The Lord deals with His disciples in the spirit of heavenly simplicity and fidelity.—The plain disparity between the temper of the disciples and the feeling of our Lord: 1. Its meaning; 2. its signs; 3. itself a sign of the betrayal, the denial, and the forsaking Him in the night of His passion.

STARKE:—Conversations in travelling should further us in the heavenly pilgrimage.—All the steps which are taken in suffering with Christ, are steps taken to glory, 2 Thess. iii. 5; 1 Pet. iv. 1; Heb. xii. 2, 3.—We should often remind ourselves of the cross.—Christ summons us to fellowship with Him, as often as we hear of His sufferings and death.—We should be of good heart (Luke xxiv. 26), remembering in our sufferings the resurrection, and expecting our redemption in patient hope.—LISCO:—They were amazed and affrighted at the way which Jesus so boldly took into the very presence and power of His enemies.—BRAUNE:—On account of their Master they were amazed; for themselves, they feared.—Jesus going before them attracted them to follow.—A secret presentiment and longing of the spirit points to fellowship with Christ upon the cross; but the flesh grievously recoils.—We must train ourselves to endure sufferings.—GOSSNER:—All nature trembles when God leads man on the way of the cross.—BAUER:—The Master going before them, what remained but that they should follow?

PART FOURTH.

THE Conflicts and Triumphs of the Lord in Judæa. Christ the Founder of the New Church.

FIRST SECTION.

THE TRIUMPHAL ENTRY INTO JERUSALEM.

CHAPTER X. 35—XI. 26.

1. *The Request of the Sons of Zebedee.* CH. X. 35–45.

(Parallel: Matt. xx. 20–28.)

35 And James and John, the sons of Zebedee, come unto him, saying, Master, we
36 would that thou shouldest do for us whatsoever we shall desire.[1] And he said unto
37 them, What would ye that I should do for you? They said unto him, Grant unto us
that we may sit, one on thy right hand, and the other on thy left hand, in thy glory.
38 But Jesus said unto them, Ye know not what ye ask: can ye drink of the cup that I
39 drink of? and[2] be baptized with the baptism that I am baptized with? And they said
unto him, We can. And Jesus said unto them, Ye shall indeed drink of the cup that
40 I drink of; and with the baptism that I am baptized withal shall ye be baptized: But
to sit on my right hand and[3] on my left hand is not mine to give; but *it shall be given to*
41 *them* for whom it is prepared. And when the ten heard *it*, they began to be much dis
42 pleased with James and John. But Jesus called them *to him*,[4] and saith unto them, Ye
know that they which are accounted to rule over the Gentiles exercise lordship over
43 them; and their great ones exercise authority upon them. But so shall it not be[5]
44 among you: but whosoever will be great among you,[6] shall be your minister: And
45 whosoever of you will be the chiefest, shall be servant of all. For even the Son of
man came not to be ministered unto, but to minister, and to give his life a ransom for
many.

[1] Ver. 35.—Lachmann, Tischendorf, [after A., B., C., D., Versions,] supply *σε* after *αἰτήσωμεν*.
[2] Ver. 38.—According to B., C.*, D., L., Δ., [Lachmann, Tischendorf, Meyer,] instead of *καί* read *ἤ*.
[3] Ver. 40.—Instead of the *καί* here, also read *ἤ*, [after B., D., L., Δ., Lachmann, Tischendorf, Meyer.]
[4] Ver. 42.—*See* the order in Tischendorf and Lachmann, [who read *καὶ προσκαλεσάμενος αὐτοὺς ὁ Ἰησοῦς*, after B. C. D., L., Syriac, Coptic.]
[5] Ver. 43.—Instead of *ἔσται* here, *ἔστιν* is the reading of B., C.*, D., L., Δ. So Lachmann, Tischendorf.
[6] Ver 44.—Lachmann, after B., C., *ἐν ὑμῖν εἶναι*, instead of *ὑμῶν γενέσθαι*.

EXEGETICAL AND CRITICAL.

See on the parallel of *Matthew*, especially *Critical Note* on ver. 20.—Christ has prepared the Twelve for His final festival journey, and for its significance as a time of crisis. He has come forth from the wilderness of Ephraim; the first band of the Galilæan pilgrims to the feast—consisting probably of the most intimate friends and dependants of Jesus, who had come from Galilee through Samaria to Ephraim—had joined Him, purposing to go on with Him through Jericho to Jerusalem. This seems to be confirmed by the fact of the presence of Salome, and her participation in the request of her two sons. This request itself shows us how mighty had once more grown the joyful excitement of the disciples' hopes: in this respect, it makes the present section a perfect contrast to the previous one. Matthew alone accompanies Mark here; and he makes Salome prominent, putting the request into her lips. According to Mark, her sons present the petition to the Lord; but the records are evidently complementary to each other. Matthew's account makes Salome only the intercessor, and with marked accommodation to the spirit of Oriental court ceremony. Hence, even according to Matthew, Christ speaks immediately,—after the mother had proffered that request which, according to Mark, is the supplication of the sons,—to these sons themselves. Mark adds to the word concerning drinking of the cup, the word concerning the baptismal bath. Matthew says, "The sitting on My right hand and on My left is not mine to give, but for whom it is prepared of My Father;" Mark says briefly, "For whom it is prepared." He also says, in his manner, "The ten *began* to be displeased." The princes of the earth also he describes in his own peculiar way. For the rest, he agrees here with Matthew very closely; and down to trifling variations, such as between Matthew's "*your* servant," and Mark's "servant of *all*."

Ver. 35. **We would that Thou shouldst do for us.**—Strong importunity, *θέλομεν, ἵνα*.

Ver. 37. **In Thy glory.** According to Matthew, *in Thy kingdom*.—These are essentially the same. But we must reject the explanation, "in that glory which will surround us when we sit by Thee."

Ver. 38. **And with the baptism.**—Peculiar to Mark. On the double meaning of the expression, *see Matthew*, xx. 22.

Ver. 40. **For whom it is prepared.**—Matthew adds, "of My Father." In Mark the emphasis lies upon the fact that the matter of the honor was already decided.

Ver. 41. **They began.**—Here again follows at once a counter feeling: the appeasing word of our Lord.

Ver. 42. **Which are accounted to rule over the Gentiles,** *οἱ δοκοῦντες ἄρχειν*.—Meyer: The essence of Gentile government, the ruling ambition, is signified; not simply *οἱ ἄρχοντες* (Gataker and others) but *qui censentur imperare; i. e., quos gentes habent et agnoscunt, quorum imperio pareant* (Beza). He justly sets aside Fritzsche's exposition: "those who think they rule." But in Wetstein's interpretation,—*qui sibi regnare videntur, revera autem affectuum suorum servi sunt*,—there is an element worth noticing.

Ver. 43. **Whosoever will be great among you shall be your minister.**—Properly the "he *will* be" has the meaning of *ἔστω*, he should be, let him be; yet also with a hint of the thought that he will be such, either in the most internal sense or in the most external. Christ is the servant of all in the centre of the Church; the Pope, in the periphery of the Church, is the involuntary result of, and protest against, a too hasty development of the kingdom of God.

DOCTRINAL AND ETHICAL.

1. *See* on *Matthew*, especially the *Critical Notes*.

2. The last known instance of the Lord's apostolical training of the sons of Zebedee. The two preceding periods were Luke ix. 54, and Mark ix. 38. Thus there is an analogy and a contrast with the apostolical education of Peter. Our history throws light in many directions: 1. As the beginning of that enthusiastic Hosanna, which found its climax in the acclamations of the palm-entry into Jesusalem. Christ had predicted His sufferings on the cross. The sons of Zebedee declare, with glowing heroism, that they are willing to connect their fate with His in the strictest manner, and that they are fully resolved to go forward: they rather, however, hope for glory with Him, than fear the shame of His cross. 2. As the last outbreak of the high-toned, noble, natural pride of the sons of Zebedee. The mother and the sons are one. But John seems to interpose especially in favor of his brother James: he might, according to antecedents, have had some sort of claim to the right-hand place; but he now (as the younger) will take his place on the left hand. 3. As an unconscious request for martyrdom with Christ. 4. As a keen test of the heroism of Peter. 5. As an illustration of the stage of transition, through which the disciples were then passing. 6. As giving the Lord occasion to characterize the nature of earthly government, and to utter His protest against all ideas of a Christian hierarchy; as well as to distinguish expressly the economy of the Father, and the creation and preordination, from the economy of the Son and redemption; and still more expressly to mark out the royal road of humility as the appointed and only way to true and abiding Christian exaltation. Phil. ii. 6 *seq.*

HOMILETICAL AND PRACTICAL.

See on *Matthew*.—What was noble and what was evil in the request of the sons of Zebedee.—The bold petition of these disciples: 1. As a fault: with regard to the error and the sin in it,—*a.* they prayed for something which, *in the sense in which they prayed for it*, did not exist in the kingdom of Christ; *b.* for something which was *not yet* existing (not before the cross); *c.* for something about which decision had already been made: possibly in their favor, so that their request was superfluous; possibly not, and then their request was vain. 2. As a pious impulse of the Spirit, which was sanctified and abundantly gratified: it was an impulse, *a.* to remain always near Him; *b.* to share His lot and serve Him; 3. to work with self-devotement for His kingdom. One was the friend of Jesus, the other the first martyr.—The cup of Christ and His baptism: *a.* the tasting of all the bitternesses of the Messianic suffering; *b.* the experience of all the external trials, or the being baptized into the shame of the cross, the death, the sepulchre, the underworld. Or, *a.* His drinking (Gethsemane); *b.* His sinking (Calvary).—Cup and baptism in the kingdom of Christ: 1. The cup and the baptism; 2. the baptism and the cup.—As the Lord corrected Peter by rebuking lessons, so He corrects the sons of Zebedee by humbling lessons: 1. By making an express distinction between the suffering of Christ and His glory; 2. between martyr-fidelity with its reward, and the divine gift and its blessedness; 3. between the economy and work of the Father, and the economy and work of the Son; 4. between the eternal fundamental principles of he kingdom of God, and their realization in the work of man's free will; 5. between the earthly State and the spiritual Church.—The displeasure of the disciples at the error of the sons of Zebedee: 1. Probably a feeling on behalf of Peter's rights; * 2. not free from envy and strife; 3. but at the same time springing from a presentiment of a higher order of things.— Above and below in the Church of Christ: 1. An above which is below; 2. a below which is above (as oft-times the first is the last, and the last first).—Contrast between the appointments of the State and those of the Church: 1. Those are legal; these rest upon the fundamental principles of pure and free love. 2. Those are symbolical; these are actual powers in life.—The repeated testimonies of Christ against a primacy.—Christ servant of all and Lord of all, Phil. ii. 6 *seq.* Real and essential dignities in the kingdom of heaven: 1. Its names or titles are powers of life; 2. its powers of life are divine fruits; 3. its divine fruits are God's gifts.—Christ the Prince of peace among His people.

STARKE:—OSIANDER:—Ministers in the Church have their own failings.—Take good heed how thou prayest.—We should never look at anything high for ourselves.—QUESNEL:—Ambition is blind, and often knows not what it wants.—OSIANDER:—The cup of affliction is bitter enough to the flesh, but it is exceeding salutary. Take it in full confidence, and it will serve to the healing of the soul.—Christ does not say that He could not give the heavenly glory, but that He could not give it to any but those for whom it was prepared, 2 Tim. ii. 11, 12.—We must not trouble ourselves as to the place which we shall occupy in heaven, but see to it that we get there.—HEDINGER:—Christ does not disparage or overturn dignities, but their pride and vanity.— Variety of gifts in the Church: these should not exalt themselves, those should not envy, Rom. xii. 3; 1 Cor. xii. 15; Jas. i. 10.— In the kingdoms of the world, a man is called great when he rules; in the kingdom of grace, when he serves many.—LUTHER:—There is nothing which more adorns and dignifies the office of a true servant of Christ than genuine humility and simplicity.—BRAUNE:—There is ever a widening interval between seeking the applause of others and the cause itself (at first, he remarks, they coalesce, or are much more concurrent).—In the result, the ambitious man forgets the cause itself, and displays his own gifts and powers; from one false step he then proceeds to another. —If in their (Zebedee's sons') love to the Lord there was an admixture of ambition, this would tend to make their love impure: the kingdom of love could not and must not tolerate such a blending.—The displeasure of the ten was a proof that they were affected by the same fault.—The promises of Christ, Rev. ii. 10, 28; iii. 21.

SCHLEIERMACHER:—Love to Christ is the measure for all the actions of men in His Church.—BRIEGER:—The kingdom of Christ is a kingdom of the cross.—Love teaches us to serve.—His serving should endear our service.—BAUER:—The whole life of the Son of Man was humble service.

* [The author here travels out of the record. There is not the slightest allusion to Peter in the narrative.—*Ed.*]

2. *The Passing through Jericho.* VERS. 46–52.

(Parallels: Matt. xx. 29–34; Luke xviii. 35–43; xix. 1–28.)

46 And they came to Jericho: and as he went out of Jericho with his disciples, and a
great number of people, blind Bartimeus, the[1] son of Timeus, sat by the highway-side
47 begging. And when he heard that it was Jesus of Nazareth,[2] he began to cry out, and
48 say, Jesus, *thou* son of David, have mercy on me. And many charged him that he
should hold his peace: but he cried the more a great deal, *Thou* son of David, have
49 mercy on me. And Jesus stood still, and commanded him to be called:[3] and they call
50 the blind man, saying unto him, Be of good comfort, rise; he calleth thee. And he,
51 casting away his garment, rose,[4] and came to Jesus. And Jesus answered and said
unto him, What wilt thou that I should do unto thee? The blind man said unto him,
52 Lord, that I might receive my sight. And Jesus said unto him, Go thy way; thy faith
hath made thee whole. And immediately he received his sight, and followed Jesus[5] in
the way.

[1] Ver. 46.—We read, with A. and *Recepta*, υἱός without the Article, and ὁ τυφλός with the Article. [Lachmann, Tischendorf, and Meyer, following B., D., L., Δ., omit it.] So also προσαιτῶν, although important Codd., including B., L., Δ., Tischendorf, and Meyer, read προσαίτης. *See* the *Notes*.

[2] Ver. 47.—Ναζαρηνός, Lachmann, Tischendorf, Meyer.

[3] Ver. 49.—Εἶπεν· φωνήσατε αὐτόν: B., C., L., Δ., Tischendorf, Meyer.

[4] Ver. 50.—Instead of ἀναστάς, Lachmann and Tischendorf read ἀναπηδήσας, after B., L., D., Δ., Vulgate, &c.

[5] Ver. 52.—Αὐτῷ instead of τῷ Ἰησοῦ.

EXEGETICAL AND CRITICAL.

See on the parallels in *Matthew* and *Luke*.—From Ephraim and the desert, Jesus, with the Twelve and His trusted Galilæan dependents—who had joined Him at this point or before—turned to Jericho, where He united His company with that of the great Galilæan-Peræan band going up to the feast, which had come from Peræa over the Jordan. Upon the question of time, and Jericho itself, and the difference among the Synoptists in regard to the healing of the blind, consult the notes upon *Matthew*. Like that Evangelist, Mark passes over the narrative of Zacchæus, and gives instead all the more exact account of the healing of the blind man. The fundamental idea of Luke's Gospel demanded that the favor shown to the rich publican should not be omitted. Matthew and Mark are so intent upon depicting the great procession to the feast in its unity, that they cannot linger upon another episode, such as that of Zacchæus, in addition to the healing of the blind man. Matthew, indeed, might hesitate through modesty to record prominently so many instances of favor shown to the publicans; and Mark would probably prefer to omit a new remembrancer of the embittered hatred which subsisted between the Jews and the Romans—writing as he did so much for Roman Christians. Moreover, the occurrence with Zacchæus was not properly a miraculous history, such as both these Evangelists mainly record at this time.—Now, while Matthew gives an account merely of the departure from Jericho, Mark mentions also the entrance. In his account of the departure, he describes the great numbers that accompanied Jesus, and records the full name of the blind man, Bartimæus, the son of Timæus. Luke joins him in saying that this man was a beggar. Mark, again, has the specific note that he, Bartimæus, began to cry aloud. The words of the people to the blind man, "Be of good courage, rise; He calleth thee."—the conduct of Bartimæus generally, and his casting away his garment, and standing up, and coming—are all characteristic touches of painting which Mark alone gives. Only Matthew records the compassion of Jesus, and the fixing His eyes upon the man. Mark also omits "Receive thy sight." The word of healing is condensed, and the conclusion is briefer than Luke's, touching only the main points.

Ver. 46. **Bartimæus.**—The patronymic בַּר טִמַּאי is made into a proper name (after the analogy of Bartholomew and others); as it is explained by the additional clause, "son of Timæus." This last seems to place Timæus among the number of well-known Christians. Meyer: Probably a Christian who afterwards attained distinction. And this might be true, notwithstanding the fact that he had allowed his son, a blind man, to beg on the highway. But, if we read with Codex A. and the *Text. Rec.*, "a son of Timæus, Bartimæus the blind man, sat and begged," it is plain that this is an account of him more precise and consistently carried out, which however seemed too full and specific to most copyists. According to it, Bartimæus, the blind man, was himself a personage well known to Christians as a monument of the Lord's miracle, as was probably also Simon the Leper; and the designation "a son of Timæus" would distinguish him, not merely from the father, but also from other sons.

Ver. 47. **And when he heard.**—He therefore believed that Jesus of Nazareth was the son of David, that is, the expected Messiah. He thus bore testimony to the widely-scattered seed of faith, and especially to the renewed stimulus given to the Redeemer's cause, since the beginning of the festal journey, amongst the masses. But the blind man might also have heard on his hill-top of the recent resurrection of Lazarus, which took place in his own neighborhood; and this might have been matter of many silent night-ponderings in his blindness.

Ver. 49. **And Jesus stood still.**—We now have reached the great crisis. He now hears the loud cry of the people—Messiah! *See* on the parallel of *Matthew*.—**Be of good comfort.**—Meyer: θάρσει, ἔγειρε, φωνεῖ σε: most affecting *asyndeton*.

Ver. 51. **Rabboni,** רַבּוּנִי, *my* Master.—If the Yod is taken paragogically, it means merely "master" (*see* Meyer); but even then it has so emphatic a sense as to be almost equal in personal reverence. Bartimæus adhered from that time to the Lord. He followed Him, praising God, Luke says; he followed Him in the way, in the procession, says Mark. He immediately joined the festal company of Jesus' triumph. It was, indeed, the triumphal procession of the Prophet, and not yet that of the High Priest: this is formed by the living Church, even as the risen saints will be the triumphal procession of the King.

DOCTRINAL AND ETHICAL.

1. *See* on *Matthew* and the previous notes.

2. The contrast in the sentiments of the people round Christ: type of the contrast between the hierarchical and the evangelical Church. In the former, the poor and wretched are threatened, and bidden to keep silence, when they cry directly to Christ; in the latter it is, "Be of good comfort, rise; He calleth thee." It was natural that those who surrounded Christ should be led, by the thought that His kingdom was beginning, into conventional notions as to the value of courtly customs and hierarchical order; but it was also natural that the mercy of our Lord towards the wretched should scatter all such mists.

3. The casting his garment away was an expression of joyous boldness and zealous haste, and a removal of all impediments.

4. Mark intimates the dignity of the crisis in which the Lord now stands, by the circumstance that He heals the blind man simply by words: "Go thy way, thy faith," etc. We know from Matthew how they are to be explained in detail; nevertheless, it is observable that Mark, who earlier records the sighing, the anointing with spittle, etc., introduces here so few intervening circumstances.

5. The Lord declared, by act and deed, that He would have no courtly state in His kingdom, no intermediate personages between Him and His dependents; that He was come, not to rule, but to minister. And, so far as this goes, our history is an acted illustration of the former section.

HOMILETICAL AND PRACTICAL.

See on *Matthew*.—The beginning of the procession of Christ was the opening of blind eyes.—Light must be diffused in the world.—The fame of Bartimæus the best fame for all men; the best reputation for all Christians. (He was a blind man, a beggar; he believed and importuned; the Lord took pity upon him, and healed him.)—With the name of Christ the names of those whom He saved are immortalized.—The most beautiful homage with which Christ was publicly hailed as Messiah: Have mercy on me!—It is a pitiable thing when the cry, "Lord, have pity on me" (the κύριε ἐλέησον, to wit), becomes a dead formula in our poor Christendom.—How Jesus can transform the harsh threateners of the wretched into compassionate comforters and helpers.—The three words of true Christian sympathy and help for the wretched: Be of good comfort, rise; He calleth thee.—Through the compassion of Jesus and nearness to Him, one is taught to preach the Gospel even unconsciously.—How the helping "Go thy way" of the Lord to Bartimæus and others becomes a glorious and encouraging announcement, "Come unto Me."—All the uncalled ceremonialists in the royal procession of Christ are unable to suppress the cry of faith sent forth to Him.—The ear of the King detects the lamenting cry of the blind beggar through all the tumult of the crowd.—Thus the royal procession is magnified by the cry of misery.—A blind beggar can arrest the course of it; a blind beggar, turned into a seeing disciple, can advance it and add to its dignity.—The true petitioners of God throw away for ever the beggar's array.—Mendicancy appears or vanishes as men are guided: 1. It appears in the ancient priestly and royal states of this world; 2. it vanishes in the kingdom of Christ. Compare with this passage John ix. 8; Acts iii. 2; iv. 34.—Men may at first hinder the beginnings of Christianity, and then agree afterwards to further it prematurely and rashly. (The first three centuries, and the three following, are examples.)

STARKE:—LUTHER:—Blindness and poverty cause a double distress: so it is in spiritual matters, when both are rightly felt and mourned over.—CANSTEIN:—The preaching of the Gospel is a perpetual announcement that Jesus is near; and we should, knowing our misery, incessantly and confidently cry aloud to Him for His mercy.—LUTHER:—Sufferers oftentimes meet with scanty sympathy and poor intercession.—CRAMER:—It would be a sore thing if the good God were as easily wearied as men are with our praying and beseeching.—QUESNEL:—We should let no opportunity pass of getting good either to body or soul, for such opportunities do not always return.—HEDINGER:—In prayer we should let nothing interrupt or divert us.—The simplicity of faith in prayer holds fast and holds out.—LUTHER:—God's call is even in spiritual things the beginning of actual cure.—He who truly wants salvation must disencumber himself of all embarrassments and come to Christ.—HEDINGER:—He who would see, must acknowledge his blindness.—LUTHER:—Faith is counted of such high dignity that salvation is ascribed to it, although the work of God.—HEDINGER:—Christ is our Physician and our Light.—Faith is the best of all medicine.—CANSTEIN:—Those who receive gifts follow their benefactors. Ought we not then to follow Christ?—He is indeed our greatest Benefactor.—RIEGER (with reference to those who murmured):—Those who stand around are often unaware how much harm they may do by light words, and how easily a tender germ is trodden down and ruined.—The inward earnestness of the blind man broke through everything. Happy he who lets himself be restrained from faith and the cry of faith by nothing under the sun.—Things are continually occurring which might have a tendency to turn us in part or wholly away from Christ. What then? So much the more does the blind cry out, and faith believe; and the more it is hindered, the more it is helped.—The Lord was not always so willing to be followed by those who were healed; but in this last journey to Jerusalem an exception was admitted. Envy was not now to be excited; it had reached its highest point. Praise, on the other hand, was now, by all the wonderful works of God, to demonstrate its power against "the enemy and the avenger."—GOSSNER:—The blind man runs to Jesus without seeing Him; so must we hasten to Him in faith, though we see Him not.

---

3. *The Triumphal Entrance of Jesus into Jerusalem.* CH. XI. 1-11.

(Parallels: Matt. xxi. 1-17; Luke xix. 29-46; John xii. 12-29.)

1 And when they came nigh to Jerusalem, unto Bethphage and Bethany, at the
2 Mount of Olives, he sendeth forth two of his disciples, And saith unto them, Go your
way into the village over against you: and as soon as ye be entered into it, ye shall
3 find a colt tied, whereon never[1] man sat; loose him, and bring *him*. And if any man
say unto you, Why do ye this? say ye that the Lord hath need of him; and straight-
4 way he will send[2] him hither. And they went their way, and found the colt tied by
5 the door without, in a place where two ways met; and they loose him. And certain
6 of them that stood there said unto them, What do ye, loosing the colt? And they
7 said unto them even[3] as Jesus had commanded: and they let them go. And they
brought[4] the colt to Jesus, and cast their garments on him; and he sat upon him.
8 And many spread their garments in the way; and others cut down branches off the
9 trees,[5] and strewed *them* in the way. And they that went before, and they that fol-
lowed, cried, saying,[6] Hosanna; Blessed *is* he that cometh in the name of the Lord:
10 Blessed *be* the kingdom of our father David, that cometh in the name of the Lord:[7]
11 Hosanna in the highest. And Jesus[8] entered into Jerusalem, and into the temple: and
when he had looked round about upon all things, and now the even-tide was come, he
went out unto Bethany[9] with the twelve.

[1] Ver. 2.—Lachmann reads οὐδεὶς οὔπω, after B., Origen, and others. [A. reads οὐδεὶς πώποτε.] Tischendorf and Meyer, after B., C., L., Δ. read λύσατε αὐτὸν καὶ φέρετε.

[2] Ver. 3.—In several Codd., B., C.*, D., L., Δ., &c., stands πάλιν. Thus the clause is made part of the answer of the disciples: The Lord will use the colt and send it back again.—Probably this was designed to soften the seeming violence of the transaction. [Elzevir and Fritzsche read ἀποστελεῖ.]

[3] Ver. 6.—Καθὼς εἶπεν corresponding to the preceding εἴπον, according to B., C., L., Δ., Lachmann, Tischendorf [Meyer].

[4] Ver. 7.—B., L., Δ., Origen, Tischendorf, Meyer, read φέρουσιν instead of ἤγαγον. Ἐπιβάλλουσιν, emphatic Present, [B., C., D., L., Δ., Vulgate, Griesbach, Fritzsche, Lachmann, Tischendorf, Meyer].

[5] Ver. 8.—Tischendorf's reading (recommended by Meyer), ἄλλοι δὲ στιβάδας, κόψαντες ἐκ τῶν ἀγρῶν, is not sufficiently supported. [Ἀγρῶν is found in B., C., L., Δ., Syriac (margin); Fritzsche, Lachmann, Tischendorf, and Meyer regard στιβάδας as the correct form.]

[6] Ver. 9.—The λέγοντες is wanting in B., C., L., Δ., [Tischendorf; bracketed by Griesbach, Lachmann].

[7] Ver. 10.—The reading, ἐν ὀνόματι κυρίου, has some important Codd. against it, but A. and others sustain it. It was probably corrected as being difficult; but the difficulty is obviated if we regard the expression "kingdom" (poetically brief, without the Article) as repeated in thought. [Meyer rejects it.]

[8] Ver. 11.—Ὁ Ἰησοῦς is an explanatory addition. [Rejected by Griesbach, Fritzsche, Lachmann, Tischendorf, Meyer.]

EXEGETICAL AND CRITICAL.

See on the parallels in *Matthew* and *Luke*.—The Evangelist translates us at once into Palm-Sunday, as to time; and, as to place, into the region between Bethany and the Mount of Olives. The departure from Jericho took place on the Friday before the Passion-Week: it was the custom to spend the night in the district of the Mount of Olives, and to keep the Sabbath there. In Bethany, on the evening of Saturday, the meal took place in the house of Simon the Leper. On Sunday morning the journey from Bethany was continued. Now, in the accounts of the Synoptists, the beginning and the continuation of the festal journey are combined in one, because it is their object to describe the important palm-procession at once as a whole. Luke, indeed, informs us of the delay of the journey on Friday in Jericho, that is, through the Lord's entrance into the house of Zacchæus; and he adds the delivery of a parable which is connected with that entrance, and with the expectation of the people that He would at once found the Messianic kingdom in Jerusalem. But it is John alone who tells us that the tarrying in Bethany occupied an interval; and to him also we owe the most particular explanation of the procession, in the passage, ch. xii. 12-29. What is peculiar to Mark is this, that he places us by his minute specialities in the very midst of the scene. He writes in the present tense: "They come nigh; He sendeth." The sending of the two he relates somewhat more circumstantially; while, with Luke, he omits the mention of the older ass, and does not join Matthew and John in their allusion to Zech. ix. 9. He alone marks the fact, that the colt stood tied by the door of a house in a place where two ways met; and he also gives most vividly the particulars connected with the loosing of the ass. Then he again gives his record in the present tense: They bring the foal; they lay their garments thereon. In his description of the strewing of branches and garments in the way, as well as of the Hosanna, he agrees now with Matthew and now with Luke; yet he alone has the στοιβάδες, and the greeting to the kingdom of the Messiah, as well as to the King. Several traits which are found in Matthew, Luke, and John, he omits. Earnest and powerful is the final narrative. Jesus comes into the city, into the temple; takes all into His eye with silent, searching glance, and returns back to Bethany in the evening with the Twelve. For this distinction between the day of the entrance and the day of the cleansing of the temple, we are indebted to Mark alone.

Ver. 1. **Unto Bethphage and Bethany.**—They are approaching Jerusalem; and the approach is so ordered, that they arrive at Bethphage and Bethany. The intermediate stations are measured from Jerusalem, the goal; consequently, Bethphage comes first, and then Bethany, for they proceed from Bethany over Bethphage to the city. But how is it we read *towards Bethany*, when the departure was from that place? First, we must bear in mind that the Sunday procession from Bethany is blended into unity with the Friday procession from Jericho. Thus the passage means, that Jesus sent His disciples forth at once from Bethany. Moreover, it may be assumed that the Bethany of that time stretched wide into the country around, and that Jesus had found a lodgment in its eastern outskirts. The district of Bethany reached as far as to join the district of Bethphage. But Bethany they had not yet arrived at: the colt was sent for from thence. Concerning Jerusalem, Bethany, Bethphage, *see* on *Matthew*. Concerning the Mount of Olives, comp. Winer and the travellers.

Ver. 2. **Whereon never man sat.**—So also Luke. This circumstance is wanting in Matthew, but perfectly agrees with his account of the mother-ass. The foal had up to this time run with its mother. Meyer discerns in this notice "an appendage of reflective tradition, based on the sacred characteristic of the animal (for unused animals were put to sacred purposes, Num. xix. 2; Deut. xxi. 3; 1 Sam. vi. 7)."—Matthew did not note the circumstance, because it was self-understood that the foal was not yet used, so long as it was a foal running with the mother. *See* the notes on *Matthew*.

Ver. 3. **And if any man say unto you.**—That this significant interchange of sayings implies previous acquaintance and private watchwords, is proved by the use of the εἰπεῖν in Mark, and in Luke of the emphatic οὕτως ἐρεῖτε. So is it with the ordering of the Passover-feast by such a particular one: εἴπατε αὐτῷ. Luke has the equivalent ἐρεῖτε, with the addition, λέγει σοι ὁ διδάσκαλος.

Ver. 4. **Without, in a place where two ways met.**—The ἄμφοδον means primarily a way encompassing a block of houses; then the street, and even a quarter of the town. The animal being fastened to the door points to the open space before the house.

Ver. 8. **Branches.**—The word στοιβάδες is an error of the transcriber; the Codd. B. D., and others, read στιβάδες. The στιβάς is a scattering of straw, reed, branches, or twigs. The plural and the cutting down point to branches of trees. According to John xii. 13, palm-leaves were strewed (as the symbol of peace).

Ver. 10. **The kingdom of our father David.**—That is, the kingdom of the Messiah as the spiritual restoration of the kingdom of David, which had become, for the Jew, a type of the Messianic kingdom, as David was a type of the Messiah. "The Messiah

Himself was also called David, among the Rabbis (SCHÖTTGEN, *Hor.* ii.)." (Meyer.)

Ver. 11. **He went out unto Bethany.**—Meyer insists on it that there is here a discrepancy with Matthew. It is a discrepancy when the definite is opposed to the definite; but not when the definite is opposed to the indefinite. This well-founded canon of hermeneutics would demolish many of the discrepancies pointed out by school criticism. Matthew and Luke wrote no diaries. There is no difference here, any more than the blending of the parts of the palm-procession into the journey of one day makes the Synoptists and John disagree. Matthew and Luke connect the cleansing of the temple with the import of the palm entry; but this Mark does not. Christ, according to his account, takes a general survey, which in its silent observation betokened the cleansing which would take place on the morrow.

DOCTRINAL AND ETHICAL.

1. *See* on *Matthew* and *Luke*.

2. The expectation of the Messiah was the expectation of His kingdom; hence the salutation of the Messiah was the salutation of His kingdom. Christ and His kingdom are not to be separated; but the kingdom of His cross and the kingdom of His glory are to be distinguished, even as the glorified Christ is distinguished from the Christ in the form of a servant. Of this gulf between the kingdom here and the kingdom there, most of the jubilants had no idea; many rose not beyond it, but plunged below.

3. The Mount of Olives a symbol.

4. The palm-procession in Mark is brief, earnest, sublime. A swift progress to the city, and to the temple; ending in a wide and silent inspection of the temple until evening.

HOMILETICAL AND PRACTICAL.

See on *Matthew*, and the preceding reflections.—Christ's goal in His royal procession: to the temple.—The significance of Christ's coming to the temple: 1. The types and promises, Exod. xl. 34; 1 Kings viii.; 2 Chron. v.; Isa. ii.; lxvi. 20; Ezek. xliii.; Hagg. ii. 3, 9; Zech. xiv. 20; Mal. iii. 1. 2. The historical visits paid to it: the child Jesus in the temple, the visit when twelve years old, the feasts, Jesus as the public Messiah in the temple, the Pentecost, the burning of the temple in A. D. 70. 3. The spiritual visitations of the temple.—The history of the temple the history of the world; the history of the temple the history of the kingdom of God.—The palm-entry into the temple, according to its external and its internal form: 1. The great procession to the great cathedral; 2. Christ the judged, and Christ the Judge, conducted by a wretched people to the deserted house of God.—Christ comes to the temple, 1. from Galilee with the ecclesiastical devout, 2. from Jericho with the enthusiasts, 3. from Bethany with His friends and servants, 4. from the Mount of Olives alone with His Holy Spirit.—Christ in the temple as the Jesus of twelve years, and as the openly-proclaimed Messiah.—Christ in the beautiful new-built temple; or, the difference between an æsthetic and a spiritual inspection of the temple.—The fearfully silent glance of Christ in the temple until evening.—The Lord's visitation of His churches: 1. He knows and sees all; 2. He sees and looks through all; 3. He looks through all, and keeps silence; 4. He keeps silence, thinking upon judgment and mercy.—Christ's entrance and exit at His temple visitation: 1. The entrance: through the city straight to the temple; 2. the exit: from the temple to Bethany.—The procession of the people with Christ to the temple.

STARKE:—Thus Jesus comes as the Lamb of God, and places Himself on the altar of sacrifice Certainly this was not the act of a mere man, thus joyfully to come, to give Himself up to His enemies, and go to confront His death.—Comp. the foal, 1 Sam. vi. 7.—CANSTEIN:—The Lord needs not that we should give Him anything, for all is always His; yet He may require it for certain purposes.—QUESNEL:—All things must be cast under the feet of Jesus.—*Nova Bibl. Tub.*:—Where Jesus is, there is life, movement, praise, and joy.—How necessary is the visitation of the churches!—HEDINGER:—The eye and the heart may well take pleasure, as in nature, so also in art, her copy. (But all in its measure and in its time.)—GERLACH:—(The foal never yet used.) This trait points to the fact that Jesus made His entrance as Priest-King.—BRAUNE:—Believers gladly place their substance at the feet and disposal of Jesus, their Master.—In the way of obedience (which the disciples followed), light always arises upon light.—The Lord now came upon the animal of peace, not as one day upon the great white horse to judgment.—Thus they received with peaceful joy the Prince of peace.—Every festal pilgrim was received with the "Blessed is He that cometh in the name of the Lord;" but the greeting befitted Him in a peculiar and higher sense.

SCHLEIERMACHER:—We must confess that, though they may not have been the same men (who first cried *Hosannah!* then *Crucify* Him), yet that it was the same people.—The oneness and interdependence of the people makes the difference of the individuals disappear.—We cannot help regarding this gross fickleness and instability as the proper characteristic of the great mass.—(Christ keeping silence in the temple till even-tide.) The boundary between the old and the new covenant came nearer and nearer: the one was to find its end, and the other was to be erected on the ruins of the former.—What thoughts touching the past must have arisen, and how deep must His emotions have been, in the consciousness of what He came to do, when He compared the magnificence and glory of the old covenant with the spiritual life of the new covenant, which, far removed from all outward demonstration, unseen and unpretending, was creating for itself its own form in sweet and gentle silence; when He compared the magnificence and glory of the external temple with the spiritual temple built of living stones, in which His spirit should dwell, and where should be established for ever the worship of His heavenly Father in spirit and in truth!

BRIEGER:—The devotion of the garments to His service intimates something extraordinary. When Jehu in the camp was to be proclaimed as king, a throne of garments was erected for him. This, with the sound of trumpets, and the cry, "Jehu is king,' made up the homage (2 Kings ix. 13). Here we have something similar, whereby homage is done to Jesus.—As a light before its final extinction blazes up once more, so Israel before their final fall lifted themselves up to Jehovah once more. But, as at Sinai they were put to shame after professing obedience (Exod. xx. 19), through making the golden calf, so here they are put to more wretched shame by so soon crying, Crucify Him! crucify Him!—Now does the Father set His Son as a King upon His holy hill of Zion, Ps. ii. 6.—Christ was a King from this hour. In all the parables from this point, His own Person is the centre. He speaks and acts as a king. (But we must distinguish between the time when the people heralded Him as king, and when God lifted Him up to His throne: between Palm Sunday and the Resurrection and Ascension.)

---

4. *The Withered Fig-tree, and the House of Prayer made a Den of Thieves. The Cleansing of the Temple.* VERS. 12–26.

(Parallels: Matt. xxi. 12–22; Luke xix. 45, 46.)

12 And on the morrow, when they were come from Bethany, he was hungry.
13 And seeing a fig-tree afar off,[1] having leaves, he came, if haply he might find anything
thereon: and when he came to it, he found nothing but leaves; for the time[2] of figs was
14 not *yet*. And Jesus[3] answered and said unto it, No man eat fruit of thee hereafter for
15 ever. And his disciples heard *it*. And they come to Jerusalem: and Jesus went into
the temple, and began to cast out them that sold and bought in the temple, and over
16 threw the tables of the money-changers, and the seats of them that sold doves; And
17 would not suffer that any man should carry *any* vessel through the temple. And he
taught, saying unto them,[4] Is it not written, My house shall be called of [by] all nations
18 the house of prayer? but ye have made it a den of thieves. And the scribes and chief
priests heard *it*, and sought how they might destroy him: for they feared him, because
19 all the people was astonished at his doctrine. And when even was come, he went out
20 of the city. And in the morning, as they passed by,[5] they saw the fig-tree dried up
21 from the roots. And Peter, calling to remembrance, saith unto him, Master, behold,
22 the fig-tree which thou cursedst is withered away. And Jesus answering, saith unto
23 them, Have faith in God. For[6] verily I say unto you, That whosoever shall say unto
this mountain, Be thou removed, and be thou cast into the sea; and shall not doubt in
his heart, but shall believe that those things which he saith shall come to pass; he shall
24 have whatsoever he saith. Therefore I say unto you, What things soever ye desire,
25 when ye pray,[7] believe that ye receive *them*,[8] and ye shall have *them*. And when ye
stand praying, forgive, if ye have ought against any; that your Father also which is
26 in heaven may forgive you your trespasses.[9] But if ye do not forgive, neither will your
Father which is in heaven forgive your trespasses.

[1] Ver. 13.—[Griesbach, Fritzsche, Scholz, Lachmann, Tischendorf, Meyer, after important MSS., read ἀπό before μακρόθεν.]

[2] Ver. 13.—Lachmann reads ὁ καιρός with the Article, following Origen and several Codd.; and thus the true meaning of the passage becomes more definite.

[3] Ver. 14.—Ὁ Ἰησοῦς interpolated.

[4] Ver. 17.—Καὶ ἔλεγεν αὐτοις, according to C., L., Δ., &c. Πεποιήκατε, B., L., Δ., Origen, [Tischendorf, Meyer,] instead of ἐποιήσατε.

[5] Ver. 20.—The order of B., C., L., Δ., Lachmann, and Tischendorf is παραπορευόμ. πρωΐ.

[6] Ver. 23.—The γάρ (for) is wanting in B., D., Lachmann, Tischendorf. The additional clause, ὃ ἐὰν εἴπῃ, is wanting in B., C., D., L., Δ., Tischendorf.

[7] Ver. 24.—Lachmann, Tischendorf, Meyer, after B., C., L., Δ., read προσεύχεσθε καὶ αἰτεῖσθε: a more comprehensive promise.

[8] Ver. 24.—Codd. B., C., L., Δ., read ἐλάβετε, instead of λαμβάνετε: accepted by Lachmann, Tischendorf, and Meyer.

[9] Ver. 26.—This verse is wanting in B., L., S., Δ., and some others. Tischendorf gives it up. Lachmann and Meyer retain it, after C. and others. But it is an interpolation which some MSS., after ver. 26, add from Matt. vii. 7, 8.

EXEGETICAL AND CRITICAL.

See on the parallels in *Matthew* and *Luke*.—Notwithstanding Mark's conciseness in his record, we can yet distinguish three days of Jesus' abode in the temple; that is, of the Messianic residence there of the King. Sunday was the day of entrance and looking around, ch. xi. 1–11. Monday was the day on which the fig-tree was cursed, the temple was cleansed, and those festal works were done by Jesus in the temple which filled up the exasperation of His enemies, vers. 12–19. Then Tuesday was the day of His conflict in the temple with all the assaults of His enemies in their several divisions, and of His departure from the temple, ch. xi. 20; xiii. 37. On Wednesday Jesus remained in concealment, as we are positively assured by John (ch. xii. 37); and probably it was then that He completed His discourse of the last things by adding those eschatological parables which Matthew communicates: unless we may assume rather that they were uttered on the night between Tuesday and Wednesday within the circle of His most confidential disciples. The allusions to night might suit such a view, Matt. xxiv 42, 43; xxv. 6, 30. The silent Wednesday of His concealment was then devoted to the preparation of His larger body of disciples, and to purposes of retired devotion.

The unity of this section lies in the narrative of

the fig-tree cursed. Mark makes it the starting-point of His account of Jesus' wonderful works in the temple during Monday. The individual particulars of these festal wonders are singled out prominently by Matthew, ch. xxi. 12–15. Therefore he brings into this second day the cursing of the fig-tree, with its withering up. Luke also indicates these festal hours, ch. xix. 47, 48. For the peculiar significance of the facts of the Greeks earnestly desiring to see Jesus, and the discourse which that occasioned, *see* the Notes on John xii. 20–36. But the Evangelist Mark takes the whole day into His view under its severe aspect. Hence he connects all this with the narrative of the fig-tree; and this section embraces the time from Monday morning to Tuesday morning. Thus, according to his account, the cursing of the fig-tree preceded the cleansing of the temple on Monday morning. With Matthew, who likewise has the narrative, it follows it; because Matthew purposed more strongly to stamp the contrast of the two temple-days—the day of peace and the day of contest. Concerning the fig-tree, Mark preliminarily remarks that it had leaves (which from afar might seem to be inviting). But in connection with the circumstance that Jesus found no figs upon it, he has the remarkable clause οὐ γὰρ ἦν, etc., the time was not yet (concerning which, *see* below). Matthew's word, "Let no fruit grow henceforth," he gives concretely: "Let no man eat," etc. He adds, that the disciples heard it. The cleansing of the temple he relates again with an ἤρξατο: He began. And he adds to the picture, that Jesus would not suffer any vessel to be carried through the temple. The explanatory word of Christ he introduces as instruction (ἐδίδασκε), and in vigorous interrogative form (οὐ γέγραπται). To the "house of prayer" he adds, "for all nations;" which Luke has not, and which reminds us of "every creature," ch. xvi. 15. The confusion of the Sanhedrim on this day, and their projects as to the manner in which they should kill Jesus—seeing that they feared the people, who did earnest homage to Jesus—he connects rightly with this day; while Luke records it more indefinitely (ch. xix. 47, 48), as also Matthew in somewhat similar manner (ch. xxi. 15, 16), and John also in another aspect of it (ch. xii. 17–19). Then follows, according to Mark, the departure of Jesus from the city. Matthew tells us that the fig-tree had straightway withered. Mark relates that it was early in the morning, as they passed by. Thus the withering had proceeded in the course of a day and night; and that, as he remarks, from the root. Matthew makes the disciples see, wonder, and speak; Mark records more precisely how Peter remembered the circumstance and spoke. The words themselves are more vivid here: Rabbi, behold, etc. Thereupon Jesus utters the word concerning the removing of mountains by faith: more concretely apprehended in Mark; more generally in Matthew. But Mark connects with this promise of Jesus the very important word concerning the hearing of prayer (ver. 24), and the condition of being reconciled with our brother (Matt. vi. 14).

Ver. 12. **And on the morrow.**—Therefore, on the Monday morning after the Sunday of the palms. —**He was hungry.**—Early departure, haste to enter the work of the day, and much else, lay at the foundation of this fact.

Ver. 13. **If haply,** εἰ ἄρα: that is, because it had leaves; since the leaves of the fig-tree appear after the fruit. Matt. xxi. 19.—**The time of figs was not yet.**—*See* the note on *Matthew.* As the tree had leaves, it promised fruit; for the harvest-time of figs, when it might have been stripped of its fruit, was not yet come. For the various explanations of this, *see* De Wette and Meyer. As καιρός signifies the full and perfect time, the meaning is clear enough. Between the period of leaf-formation and the time of fig-harvest, one might seek for figs from a tree standing exposed. But not till the καιρός had come could the tree be stripped. Thus the οὐ γὰρ is not an explanation of the circumstance that it had no figs, but of the Lord's coming and seeking, by which it appeared that the tree had only produced its leaves. The expression, "He found nothing but leaves only," signifies that He saw with displeasure that, as a worthless tree, it had nothing but leaves upon it. This He might conclude from the fact that the time of harvest had not yet come, and, therefore, that it was not already stripped of its fruit. According to Meyer, the meaning is, that the tree could not yet have borne fruit. "If it had been the time of figs, He would have found fruit besides the leaves." * But then a premature doom would have been pronounced on the tree. The early display of leaves was certainly irregular; but if it had been a certain sign of its dying, the Lord would not have sought fruit upon it. If it could put forth leaves, it must have been able previously to set its fruit.

Ver. 14. **And Jesus said unto it.**—Properly, answered and said. Bengel: *arbori fructum neganti.*

Ver. 16. Concerning the temple, *see* on *Matthew.* —**And would not suffer that any man should,** ἵνα; the toleration of evil is the procurement of it.—**Any vessel.**—No man durst carry tools and implements through the sacred precincts of the temple, that is, through the fore-court. Was it intended to avoid a circuitous route, as in a great city profane passages may be made through holy places? But the temple space was not in the way of such passing. Many, however, might bring their implements of toil with them at their devotions, in order to have them conveniently at hand. The carrying them through was, therefore, not literally a passing through with them, but rather the having them at hand; and it is opposed to the business of money-changing and selling doves which was carried on within the temple itself. According to Lightfoot and Wetstein, the Rabbins afterwards forbade the same thing.

Ver. 17. **Of all nations.**—The prediction of the prophets, that the temple should be a house of prayer for all nations, had a higher meaning (*see* Isa. ii. and other passages). There must be a distinction, however, between the Israelite bondsmen who brought their offerings (Lev. xvii. 8; xxii. 19; Ezra ii. 43; vii. 7), and the later proselytes of the gate; the relative recognition of these latter had given occasion to the symbol of the Court of the Gentiles. Therein lay the germ of the universality of the religion of promise. *See* on *Matthew.* That the additional clause occurs only in Mark, is not to be accounted for only on Gentile-Christian grounds; for it is wanting in Luke. It is peculiar to Mark that he everywhere lays stress upon the universality of the Gospel.†

* ["Οὐ γὰρ ἦν καιρὸς σύκων gives the reason why Jesus found nothing but leaves. If it had been the season for figs (viz., *June*, when the early fig, *Boccore*, ripens), he would have found fruit besides leaves, and would not have been deceived by the unseasonable (abnormal) leafage of the tree." Meyer, *in loc.*—*Ed.*]

† On the harmony here, Starke says: This was the third time that He thus cleansed the temple. The first time is

Ver. 18. **Sought how they might destroy Him.**—This was their counsel on Monday: that Jesus should die, had been already previously decided (John v. 16 ; vii. 32; x. 31; xi. 45). They now confusedly took counsel about the *how ;** since it seemed almost an impossibility, on account of the people, on this day of His wonderful ascendancy in the temple. Then again on Wednesday: "not on the feast-day," although Judas had preliminarily dealt with them on the Sunday concerning the matter. The Palm Sunday may have made Judas suspicious again, or brought his promise into doubt. Then he came on Thursday evening, after a new crisis had come (the departure of Jesus from the temple), and his exasperation had become complete.

Ver. 20. **They saw the fig-tree dried up from the roots.**—*See* on *Matthew.* Meyer naturally finds here another discrepancy with Matthew. Matthew is inexact in his record, only on account of a higher end that he contemplated in his narrative. Nor does Mark say that the withering had just then taken place, or been finished. The tree was now in a marvellous manner dried up; and that, as he adds, from the roots—from its diseased root upwards, throughout.

Ver. 22. **Faith in God.**—Trust towards God, πίστις Θεοῦ (Genitive of the object). More general view of faith, with reference to the personal source of miraculous power, the almighty God of the covenant: ch. ix. 23. Compare Matt. xvii. 20; Luke xvii. 6.

Ver. 24. **That ye receive them.**—That is, in the divine confidence of faith that is already received which in external reality has yet to come: Heb. xi. 1. The prayer of faith is heard: as prayer in the name of Jesus, John xiv. 13, 14; xvi. 23, 24, 26; or, as the prayer of a holy society, the Church, Matt. xviii. 19; or, as the prayer of the Holy Ghost, Rom. viii. 26–28.

Ver. 25. **When ye stand praying.**—Comp. Matt. v. 23, 24, and vi. 14, 15. As the word concerning the faith which moves mountains might have originally been uttered in more than one connection, so also that concerning the forgiveness of others, as the condition of all true offering of prayer, and its answer. But in this place, where Jesus connected this strongest assurance of the marvellous power of faith with the cursing of the fig-tree, it seems inevitable that He should declare how such a faith could not be sundered from a placable love; that it should never be used in the service of hate and fanaticism.

DOCTRINAL AND ETHICAL.

1. *See* on the parallel in *Matthew*, and also the previous notes.

2. The so-called cursing of the fig-tree is the rather to be regarded as a grand prophetic act, because Christ, as Christ, now stood at the climax of the palm festivity, and it was obvious that all Israel might now do Him homage. This symbolical act at such a crisis was a sure sign that He was perfectly conscious of the situation of things; as also was the weeping over the city during the festal procession according to Luke.

3. The cleansing of the temple at the beginning and at the end of Christ's pilgrimage, the earnest of a manifold cleansing of the Church from Gentile and Jewish perversions.

4. The declaration of the curse in its sacred form, a revelation to explain its real nature, and thereby to remove it; as contrasted with man's curse of evil wishing.

HOMILETICAL AND PRACTICAL.

See on *Matthew*.—The fig-tree a figure of Israel, and a warning sign to the Church: 1. As the fruitful fig-tree, which sets forth fruit sooner than leaves. So Israel. It had faith, and the works of faith, before it had the ceremonies of faith. So the early Church. 2. As the unfruitful fig-tree, which had an adornment of leaves, promising fruit deceitfully. So the Israel of the time of Jesus, and so the external Church of later times and the last.—The cursing of the fig-tree in its relation to the cleansing of the temple: 1. An indication of the morning thoughts of the Lord concerning Israel; 2. a prelude to the coming expurgation of the temple; 3. a prophetic token (for the hopeful disciples, concerning the coming solemn issue of things).—The judgment of Jesus upon the fig-tree, and His judgment upon the temple with its service.—Christ hungering on the morn of His greatest day of honor: or, the great sign of the spiritual purity and freedom of the kingdom of Christ.—The Lord's hunger on the temple-mountain, and His thirsting on Calvary.—How zeal for the Lord should keep itself pure from hatred against men.—Only in the spirit of reconciliation can the Christian execute the judicial office.—The flames of Christ's wrath a loving zeal, which is always one with the spirit of reconciliation.—We cannot help others in the way to heaven by the hateful and tormenting fury of fanaticism.

STARKE:—Christ knows what the feeling of the hungry is.—If we endure hunger, we should not murmur, remembering Him.— CANSTEIN: — Christ demands nothing of man, if he has not had time; nor does He come to seek till the time is up.— OSIANDER:—Hypocrites have a semblance of godliness, but no true fruits of faith; and so, if they repent not, they must perish. — HEDINGER: — We must rid the Church of every abuse, and spare no man.— QUESNEL:—Every believer is a temple of God, and must entertain the same zeal for his own soul's purity as Jesus displayed for the purity of the visible sanctuary.—OSIANDER:—The churches which celebrate a false worship of God are dens of thieves; they wrest for themselves the goods of simple people, and slay their souls.—Those who devote themselves to the correction of ecclesiastical abuses have commonly to encounter great opposition, their lives being sometimes laid in wait for.—An evil conscience must always tremble at itself, and is never bold in its work.—QUESNEL:—The truth everywhere makes a division among the people; some think to oppress it, while others hear it with wonder and faith.—GERLACH:—If you do not find that your believing prayer is granted, ask yourself what lies within that hinders your being heard.—BRAUNE:—Benevolent and like a Creator were all His miracles.—This is the only one which punishes and hurts, but it is performed on an inanimate object. It was designed to set lumi-

John ii.; the second time on the day before this, immediately after His entrance, Matt. xxi. 10, 12.

* [This would be indicated by the Future, ἀπολέσουσιν, of the Received Text; the Subjunctive, ἀπολέσωσιν, adopted by Lachmann and Tischendorf, would imply that the purpose itself to put Christ to death was now formed. —*Ed.*]

nously before us the reality of the divine punishments.—He pronounced here upon the tree that which, in the parable of the barren fig-tree, the vine-dresser had spoken of as in store for it.—Enmity to man suffers not the philanthropy of God to reach us. —Faith and reconcilableness go together.—SCHLEIERMACHER:—All that pertains to the community of Christian life and fellowship should be so ordered as to be free from all reference to the outward commerce of this world (on the cleansing of the temple). —GOSSNER:—Words, oral prayers, formularies, external exercises without the spirit, good wishes and mere resolutions, are mere leaves, if the Spirit of God does not invigorate them, and they bear no fruit.

SECOND SECTION.

THE DECISIVE CONFLICT OF JESUS WITH HIS ENEMIES IN JERUSALEM, AND HIS WITHDRAWAL TO THE MOUNT OF OLIVES.

CHAPTERS XI. 27—XIII. 37.

1. *The Attack of the Sanhedrim; or the Question concerning Christ's Authority, and His Counter-question concerning the Baptist's.* CH. XI. 27-33.

(Parallels: Matt. xxi. 23-27; Luke xx. 1-8.)

27 And they come again to Jerusalem: and as he was walking in the temple, there
28 come to him the chief priests, and the scribes, and the elders, And say[1] unto him, By
what authority doest thou these things, and who gave thee this authority to do these
29 things? And Jesus answered and said unto them, I will also ask of you one question,
30 and answer me, and I will tell you by what authority I do these things. The baptism
31 of John, was *it* from heaven, or of men? answer me. And they reasoned with themselves, saying, If we shall say, From heaven; he will say, Why then[2] did ye not believe
32 him? But if[3] we shall say, Of men; they feared the people: for all *men* counted John,
33 that he was a prophet indeed. And they answered and said unto Jesus, We cannot
tell. And Jesus answering,[4] saith unto them, Neither do I tell you by what authority I
do these things.

[1] Ver. 28.—Tischendorf reads, with B., C., L., Δ., ἔλεγον, and ἤ for καὶ (τίς) with B., L., D.
[2] Ver. 31.—The οὖν is wanting in A., C.*, L., Versions, Lachmann, Tischendorf, Meyer.
[3] Ver. 32.—The ἐάν is wanting in the best Codd.; omitting it, the sentence takes a very characteristic interrogatory form.
[4] Ver. 33.—The ἀποκριθείς is wanting in B., C., [L., Tischendorf, Meyer,] and elsewhere varies in its position.

EXEGETICAL AND CRITICAL.

See on the parallels of *Matthew* and *Luke*.—According to Mark's representation, this day of Christ's conflict falls on Tuesday of the Passion Week. But the conflict is subdivided into three parts: 1. The official demand as to Jesus' abode and supremacy in the temple, exhibited in the question of the Sanhedrim touching His authority; with its reply, as in our present section. 2. The ironical acknowledgment, on the side of the inimical party, of Christ's Messianic dignity, exhibited in a series of tempting questions and answers; with the great counter-question of Jesus. 3. The Lord's words to the people, and departure from the temple. Mark's account has in our text no prominent peculiarities; he agrees rather with Luke than with Matthew. His vivid style of delineation is seen in the trait that Jesus went round about the temple, while according to Matthew, He was in the act of teaching (though these are not inconsistent with each other); as also the second clause of the Sanhedrim's pondering—"But if we shall say." The Evangelist's choice of the expression λέγει αὐτοῖς, ver. 33, seems appropriate; while Matthew says ἔφη, and Luke εἶπεν. As the Sanhedrim refused Him a decisive declaration concerning John, who had prophetically authenticated Him as the Messiah, He also refused to them the decisive declaration they sought. This was, however, in itself decisive; but not in the form of an express statement.

Ver. 27. **Doest Thou these things?**—*See Matthew.* This meant, doubtless, the public appearance and work of Jesus in the temple under the Messiah-name which the people gave Him; amongst the rest, certainly, as an individual act, the cleansing of the temple also. The law ordained that prophets were to be tried, Deut. xiii. 1. The most essential requisite was agreement with the faith of the God of Israel; the accidental requirement was the performance of miracles. The latter was not valid without the former; but it was not said that the former without the latter was not valid. (Comp. Deut. xviii. 20; Ezek. xiii. 1). The Sanhedrim could hold themselves justified only in asking for the authority of Jesus. They could not deny that He had approved Himself by miracles. They were disposed, however, to make it a reproach, that He taught other gods, and a new religion. Hence they ask Him: 1. After the divine source of His power, prophetic inspiration; 2. after

His theocratic authentication. By the latter the former also was approved, and therefore Jesus appealed to John. John was the most recent monument of the truth and validity of the prophetic order in Israel. And this John had marked Him out as the Messiah. They had been compelled to allow his validity as a prophet, although they did not afterwards acknowledge him. They would entangle Jesus by making Him appeal to His divine dignity; but the word of Jesus entangled them and smote them at the same time. It was a reference to His theocratic legitimation, the bearer of which they durst not openly impeach; and at the same time a remembrancer that they themselves had, since the days of John, been falling deep into apostasy.

Ver. 31. **If we shall say.**—The abrupt form is expressive, and more significant than the full unfolding of it in Matthew and Luke, "We fear," which certainly declares the motive of their silence.

Indeed (of a truth).—According to the reading ὄντως ὅτι, which Tisch. adopts from B. C. L., Meyer translates "They were inwardly sure that John was a prophet." But A. D. and others form a counterpoise; as well as the consideration that this would attribute to the people altogether, and as a whole, the full and believing acceptance of John.

DOCTRINAL AND ETHICAL.

1. *See* on the parallels.

2. The counter-question of Jesus arose as the simple consequence of the question addressed to Him. That question was addressed to His theocratic authority. This was already involved in the authentication by John. If they acknowledged John, they must acknowledge also his witness to Jesus as the Messiah. If they did not acknowledge him, they were in a theocratic sense rebels; and Christ could, in the consciousness of His real, human-divine authority, transcending all theocratic authorization, refuse to give them an answer.

3. From heaven or of men.—Divine mission or human enthusiasm. The antithesis is here laid down, with reference to the contrast between the divine and the human in the human sphere, and does not prejudice the union of the divine and human in the Christological sphere.

HOMILETICAL AND PRACTICAL.

See Matthew.—Christ in His temple assaulted by the official rulers of the place.—Vainly would hierarchical official authority suppress the divine mission of Jesus.—The misuse of spiritual prerogatives against the rights of the Spirit of Christ a guilt which brings after it the severest punishments: 1. Misuse of dignity calls down the judgment of disgrace; 2 misuse of office calls down displacement and rejection from office.—The Spirit of Christ triumphs over the false spirituality of His enemies: 1. With His counter question opposing their question; 2. with His counter declarations against their declarations.—The authority of Christ to take possession of the temple of God as opposed to the impotence of His foes: 1. The authority: *a.* His theocratic authority; *b.* His personal divine-human authority; *c.* the authority which rose out of His actual Passion-conflict. 2. The impotence of His foes: *a.* as rejecters of the God-sent Baptist, forsaken of human justice; *b.* as rejecters of Christ, forsaken of the Spirit; *c.* as enemies and murderers of Christ, forsaken of God in His government of the world.—The obedience of Christ as confronting the Jewish priesthood, an emblem of Christian faith confronting churchly office: 1. The Lord regards the office as under the condition of obedience to the revelation of God, because it issues from that revelation; 2. He regards Himself as under the obligation to obey the revelation of God, because He is the consummation of it. Or, 1. In His suffering a question; 2. in His declining to answer; 3. in His willingness to submit to officials, so long as their rejection is not complete. —The heavenly prudence of the Lord in its triumph over the human wisdom of His enemies.—How the spirit of the New Covenant confronts the false representatives of the Old Covenant in God's temple: 1. With the clear word of knowledge; 2. with the firm word of assurance; 3. with the sharp word of judgment; 4. with the abundant word of life and of freedom.

STARKE:—*Nova Bibl. Tub.:*—Zeal for God's house and for its purity is sure to awaken enemies.—Conscience bears witness against the worst of men: they are their own accusers, judges, condemners.—OSIANDER:—They who will not suffer the Church's amendment in rule and discipline must fall.—CANSTEIN:—When those in the teaching and ruling office are unfaithful to their calling, and God raises up others extraordinarily, the former take all pains to deny to the latter the power that God Himself has given them.—HEDINGER:—The good need prudence in their intercourse with cunning and wicked people, lest their simplicity and openness bring harm to them and their cause.—QUESNEL:—Miserable case when the men of light use their knowledge of the truth to oppose that truth.—How many will not in religious matters be sincere, and reveal the truth, lest they be assaulted and tried!—*Bibl. Wirt.:*—The scorners of the truth, God will in the end count not worthy of the truth they scorn; but, instead of it, will send them strong delusions, that they should believe a lie, 2 Thess. ii. 11, 12.

BRAUNE:—He might have appealed to many prophets (yet not in the same sense as to John). They would then have said: But that was in a former age. He takes the latest example (of a prophetic vocation)

---

2. *The Parable concerning the Counsel of the Sanhedrim against the Messiah.* CH. XII. 1–12.

(Parallels: Matt. xxi. 33–46; Luke xx. 9–17.)

1 And he began to speak[1] unto them by parables. A *certain* man planted a vineyard,
and set an hedge about *it*, and digged *a place for* the wine-fat, and built a tower, and
2 let it out to husbandmen, and went into a far country. And at the season he sent to

the husbandmen a servant, that he might receive from the husbandmen of the fruit of
3 the vineyard. And[2] they caught *him*, and beat him, and sent *him* away empty
4 And again he sent unto them another servant: and at him they cast stones,[3] and
5 wounded *him* in the head, and sent *him* away shamefully handled. And again[4] he sent
another; and him they killed, and many others; beating some, and killing some.
6 Having yet therefore one son, his well-beloved, he sent him also last unto them, saying,
7 They will reverence my son. But those husbandmen said among themselves, This is
8 the heir; come, let us kill him, and the inheritance shall be ours. And they took him,
9 and killed *him*, and cast *him* out of the vineyard. What shall therefore the lord of the
vineyard do? He will come and destroy the husbandmen, and will give the vineyard
10 unto others. And have ye not read this scripture: The stone which the builders re-
11 jected is become the head of the corner: This was the Lord's doing [from the Lord],
12 and it is marvellous in our eyes? And they sought to lay hold on him, but feared the
people; for they knew that he had spoken the parable against them: and they left
him, and went their way.

[1] Ver. 1.—Lachmann, Tischendorf, [Meyer] read λαλεῖν instead of λέγειν, following B., G., L., Δ., [Syriac, Vulgate].
[2] Ver. 3.—Lachmann, Tischendorf read καί, after B., D., L., Δ. Meyer: from Matt. xxi. 35.
[3] Ver. 4.—The reading of B., D., L., [Δ., Lachmann, Tischendorf, Meyer,] κἀκεινον ἐκεφαλαίωσαν καὶ ἠτίμησαν, does not seem thorough enough, as opposed to the climax supported by Cod. A. and others, viz., beating and sending empty—wounding in the head and sending home shamefully handled.
[4] Ver. 5.—Codd. B., C., D., L., Δ. omit πάλιν.

EXEGETICAL AND CRITICAL.

See the parallel passages in *Matthew* and *Luke*.—Mark relates only the second of the three parables, which Christ, according to Matthew, connected with His rejection of the commission of the Sanhedrim, for the purpose of indicating to them what He awaited at their hands, and how they, as the murderers of the Messiah, should be subjected to the punishment of losing the Messianic kingdom. It is the very parable in which they are made to appear as the murderers of the Messiah in connection with the persecutors of the prophets. In the first verse, we obtain a hint from Mark that Jesus delivered several parables (ἐν παραβολαῖς λέγειν) before His opponents. Mark is, further, more exact than Matthew in the climax of the messages sent by the lord of the vineyard. According to him, the first servant is beaten upon the back, and sent empty away; the second is wounded in the head, insulted, and sent away covered with disgrace; the third is killed. This triple fate is then met by many others. In consequence of this conduct the lord of the vineyard despatches his son; and of him Mark observes that he was the only son. From Matthew we learn that servants were twice sent,—on the first occasion in smaller, on the second, in greater numbers; and their fate is to be beaten, killed, stoned. Luke records only an increased abuse of the several servants despatched. The actual ground-thought is in each case the same: repeated messages, increased injuries, and, as a consequence, augmented hardening of heart and rebellion. Then we have the opposition between the sending of the servants and the sending of the son,—between the generous hope of the lord, that pious fear and remorse would be manifested, and the flagitious design respecting the inheritance on the part of the vinedressers. Christ, according to Matthew, makes His enemies pronounce judgment, and declare what would be the dealing of that lord with his servants; according to Mark, the condemnation is expressed by Christ Himself. The passage from the Psalms, Mark quotes in conclusion, as does Luke; the citation from Isaiah, introduced by Matthew, is not here given. And further the μὴ γένοιτο, spoken by the opponents in Luke xx. 16, is wanting. Graphic narrative and a freshness of delineation are the characteristics of Mark in this passage, as in others.

Ver. 2. **Of the fruit.**—The stipulated portion of the product. For the agreement of Matthew with Mark in this passage, consult *Note* on *Matthew*.

Ver. 4. **And again he sent.**—We admit, there is undoubtedly a kind of periodic succession in the missions hinted at; but this is not to be settled in an external, petty way, of which an example is presented in Meyer.—**At him they cast stones.**—'Εκεφελαίωσαν is to be explained in accordance with the difference between it and the simple ἔδειραν. Beating with sticks upon the back, casting stones at the head, marked the first gradation, to which the second pair corresponded,—being sent away empty, shamefully disfigured. As this word, in other collocations, means simply to recapitulate, to relate summarily, we must interpret here according to the context. Meyer says, Mark has confounded κεφαλαιόω with κεφαλίζω. But the latter would have been too strong; and it is possible that the verb before us might have recommended itself to him as capable of bearing two senses, and this double-force we have endeavored to indicate. Wakefield's interpretation, "They made short work of him," is too one-sided.

Ver. 9. **Killed him and cast him out.**—The order is reversed in Matthew and Luke. Grotius and De Wette make it a hysteron-proteron. Meyer says, it is only another description.

He will come and will.—Kuinoel, following Vatablus, makes this the reply of the Pharisees in Matt. xxi. 24. It is plain that Mark gives a more brief account of the matter. The Lord spoke the judgment which His parable forced from the lips of His enemies. *See Note* on *Matthew*.

Ver. 12. **For they knew that He had spoken against them.**—Meyer would make these words, as well as in Luke, apply to the people and not to the members of the Sanhedrim. He intends this explanation to account for the apparent want of the proper succession in words. According to some commentators, these words should follow κρατῆσαι. But the order presents no difficulty at all. They would have seized Christ at once very willingly, and yet they ventured not, etc. This is only a reflection; and our words present the key, the concluding explanation. Their common purpose, to put the Messiah to death upon the first favorable occasion, rose in these and similar moments of exasperation to such a pitch, that they would have gladly seized Him on the spot, and killed Him, if they had only dared to do so.

DOCTRINAL AND ETHICAL.

1. Upon the import of the parable, *see* the remarks upon the passage in *Matthew*. The planting of the vineyard is to be looked upon as the promise and the law, or generally as the covenant-word in its identity with believing hearts. The hedge is not the law in itself, but is to be interpreted as being that external institution by which Israel was separated from the other nations (Eph. ii. 14); the wine-press, or tank, considered in connection with the altar of sacrifice and the martyrdom of the prophets, indicates the inner side of the congregation; and hence we are led to consider the tower, typifying civil order, law, and protection, as the opposite of the wine-press. The wine-fat is sunk into the earth and hidden; the tower rises on high, apparent to every eye, the sign of the vineyard.

2. We must remark, further, that we have here pictured the gradual augmentation of selfishness, of hostility to, and revolt from, the Lord, on the part of the theocratic servants and vassals of God. This representation presents at the same time a type of the climax of injuries inflicted upon the prophets, and above all, of the climax of the Lord's magnanimity, as opposed to the disgraceful conduct of the servants. The struggle of divine grace with the obdurate unbelief of the administrators of His plan of mercy divides into two periods: 1. The period of long-suffering; and 2. the period of judgment. The first era has two chief periods: *a.* The Establishment, *b.* the Missions; which we may divide into, 1. The missions of servants, rising by a threefold climax; 2. the mission of the Son, in which, again, three points present themselves: A. The wicked proposal; B. the murder of the Son; and C. the casting of his corpse forth out of the vineyard. But, in the same manner, are three points to be observed in the Judgment: 1. The destruction of the evil-doers; 2. the entrusting of the vineyard to others; and 3. a donation of the vineyard to others, instead of a relation of vassalage.

3. The nature of the theocracy.—On the one side, it had a political, national end; on the other, a religious: and therefore the lord demands not all the fruit, but only a portion. The transformation of the theocracy into hierarchy: 1. The servants of God begin by converting His vineyard, which, under the condition of feudal service, He had let out to them, into a private possession. 2. They treat the prophets and reformers, who desire to call their condition of dependence back to their recollection, as enemies, and so treat mediately the Lord as an enemy. 3. They killed the son and heir, not in ignorance, but knowing him to be the heir, and actually because he was the heir: so evil-disposed were they.

4. The prospect, which the Lord presented, of the vineyard being handed over to strangers, to the Gentiles, must have exasperated the Sanhedrim almost more than the proclamation of their own downfall.

5. The parable before us is illustrated and expanded by the parables which Matthew makes precede and follow. If we examine the idea of this parable, we shall find that the germs of the two other parables are contained in the one before us.

6. Christ the beloved, the only Son, that is, the only-begotten Son of God; Christ, the last sent, is a mark of the revelation being perfected; Christ, the corner-stone, indicates the perfected Redeemer and Head of the Church.

HOMILETICAL AND PRACTICAL.

See the foregoing Reflections, and the *Commentary* on *Matthew*.—The mournful, historical fact that the administrators of the sacred things of God fail so often to attain salvation; or, the *night side* of the priesthood.—The history of the priestly office under the old economy, a perpetual symbol of warning to the priestly (ministerial) office under the new.—The contest which the Lord, from the remotest ages, has been engaged in with the unfaithful servants of His word and His grace.—The immemorial contrast between unfaithful officers of God and faithful messengers from God.—How the gracious generosity of God strives with the obdurate unbelief of men up to the moment of final decision.—The final purpose of God (They will reverence My Son), and the last purpose of the rebellious servants (This is the heir; come, let us kill him, etc.).—The Lord in heaven is willing rather to have the appearance of folly in sending His Son, than that His grace should not be revealed to the uttermost.—Grace in highest glory appearing alone, to the apparent neglect of wisdom, justice, and omnipotence, and yet, at that very moment, uniting in itself all the attributes of wisdom, justice, and omnipotence.—How all the perfections of God are comprehended in the glory of His grace: 1. By seeming to vanish in it; 2. by again appearing, glorified in it.—The last point by which God's grace seeks to obtain a hold, is pious fear in men.—Finally: Christ the last mission of God's grace to mankind, John iii. 16; Heb. x. 26, 27; xii. 18.—The contradiction in the words, This is the heir, let us kill him; or, the remnant of faith in unbelief, making unbelief damning.—To the exercise of long-suffering succeeds that of judgment.—The heir and the inheritance cannot be separated.—The murder of the heir converted into the glorification of the inheritance.—The parabolical statement of Christ's glorification, a supplement to the parable of His rejection.—The determination of God as to the wicked counsel of the opponents of Christ: 1. Their counsel allowed; 2. defeated; 3. turned to the service of God's design.—The theocracy as a building of God: 1. A completed building; 2. a preparation for a second building.—Christ, the great miracle of God.—The enmity manifested towards the Lord's word, enmity shown to the dazzling brightness with which the picture of His enemies was drawn.—The wicked shudder before the picture of their own life.—The impotency of Jesus' foes.—Jesus' address before the people; or, the fault of the priests, and the fault of the laity: 1. Difference; 2. connection.

Hedinger:—God spares neither labor nor expense in sustaining and extending His Church.—Be fruitful in good works.—The fate of the servants sent into God's vineyard.—Osiander:—The more frequently the obdurate are called to repent, the more insane and senseless is the position assumed by them.—The riches of the goodness and long-suffering of God in sending faithful servants, who are zealous to the very death for His house.—The witnesses of the truth.—O that the pious would stir one another up to goodness with the same industry that the godless excite one another to wickedness!—CANSTEIN:—Sin is very frightful: it ceases not where it has begun; one sin springs from another.—QUESNEL:—So many deadly sins, so many murderous acts against Jesus Christ.—CANSTEIN:—The enemies of the truth can, no doubt, in some manner say such in itself is truth; yet their answer proceeds not from truth, because their hearts are not temples of truth.—*Nova Bibl. Tub.*:—God and His grace are bound to no people.—What the proud generation of Satan rejects, laughs to scorn, tramples under foot, that God raises in defiance of it, to the glory of Himself.—The world, despite its efforts, cannot execute its malice and wickedness sooner than God, from hidden reasons, permits.

LISCO:—That the only Son is sent, and sent the last, magnifies both the love of the Lord and the offence of the servants.—BRAUNE:—Official sins: The wine-press is the ministerial office, which should express the letters, the peel covering the divine word, which should expound the divine word, the fruit of the vine, and make wine from it to refresh the heart. (Let it be remarked that this interpretation is not sufficient; comp. *Doctrinal Reflection*, 1.) Isa. v. 1 2. Fates of prophets: Micaiah was scourged (1 Kings xxii. 24), and also Jeremiah (Jer. xxxvii. 15) Isaiah, Amos, and others were killed (1 Kings xviii. 13); Zechariah was stoned (2 Chron. xxiv. 21); and we find in Nehemiah (ix. 26) that the prophets of God had been slain: Acts vii. 52; Heb. xi. 36-38.—The judgment of Jesus in the Pharisees' mouth (The Lord will come, etc.), the first note of the fearful cry, His blood be on us, and on our children (Matt. xxvii. 25).—The world's salvation is, nevertheless, triumphant. From the Jews it passed to the Gentiles, from the benighted east to the clear west, from the enervated south to mighty north; and when yet farther?—Still God's kingdom remains.—They raged, but a hook had been put into their nose, and a bridle into their lips (Isa. xxxvii. 29).

SCHLEIERMACHER:—Truth we owe to men, yet we are ourselves bound by it according to our ability.—In every circumstance we must let love point out how we can render the best service to the truth in dealing with each individual.—BRIEGER:—Let us go forth, therefore, unto Him, etc.: Heb. xiii. 13 (referring to the heir being cast out of the vineyard); Isa. xxviii. 16.

---

3. *The Cunning Attack of the Pharisees and Herodians, and their Defeat.* VERS. 13-17.

(Parallels: Matt. xxii. 15-22; Luke xx. 20-24.)

13 And they send unto him certain of the Pharisees and of the Herodians, to catch
14 him in *his* words. And when they were come,[1] they say unto him, Master, we know
that thou art true, and carest for no man: for thou regardest not the person of men, but
15 teachest the way of God in truth: Is it lawful to give tribute to Cesar, or not? Shall
we give, or shall we not give? But he, knowing their hypocrisy, said unto them,
16 Why tempt ye me? bring me a penny, that I may see *it*. And they brought *it*. And
he saith unto them, Whose *is* this image and superscription? And they said unto him,
17 Cesar's. And Jesus answering, said unto them, Render to Cesar the things that are
Cesar's,[2] and to God the things that are God's. And they marvelled at him.

[1] Ver. 14.—Lachmann, Tischendorf, after B., C., L., Δ., read καὶ οἱ ἐλθόντες instead of οἱ δὲ ἐλθόντες.
[2] Ver. 17.—Lachmann, after A., D., reads ἀπόδοτε τὰ Καίσαρος Καίσαρι; Tischendorf and Meyer, after B., C., L., Syriac, read τὰ Καίσαρος ἀπόδοτε Καίσαρι.

EXEGETICAL AND CRITICAL.

Comp. the parallels in *Matthew* and *Luke*.—The turning-point here is the ironical acknowledgment of Jesus' Messianic dignity on the part of the Jewish rulers, after that they, in their attempt to overcome Jesus by the assertion of their authority in the presence of the people, had been covered with shame. It forms, consequently, the second section of our Lord's strife in the temple on the Tuesday of the Passion Week. In this history of the temptation, the object of which was to entangle the Lord, two chief attacks are specialized by Mark: the attack made by the Pharisees in connection with the Herodians, or the history of the tribute-penny; and the attack of the Sadducees. In the latter, however, the question of the scribes leaves no longer an impression of malicious temptation, but draws the transactions to a close with an example of the triumph of Christ over many minds among the scribes and Pharisees. It is, nevertheless, the same history, written more from the bright side, while Matthew pictures it from the darker side. This individual was better than his party who had despatched him to tempt Christ: he made no concealment of the effect which the wisdom of Christ made upon him. This history is allowed by Luke to pass unnoticed. The cunning shown in the temptation now under consideration, is distinctly emphasized by each of the three Evangelists, Matthew and Mark giving the additional fact of the union between the Pharisees and Herodians to effect their ends. Matthew states that those who were sent were *disciples* of the Pharisees, and consequently young persons; from Luke it appears they were worldlings, who could only feign scruples of conscience. At the outset, the lively addition characterizes Mark, "Shall we give, or shall we not give?" The rest of the narrative is quickly sketched, and remarkably graphic. In the conclusion he is shorter than Matthew and Luke.

Ver. 13. **And they send unto Him.**—Those mentioned in the preceding section, the Sanhedrim, are intended. But Matthew represents with proprie ty the Pharisees as the most active in the transaction.—**To catch Him.**—'Αγρεύειν refers primarily to the chase.

Ver. 15. **Shall we give?**—Important application of the question to their conduct. They appear, moreover, anxious to place the negation in His mouth.

Ver. 17. **The things that are Cæsar's.**—The order of the words in Mark is peculiar; the construction is more cautious, and yet more lively.—**And they marvelled at Him.**—The young aristocratic portion of the population of the capital had not, in its pride, expected such a blow from the Galilæan Rabbi. Matthew informs us that they felt themselves overcome: in Mark this is implied.

DOCTRINAL AND ETHICAL.

1. *See Matthew.*

2. The feigned alliance of hostile parties against Christ, a measure of the greatness of their hatred to Christ. Mark has already (ch. iii. 6) recorded the decision of the alliance. Compare the friendship of Pilate and Herod, as recorded in Luke.

3. Students and young nobles are often caught in the dangerous currents of their day. They are often, through their warm, generous feelings, misled and deceived.

4. Christ remains unmoved by the excitement; and what was confused, becomes, by a reference to manifest right, disentangled.

5. The word of Christ undermined, further, the alliance between the two allied-hostile parties. The Pharisees were not willing to give to the Emperor what belonged to him; the Herodians gave not to God what was God's, not even in appearance.

HOMILETICAL AND PRACTICAL.

See the notes on *Matthew.*—Perfect rest and calmness is the perfect action and quickness of the spirit.—The spiritual presence of Christ fills the present with the might of eternity.—How a stream of light from Christ can become a piercing lightning-flash.—Hypocrisy, the original sin of an impure patriotism and feeling of false freedom.—The majesty with which Christ investigates the rights of Cæsar: 1. The free examination; 2. the just recognition; 3 the holy reservation.—Christ and the young nobility of Jerusalem: 1. How little they knew; 2. how royally He revealed Himself to them.—Students and earnest youths often the unconscious and deceived tools of impure endeavors.—Divine simplicity and integrity always triumphant over human and devilish cunning.—Speak the truth without seeking to please or to injure any one.—Amazement may form, particularly with youthful and deceived minds, the beginning of wisdom.

STARKE:—*Nova Bibl. Tub.*:—The meanest kind of persecutors betake themselves to the secular authority.—Truth must frequently find that hypocritical professors unite with worldlings against her.—HEDINGER:—Every station has its rights. Fear God. Honor the king: 1 Pet. ii. 17.—CANSTEIN:—The Pharisees flattered the Lord to destroy Him: He, however, put them to shame to bring them to salvation.—BRAUNE:—Those who, from their knowledge, should have been the friends of truth, are the first in enmity against the King of truth. (Pharisees and Herodians.) No one should allow himself to be employed to vex others: this is especially the duty of young persons towards noble, venerable men.—They thought He had within Him the spark of vanity, and that He would destroy Himself in His zeal for God's honor and His own personal dignity, which they presented in combination. So do men strive to entangle one another by praise.—*See* Braune's extract from CLAUDIUS' *Asmus*, p. 316.

SCHLEIERMACHER:—It were a different case if ye had never received the money, if ye had perilled blood and life for independence; but if ye have suffered the halter to be bound round your neck, and have not made any opposition, then bear the yoke.—Ye are giving your approval to the external regulations under which ye are living, as is sufficiently evident from your use of the money.—(God, what is God's.) He would remind them that they had other wealth, and were in undisturbed possession of the same.—They should distinguish between the tributary condition and the spiritual.—GOSSNER:—Out of hypocrisy they state the truth, in order to overthrow the truth.

---

4. *The Attack of the Sadducees, and their Overthrow.* VERS. 18–27.

(Parallels: Matt. xxii. 23–33; Luke xx. 27–40.)

18 Then come unto him the Sadducees, which say there is no resurrection; and they
19 asked him, saying, Master, Moses wrote unto us, If a man's brother die, and leave *his*[1]
wife *behind him*, and leave no children, that his brother should take his wife, and raise
20 up seed unto his brother. Now there were seven[2] brethren: and the first took a wife,
21 and dying left no seed. And the second took her, and died, neither left he[3] any seed
22 and the third likewise. And the seven had her, and left no seed:[4] last of all the wo-
23 man died also. In the resurrection therefore, when they shall rise, whose wife shall
24 she be of them? for the seven had her to wife. And Jesus answering, said unto them,
Do ye not therefore err, because ye know not the scriptures, neither the power of God?
25 For when they shall rise[5] from the dead, they neither marry, nor are given in marriage;
26 but are as the angels which are in heaven. And as touching the dead, that they rise:
have ye not read in the book of Moses, how in the bush God spake unto him, saying, I

27 *am* the God of Abraham, and the God of Isaac, and the God of Jacob? He is **not**
the God of the dead, but the God[6] of the living: ye therefore do greatly err.

[[1] Ver. 19.—The αὐτοῦ after γυναῖκα is omitted by B., C., L., Δ., Meyer.]
[[2] Ver. 20.—After ἑπτά, Elzevir and Fritzsche have οὖν; it is not found in A., B., C., E., F., L.]
[[3] Ver. 21.—Instead of καὶ οὐδε αὐτὸς ἀφῆκε, B., C., L., Tischendorf read μὴ καταλιπών.]
[4] Ver. 22.—The reading, καὶ οἱ ἑπτὰ οὐκ ἀφῆκαν σπέρμα, [omitting ἔλαβον αὐτὴν and the second καί,] is strongly supported by B., C., L., Δ., [Tischendorf]; but the demands of the context go to strengthen the Codd. which give the other reading. That no seed was left by the seven, is in and for itself of no importance; it is merely the occasion of the seven taking the same woman to wife.
[5] Ver. 23.—Ὅταν ἀναστῶσι is omitted by B., C., L., Δ. Lachmann puts it in parenthesis; Cod. A., &c., support it; and the consideration, that its omission is easier to account for than its insertion, is an additional argument in favor of this reading.
[6] Ver. 27.—Θεός is wanting with ζώντων in A., B., C., D., Griesbach, Lachmann, and Tischendorf. [Tischendorf omits ὑμεῖς οὖν, after B., C., L., Δ.]

EXEGETICAL AND CRITICAL.

See Matthew, and the parallel in *Luke*.—In this section, Mark's individuality appears only in the more pictorial description of the seven successive marriages; in special supplemental strokes; in the more positive tracing of the error of the Sadducees up to a want of knowledge of the Scriptures and to unbelief; and in the final statement, Ye therefore do greatly err. While the immediate effect of Christ's word is not presented till the Evangelist comes to relate the next history.

Ver. 23. **When they shall rise.**—The immediate, special reference is to the seven. Perhaps doubt is also expressed.

Ver. 26. **How in the bush**; that is to say, in the appropriate passage, where the thorn-bush is spoken of—which ye will find something of a thorn-bush.

DOCTRINAL AND ETHICAL.

1. Comp. *Matthew*, and the conclusion of the Apostles' Creed, Resurrection of the body, etc. John v.; 1 Cor. xv.; 2 Cor. v.; Dan. xii., etc. Comp. the doctrine of the Scripture on the Resurrection, as unfolded in the works upon Biblical Theology, and the teaching of the Church as given in works on Dogmatics; the hopes of immortality cherished by the nations, recorded in histories of religion. Comp. the proofs of an immortality. The writings bearing on the topic from PLATO's *Phædo* down.

2. Unbelief has always two springs: 1. The want of historic faith (Ye know not the Scriptures); 2. the want of personal faith (Ye know not the power of God).

3. Belief in immortality and belief in angels, or a world of spirits, are most intimately united: so also the respectively opposed elements of unbelief.

4. Unbelief is, on the one hand, united with rude sensuality ("marrying" in that world too); and, on the other, with a wild phantasy (indulging in phantasies upon the future state), and a carnal view of the uniformity obtaining throughout God's universe (*tout comme chez nous*).

5. Unbelief, which attacks one part of the truth, understands nothing of that part upon which it intends to support itself in attacking.

6. They tempted the Lord to the abandonment of the doctrine of the resurrection, or to the retaining of it, coupled with polygamy in the future as its consequence. They supposed, He must either state an absurdity, or be struck dumb by their supposed *deductio ad absurdum*. But they had political designs in addition. Comp. *Matthew*. They intended that, by a denial of the resurrection, He should deny His work, or should present Himself as an enthusiast, and yield up to the profane world the secret of His hope. Christ sent the especially "wise" home as the especially "foolish."

HOMILETICAL AND PRACTICAL.

Comp. *Matthew*.—The Sadducees constitute the historical counter-picture to the Pharisees.—The Sadducees, the deniers of immortality, are immortal.—They invented an improbable, indecent tale to deny a most trustworthy and glorious reality.—They find in the Bible a thorny bush indeed, but not the burning bush.—The sentimental expectations of a bodily sight and possession are not tenable: 1. Too great for the reason; 2. for faith too little; 3. for both preposterous.—The external revelation is not in itself weak through too strong faith, but through credulity springing from too little faith, which believes, 1. Many things, but not much; 2. the extraordinary, but not the miraculous; 3. the spectral, but not the spiritual; 4. the earthly in heavenly hue and dress, but not the heavenly as the glorification of the earthly.—The Sadducees and their faith: I. How they attack faith (while they propound the most improbable views), either, 1. with an improper explanation of Scripture and of the law, 2. with an improper picture of life, and 3. with an improper view of the world; or, 1. with improper reasoning, 2. with improper wit. II. How faith replies: with, 1. a deeper exposition of Scripture, 2. higher pictures of life, 3. a holier contemplation of the world in the light of God.—They say, our unbelief comes from our knowing: He says, it comes from your not knowing.—The belief in the angels makes the belief in the resurrection a necessity.—One truth of faith explains and strengthens another.—Unbelief in immortality a radical error: 1. A positive confusion; 2. a positive mistake.

QUESNEL:—The devil gives the Christian no rest. If one temptation does not entangle, another is tried; hence watchfulness is essential.—HEDINGER:—Preformed opinions constitute a hindrance to the truth. —Oh that there were none among Christians who doubt the resurrection! If they venture not to acknowledge their doubt, they manifest nevertheless by their deeds that they believe in no other life.—The thoughts of carnal men regarding the heavenly life are carnal and disreputable.—CANSTEIN:—Christians must stir themselves up, in thinking of the eternal life, to separate themselves ever more and more from the lusts of the body and fleshly-mindedness.

BRAUNE:—It was the extreme fleshly-minded (the Sadducees) who could not comprehend the reality and truth of the spiritual world.—The Gospel of the Risen One has brought forward more clearly for the spirit of man the kingdom of God and the hope of resurrection, of which we have frequent relations in the Acts of the Apostles, where the Sadducees repeatedly appear as foes.—The Saviour unites the Scriptures and the power of God. Hence comes Augustine's statement, The more we see of the Scripture, the more we die to the world; the more we live to the world, the less we see.—"Reason digs beside (Scripture), Frivolity stalks by, and Pride flies away over" (Zinzendorf). Many of the Rabbis dreamed of marriages according to passages in the prophets, as Isa. lxv. 20, 23, where we read of a new heaven and a new earth; and this was not once deemed base by the Pharisees.—Of marriage, accordingly, that alone remains which was spiritual, just as sex in regard to physical distinctions is lost, and that alone remains which had spiritually been developed for the distinction between sexes, consisting in the development of what relates to spirit, and in that which lays hold of the mind's most inner nature, continues undoubtedly for ever.—Death breaks all bands, but destroys not existence.

BRIEGER:—He who has not in various ways experienced that God is the Living One, cannot from the heart believe in any resurrection. Is God called the God of Abraham? much more must He be called the God of Jesus Christ, John v. 29; 1 Cor. xv. 19; Rom. xiv. 8.

GOSSNER:—One sort of evil men after another come to Jesus to trouble Him, to tempt Him, instead of seeking their salvation from Him.

---

5. *The Scribe, first tempting, then half won.* VERS. 28–34.

(Parallels: Matt. xxii. 34–40; Luke xx. 39.)

28 And one of the scribes came, and having heard them reasoning together, and perceiving[1] that he had answered them well, asked him, Which is the first commandment
29 of all? And Jesus answered him, The first of all the commandments *is*,[2] Hear, O Israel;
30 The Lord our God is one Lord: And thou shalt love the Lord thy God with all thy heart, and with all thy soul, and with all thy mind,[3] and with all thy strength. This *is*
31 the first commandment.[4] And the second *is* like, *namely* this,[5] Thou shalt love thy
32 neighbour as thyself: there is none other commandment greater than these. And the scribe said unto him, Well, Master, thou hast said the truth: for there is one God;[6] and
33 there is none other but he: And to love him with all the heart, and with all the understanding, and with all the soul,[7] and with all the strength, and to love *his* neighbour as
34 himself, is more than all whole burnt-offerings and sacrifices. And when Jesus saw that he answered discreetly, he said unto him, Thou art not far from the kingdom of God. And no man after that durst ask him *any question.*

[[1] Ver. 28.—Lachmann reads ἰδών for εἰδὼς, after C., D., L.]

[2] Ver. 29.—Many variations. Tischendorf, adopting B., L., Δ., reads ὅτι πρώτη ἐστίν; Griesbach, ὅτι πρώτη πάντων ἐντολή, after A. and Minusculi.

[[3] Ver. 30.—Tischendorf, following D. and some Minusculi and Versions, omits καὶ ἐξ ὅλης τῆς διανοίας.]

[4] Ver. 30.—Αὕτη πρώτη ἐντολή omitted by Tischendorf, following B., E., L., Δ.; retained by A., D., &c.

[5] Ver. 31.—Tischendorf reads simply δευτέρα αὕτη, and so B., L., Δ.; this means, "this is the second in importance." Lachmann, and the majority of the MSS., retain ὁμοία αὐτῇ.

[[6] Ver. 32.—The best MSS. omit Θεός after ἐστι.]

[[7] Ver. 33.—Tischendorf, following B., L., Δ., omits καὶ ἐξ ὅλης τῆς ψυχῆς. Meyer defends the reading.]

EXEGETICAL AND CRITICAL.

Comp. *Matthew.*—The peculiarities of Mark: Matthew causes the tempting Pharisees, who were for the moment influenced by friendly feelings towards the Lord because He had put the Sadducees to silence, to advance; while Mark brings forward into the light their representative, a well-meaning scribe, whom Matthew designates more specifically as a lawyer. Matthew emphasizes the temptation, Mark the questioning; and, in addition, the transaction is clothed in a much richer form than in the Gospel by Matthew. The statement of Jesus is first introduced, that the greatest commandment is to hear that God is one, as therefrom proceeds the unity of the commandment of love out of the unity or absolute simplicity of the entire inner life. To this succeeds the joyful assent of the scribe, and his well-nigh literal repetition of the Lord's words. And, lastly, the recognition by Christ that he had answered discreetly; to which the declaration is appended, that he was not far from the kingdom of God. The observation that the Jews dared not question further, forms the conclusion of this section in Mark. Luke appends this remark to the question of the Sadducees, Matthew to the counter-question of Christ. Considering the meaning, these three narratives form but one whole. For, after the Sadducees had been defeated, the hope to overcome Him was already destroyed. The temptation here narrated was only an ambiguous after-game, probably half devoted to the attempt of inducing Christ to allow Himself, in spite of all, to be won over as a partisan to the party of the Pharisees. But when Jesus had put His counter-question, to which no reply could be given, the mouths of His opponents were finally closed. Upon the allegation of Meyer, that a difference exists between Mark and Matthew, comp. *Note* to Matthew's account.

Ver. 28. **The first commandment of all.**—The first, and that in the sense of the chief importance. *See* Note upon *Matthew.* "The Jews enumerated six hundred and thirteen ordinances; three hundred and sixty-five prohibitions, according to the days of the year; two hundred and twenty-eight commandments, according to the parts of the body. The Pharisees distinguished between lesser and greater commandments." Braune.

Ver. 29. **Hear, O Israel; The Lord:** Deut. vi. 4, 5.—Jesus gives the introduction to the ten commandments as the first command itself, not in so far as it forms one of the commandments, but in so far as it is the principle of the commandments,—finding its full exposition in the words: And thou shalt love, etc. The inner idea of the introduction has been explained already in Deuteronomy, from which the citation is drawn. Directly in opposition to this *qualitative* conception, the modern Jews reckon, according to their division, the words: Hear, O Israel, etc., *quantitatively*, as the first commandment. Upon this division, as well as generally upon the various divisions of the decalogue, comp. GEFFKEN, *Ueber die verschiedene Eintheilung des Dekalogus*, Hamburgh, 1838, p. 9 *seq.* "This principle of all duties was termed specially, קריאה, or sometimes, after the initial word, שְׁמַע; and the words were usually recited daily, night and morning; *see* VITRINGA, *Synagoga Judaica*, 2, 3, 15; BUXTORF, *Syn.* 9." Meyer.

Ver. 30. **With all thy heart.**—The Hebrew text has the three following specifications: with all thy heart, and with all thy soul, and with all thy strength (מְאֹד, a might which is at once the manifesting of strength, and employing of strength; Gesenius, *robur*, *vehementia*). Instead of the first word, heart, the Septuagint reads, διάνοια; the second is of the same tenor; and the third it properly renders δύναμις. Christ's quotation, as given by Matthew, follows the original text in the first and second word, heart, soul; but substitutes, with a fulness of meaning, for the third, διάνοια, the moral might of consciousness, of will. In Mark, the one word is expressed by two, διάνοια and ἰσχύς (=מאד). On the contrary, in Mark, the scribe divides the first conception (heart) into two, καρδία and σύνεσις; while the lawyer, in the narrative in Luke x. 27, where we have a similar, though not identical, interview, speaks as Jesus here does. Only ἰσχύς precedes διάνοια. From all this, it is evident that a freer mode of handling the Old Testament text prevailed in the apostolic circle; moreover, it is worthy of being noted that no Gospel contains the δύναμις of the Septuagint. Whether the differences are only "variations of the Greek tradition," occasioned by the habit of quoting from memory, or different points of view, is doubtful. In any case, it is noteworthy that the philosophizing Septuagint has explained καρδία by διάνοια; while, according to Matthew, Christ, spiritualizing ἰσχύς, gives its force as διάνοια, which is preceded by the heart and soul. Mark and Luke exegetically unite διάνοια and ἰσχύς. The lawyer, to indicate his legal stand-point, adds to καρδία, which the Septuagint had converted into διάνοια, the σύνεσις. Upon biblical psychology (upon which Roos, Beck, and Delitzsch have written), comp. *Note* upon *Matthew*.

Ver. 33. **With all thy understanding.**—Signification of the intelligence, as it develops into understanding.

Burnt offerings and sacrifices.—Ps. li.; 1 Sam. xv. 22; Hos. vi. 6. This very comparison proved that the lawyer was overcome by an emotion of courageous faith, the giving utterance to which might have easily caused offence to his companions. t was in this situation a testimony.

Ver. 34. Discreetly, νουνεχῶς: with knowledge and understanding.—Attic, νουνεχόντως; the opposite, ἀφρόνως.

DOCTRINAL AND ETHICAL.

1. *See* remarks upon *Matthew*.—From the unity and spiritual harmony of God proceeds the essential unity of His law in one principle—love. This principle has already been brought into view in Deuteronomy. The true covenant-God, as the one God and the one Lord over hearts and in them,—this makes one life-experience, one life-motive, love. So appears the royal law as given by James (ch. ii. 8) and Paul (Rom. xiii. 10). Upon the element of temptation in this question, comp. *Note* on *Matthew*. *In the passage before us, religion is declared to be the central, concentrated direction of the whole man, especially of his soul's powers, to the one God.*

2. The man, in whose inward parts the law of God has been by love inscribed, loves at first from the heart, in the very core of his being; next, notwithstanding the varying frames of his soul, in his soul likewise, in the disposition of his soul-life; and then in his practical intelligence or mode of thought,—in the practical resolutions and purposes of his life, with which all the powers of his life (as members and instruments of righteousness) enter into, and are spent in, the service of love.

3. BRAUNE:—These two commandments point to the two tables of the law. Upon the first are five laws, concerning God's glory, God's likeness, God's name, God's day, God's representatives; upon the second, five concerning person and life, marriage and household peace, goods and chattels, honor and right, and the heart of man. The two tables are one; containing the commandments of one, inseparable, heavenly law of love.

4. To be rational (discreet), the Lord here calls, not to be far from the kingdom of God. The reason, ideally conceived, is the faculty of understanding or perceiving the divine in its ideas. This faculty perceives the idea of love in the law. Discretion and subtilty mark the contrast between the true and false use of reason.

5. Thou art not far from the kingdom of God.—He who recognizes the law in its spiritual meaning, and in opposition to external forms and ceremonies (more than burnt-offerings and sacrifices), is on the road of the Spirit (rational in a moral sense), and on the way of return from self-righteousness and of turning back to self-knowledge, which conditions the entrance into the kingdom founded by Christ. Not far from, that is, near. What was still wanting was, the full surrender to his conviction, or the actual following of Jesus. This transaction is, accordingly, a sign and presage of Christ's victory in the centre of His enemy's camp.

HOMILETICAL AND PRACTICAL.

See Matthew.—The three unities in religion, a type of the Trinity of the one God: 1. The one God; 2. the one faith (giving heed to Christ's word); 3. the one commandment.—The unity of God is not mere individuality, nor singleness, but chiefly, His being alone and His being one, to which the unity of man in the simplicity of the faith must correspond.—Man is really a unity in obedience, when his inner life, in the trinity of heart (feeling), of soul (the will) and of reason or intelligence, is at one with itself and with God's word.—Unity and trinity, the secret of all spiritual life: 1. Of the highest life above us; 2. of the deepest life within us; 3. of the richest life around us.—In the true love of God and his neighbor, man would re-obtain his true self-love, and recover from his diseased self-love.—Thou art not far from the kingdom of God; or, the tempter transformed into the disciple. Or a meaning-fraught word,—1. of recognition, 2. of warning, 3. of encouragement.—Christ explained in the temple-court, in the circle of those who hated Him, the great law of love, as He upon the night of betrayal instituted the meal of love, and upon Golgotha overcame the curse of the entire world-hate, by His act, by His suffering, and by His sacrifice of love.

CANSTEIN:—Good men may be often so misled as to permit themselves to be employed against Christ: for such we must have compassion, pray for them, and endeavor to deliver them.—QUESNEL:—True religion consists in hearing, believing, and loving.—As thou lovest thyself, so act with thy neighbor.—HEDINGER:—Who can withstand the truth? Where but a little good-will is found, it pierces through. But ah! how hard the hearts that strive against her!—OSIANDER:—External ceremonies are no doubt good; but where they are found without love, they are only a mantle covering secret sin, and will be rejected by God.—*Bibl. Wirt.*:—Courage, ye teachers and preachers! God moves the heart of many a one, who has not known the fact, in a sermon, so that he goes forth better than he came in.—He who recognizes the worth of love, and what it is, is near the kingdom of God; but he who has experienced love, is in it.—HEDINGER:—Whosoever is, in the beginning, obedient and true to the divine leadings of grace, of him is there hope that he is won.—He who is near, is not therefore within the kingdom, Matt. vii. 13.—CANSTEIN:—Truth conquers.—QUESNEL:—A silence of contentedness and obedience is a wholesome silence; but that of rude ignorance and obstinacy is a damning silence.

RIEGER:—Upon the commandment of love to God and to our neighbor is all dependent; and yet God, on account of man's lost state, could not leave all to be dependent on this alone, but had to reveal many other, special, explicit commandments, and make us conscious of our captivity to sin by them. Not till that institution (these laws) has fulfilled its part, can we be brought by the grace of Christ under the law of the Spirit.

LISCO:—All external sacrifices are only weak types of the one perfect sacrifice, the perfect surrender of the heart to God.—With thy earnest moral striving, thou art upon the way by which the kingdom of God may be reached; for thou recognizest the existence of true piety, and deceivest thyself not with an external righteousness by works. The entrance is by faith alone in the Saviour, who is the Way, John xiv. 6.—GERLACH:—Through a living acquaintance with God's law, through heartfelt affection for its chief commandment, love, man comes *near* to the kingdom; but to come *into* the kingdom, he needs the knowledge of God, by which alone the conflict between pleasure in the law, and its constant transgression, can be stopped.—BRAUNE:—God is one, says Paul, Gal. iii. 20, to prove that law and promise are eternally one. So, too, says the Lord here, in that He calls to His support the fundamental doctrine of the law: Hear, Israel, etc. It is always the heart upon which God first looks.—The second command is the proof of the first. "If a man say, I love God," etc., 1 John iv. 20.—God says, No God beside Me; but man must say, Other men beside me.—On God's account we are bound to love our neighbor as ourselves.—Thou *shalt*: it is accordingly no merit if thou do so; but it is sin if thou neglect. Thou shalt *perfectly*: It is not a portion which suffices. This must drive us to Him who fulfilled this law, and helps us to fulfil.—The Master gives measured praise: of beautiful views and fine declarations He never makes too much, but recognizes these in all relations in such a way as to encourage to progress.—Let each take heed, that in his case the separation between knowing and doing, between the acknowledgment of the faith and the work of faith, become not fixed, and ever grow more terrible.

SCHLEIERMACHER:—*See* his *Sermons*, vol. iii. p. 765 ff.—BRIEGER:—To love God, who is the Love and the Life, is to live godly. But he who lives in and with God, or godly, loves also what God loves.—Love is the only self-sacrifice, and it is the only sacrifice that God wishes.—GOSSNER:—One God, one heart, one love.

---

6. *The decisive Counter-question put by the Lord to the Scribes.* VERS. 35–37.

(Parallels: Matt. xxii. 41–46; Luke xx. 41–44.)

35 And Jesus answered and said, while he taught in the temple, How say the scribes
36 that Christ is the son of David? For David himself said by the Holy Ghost, The Lord
said[1] to my Lord, Sit thou on my right hand, till I make thine enemies thy footstool.
37 David therefore[2] himself calleth him Lord; and whence is he *then* his son? And the
common people heard him gladly.

[[1] Ver. 36.—Some MSS. read λέγει ("the Lord said") instead of εἶπεν; Meyer asserts that εἶπεν comes from Matthew Luke, and the cited passage in the Psalm.]
[[2] Ver. 37.—The οὖν is wanting in B., D., L., Δ., Syriac, Tischendorf; bracketed by Lachmann.]

EXEGETICAL AND CRITICAL.

See Matthew, and the parallels in *Luke*.—The great counter-question which Jesus, after all the tempting questions of His enemies, addressed to the Pharisees, is brought forward by Matthew in all its historic importance as the decisive, concluding interrogation put to the Pharisees. In Matthew, accordingly, this question has the form of a discussion of rabbinical disputation; and without doubt this is the original, historical form of the matter. Much of this external form has been rubbed away by Mark; yet he points out by the words, "Jesus answered," that the statement contained a reply to some question already put, with a view to try the Lord. Consequently the last is referred to. In this way, the preceding discussion also gains a new illustration; for which, consult the explanation of this last temptation. Mark, in allowing the form of the disputation to pass unnoticed, causes Christ's spiritual triumph to stand out all the more strongly to the view; just as he presented the preceding narrative likewise from its bright side.

Ver. 35. **While He taught in the temple.**—The last address Christ made to the Pharisees was a word intended for the whole people; and this is in Mark's mind the most weighty point: and from this view we see that His triumph, and the humbling of His enemies in the presence of the multitude, are implied as matters decided from the very outset.

Ver. 37. **And whence is He then his son?**—This question was intended to say to the Pharisees especially, that the Son of David, or the Messiah, as David's Lord, must, according to the Scriptures, be of divine dignity; while to the people especially it was intended to say, that He was not to be David's son in the sense that He had been appointed, as they expected, to found an external Messianic kingdom, after the nature of David's kingdom. But the one conception cannot be severed from the other.—He who brings in a divine kingdom must introduce one of a different nature from an earthly one: he who introduces one of another, higher nature, must introduce a divine.—**Heard Him gladly.**—Not merely in the common sense, but with special reference to His divine dignity as the Messiah, was it that they listened to Him. The people were in the best mood for doing, and were on the point of doing, homage to Him.

DOCTRINAL AND ETHICAL.

1. *See Matthew* and the foregoing remarks.

2. In their last question, the Pharisees gave the Lord to understand that if God be only One, He (Jesus) could not be God's Son, and desired in this way to force Him either to offend against monotheism, or to deny His own dignity. Christ, by His counter-question, lays down this proposition: Christ as David's son, and at the same time David's Lord, could not be man simply, though He is a real man. For David calls Him, not in a general way, his Lord; but Lord, *the* Lord, directly, and positively. At the same time, Jesus reveals to them mediately, by means of Ps. cx., that His kingdom is not of the same nature as David's, of a worldly character; that He should triumph over all His foes, and sit down upon the right hand of Majesty on high,—a declaration which comes distinctly and triumphantly forward in His trial before Caiaphas, ch. xiv. 62. *See* HAMANN'S *Golgotha*, and *Scheblimini*.

3. Matthew marks chiefly the conviction which the last counter-question of Christ produced, made apparent by the silence of His opponents: Mark brings into prominence this presage of His victory over the rulers of the people, and the perfect spiritual might by which Jesus subdued His enemies. Hence, Mark notes this was a moment when Christ needed but to move His finger, and the whole hierarchy was overthrown, the people lay at His feet. And this was indeed no mere Galilæan triumphal entry, in which a few individual friends from Bethany and Jerusalem were mingled; but it was the Jewish people, who were assembled for the Paschal feast. It was the intensified repetition of the scene in Galilee, of which John gives the account, ch. vi. But Jesus wished to rule over the spirit, and through this rule establish a kingdom. The Israelitish authorities denied Him homage, in suppressed rage, in demoniacal silence. He retired, accordingly, now, in His full, decisive spirit-conquest over them, in secrecy, after He had finished His spiritual judgment in denunciations of woe, and in His decision regarding the gifts cast into the temple-treasury.

HOMILETICAL AND PRACTICAL.

The people heard Him gladly. One of the many beautiful, solemn moments which Israel lost, deceived principally on this matter by its priesthood. (Similarly upon the days of palms. The general repentance after the Feast of Pentecost, Acts v. The great moment in the life of Paul, Acts xxii. 22. A similar one in the life of James, according to HEGESIPPUS, in EUSEB. ii. 23.)—The mystery in the life of Jesus induces and allures unprejudiced minds to sink themselves into its depths.

STARKE:—The Holy Scriptures contain very deep mysteries.—If a true Christian is to be formed out of a Pharisee, the knowledge of Christ in His humanity and divinity must spring up within that man.—QUESNEL:—It is only faith which is able to unloose these knots (*i.e.*, unite divinity and humanity).

BRAUNE:—What think ye of Christ? This question is the sum of the law and the Gospel. He had *been questioned*, first, as to the tribute, from political motives; then regarding marriage and the resurrection, because of philosophical views; then concerning different commandments, on ethical grounds. He now *asks* the life-question of centuries (which springs from the centre of religion): Rom. ix. 5; 1 Cor. xv. 25; Acts ii. 34; Heb. i. 13.—Had Moses been superior to Christ, then had the chief question been, What is the chief command of the law? Because this is not the case, the question regarding the Saviour remains the chief and life-question. According to Christ's view of the case, however, that first query, conceived not according to the law, but according to the Gospel, belongs to this second.

SCHLEIERMACHER:—He does not say, If He is his son, how is He then his Lord? but reversed, If he himself names Him his Lord, how is He then his son? He consequently represents the first as the greater (and yet it is the latter which forms the concluding point, inasmuch as He wishes to call upon them to give up their conception of the Messiah for the Old Testament conception of Him, which His life had exemplified).

BRIEGER:—The Pharisees having interrogated Him as to His *power*, He interrogates them as to His *person* (for they knew, it is properly remarked, that the people considered Him the Messiah).—It was now recognition or rejection. By this question Jesus wishes to lead them to decide.—The throne of God, at the right hand of which the Anointed is to seat Himself, is the throne "high and lifted up," spoken of by Isaiah, ch. vi.,—the *heavenly* throne, Ps. ix. 7; lxviii. 18; xxix. 10. It is the symbol of His rule over heaven and earth, Ps. ciii. 19; Rev. iii. 12; 2 Tim. ii. 12.

7. *The Lord's Public Admonition to beware of the Scribes.* VERS. 38–40.

(Parallels: Matt. xxiii.; Luke xx. 45–47.)

38 And he said unto them in his doctrine, Beware of the scribes, which love to go in
39 long clothing, and *love* salutations in the market-places, And the chief seats in the syna-
40 gogues, and the uppermost rooms at feasts; Which devour widows' houses, and for a
pretence make long prayers: these shall receive greater damnation.

EXEGETICAL AND CRITICAL.

See Matthew, and the parallels in *Luke*.—Mark, like Luke, gives us, of the great denunciatory speech against the Pharisees and scribes which Matthew records, but a very brief warning against the scribes. And how exactly accordant with the intention of his Gospel! It was only the Jewish Christians, for whom Matthew wrote, who *could* at once, and at that time, be summoned to gaze upon the pharisaic Judaism in all the blackness of its sunken state; for young Gentile Christians, the great punitive speech was to a certain extent unintelligible, and was besides too strong food. Hence the picture of the scribes is briefly given in their three principal features: ambition, avarice, and hypocritical external piety. The address is made up of the introductory word of warning by the Lord against the Pharisees, and of the first woe denounced by Him against them. The expression in Matthew, "Do not ye after their works," is here, "Beware of them." The religious enlarging of the garments, as Matthew relates it, is here briefly given in the going about in long clothing. The seeking of greetings precedes the desire for the chief seats in the synagogue, and the civic seats of honor; while the anxious listening for the salutation of Rabbi is passed over. With these chief seats at festivals is admirably united the devouring of widows' houses, under pretence of long prayers, according to the first woe of Matthew. The address to the Pharisees, which we find in Matthew gradually passing into a direct, pointed attack, is here everywhere changed to the representation in the third person. Mark agrees almost verbally with Luke.

Ver. 38. **Which love,** θελόντων.—Meyer: "Demand, claim." But they did not first claim the walking about in long robes: they actually did this; and that, too, with pleasure, consciousness, and deliberation. They loved this, had pleasure in this.—**In long clothing.**—Gerlach: "Because they imitated the priests, who were the nobles of the Jewish people." But are not the priests themselves included? Braune: "Because they imitated the venerable matrons." Jewish Rabbis imitate women! The reference is undoubtedly to their wandering about the streets and public places with marks of distinction significant of religiousness, in long robes of office and rank; hence also in gowns and robes of various orders.

Ver. 40. **Which devour.**—Grotius, Bengel, [Lachmann], and others, make a new sentence begin with οἱ κατεσθίοντες. As administrators, guardians, representatives of unprotected widows (Theophylact); or also by embezzling the funds of the temple-foundations.—For the more lengthened denunciation, *see Matthew*.

DOCTRINAL AND ETHICAL.

1. *See Matthew*.—We have here three points of contrast: 1. Public appearance,—the proud walk in long trailing garments (devotion), the love of greetings (frivolity). 2. Demeanor in society,—love of the chief ecclesiastical seat, and at the same time of the places of honor at banquets and festive entertainments. 3. Personal and secret conduct,—the appropriation of the goods of the poor, under the veil and pretence of long prayers, and of supplications for the poor.

HOMILETICAL AND PRACTICAL.

Comp. *Matthew*.—The scribes distinguished as the worst of the Pharisees.—The false scribes are considered in three different ways, apart from the Scriptures:* 1. Upon the streets; 2. in business and at banquets; 3. as the appropriators of inheritances in families, and by secret means.—The veil of hypocrisy is a transparent covering: 1. The covering, *a.* the long robes, *b.* the long prayers; 2. the transparency of the covering, *a.* the walking about to be seen, *b.* the lust for the seats of honor, festive banquets, and unrighteous gain.—The hypocrite's terrible picture: 1. His public appearance contradicts his secret conduct; 2. his external importance, and desire to be important, is in contradiction to his internal emptiness and unworthiness.—The extent to which a hypocritical profession is carried, is the measure of approaching punishment.—Satan, who clothes himself as an angel of light, and plays the part of man's friend, is the archetype of all hypocrisy.

STARKE:—As sinners are distinguished, so are their punishments.—The confession of sin mitigates the judgment; to hide sin, under the pretence of God's service, makes the judgment heavier and more terrible, Prov. xxviii. 13.

BRAUNE (upon the long clothing):—Somewhat as formerly many clergymen were wont to seek especial dignity from the size of their wigs, and the monks from their cowls and rosaries.—STIER:—Satan was the first who exalted himself to be brought low (the opposite of Christ).

SCHLEIERMACHER:—They used their piety only for external profit.—BRIEGER:—It is to be remarked, that Jesus pictures forth not individual scribes, but the whole sect. There were not wanting a few in whom better tendencies were to be found; *see* vers. 28–34.—The warning has a twofold intention: first, we are not to allow ourselves to be deceived by them; second, we are not to imitate their conduct.

* [There is a play here upon words in the original. *Schrift*gelehrten ausserhalb der *Schrift*.—*Ed.*]

8. *The Widow's Mite, and our Lord's view of the Piety and Good Works of the Jews.* VERS. 41–44.

(Parallel: Luke xxi. 1–4.)

41 And Jesus[1] sat over against the treasury, and beheld how the people cast money
42 into the treasury: and many that were rich cast in much. And there came a certain
43 poor widow, and she threw in two mites, which make a farthing. And he called *unto
him his disciples, and saith unto them, Verily I say unto you, that this poor widow hath
44 cast more in than all they which have cast[2] into the treasury: For all they did cast in
of their abundance: but she of her want did cast in all that she had, even all her living.

[[1] Ver. 41.—Ὁ Ἰησοῦς wanting in B., L., Δ., Tischendorf, Meyer; bracketed by Lachmann.]
[[2] Ver. 43.—Lachmann, after A., B., D., Origen, reads ἔβαλεν τῶν βαλλόντων.]

EXEGETICAL AND CRITICAL.

See the parallel passages in *Luke*.—This apparently trifling history is of inestimable importance. It shows how the Lord, in perfect quiet of spirit, can still seat Himself in the temple, after He had ended His great day's work in it, namely, after the silence of the Sanhedrim regarding His person, in which its rejection of Him lay,—after He had opened His mouth, and pronounced the great denunciations, and with these had, as theocratic King, whom the authorities of Israel rejected, taken His departure from the temple. In this He seems like a deposed king, who seats Himself, as he leaves, on the lowest step of his palace, not to weep on account of his fall, but to bless the poor child of a palace-domestic; or like one excommunicated, who is able, under the new burden of its fanatical ban, to judge with the greatest mildness, and freedom from prejudice, that religious society which cast him out. It is the divine manifestation of His freedom from all fanatic disposition and exasperation, with which He had fought through the great decisive epochs, made His denunciatory speech, and presented His great judgment-picture. In this sunlike clearness and purity, the old Catholic Christians did not in general leave the heathen temples, and but few of the old Protestants the temples of Roman Catholicism. This eternally figurative import is gained by our passage in consequence of its position. In itself, however, it shows us, in a most instructive narrative and act of our Lord, how His eye —and how, consequently, God's view, and the Spirit's —rests upon the treasury of the Lord, and marks the act and manner in which we give. Luke has recorded this circumstance likewise; but Mark presents it more picturesquely and more fully. The Lord's seating Himself opposite to the treasury, the statement of the worth of the mite, the summoning of the disciples to Himself, and the sublime elevation of tone characterizing the decision,—in all this we see plainly how important Mark deemed the history. It stands there to show that the Lord has His eye upon the offerings in His temple; and that, amid all the chaff of seeming religion, He finds out the noble grain of spirituality and truth.

Ver. 41. **The treasury,** γαζοφυλάκιον.—The sacrifice-fund is meant, which was distinguished from the proper temple-treasury, but yet, as belonging to it, was denoted by its name (JOSEPHUS, *Ant.* xix. 6, 1). The Rabbis tell us that this treasury consisted of thirteen **brazen chests** (שׁוֹפָרוֹת, "trumpets;" certainly not because the chests themselves were trumpet-shaped, but because the mouths through which the money was cast into the chests were wide at the top and narrow below). They stood in the outer court of the women. This offering-fund received also the voluntary gifts for the temple. LIGHTFOOT, *Hor.*: "Nine chests were for the appointed temple-tribute, and for the sacrifice-tribute (that is, money-gifts, instead of the sacrifices); four chests for freewill-offerings, for wood, incense, temple-decoration, and burnt-offerings." Before the Passover, freewill-offerings, in addition to the temple-tax, were generally presented. No one, we may easily suppose, entered the temple without putting something in. This is also the custom in the synagogue. The Church has taken an example from this habit.—**Many that were rich cast in much.**—They were not content to give only copper, which was the general offering, but presented silver. Or, perhaps, gave in copper, because a large gift in that metal was of greater bulk, and made more noise.

Ver. 42. **A certain poor widow.**—She is singled out from the whole crowd of donors.—**Two mites,** λεπτόν.—The very smallest copper coin. Two made one Roman quadrans, which was equal to the fourth of an as: ten or sixteen ases were equal to a denarius, which is equivalent to about five groschen, four pfennigs Prussian money (6½ *pence, nearly*). An as in Cicero's time was worth nearly four pfennigs (*or nearly a halfpenny*); hence the quadrans would be one pfennig (*one-tenth of a penny*,) and the mite half a pfennig. She gave two; and Bengel remarks, she could have kept one. "The rabbinic injunction, '*Non ponat homo* λεπτόν *in cistam eleemosynarum*,' is of no force here, because alms were not under consideration." Meyer. Nevertheless, the inference drawn by Schöttgen is by no means foreign; only it is probable this rabbinic habit became, at a later period, the matter of rabbinic legislation.

Ver. 43. **More in than all they.**—That is, in proportion to her means, as the Lord Himself immediately explains.

DOCTRINAL AND ETHICAL.

1. *See Exegetical Note.*

2. Jesus, to a certain degree as stranger, or observer of a religion now become foreign to Him, presents us with an ever-enduring example of the way in which one should, in the spirit of Christianity, look upon and judge all religious systems and associations. Such was the conduct of Paul at Athens, Acts. xvii. He found out the altar of the Unknown God.

3. The last object on which our Lord's eyes rested in the temple.—The widow's mite. It is not said that the gifts of the others were worthless. Many possessed, no doubt, no worth (Matt. vi. 1); others, a greater or a lesser. The greatest value, however, attached itself to the widow's mite.

4. And how much interest may that mite, in the course of the entire history of the Church, have accrued?

HOMILETICAL AND PRACTICAL.

See Doctrinal Reflections.—The Lord's sublime peace of soul in leaving the temple, where He had met no recognition.—The humble resting-place of the Lord at the temple-gate, after He had been refused the throne.—The backward glance of mildness which the Banished cast upon the Church system by which He had been banished.—Christ's example teaches the heaven-wide distinction between godly zeal and ungodly fanaticism.—The Lord's eyes are upon all offerings.—The mite of the widow as a gift: 1. The smallest gift; 2. the largest gift.—The freewill-offering of the heart, the real inner existence and life of the temple.—Christ observes with emotion the dying embers of the expiring fire of God in the temple.—The distinction between the treasury of the Lord in the law-church and Gospel-church (there, chiefly intended for symbolic temple necessities; here, chiefly for the poor. See the lame beggar at the Beautiful gate of the temple, whom Peter heals).—The ancient estimable institution of Church alms.—*Christo in pauperibus.*

STARKE:—CANSTEIN:—The Lord Jesus pays attention, without doubt, to men's alms; hence they should be willing to give, and take earnest heed how they give.—*Bibl. Wirt.*:—Christians must willingly deposit in God's treasury, and contribute to the support of God's service—churches, schools, the poor, 2 Cor. ix. 7.—J. HALL:—Where distribution is made to the poor, there Jesus pays attention, and takes pleasure therein.—O God, I have only two mites, a body and a soul.—CANSTEIN:—Christ remarks a compassionate and believing heart, when alms are being given.—*Nova. Bibl. Tub.*:—God's opinion regarding good works is infinitely different from that of men. Those who give the most, give often the least; and those who give the least, the most.—Servants must not exclude themselves from alms-giving.

BRAUNE:—He says, Verily I say unto you, because He wishes to make His judgment abide, as though it were a dogma and fundamental principle in His divine kingdom.—How she must have fixed her trust upon God, and not have cared for the morrow; since she did to-day, what to-day brought with it, Mal. i. 8; ver. 14.

SCHLEIERMACHER:—If there had only been many such to give as this poor widow, who was ready to contribute all that she could claim as her own, to the support of God's service, then might a purer zeal have developed itself, which had been far from degenerating into that tempest which destroyed the temple, and had contributed rather to prevent the downfall. This extreme tendency to externals on the part of the many was the first germ of destruction to that people.

---

9. *Jesus' Departure from the Temple. His Retirement to the Mount of Olives; and His Address concerning the Last Things.* CH. XIII. 1–37.

(Parallels: Matt. xxiv. and xxv.; Luke xxi. 5–38; Revelation.)

1 And as he went out of the temple, one of his disciples saith unto him, Master, see
2 what manner of stones and what buildings *are here!* And Jesus answering,[1] said unto
him, Seest thou these great buildings? there shall not be left one stone upon another,
3 that shall not be thrown down. And as he sat upon the Mount of Olives, over against
4 the temple, Peter, and James, and John, and Andrew, asked him privately, Tell us,
when shall these things be? and what *shall be* the sign when all these things shall be
5 fulfilled? And Jesus answering them, began to say, Take heed lest any *man* deceive
6 you: For many shall come in my name, saying, I am *Christ;* and shall deceive many.
7 And when ye shall hear of wars, and rumours of wars, be ye not troubled: for *such*
8 *things* must needs be; but the end *shall* not *be* yet. For nation shall rise against
nation, and kingdom against kingdom; and there shall be earthquakes in *divers* places,
9 and there shall be famines and troubles:[2] these *are* the beginnings of sorrows. But
take heed to yourselves: for they shall deliver you up to councils; and in the synagogues ye shall be beaten: and ye shall be brought before rulers and kings for my
10 sake, for a testimony against them. And the Gospel must first be published among all
11 nations. But when they shall lead *you*, and deliver you up, take no thought beforehand what ye shall speak, neither do ye premeditate;[3] but whatsoever shall be given you
12 in that hour, that speak ye: for it is not ye that speak, but the Holy Ghost. Now,
the brother shall betray the brother to death, and the father the son; and children shall
13 rise up against *their* parents, and shall cause them to be put to death. And ye shall be
hated of all *men* for my name's sake: but he that shall endure unto the end, the same
14 shall be saved. But when ye shall see the abomination of desolation, spoken of by

Daniel the prophet,[4] standing where it ought not, (let him that readeth understand,)
15 then let them that be in Judea flee to the mountains: And let him that is on the house-
top not go down into the house,[5] neither enter *therein*, to take anything out of his
16 house: And let him that is in the field not turn back again for to take up his garment.
17 But woe to them that are with child, and to them that give suck, in those days!
18, 19 And pray ye that your flight be not in the winter. For *in* those days shall be
affliction, such as was not from the beginning of the creation, which God created, unto
20 this time, neither shall be. And except that the Lord had shortened those days, no
flesh should be saved: but for the elect's sake, whom he hath chosen, he hath shortened
21 the days. And then, if any man shall say to you, Lo, here *is* Christ; or, lo, *he is*
22 there; believe *him* not: For false Christs[6] and false prophets shall rise, and shall show
23 signs and wonders, to seduce, if *it were* possible, even the elect. But take ye heed:
24 behold, I have foretold you all things. But in those days, after that tribulation, the
25 sun shall be darkened, and the moon shall not give her light. And the stars of heaven
26 shall fall,[7] and the powers that are in heaven shall be shaken. And then shall they see
27 the Son of man coming in the clouds, with great power and glory. And then shall
he send his angels, and shall gather together his elect from the four winds, from the
28 uttermost part of the earth to the uttermost part of heaven. Now learn a parable of
the fig-tree; When her branch is yet tender, and putteth forth leaves, ye know[8] that
29 [the] summer is near: So ye, in like manner, when ye shall see these things come to
30 pass, know that it is nigh, *even* at the doors. Verily I say unto you, That this genera-
31 tion shall not pass, till all these things be done. Heaven and earth shall pass away:
32 but my words shall not pass away. But of that day, and *that* hour, knoweth no man,
33 no, not the angels which are in heaven, neither the Son, but the Father. Take ye
34 heed, watch and pray:[9] for ye know not when the time is. *For the Son of man is* as a
man taking a far journey, who left his house, and gave authority to his servants, and to
35 every man his work; and commanded the porter to watch. Watch ye therefore: for
ye know not when the master of the house cometh, at even, or at midnight, or at the
36 cock-crowing, or in the morning: Lest, coming suddenly, he find you sleeping
37 And what I say unto you, I say unto all, Watch.

[[1] Ver. 2.—Ἀποκριθείς is wanting in B., L., Versions, Tischendorf, Meyer; found in A., K., Lachmann, Fritzsche; ὧδε before λιθος supported by B., D.; received by Griesbach, Lachmann; omitted in A. and Tischendorf.]

[2] Ver. 8.—Lachmann and Tischendorf, on the authority of B., D., L., have omitted καὶ ταραχαί. Meyer would retain the words, and says, they have been left out by mistake; the scribe's eye running forward to the ἀρχαί following.

[3] Ver. 11.—Μηδὲ μελετᾶτε, omitted by B., D., L., Tischendorf; Meyer would retain them.

[4] Ver. 14.—Τὸ ῥηθὲν ὑπὸ Δανιὴλ τοῦ προφήτου, wanting in B., D., L., Coptic, &c. It is easy to see how they might be interpolated from Matthew; but their omission would be difficult to explain.

[[5] Ver. 15.—B., L. omit εἰς τὴν οἰκίαν. Lachmann brackets it.]

[6] Ver. 22.—Tischendorf omits, improperly, ψευδόχριστοι καί. So D.

[7] Ver. 25.—A., B., C., &c., read, ἔσονται ἐκ τοῦ οὐρανοῦ πίπτοντες. Lachmann, Tischendorf.

[8] Ver. 28.—A., B., D., L., Δ.: γινώσκεται.

[9] Ver. 33.—B., D. omit καὶ προσεύχεσθε; Lachmann and Tischendorf follow.

EXEGETICAL AND CRITICAL.

See Matthew.—In our Gospel, the time and situation in which Christ delivered His great eschatological address present themselves, as is the case with Matthew. Upon Tuesday evening, immediately after His departure from the temple, the first introductory words were exchanged between Jesus and His disciples. Jesus declared Jerusalem's destruction. Thereupon He seats Himself in the circle of His most trusted followers upon the Mount of Olives, and reveals the eschatological import of Jerusalem's being destroyed. Hence it is exceedingly probable that this revelation by Jesus is a night-speech, or rather midnight address, succeeding the night-conversation which He had held upon His evening walk to Bethany, on the summit of Olivet, sitting opposite to the temple.

The three chief divisions of the address are, by all the Evangelists, distinctly enough marked: 1. The universal eschatological world-course to the end; 2. the destruction of Jerusalem, with its succeeding days of trouble and contest, or the succeeding period of the Church of the Cross (the Christian Church), which period may be regarded also as a distinct division; 3. the indication and commencement of the world-end. The beginning of the first part is marked by Jesus' warning against being seduced by the pseudo-Christs (Mark, ver. 5); the end by the promise, "He who endureth," etc. (ver. 13). The beginning of the second part is indicated in Mark and Matthew by the reference to the abomination of desolation; in Luke by the investing of the city (Luke xxi. 20): the close is here shown by the words, "For in those days shall be," etc. (Mark, ver. 19); in Luke, ver. 23, the statement is—a time of wrath upon Israel. The interval between the destruction of Jerusalem and the end of the world, distinguished as the period of mitigated judgment, is brought forward in the words, "Except the Lord had shortened those days" (Mark, ver. 20): the close, according to Mark, is given in the exclamation, "Behold, I have foretold you all things;" according to Matthew, in the words, "Where the body is," etc. The chief point in this statement regarding the interval, in Mark and Matthew, is the warning against the false Christs; in Luke, the sufferings of the Jews, the treading under foot of Jerusalem, until the times of the Gentiles be fulfilled. The beginning of the section upon the world-end is brought most prominently forward by Mark—"In those days" (ver. 24); Matthew similarly; Luke, with a short καὶ ἔσται, a Future, which is connected with the Preterite of the fulfilment of the times of the Gentiles. All three Evangelists mark the end of this period as the deliverance of the faithful. The Son of Man, according to Matthew and Mark, appears and sends forth His angels to gather in His chosen. Luke makes this known in the words, Lift up your heads, for your salvation draweth nigh. To this succeeds the practical application of the speech in the parable of the fig-tree. The eschatological discourse of Mark's Gospel agrees most with Matthew; yet it is on the whole shorter, in particular points more circumstantial, and picturesque. Particularly strong is the call in Mark to foresight, to attention, and watchfulness, vers. 5, 9, 23, 33, 35, 37. The comparative characterization, however, will be most appropriately added to the consideration of the various sections. For the literature upon thi portion, *see Matthew*. Worthy of special notice is EBRARD'S tract: *Adversus erroneam nonnullorum opinionem, qua Christi discipuli existimasse perhibentur, fore, ut universale judicium ipsorum ætate superveniret*, Erlangen, 1842.

A. *The Occasion.* VERS. 1–4.

(Parallels: Matt. xxiv. 1–3; Luke xxi. 5–7.)

Mark brings before us a single speaker, who pointed out to the Lord the splendor of the temple; while Luke speaks of several, Matthew of the disciples in general. One might imagine it was Andrew who furnished in this manner the occasion, entering as he did this time into the circle of the intimate few. If it were not he, then it was most probably Peter. What the disciples bring before the Lord—interceding, so to speak, for the temple—is, according to Matthew, the building itself (the structure being perhaps, in some part, in process of reconstruction); according to Luke, the beautiful stones and the gifts; according to Mark, the greatness of the stones and structures. Braune: According to Josephus, the stones were, in part, twenty-five ells long, twelve broad, eight high. The thought that such a building should be destroyed, was too sad for them; and the precious stones alluded to by Luke, the consecration-presents of piety, upon the walls and in the courts, testified to a continued respect for the temple. The reply of the Lord is here very lively, Dost thou see these buildings? The seat upon the Mount of Olives is marked as a position *over against the temple*. Of the circle of the disciples who interrogate the Lord, we learn this only, that they are His trusted friends, and that Andrew was on this occasion present, in addition to Peter, James, and John. The two questions, regarding the destruction of Jerusalem, and the sign of the end of the world, given by Matthew, are likewise given by Mark, yet in a different form.

Ver. 2. **One stone upon the other.**—Meyer: "There would not be one stone left upon another, which should escape, in the further prosecution of the work of destruction, being torn down." But this is the depicting of a *regular* breaking down of a house, in which the chief thing is to separate one stone from another, down to the very last. Here, on the contrary, we have the picture of a violent destruction, in which many stones, as all know, remain lying upon one another, yet is each torn from his place and broken. In other words, καταλύεσθαι refers not merely to the mass of the temple, but also to the single stones: the temple should be so thoroughly destroyed, that each stone should be destroyed. Of course this strong expression is not to be pressed literally.

Ver. 3. **Over against the temple.**—The summit of Olivet made a *vis-à-vis* to the temple's pinnacle. *See* books of travel.—**And Andrew.**—*See Matthew.*

Ver. 4. **When shall these things be, and what,** etc.—The subject of the two distinct questions is here indicated in a twofold manner: ταῦτα and ταῦτα πάντα; ἔσται and μέλλῃ συντελεῖσθαι.—**When all these.**—Not once more the destruction of Jerusalem (Meyer). By Grotius and Bengel, πάντα ταῦτα is referred to the whole world. We understand it of all things which formed part of the Jewish regime, and which, according to the view of the disciples, were connected with the destruction of Jerusalem.

B. *The World's Course to the World's End in general. The Last Things of the Christian, or the Christian Signature of the End of the World.* VERS. 5–13.

(Parallels: Matt. xxiv. 4–14; Luke xxi. 8–19.)

Mark begins again with an ἤρξατο λέγειν. The warning against the pseudo-Christs is common to all the Synoptics. Luke alone has the addition, that the time draws near: the indication of the chiliastic (millenarian) element. The representation of the wars of the nations is in Mark the shortest. The signs of the world's development are given by Luke most complete: earthquakes, famines, pestilences, terrors, and signs in the heavens. Mark, with Matthew, omits the terrific things and signs in heaven, also the pestilences, and has instead ταραχαί, pointing out (from the Roman stand-point) chiefly the political condition of the world. After Mark has with Matthew denoted this as the beginning of sorrows, we have a second, Take heed unto yourselves, introduced. And now he depicts more fully than Matthew the persecutions of the Christians, giving, as does Luke, a view of these which had been already given by Matthew in the instructions to the Apostles, ch. x. 17, 18. These were very weighty words for the Roman Christians, at a time when the martyrdom of Peter and Paul, in Rome, was about to take place. Then, as early as the 10th verse, he gives the *concluding* statement of Matthew regarding the preaching of the Gospel in all the world; and appends the rules of conduct for the persecuted, which we find in Matt. x. 19. To this succeeds the presaging of fraternal hatred, and the detestation of the Christians, occurring Matt. x. 21. None the less does the concluding portion of that statement form here the conclusion: He who endureth, etc. Matthew has this final word once again in this passage; and this circumstance, as well as the connection between Mark and Luke, speaks for Mark's accuracy, and proves that all the various portions recorded by him have their proper place in this address. The words, Matt. xxiv. 10-12, are omitted by Mark, probably because they are implied in the statements already made.

Ver. 5. **Take heed lest, etc.; for many shall come.**—This warning against pseudo-Christs, pseudo-Christianities, false prophets, and false prophecies, being placed at the head, denotes that it is an essential point of view from which to contemplate Christian eschatology.

Ver. 7. **But the end shall not be yet.**—Meyer: "The end of the calamities, not of the world." But the end of the calamities is really the end of the world.

Ver. 8. **Troubles** (terrifying confusions), ταραχαί,—Mark alone gives this. The word denotes primarily a shock, or commotion (John v. 4); then a commotion of mind, overwhelming, a fright; and hence, with respect to political circumstances, public terrifying confusion, anarchical conditions of states, tumults, etc.

Ver. 9. **Ye shall be beaten.**—The question is, whether the construction be, Ye shall be delivered up to councils and synagogues; shall be beaten, etc. (Luther, Meyer), or as in the English text, with Bengel and others. Against this latter construction, Meyer says, the idea of motion lies not in δαρήσεσθε, but it does in εἰς. Meyer says, further, the scourging took place regularly in the synagogues. Then it is certainly a striking picture of fanatic maltreatment, if it had been already inflicted upon the way to the synagogues (Acts vi. 12; xxi. 30, 31). According to Meyer's construction, in councils and synagogues, we have a tautology. The view, however, is this: The trial and condemnation took place in the councils or ecclesiastical courts, which were annexed to the synagogues; and the condemned were then led into the synagogues, or congregations, to be beaten: fanaticism could not, however, restrain itself: they were scourged even on their way thither.—**For a testimony against them.**—*See Matthew.*

Ver. 10. **Among all nations.**—A result of the above-mentioned martyrdom. Through sufferings the Gospel was to be spread among all peoples. This is, accordingly, the end of their trials. Not till this be fulfilled does the *end* of the woes come, as distinguished from the ἀρχαί.

Ver. 11. **When they shall lead you.**—Rules for conduct. Above, it was **Take heed**; here, **Take no thought.**—Be on your guard against the seductions of the pseudo-Christs; be not anxious because of the threats of open foes. "Μελετᾶτε, the regular word for the committing to memory of a speech *see* WETSTEIN; the opposite of extempore." Meyer Comp. *Matthew.* Take no thought, *how or what*, as the more objective mode of Matthew puts it. Here equally a double prohibition in a more subjective form: Take no thought beforehand; do not trouble yourselves on account of it.—**For it is not ye that speak.**—*See Matthew.*

Ver. 13. **He that shall endure.**—Meyer explains by the context: In confessing My name. Compare the διὰ τὸ ὄνομά μου. Nevertheless, the endurance refers to the entire state of trial, which they should pass through faithfully; of course, confessing Christ. It is from sufferings that confession receives its name, as *the Confession.*

C. D. *The Destruction of Jerusalem, and the interval between this and the End of the World; or, the World's Course to the End from the predominating point of view of the Jewish Theocracy.* VERS. 14-20; VERS. 21-23.

(Parallels: Matt. xxiv. 15-21; 22-28; Luke xxi. 20-23; 24.)

The presage of the destruction of Jerusalem is given more briefly than by Matthew, still in biblical form; not as in Luke, who declares plainly the besieging and destruction of the city. The direction to flee is the same as in Matthew, only more exact. From the command, Pray that your flight be not in winter, he leaves out the additional statement of Matthew, Nor yet upon the Sabbath, as it was less easy to be comprehended by the Roman Christians. The description of this one great tribulation is expressed in a richer dress than by Matthew. In describing the appearance of the false Christs and prophets, he omits the details: If they say, Lo, he is in the wilderness, etc.; also the picture of the last judgment, the lightning, and the eagles. On the other hand, his conclusion is in the highest degree impressive: ὑμεῖς δὲ βλέπετε, ver. 23.

Ver. 14. **Where it ought not.**—*See Matthew.*

Ver. 19. **Shall be affliction.**—The very days themselves. Stronger expression: It will be the characteristic of those days that they are tribulation itself.—**From the beginning of the creation, which God created.**—This not a merely stronger emphasizing of the conception, Creation. The κτίσις which God created, forms an opposition to the κτίσις of men, the city Jerusalem and her hierarchy, which was now falling, while the former should endure. Similar is the expression regarding the elect: Whom God hath chosen,—who are, and shall remain, chosen. And just so we have a twofold reference to the shortening of the days: Although they are the days of vengeance, He has shortened them as such, and made them endurable. *See Matthew.*

Ver. 23. **But take ye heed.**—Ever-repeated emphasizing of the greatness of the temptation.

E. *The End of the Cosmos.* VERS. 24–27.

(Parallels: Matt. xxiv. 29–31; Luke xxi. 25–28.)

Mark, as well as Matthew, draws a very sharply defined distinction between the time of the destruction of Jerusalem, and the time when the sign of the end of the world shall appear. Mark: After that tribulation (the destruction of Jerusalem), in the period of the *shortened days*. Here he has omitted the εὐθέως of Matthew. The fall of the stars he expresses differently from Matthew. He passes over the picture of men's consternation at the appearance of the Son of Man, which Matthew gives; also the summons of the great trumpets. And the expression, "From one end of heaven to the other," runs, in his narrative, "From the uttermost part of the earth to the uttermost part of heaven."

Ver. 24. **After that tribulation.**—Meyer holds that, according to Mark, the appearing of the Son of Man should occur immediately after the destruction of Jerusalem. According to the text, however, after the destruction, follow only "those days," and these endurable. Between *those days* and *that day* is a great difference, which Meyer's exegesis has not noticed.

F. *The Parable of the sudden irruption of the Catastrophe, and the Exhortation to Watchfulness.* VERS. 28–37.

(Parallels: Matt. xxiv. 33–50; Luke xxi. 29–36.)

To the end of ver. 32, Mark writes to quite the same import as Matthew; then, however, a different statement comes in: Of that day and that hour know not the angels, neither the Son. At this point the three Synoptics separate and take different ways. Matthew represents the Lord as here pointing back to the days of Noah, as being symbols of the days of the world's end. The surprise of that day is depicted by him in a particular way. The parable of the midnight has its characteristic point in the coming thief; and, succeeding this, is another parable of the lord who, in coming home, surprises his servants. Mark has the exhortation, Watch, for ye know not, etc., which is found in Matthew. But then he adds a parable, peculiar to himself, of the lord going away upon a journey, appointing special duties to his trusted servants: and in this parable the chief person is the lowest servant, the porter, who must keep watch; while Matthew makes him the steward, who had charge of the house. It is evident that the parables are distinct. Matthew selected the steward, because watchful honesty seemed to him the chief thing; Mark selected the porter, because honest watchfulness seemed to him the chief thing. Matthew may have had before him, in his selection, the picture of the Jewish high-priest; and Mark, the picture of a porter attached to some noble Roman house. Mark notices the different hours in which the master may return, marking them out sharply by the statement of the divisions of the night. Luke brings prominently forward the common danger to man,—the heart must not be overcharged, etc.; the momentous day is compared by him to a snare (παγίς). Mark concludes with the word, Watch!

Ver. 28. **That the summer.**—"Τὸ θέρος, also in *Test.* xii. *Patr.*, is the symbol of the Messianic time." Meyer.

Ver. 30. **This generation.**—According to Meyer, the (then) present generation. *See Note* on *Matthew*. The generation which has these signs under observation. Had the generation of that time been meant, then the end of the time at least could have been specified; while Christ says, on the contrary, the day and the hour knoweth no man.

Ver. 32. **Neither the Son.**—An admission, which Meyer, in considering the human limitations in which the Son of Man moved on earth, places in its due position. Athanasius says, Jesus did not know as a human being; Augustine, He did not know it to impart to His disciples. For other interpretations, consult Meyer. Respecting our own interpretation, Meyer judges falsely or inaccurately. We assume that the Son, as God-man, knew not that day in His present daily consciousness, because He willed not to pass beyond the horizon of His daily task to reflect upon that day (*see* LANGE's *Leben Jesu*, ii. 3, p. 1280); because He preferred, accordingly, the limiting horizon of His holy, human observation and knowledge, which widened from day to day, to a discursive pedantic polyhistory, or preternatural pretension of knowing everything, the dim opposite of dynamic omniscience. *Self*-limitation in the knowledge of all chronological, geographical, and similar matters, is quite different from an absolute "limitation" of the theanthropic omniscience of Jesus. *See Matthew.*

Ver. 34. **As a man taking a far journey.**—According to Meyer, a part of a speech, "made up of the different rôles which formed the links between the several heads of the speech." Why not a special parable? Or, is a porter or a guard of a house formed by uniting the rôles of a house-proprietor and a house-steward? and out of a thief and a master of a house do we get, again, a master of a house? We assume, simply, a distinct, though connected, parable. In Matthew, the householder himself is first, then the steward, summoned to watch; in Mark, the house-watch or porter, to guard the house.—**As a man taking,** etc.—The anantapodoton [*i.e.*, the apodosis to be supplied] is found simply in the omitted ἐστί. It is as with a man who took a journey. The whole emphasis falls then upon the finite verb, in accordance with the participles following, viz., upon the injunction which the lord gave the porter to watch.—**Authority to his servants.**—A proof that we have here to do with another parable. The parable of the servant, to whom the highest authority was entrusted, is recorded by Matthew.—**And commanded the porter to watch.**—After he had given all the orders concerning the internal affairs, he gives finally, at the door, to the porter, the additional command to watch: this is the point of the parable. Contemplating them with reference to the Church this side of eternity, the porters are, of course, the Apostles of Christ, together with the body of Christians,—a different aspect from that in which the servant of Christ may be preëminently considered a steward.

Ver. 35. **At even, or at midnight.** — The four night-watches. *See* WINER, *Nachtwache* (Night-watch); the author's *Commentary on Matthew;* WIESELER, *Chronol. Synopse*, p. 406. The uniform thought is, The Lord comes in the night-season, in a dark, sad time; and it is not known in what stadium or moment of this time. He comes quite unexpected. From different stand-points, these periods (ὀψέ = 9 o'clock; μεσονύκτιον = 12; ἀλεκτοροφωνία = 3; πρωΐ = 6) may denote the same unexpectedness:—the evening, the evening of the old world (Matt. xx. 8); the midnight, the frame of mind of the slumbering Church (Matt. xxv. 6); the cock-crow, the voice of the watchers (Isa. xxi. 11); the morning, the dawn of Christ's appearing, the breaking into day of the new world (Mal. iv. 2).

DOCTRINAL AND ETHICAL.

1. Comp. the parallel in *Matthew.*—It is significant that Mark gives prominence to the *size and strength*, Luke *the beauty*, Matthew the restoration and *apparent theocratic rebuilding*, of the temple. All this could not save it.

2. The eschatological speech of the Lord, the germ of John's Apocalypse; the New Testament exposition and form of the Old Testament ideas and symbols; the opposite and corrective of all apocryphal Apocalypsism (Comp. LUCKE, *Versuch einer vollständiger Einleitung in die Offenbarung des Johannes und in die apokalyptische Literatur überhaupt*, Bonn, 1848; AUBERLEN, *Der Prophet Daniel und die Offenbarung Johannes*, 2d ed. Basel, 1857.*) The eschatological hymns. Eschatology in dogmatic theology.

3. *Neither the Son.*—Comp. the topic Agnoetism in the History of Doctrine. Dogmatic theology has not reached the point of being able to do perfect justice to the œconomic and dynamic import of the Son's not knowing. In order to succeed in this, we must not carry the old human finiteness into the Logos, which men have deemed to be a further development of dogmatic theology; but we must do justice to the fact, that His divine nature transforms His human finiteness into the theanthropic condition and mode. Leo the Great says, "*Humana augens, divina non minuens.*" No safety can lie in the "*minuere divina.*" Not to know, and ignorance, are two entirely distinct things.

4. The strong emphasizing of Christ's exhortation, Watch!—According to this Petrine gospel, Christ's servants, above all Peter, should be the doorkeepers not so much of heaven as of the Church on earth, and should keep her awake, watching for the day of judgment.

5. Three is the number of the Spirit, four the number of the world. At the revelations of His personal spirit, Christ was attended by three trusted friends; at the unveiling of the world's fate He has four.

6. JOSEPHUS, *De Bello Jud.*, should be used with this passage; particularly the history of the destruction of Jerusalem. *See* VON RAUMER'S *Palästina;* also BRAUNE, p. 353.

* "Prophecies of Daniel and the Revelation of St. John, viewed in their mutual relationships," Edinburgh, T. & T. Clark.

HOMILETICAL AND PRACTICAL.

See Matthew.—General thoughts upon the entire passage.—Homily upon the Lord's speech concerning the end of the world, according to the preceding division.—The Judge has already announced Himself.—The last judgment in its presages: 1. The one great presage: the destruction of Jerusalem; 2. the continuous presages: the days of less terror in the New Testament seasons of trial; 3. the last presage, as signal.—The world's state and course between two great judgments, the destruction of Jerusalem (the symbolical end of the world), and the real end of the world in a place of judgment: 1. The picture of the state itself; 2. the misapprehension of the state. The world does not observe the forbearance, the administration, the approach of justice-dispensing righteousness.—The coming of Christ in our time with the baptism of the Spirit and of fire: 1. A true coming; 2. reminds us of His first coming; 3. an indication of His last coming.—The final words of Christ in His speech upon the end of the world: 1. Take heed unto yourselves; 2. Beware; 3. Watch.—The last day, a day which makes all things clear.—The day of the great revelation and the great appearance: 1. The great revelation of the old appearance (the phenomenal and visionary world); 2. the great appearance of the old revelation.

Upon A. Vers. 1-4.

See Matthew.—The exit of Jesus from the temple of His people: 1. A decisive step; 2. a melancholy farewell; 3. a decisive token; 4. the certain pledge of the rebuilding.—The prospect from the Mount of Olives of the temple and the city; or, the great difference between the sensuous (æsthetic) and a spiritual prospect from the Mount.—The Lord's repeated survey of the city from the Mount of Olives: 1. A look of a compassionate heart, during which the tears fall, Luke xix. 41; 2. a look of the solemnly earnest spirit in which the tears must disappear (here).—Jesus sitting in the circle of His four disciples upon the Mount of Olives; or, the night-conversation on the end of the world and the judgment, ever sad, yet solemnly joyous, because of its anticipations.—The great mystic discourse upon the last time: 1. Much overlooked; 2. much falsified; 3. ever of force; 4. ever efficacious; or, 1. in the world ever falsified and darkened; 2. in the Church continually illuminated and deepened.

STARKE:—*Bibl. Wirt.:*—Men's degeneracy, to be bewitched with the seeming reality of this world, and to forget, what they should necessarily consider, the statements of God's word.—*Nova Bibl. Tub.:*—If the wind of God's judgments storm around, there is nothing so firm, nothing so magnificent, as not to be torn down and destroyed. How many thousands of the fairest cities, of the most gorgeous palaces, of the most impregnable castles, have experienced this, lying now, because of their sins, in heaps!—Is this the city of which men say, It is the all-beauteous, on account of which the whole land rejoices, etc.? Lam. ii. 15 and 17.—CANSTEIN:—When we gaze upon great and glorious structures of this world; let us ever remember that a time will come when these shall be no more, and that nought is abiding but that which is not seen, 2 Cor. iv. 18.—At the house of God judgment must take its beginning, 1 Pet. iv. 17.—It is edifying to speak of the divine judgments, of the destruction of all that is splendid, yea, of the end, even, of this present world.

Rieger:—In the minds of the disciples these two things [rather, these three, the destruction of the temple, Christ's future, and the world's end,] must have become confused, or they must at least not have been able to distinguish between them accurately [still in some measure. *See* above.] Just as now, in our belief of the future coming of the Lord to judge the quick and dead, many things also are united into one, which, nevertheless, the result itself might separate into distinguishable representations and periods.—The Lord Jesus, in His answer, has not explained it so fully, etc., because Jerusalem's judgment was such a famous symbol and earnest of the end of the world.

Braune:—Comp., regarding the speedy coming of the Lord, Isa. xiii. 6; Ezek. xxx. 3; Joel ii. 1; Matt. xvi. 27; Phil. iv. 5; 1 Pet. iv. 7; 1 John ii. 18; Rev. i. 3; iii. 11. Quotation from Hamann's writings: "The death of every man is the time when the revelation of the Lord's coming is partly fulfilled to the soul. In this sense, it is literally true that the time of fulfilment is near." In the fragments of Jerusalem the last judgment is reflected.

Schleiermacher:—It was His object to represent all the institutions of the old covenant as something dedicated to destruction, in order to direct their attention by so much the more to the spiritual.—Hence we have to mark, that everything external in the Christian community is nothing else, and can and should be nothing else, than a shell, a covering in which the spiritual presents itself and works.—We find that the striving after externalism was soon renewed in the Christian Church.

Brieger:—The temple was the pride of the blinded people.—The destruction of Jerusalem is in a certain measure to be understood as a world-judgment. It befalls that people, namely, who for two thousand years had represented the human race. In the downfall of Jerusalem is depicted the downfall of the whole world (as in the exit of the Christians from Jerusalem is depicted the great deliverance of the believers in the last time).

Upon B. Vers. 5–13.

The foresight and fearlessness which the Lord enjoins upon His people in looking for His coming (or the end of the world): 1. Foresight in respect to the deceptive delusions of false Christs (spiritual delusions); fearlessness as to the threatening terrors of war and all the world-plagues (temporal terrors). 2. Foresight as to the enemies of the gospel, and as to their treachery; fearlessness as to the gift of tongues, and the power to reply. 3. Foresight as to temptations thrown in our way by our nearest relatives and the world; fearlessness as to the certain deliverance of the enduring Christians.—Take heed that no man deceive you; or, Antichrist comes before Christ comes, 2 Thess. ii.—The succession of signs: 1. False signs, and yet signs [false Christs, ver. 6]. 2. Weak signs, and yet sad signs [the wars; the end *not* yet, ver. 7]. 3. Stronger signs: national, political, terrestrial, physiological revolutions [the beginning of the woes, ver. 8]. 4. Striking signs [persecutions of Christians, ver. 9]. 5. The decisive sign [the gospel is preached among all people throughout the world].—The contradictory nature of the signs: 1. Signs which do not appear terrible, but enticing, and yet are to the utmost terrible; signs which appear to the utmost terrible, and yet are not so 2. Saddening signs. 3. The great, joyful signs, ver. 10.—The great rules for our conduct, in looking forward to the last time, and in the midst of its signs: 1. Foresight; 2. fearlessness; 3. simplicity and a spiritual walk; 4. steadfastness.—The Lord's faithful admonitions.—There is an overcoming of these troubles.

Starke:—In His teaching, Christ has regard not so much to what He knows, as to what is useful to, and necessary for, His hearers.—It does not behove us to know time and hour, but to observe the signs antecedent to the judgments of God.—*Nova Bibl. Tub.*:—Alas! how many good men has the pretence of Christ's name,—viz.: false hopes, outward show, seeming representations, fleshly accessories, etc.,—already misled, that they have fallen away into sad by-paths, and have been ruined!—The doctrine of the Last Things no useless doctrine.—Quesnel:—He who properly understands this present world, how it is disposed and what end it shall meet, is always self-possessed regarding it, and is terrified by nothing.—Wilt thou save thyself from the awful judgments of God, then be not anxious regarding the judgments and wrath of man.—The gospel-trumpet must be blown before the archangel's trumpet is heard.—Cramer:—God will not forsake His own people in the time of persecution.—In the defence of the truth, we must not look at our own weakness, nor the foes' might and strength, but we must consider the power of the truth and God's promise.—Osiander:—Imagine not thou art not bound to learn aught, etc.—Quesnel:—Faith gives us as many fathers, brothers, and sisters, as there are Christians; unbelief changes those friends whom nature has given us into enemies, betrayers, and executioners.—The most dangerous temptation is that which comes from parents.—Osiander:—It is a mark of false religion that it is bloodthirsty.—The end crowns.—Gerlach:—No man can reckon more certainly upon the assistance of the Holy Spirit than those who confess Jesus' name in the time of their utmost peril.—Stier:—The end is patience, the saints' weapon (Rev. xiii. 10; xiv. 12), as the beginning is foresight (Matt. iv.).—Braune: 2 Tim. iv. 16, 17.—The end comes not before the Gospel has finished its course. The nearer this completion approaches, the more certainly is the Lord's coming near.—Schleiermacher:—We should expect no other than Christ.—All may perish; we are sure that He and His kingdom will remain.—Brieger:—The Lord's communication includes in itself the nearest and the most remote; hence He speaks to those nearest, and to those farthest from Him.—As the hate of the world witnessed for Him, so does He witness for His own people.—The final winding-up is to be introduced by means of the Gospel.—The being saved is of the same import as being received to glory.—Gossner:—He who possesses the rights of a citizen of heaven, can remain unterrified though it should storm beneath heaven.

Upon C. D. Vers. 14–20, 21–23.

See Matthew.—Even in His great judgments is God's mercy revealed: 1. It warns of the judgments, and indicates the signs of their coming; 2. it opens a way of escape, and exhorts to use that way in flight; 3. it points to prayer as the means to mitigate that judgment; 4. it has its eye fixed upon innocent sufferers; 5. it breaks the judgment off, and puts bounds to it, for the sake of the elect; 6. it warns against falling away to Antichrist, as the falling beneath the heaviest, the most fearful judgment.—The abomination of desolation, or the judgment inflicted on the holy place, a great admonitory sign: 1. The sign of the end of a now hoary period (and form of belief; or of a long series of judgments, which point forward to the last judgment); 2. the sign of a decisive separation between an old and new period; 3. the prognostic of a new period.—The prophet Daniel; or, the eternal spirit of the Lord in the old covenant, has foretold the end of the old covenant. (*See* Isa. lxvi. 3; Jer. xxxi. 31; Ezek. xxxvi. 26; comp. 2 Cor. iii. 13; Heb. viii. 7, 8).—The Spirit of the Permanent in the Church is the prophet of the downfall of her transitory forms (especially in the Middle Ages). —Whoso readeth, etc.: The old Scripture-word shows to all time the signs of the present and the future.—The flight to the mountains: The entire life of the Christians is a fleeing to the mountains.—In a season of distress, the saving of the trifling and the unessential (the clothes) has as its result the loss of the great and the essential (the life and soul): 1. *The fact* (in conflagrations, in times of war, in political convulsions, in times of religious crises). 2. *The reason:* because the small and trifling is the net which keeps men entangled in the old system and its judgment (Lot's wife, the Jews, the Middle Ages).—Woe to those with child, etc.: The Lord's compassion towards the special sufferers among mankind in the judgments inflicted on the specially sinful part of mankind.—The alleviations of the divine judgments which God has given to men: 1. Compassion (ver. 17); 2. prayer (ver. 18); 3. the steadfastness of the elect (ver. 20).—For the sake of the elect, *whom God has chosen*, God endures the world in sparing patience (*see* Rom. ix. 22).—The surest signs of the judgment which runs through the New Testament period of grace are the false Christs, the signs of the false Christs, and the hopes placed in them: 1. Among the Jews; 2. among Christians themselves.—The tendency to believe in false Christs is the most awful result of the rejection of Christ that is to be seen in the life of Israel, John v. 43.—The great temptations of the period which is hastening to its end: 1. Perceived beforehand; 2. declared beforehand; 3. overcome beforehand.—Foresight regarding the lying pseudo-Christian system, the salvation of Christianity in the last days.—Foresight the first and last means in preserving faithfulness during the last days.—Caution: 1. Regarding excited preachers who pretend to make Christ visible in themselves or in others, in this or that person or thing (See here or there); 2. regarding persons who will attest themselves as new saviours by means of deceptive signs and wonders (2 Thess. ii. 10, 11; Rev. xiii. 13).—The end of the world's history: unceasing self-confusion, self-blinding, and self-separation of the great majority from Christianity, and self-abandonment to pseudo-Christian systems.

STARKE:—CRAMER:—If we see even the greatest distress awaiting us, we should not allow ourselves by this to be turned aside from God and His love.—In public, national calamities, the majority think only of saving their goods and lives; few are anxious to make sure of their souls and salvation.—QUESNEL: —By far the most useful flight in the day of divine wrath is to flee the fleeting pleasures of the world, and escape from conformity to it, Ps. xc. 11.—*Nova Bibl. Tub.*:—God spares even this wicked world for the sake of His elect.

RIEGER:—Sad periods in the world's course are turned to their own benefit by false prophets.—LISCO: *Take heed unto yourselves*;—an exhortation applicable to much more than the external danger of temptation, seduction, and falling away.—BRAUNE:—Luke, vers. 22, 23; Deut. xxviii. 15; Mal. iv. 1. *Lo, here is Christ*,—a voice which allures to itself; *or there*, —a voice which, unpartisan-like, points to others, and is accordingly still more dangerous—these voices are not to lead disciples astray.—Signs and troubles are no certain marks of Christ and His prophets: they are only indications of the connection of the individual with the spiritual world; they may be indications either of light and truth, or of darkness and lies.—Prove the spirits, whether they be of God.

SCHLEIERMACHER:—When we see how many imperfections have appeared in the Christian Church, one might be easily tempted to say, The light is not yet the right light. The true believer is, however, assured that the Christian faith has no share in all these imperfections; that it is the natural ruin of mankind alone which is the fountain of these, and this cannot all at once be removed.—God's kingdom is the spiritual temple of God, which needs not the external, and is raised above all external accidents, and which, where it has been once built, must endure to the end of days.

BRIEGER:—Not in the winter. It is well known that Jerusalem was destroyed in August.—The same sin, rejection of the Holy One, which brought Israel to its downfall, will cause the world's overthrow, so soon as *its* measure is filled.—The urging of precaution appears so much the less needful, inasmuch as He Himself says, it is impossible to deceive them. We may explain this in the following manner: God's acts do not *exclude* men's action, but *include* it (and that, too, not in the form of natural compulsion, but of the bond of love).—GOSSNER:—How must we ever fear to give our adherence to a false Christ!

Upon E. Vers. 24-27.

See Matthew.—The last day according to the Lord's announcement: 1. The great day of death, when the lights of heaven grow pale; 2. the judgment-day, when the Crucified appears in the glory of the world's Judge; 3. the great feast-day, when the Lord gathers His chosen by His angels from all ends of this and the other world.—Man's calamity completes itself at the end in the world's calamity.—As the sun was darkened at Christ's death, so will the entire starry world belonging to this earth grow dark in the death-hour of aged humanity.—The stars will fall from heaven. With mankind, not merely the earth, but also the planetary system which belongs to earth according to its old form, shall be dissolved, and assume a new shape.—When sun, moon, and stars shine no more, will Christ appear, and illuminate with His brightness the last day.—The last day the grand day of festival for perfected Christianity: 1. The creature-lights grow pale; the Lord appears as the festive light of His own day; 2. the impersonal being of the world disappears;* the glorified personality of Christ appears, and manifests His personal kingdom; 3. the wicked are shut out, and

* [Does this mean: The kingdom of materialism, or that "flesh and blood" which cannot inherit the kingdom of God?—*Ed.*]

have vanished; and all pure spirits are united; 4. Heaven's angels are the servants at the feast: all the elect shall be assembled who are upon the earth and in heaven.—The last day is, for the chosen of the Lord, the dawn of their blessed immortality, Job xix. 25.

STARKE:—QUESNEL:—O wished-for day of the elect! O long-desired purification, through which they shall be gathered by Jesus into the union of His body, His Spirit, and His glory!—OSIANDER:—Should we die in a strange land, yet shall we be assuredly gathered to Christ, our Head, at the last day, 2 Cor. v. 10.

BRAUNE:—Rev. i. 1; ch. xxii. 6 ["Shortly, quickly"]; Hagg. ii. 6–8 ["Yet once, it is a little while"]; Eccles. xii. 2; Isa. xiv. 12 ["How art thou fallen"]; Isa. xxxiv. 4 ["All the host of heaven shall be dissolved"].—The destruction of the creature will be an exodus into eternity.—STIER:—To the end of heaven. "Because earth and heaven now incline wonderfully to one another."

BRIEGER:—Ezek. xxxii. 7, 8; Joel ii. 3, 4; Dan. vii. 13; Acts i. 11; Heb. i. 14; Matt. xiii. 41, 42.—BAUER:—These violent things are only the heralds in the Lord's service.

Upon F. Vers. 28-37.

See Matthew.—The fig-tree with its late leaves is also a picture of the onward-hurrying judgment, upon the guilty Church (ch. xi. 12), upon the unrepentant Church (Luke xiii. 6), upon the fickle Israel (Hosea ix. 10).—The fig-tree according to its varied signification: 1. The early figs, the formation of fruit before the leaves shot forth: the early conversion of Israel and the elect. 2. The fig-tree unfruitful in the rich vineyard: a dying professing Church (and this is true of individuals) in the midst of the ever-living kingdom of God. 3. The fig-tree unfruitful, and yet pretentious with its leaves on the roadside; or, a church (congregation) without spiritual fruit, in the hypocritical covering of pious forms, fallen under judgment. 4. The blooming fig-tree, a prognostic of the summer's harvest; or, the theocratic, ecclesiastical, and cosmical indications of judgment as presages of the approach of the final judgment.—The holy certainty of believers respecting the day of the Lord strengthened and elevated through their ignorance of the time and hour: 1. The certainty, *a.* as to signs, *b.* as to His speedy coming, *c.* as to His unexpected coming, *d.* His coming during the life of a living Christian generation, *e.* in order to the destruction of the world, *f.* in order to fulfil His declaration respecting the necessity of watching. 2. Strengthened and increased through their ignorance: *a.* an ignorance regarding the day and the hour, to which He had voluntarily subjected Himself for their sakes; *b.* an ignorance regarding the time, to which He had subjected them for His own sake.—Christ's not knowing rests upon His knowing rightly [in a natural manner], or upon the holy *extension* of His range of vision.*—What Christ *may* not know, what angels *cannot* know, Christians should not *wish* to know.—The last day, the deep secret of the Father: Of the Father in His Creator-fulness, and in His gracious design; 2. of the Father in His preparing grace, and in His commands to the Son; 3. of the Father in the greatness of His patience, and the majesty of wrath.—The knowledge of Christ in itself exalted above the knowledge of men and of angels, is, on our behalf, a circle of holy self-limitation within the Father's omniscience.—Because He cannot deny anything to His own, He has denied Himself a knowledge of this.—The holy and useful uncertainty of the Church regarding the last day is to be compared with the holy useful uncertainty of individual men regarding the day of their death.—Through this holy uncertainty, we should be certain of our own salvation. Every day should for the Christian bear something like the appearance of the last day.—Christianity is a door-keeper's office, as regards the future coming of the Lord.—Christ's alarm-call, or summons to all Christians for all time to watch!—Slumbering, in respect to the Lord's coming, is a danger fraught with death; while watchfulness is a fundamental condition of life.—Christianity is a constant living in the experience of judgment and redemption: 1. Judgment: *a.* a coming from judgment [Lange alludes, apparently, to the rise of Christianity at the time Judaism was subjected to judgment. Translator], *b.* an acting under judgment, *c.* a preparing for judgment. 2. Redemption: *a.* from the time onward, that the work of redemption was ended, *b.* proceeding under the cheering hope of redemption, *c.* looking forward to redemption.

STARKE:—Spring is a beautiful image: in the shrubs bursting into life, we are reminded of the coming of Christ, of the glorious judgment day, and the joyful resurrection from the dead.—QUESNEL:—Who is certain that he is not sooner to appear before God, his Judge, than summer is to come? If he meet not God to be condemned, the joyful everlasting summer will follow.—We have seen many things in our lives pass away: is that not a proof that all things fade away?—God has concealed from all creatures the time of His judgments; hence is many a one ruined in his calculation.—Beware of security! watch and pray!

BRAUNE:—Heaven and earth pass as leaves upon the world-stem in the harvest of the world-season: God's people are the sap, and God's word the power, which carries new life to all.—Jas. v. 7, 8: "I do not know." Will it be too hard for thee to say this? If so, Christ is not thy Lord.—The watching of the Christian must be also prayer (and *active watchfulness* will be at the same time prayer).—BRIEGER:—The kingdom of God, which will at last appear in power and glory, is to be compared with the joy-fraught summer.

* [Lange's thought seems to be, that the *voluntary* ignorance of Christ, which was a part of the voluntary humiliation to which the divine nature was subjected in its union with the human, was for the purpose of making possible a *gradual* growth in His theanthropic consciousness. For, had there been from the instant of the miraculous conception (the *punctum temporis* when the union of the two natures began) onward through infancy, childhood, and youth, the omniscient consciousness of the eternal Logos, of course it would have been contradictory to say that Christ, the God-man, "increased in wisdom" (Luke ii. 52), or that He did not know the time of the last judgment.—*Ed.*]

THIRD SECTION.

THE PASSION OF CHRIST, AND HIS REST IN THE GRAVE. THE RETIREMENT INTO THE STATE OF THE DEAD. THE LION OF THE TRIBE OF JUDAH AS THE PASCHAL LAMB.

CHAPTER XIV. 1—XV. 47.

1. *The Preparation for the great Passover. The Supper.—The helpless impotency of wickedness in the old Church of God. The determined genius of wickedness in the new Christian Church. The Anointing of the Lord at the Feast preparatory to His Death; and the sale of the Anointed, or the Treachery, matured at the Feast-table.* CH. XIV. 1–11.

(Parallels: Matt. xxvi. 1–16; Luke xxii. 1–6; John xii. 1–8.)

A. *The weak Indecision of the Enemies.* VERS. 1, 2.

1 After two days was *the feast* of the passover, and of unleavened bread: and the
chief priests and the scribes sought how they might take him by craft, and put *him* to
2 death. But[1] they said, Not on the feast-*day*, lest there be an uproar of the people.

B. *The holy Presentiment of the Female Disciple.* VERS. 3–5.

3 And being in Bethany, in the house of Simon the leper, as he sat at meat, there
came a woman, having an alabaster-box of ointment of spikenard, very precious; and
4 she brake the box, and poured *it*[2] on his head. And there were some that had indigna-
tion within themselves, and said,[3] Why was this waste [loss] of the ointment made?
5 For it might have been sold for more than three hundred pence, and have been given
to the poor. And they murmured against her.

C. *The Lord's holy Decision.* VERS. 6–9.

6 And Jesus said, Let her alone; why trouble ye her? she hath wrought a good
7 work on me. For ye have the poor with you always, and whensoever ye will ye may
8 do them good: but me ye have not always. She hath done what she[4] could: she is
9 come aforehand to anoint my body to the burying. Verily I say unto you, Whereso-
ever this[5] gospel shall be preached throughout the whole world, *this* also that she hath
done shall be spoken of for a memorial of her.

D. *The Disciple's wicked Decision.* VERS. 10, 11.

10 And Judas Iscariot,[6] one of the twelve, went unto the chief priests, to betray him
11 unto them. And when they heard *it*, they were glad, and promised to give him
money. And he sought how he might conveniently betray him.

[1 Ver. 2.—Lachmann, Tischendorf, after B., C.*, D., read γάρ instead of δέ.]
[2 Ver. 3.—Lachmann, Tischendorf, B., C., L., Δ. omit κατά.]
[3 Ver. 4.—Codd. B., C.*, L. want καὶ λέγοντες; Cod. A. has it.]
[4 Ver. 8.—Codd. B., L. want αὕτη.]
[5 Ver. 9.—Codd. B., D., L. want τοῦτο; Lachmann brackets and Tischendorf omits.]
[6 Ver. 10.—Codd. B., C., D., Lachmann omit the article before Ἰούδας and Ἰσκαριώτης.]

EXEGETICAL AND CRITICAL.

Comp. the notes on *Matthew*.—The peculiarities of Mark in the history of the Passion generally are: life-like pictures, sharply-defined features, original statements of particulars. Peculiarities in this section. The two indications of Jesus' approaching death, namely, the indecisive deliberations of the Sanhedrin, and the anointing in Bethany, are found united in Mark, as in Matthew; yet he expresses himself regarding the decision of the leaders of the council much more briefly than Matthew,—more decidedly, however, than Luke. In the history of the anointing, he mentions, with John, a fact in addition to the statement as given by Matthew that Jesus sat at the table. Moreover, he describes the ointment more exactly. And, besides, to him we owe the fresh trait, that the woman broke the alabaster-box; according to several codices, the additional remark is made, that the ointment ran down from His head. In respect to diversity of statement, he assumes an intermediate position between John and

Matthew. John names Judas as the murmurer; Matthew, the disciples; Mark says, "some." With John, he declares the value to be three hundred denarii, and adds the strong word ἐνεβριμῶντο. To the words, Ye have the poor with you always, he appends,—And whensoever ye will, etc. To him again is the clause peculiar, She hath done what she could. The idea that this female disciple anticipates the anointing of Jesus for burial is here more clearly expressed. Peculiarly lively is the expression in regard to the preaching of the Gospel εἰς ὅλον τὸν κόσμον (Matthew, ἐν ὅλῳ, κ.τ.λ.). The treacherous visit of Judas to the high-priest is more briefly given than in Matthew. He does not name the traitor's question, neither the thirty pieces of silver; yet he emphasizes the joy of the chief priests.

Ver. 1. **The feast of the Passover, and of unleavened bread.**—A double feast-season. *See Matthew.* Comp. Luke's expression.—**After two days.**—Probably on Wednesday in the Passion Week, not on Tuesday (*see Matthew*). The anointing in Bethany was on the previous Saturday. The question is now, In what relation do the sitting of the council and the anointing stand to one another? We could imagine that the first history brings before us the chief priests, how undecided they still are; the second shows how Judas comes and gives advice. We must then assume that the thought of treachery had been brooded over by Judas from Saturday in the preceding week till at least Wednesday in the Passion Week, and came then first to maturity. The remark of Matthew, ver. 14, seems to speak against this, "Then Judas went unto." Judas had undoubtedly gone much earlier to the high priests. To this the statement points, "how they might take Him by craft." If they had just now decided, "Not on the feast-day," this is explained by the great triumphs which Jesus, on Palm Sunday, on Monday, and Tuesday, had celebrated over them; and with this, besides, the fact agrees well, that Judas had begun to hesitate during these days. The connection of the two recitals lies, accordingly, in the antithesis of the previous anticipation of the crucifixion on the part of the Lord and the strong presentiment of the female disciple, on the one side, and the much subsequent indecision and short-sightedness of His foes, on the other. But the second point of relation is this, that we see from the first narrative how far the foes had of themselves come; from the second, how Judas drove them to take their boldly wicked step, and succeeded in giving them the last impulse. They said, "Not on the feast-day;" Judas, on the contrary, bethought himself of the first, best opportunity.

Ver. 3. **Of spikenard, very precious.**—Upon πιστικῆς, comp. DE WETTE, MEYER, LUCKE on *John*, vol. ii. p. 493. Not drinkable (πιστός), but veritable, real. Upon the nard, comp. *Matthew.*—**Brake the box** (bottle, or flask).—The narrow neck of the small flask. She did not wish to keep or hold back anything: offered up all, gave all away.

Ver. 4. **There were some.**—*See Matthew.* Mark presents, without a doubt, the most accurate historic picture, John defines most sharply the motive, Matthew gives the specially practical historic form.

Ver. 5. **And they murmured against her.**—De Wette: They scolded her. Meyer: They addressed her harshly. In ἐμβριμάομαι lies especially the expression of a passionate feeling which we strive to keep back in the utterance.

Ver. 8. **She is come aforehand.**—Προλαμβάνειν is the chief conception, not μυρίσαι; hence we see the error of Meyer's note, "A classic writer would have said, προλαβοῦσα ἐμύρισε."

Ver. 10. **One of the Twelve.**—Made prominent, as in Matthew. The tragic point lies not only in this, that one of the Twelve was false, but that he committed that most wicked act of treachery which was the particular sting in the sufferings of Christ. In a wider sense, he extended himself through the whole sufferings of Christ; for the treachery of the disciple who betrayed the Lord to the chief priests, led to the betrayal, on the part of the Sanhedrim, of Christ to the heathen power.

Ver. 11. **Were glad.**—They shuddered not, as the traitor laid before them his black design. They understood him. But Judas knew how to lead them still further into wickedness. He filled them with a satanic joy. And while they were still hesitating to take the last step, assuredly not from dread of the sin, but for fear of the people, Judas was watching for the first opportunity to accomplish his purpose.

DOCTRINAL AND ETHICAL.

1. *See Matthew*, and the parallel passages in *Luke*.

2. Judas the betrayer, because he had been most offended at the thought of the death and cross of Christ; Mary the commended disciple, because she was the first that was found possessing a self-sacrificing courage like His own in His way to death.

3. The treachery which springs up in the midst of the disciples of the Evangelical Church surpasses the wicked counsel of the hierarchies in the Middle Ages. The secret and open apostasies from the Evangelical Church to Romanism.

HOMILETICAL AND PRACTICAL.

Comp. *Matthew.*—The council in Jerusalem, and the supper in Bethany, in their relation to the central point of Christ's death; or, a picture of the uniting of all threads of ancient history in this death.—Not out of the camp of the foes, but out of the circle of the disciples, came the last decision regarding the death of Jesus.—Judas, the enslaved, and yet free, instrument of the deepest revelation of wickedness.—The faithless disciple of Jesus an instructor of the chief council in the way of destruction.—The unexpected turning-points in life, how they rise out of the depths of the spirit-world: 1. Out of the realm of light (Mary); 2. out of the realm of darkness (Judas); 3. out of the struggle between the two.—The ointment in the house at Bethany a savour of death unto death.—Greed in its demoniac greatness: 1. A child of perfected unbelief as to Christ, God, and mankind; 2. a father of treachery, which has often injured the saints; 3. a companion of avarice, envy, anguish, audacity, despair.—Judas determines to take the best opportunity he can to betray the Lord, *i. e.*, in the sanctuary of His secret prayers.—Judas the calculator, and his miscalculation.—The estimation of Mary, and the estimation of Judas. The presentiment-filled spirit in its clear foresight as opposed to the selfish mind in its blindness.—The most multiplied purposes and projects, and over them the deep design of God.—Woman is here again before man, as is so often the case in the Gospel history.

STARKE:—HEDINGER:—Satan rests not till he has injured Christ and His cause in life, honor, and possessions.—At feast-seasons the devil generally excites the greatest uproar against Christians.—HEDINGER:—Nothing is wasted upon Christ. Miserable parsimony, when we refuse Him anything.—The prating of a fault-seeker can soon move others to join.—QUESNEL:—The pious must remain silent regarding the world's judgment. God will speak and conduct their affairs.—Behold, how the godless rejoice if they get an opportunity of fulfilling their wicked wish!—GERLACH:—The greatest praise ever spoken by Jesus regarding an act.—BRAUNE:—The Sanhedrim required him to point out Jesus' tarrying-place. And Judas is ready to do it.—BRIEGER:—Exactly what the enemies wished least of all to do, that must they.—To an uproar it came, only to the advantage of hell.—The greatest, most direct, most difficult, but the most blessed thing that ever a sinful being was able to do, namely, to receive the Lord's word in all simplicity and proceed to act, this did Mary; and this shall maintain her memory on earth till the end of time.—GOSSNER:—*She hath done what she could.* From this may every one take comfort, that nothing more than faithfulness is asked from them.—BAUER:—The deeds of love are often in the world turned into shame, because others turn them into an occasion to do evil.

---

2. *The Feast of the Passion, and of Victory.—The Paschal Lamb and the discovered Traitor. The Last Supper and the Lord's Triumph over the Traitor. The Prediction of the Disciples being offended, and of their denying Him.* VERS. 12-31.

(Parallels: Matt. xxvi. 17-35; Luke xxii. 7-38; John xiii.—xvii.)

A. *The Disciples' Passover-thought.—Unguardedness and Foresight; or, the Jewish Custom and Christ's Spirit.* VERS. 12-16.

12 And the first day of unleavened bread, when they killed the passover, his disciples
said unto him, Where wilt thou that we go and prepare, that thou mayest eat the pass-
13 over? And he sendeth forth two of his disciples, and saith unto them, Go ye into the
14 city, and there shall meet you a man bearing a pitcher of water: follow him. And
wheresoever he shall go in, say ye to the goodman of the house, The Master saith,
15 Where is the guest-chamber, where I shall eat the passover with my disciples? And
he will show you a large upper room furnished *and* prepared: there make ready for us.
16 And his disciples went forth, and came into the city, and found as he had said unto
them: and they made ready the passover.

B. *The Lord's Passover-thought.—The Passover, and the hardened and discovered Traitor in the circle of Disciples. The Lord's clear perception of the secret designs of the Traitor.* VERS. 17-21.

17, 18 And in the evening he cometh with the twelve. And as they sat and did eat,
Jesus said, Verily I say unto you, One of you which eateth with me shall betray me.
19. And they began to be sorrowful, and to say unto him one by one, *Is* it I? and another
20 *said, Is* it I?[1] And he answered[2] and said unto them, *It is* one of the twelve, that dip-
21 peth with me[3] in the dish. The Son of man indeed goeth, as it is written of him: but
woe to that man by whom the Son of man is betrayed! good were it for that man if
he had never been born.

C. *The new Passover.—The Lord's fulness of Love on the night of the Betrayal.* VERS. 22-25.

22 And as they did eat, Jesus[4] took bread, and blessed, and brake *it*, and gave to them,
23 and said, Take, eat:[5] this is my body. And he took the cup, and when he had given
24 thanks, he gave *it* to them: and they all drank of it. And he said unto them, This is
25 my blood of the new[6] testament [covenant], which is shed for many. Verily I say unto
you, I will drink no more of the fruit of the vine, until that day that I drink it new in
the kingdom of God.

D. *A new Passover upon a new Night of Terror, and upon the Death of the First-born.* VERS. 26-31.

26 And when they had sung an hymn, they went out into the Mount of Olives.
27 And Jesus saith unto them, All ye shall be offended because of me this night:[7] for it is
28 written, I will smite the Shepherd, and the sheep shall be scattered. But after that I

29 am risen, I will go before you into Galilee. But Peter said unto him, Although all
30 shall be offended, yet *will* not I. And Jesus saith unto him, Verily I say unto thee,
That this day, *even* in this night, before the cock crow twice, thou shalt deny me thrice
31 But he spake[8] the more vehemently,[9] If I should die with thee, I will not deny thee in
any wise. Likewise also said they all.

[1] Ver. 19.—Καὶ ἄλλος, μήτι ἐγώ; omitted by B., C., L., Versions, Vulgate, &c.; probably because the words were deemed superfluous, and that the construction was inadmissible. (We suppose εἱς to be supplied with the first μήτι ἐγώ.)

[2] Ver. 20.—The evidence against ἀποκριθείς is quite conclusive; [rejected by Lachmann, Tischendorf.]

[[3] Ver. 20.—Lachmann, after A. and Versions, reads τὴν χεῖρα after εμοῦ.]

[[4] Ver. 22.—Ὁ Ἰησοῦς is wanting in B., D., Versions; bracketed by Lachmann; rejected by Tischendorf.]

[5] Ver. 22.—Φάγετε must be struck out, on the authority of A., B., C., &c.

[6] Ver. 24.—Καινῆς is wanting in B., C., D., L., &c. Tischendorf rejects it, but it is retained by Lachmann. The uncertainty of the reading even in Matthew excites suspicion, that the Pauline tradition gave rise to it; for "the blood of the testament [covenant]" can mean nothing else than "of the *new* testament."

[[7] Ver. 27.—Ἐν ἐμοὶ ἐν τῇ νυκτὶ ταύτῃ. B., C.*, D. want these words. A. has them. Lachmann retains ἐν ἐμοὶ, and brackets ἐν τῇ νυκτὶ ταύτῃ.]

[[8] Ver. 31.—B., D., L., Lachmann, Tischendorf read ἐλάλει for ἔλεγε.]

[[9] Ver. 31.—B., C., D., L. want μᾶλλον; Lachmann, Tischendorf omit it.]

EXEGETICAL AND CRITICAL.

Comp. *Matthew* and *Luke*.—The unity of these sections is to be found in the contrast between the disciples' unprepared state of mind, and the ever clear perception which the Lord had of what lay before Him. Next, we have the opposition between the Passover and the Supper, the great institution of love, and of treachery; finally, the contrast between the faithful care with which the Lord warned the disciples, and their presumptuous self-deception respecting the fact of their own weakness. Peculiarities of Mark:—Exact statement of the day, ver. 12, with Luke. He brings forward (what is passed over by Matthew) the sending of the two disciples, but does not name them, as Luke does; and this again is to be traced back to Peter's modesty, for Peter was one of those sent. The direction of Jesus also,—in Matthew, Go ye πρὸς τὸν δεῖνα,—is given here in a more expanded form, as also in Luke: the description of the man with the water-pitcher, who should meet them at the gate of the city, and the directions which they were to follow. He passes over, in his description of the Passover, the special narrations of Luke and John, and hastens forward with Matthew to the detection of the traitor. The indication of the betrayer has been already given: He who eateth with Me, ver. 18. The peculiar ἤρξαντο again, ver. 19. The audacious question of Judas, Is it I? which Matthew introduces, Mark omits, as he has previously omitted his words to the chief priests. In the celebration of the Supper, he agrees, excepting in a few trifling deviations, with Matthew. Peter has, through Mark, directed attention to the fact concerning the cup, "And they all drank of it." In recording, "Shed for many," Mark allows, "For the remission of sins," to fall out. The words concerning the new cup in the kingdom of God he causes to follow the words of the institution of the Supper, as is the case in Matthew, but more briefly expressed. The remark (recorded by John) to the disciples, "Ye cannot follow Me now," in Mark (and Matthew), runs, "All ye shall be offended because of Me." Peter's vow, "I will follow Thee," as given by John, is extended in Mark, "Although all shall be offended, yet will not I;" shorter than in Matthew. The statement in John, "I will lay down my life for Thy sake," stands in Mark, "If I should die with Thee," etc., as in Matthew. The prediction that they would deny Him follows this asseveration in John, but precedes it in Mark and Matthew; in this latter case, the asseveration was, of course, more presumptuous. Mark alone has the more definite signal, "Before the cock crow twice." The particular features which are introduced by Luke before this transaction, and which bring Peter still more prominently into view, are not related by Mark. He and Matthew present the strongest statement of the occurrence (an affirmation of faithfulness *after* the declaration of the denial).

Ver. 13. **Two of His disciples.**—Peter and John. Comp. *Luke*.—**And there shall meet you.**—The description is as mysterious as in the despatching of the disciples to bring the colt. So, again, is the prominence given to the talismanic word εἰπεῖν, to be noticed. Quite groundless is the view of Meyer (rationalizing), that we find in the wonderful manner in which the supper is ordered, as recorded by Mark and Luke, an evidence of the later origin of this account. In this passage Matthew has only hinted at what the other two have explicitly stated. *See Matthew*.—**A man.**—It is a very mistaken conclusion, if, from the fact that it was a slave's employment to carry water (Deut. xxix. 11; Josh. ix. 21), we conclude this man was a slave.

Ver. 14. **Guest-chamber,** τὸ κατάλυμά μου.—The reception-room, which is appointed for Me. With the word lodgings, the conception of a separate house is united. Much nearer the idea is, "My quarters."

Ver. 15. **A large upper room.**—The form ἀνάγαιον is best supported. Meyer: "In meaning, it is equivalent to ὑπερῷον, עֲלִיָּה, upper room, place for prayer, and assembling together." But, we must undoubtedly conceive of the "upper room" as being on the second floor: the Alijah, on the contrary, is a tower-like erection upon the flat house-roof (*see* 2 Kings iv. 10; comp. Acts x. 9). The learned Winer, too, has no clear idea of the Alijah. Comp. articles, "Houses, Roof." On the contrary, Gesenius: "עֲלִיָּה, *cubiculum superius, conclave, super tectum domus eminens; ὑπερῷον*;" and De Wette, *Archäol.* p. 146.—**Furnished** (provided with pillows).—That is, with pillow-beds laid around the table, as the custom of reclining at meals required.

Ver. 17. **With the Twelve.**—The two messengers have returned and announced that all ready.

Ver. 18. **One of you which eateth with Me.**—The expression of grief. *See* John xiii. 18. Reference to Ps. xli. 10.

Ver. 20. **That dippeth with Me in the dish.**—Meyer: "He was one of those lying closest to Jesus, eating, namely, out of the same dish." There fore, no very definite description. Yet the Passion meal was not the ordinary eating from a dish. The head of the family distributed the portions. The case is thus to be conceived: Jesus was about to hand Judas his portion. Now it is a psychological fact, that an evil conscience causes the hand to move with an uneasy motion, even at the moment when one succeeds in showing a hypocritical face full of innocence and calmness. The hand, in opposition to the steady countenance, makes a hypocritically tremulous motion. So, accordingly, does the traitorous hand of Judas, betraying him, hastily extend itself, it would appear, to meet the Lord's hand, as it is still in the dish, in order with feigned ease to receive the sop. The three statements—He who dippeth with Me in the dish (Matthew, and almost identically Mark); To whom I shall give the sop (John); and, The hand of My betrayer is with Me on the table (Luke),—agree, therefore, as regards the actual state of the case.

Ver. 24. **And He said unto them, This is My blood.**—That our Evangelist makes this expression follow the drinking creates no difference between Matthew, and Luke, and Mark. Because Mark, namely, wished to make this the prominent fact, that all the company in rotation drank of the cup, he represents the Lord as speaking these important words while the act of drinking was being performed; from which it is self-evident, that He speaks them while the cup was passing round.

Ver. 31. **Spake the more vehemently.**—We understand this not quantitatively,—he made regarding this many additional statements,—but qualitatively, of the increasing force in expressing himself, as the following sentence shows.

DOCTRINAL AND ETHICAL.

1. *See Matthew.*

2. As the first Old Testament Passover was celebrated before the actual exemption and deliverance of the Israelites in the Egyptian night of terror, in the believing certainty of their salvation, so was also the New Testament Passover, the Supper, celebrated in the certainty of actual preservation and deliverance, before the outward fact, the death and resurrection of Christ. Exactly thus, in the justification of the individual sinner, does the celebration of his salvation from condemnation precede the completion of his salvation in sanctification.

3. The way and manner in which Jesus unites with the celebration of the Supper the announcement that His disciples should be offended because of Him, and His solicitude for their preservation and restoration, brings before us the relation subsisting between this preservation and that of the first-born in Egypt, for whom atonement had been made. The disciples, too, must the destroying angel pass by. No doubt, because Christ, who is the First-born in an especial sense, presents Himself a sacrifice for them. But this First-born, too, wins back His life from death.

4. Three Passovers: The typical Passover of the typified deliverance; the actual Passover of the real deliverance, finished in principle, pointing to the completion in life; the coming Passover in the kingdom of God, the celebration of the perfected salvation.

5. The detection of Judas, and the announcement of the stumbling of the disciples after the Supper, is a sign that the Supper is appointed to exclude the apostate and the hypocritical, to strengthen, establish, and restore the weak.

6. The celebration of the Supper: 1. The external preparation, and the internal ("One of you"); 2. the celebration itself; 3. the practical improvement ("In this night").

7. The Lord changes the Passover into the Supper: Christ's disciples now make with great willingness a Passover out of the Supper, in various ways A simply ecclesiastical meal of custom; a simply memorial meal; a dogma-teaching meal; a meal falsely alleged to be capable of removing guilt.

HOMILETICAL AND PRACTICAL.

See Matthew.—The pious recollection of the disciples, and the holy thought of the Lord (paschal lamb, the Last Supper).—The quiet, hidden friend of Christ in the city of His foes, and the concealed enemy of Christ in the disciple-band.—Both brought to view by Christ.—The Lord's Supper a celebration of salvation in the confidence of faith: 1. Outwardly, a pre-celebration; 2. inwardly, an after-celebration.—The holy appointment and efficacy of the Supper: 1. Revelation of hearts (acknowledgment of sins, and confession of faith); 2. the affrighting of sinful consciences; 3. the exclusion of the wicked; 4. the celebration of the pardon and the establishment of believers; 5. the determining of the future path; 6. the restoration of the erring.—The self-exaltation with which Peter goes forth after the Supper, is a sign that he had not yet properly understood it.—Peter, before and after the Supper, and during its progress; pointing to a mistaking of the Supper in its symbolic import.—The disciples forget too soon after Judas' departure how much they have in common with him.—The consciousness of success, with which the Lord looks to the coming season of the perfect reunion of His disciples and Himself, being fully assured that all their temptations and conflicts could not prevent this result.

HEDINGER:—At the approach of death, life-endangering perils, and other misfortunes, God's word and sacrament are the best anointing and refreshment. Happy is he who consecrates his room to Jesus as a household church, or entertains Him oft in His poor members.—If we hazard all to obey God, we shall find it as the Lord hath promised before.—OSIANDER:—Who serves, believes, and obeys Christ, shall be deceived in nothing.—CANSTEIN:—Whosoever receives the holy Supper aright, receives in it an assurance of the coming eternal glory.—OSIANDER:—In suffering and trouble look at redemption.—He will not break the bruised reed. So gracious is Jesus, that he promises consolation to, and addresses in the language of promise, even the stumbling disciples.—HEDINGER:—He who relies too much on self, is building on sand.—Whosoever in a deliberative assembly introduces anything evil, may easily (in a greater or less degree) bring all the others over to his own side, so that they all express the same views.

BRAUNE:—If amongst His friends there was a secret foe, there were many secret friends amongst His foes.—The traitor proceeds to complete his transgression, and Jesus proceeds to the institution of the sacrament of the Atonement.—IGNATIUS:—The Supper is a remedy bringing immortal life, an antidote to death.—Mark, who was most intimate with Peter, gives Jesus' words thus: Before the cock crow twice, thou wilt thrice deny Me. The third part of the night, from twelve to three, was called the cock-crowing: before this should end, Peter would have thrice denied the Lord.

BRIEGER:—In the Passover, Christ is shadowed forth from every side. According to the law, the paschal lamb must be set apart on the tenth day of the month Nisan. And upon the tenth of this month, upon the so-called Palm Sunday, Christ made His triumphal entry, etc. (Add to this, that Jesus died about the ninth hour, almost the time when the paschal lamb was usually slain; that all the people put Him to death, as every head of a family slew a lamb; that the roasting-spit for the lamb had the form of a cross; that no bone of the lamb should be broken.)—How precious the promise, that He, as the Risen One, should go before them into Galilee! But they have ears for nothing. They regard only that word which charges them so hardly, and so deeply wounds. The Apostles were now occupied so entirely with themselves, that they were unmoved by what was immediately to befall their Lord.—However, if they had not observed the statement that the sword should fall on Him, they could not have had regard to the promise of His resurrection.—GOSSNER—Christ can raise the hymn of praise, although He knows His disciples are about to betray Him, etc. We must not be restrained from praising God because of anything.—BAUER:—His body, His blood; that is, receive His life.

---

3. *Gethsemane and the Betrayal; or, the Lord's sorrow of Soul.—The coming of the Traitor.* VERS. 32–42.—*The Betrayal and its Effect. The Arrest of the Lord. The Flight of the Disciples.* VERS. 43–52.

(Parallels: Matt. xxvi. 36–56; Luke xxii. 39–53; John xviii. 1–11.)

A. *Gethsemane.* VERS. 32–42.

32 And they came to a place which was named Gethsemane: and he saith to his dis-
33 ciples, Sit ye here, while I shall pray. And he taketh with him Peter, and James, and
34 John, and began to be sore amazed, and to be very heavy; And saith unto them, My
35 soul is exceeding sorrowful unto death: tarry ye here, and watch. And he went for-
ward[1] a little, and fell on the ground, and prayed that, if it were possible, the hour
36 might pass from him. And he said, Abba, Father, all things *are* possible unto thee;
37 take away this cup from me: nevertheless not what I will, but what thou wilt. And
he cometh, and findeth them sleeping, and saith unto Peter, Simon, sleepest thou?
38 couldest not thou watch one hour? Watch ye, and pray, lest ye enter into temptation:
39 the spirit truly *is* ready, but the flesh *is* weak. And again he went away, and prayed,
40 and spake the same words. And when he returned, he found them asleep again, (for
41 their eyes were heavy,) neither wist they what to answer him. And he cometh the
third time, and saith unto them, Sleep on now, and take *your* rest: it is enough, the
42 hour is come; behold, the Son of man is betrayed into the hands of sinners. Rise up,
let us go; lo, he that betrayeth me is at hand.

B. *The Betrayal.—The Arrest. The Flight of the Disciples.* VERS. 43–52.

43 And immediately, while he yet spake, cometh Judas,[2] one of the twelve, and with
him a great multitude, with swords and staves, from the chief priests, and the scribes,
44 and the elders. And he that betrayed him had given them a token, saying, Whomso-
45 ever I shall kiss, that same is he; take him, and lead *him* away safely. And as soon
as he was come, he goeth straightway to him, and saith, Master, Master;[3] and kissed
46, 47 him. And they laid their hands on him, and took him. And one of them that
stood by drew a sword, and smote a servant of the high priest, and cut off his ear.
48 And Jesus answered and said unto them, Are ye come out, as against a thief, with
49 swords and *with* staves to take me? I was daily with you in the temple teaching,
50 and ye took me not: but the Scriptures must be fulfilled. And they all forsook him,
51 and fled. And there followed him a certain young man, having a linen cloth cast about
52 *his* naked *body*; and the young men[4] laid hold on him: And he left the linen cloth,
and fled from them naked.

[1] Ver. 35.—The remarkable difference between προσελθών and προελθών is found here, just as in Matthew. Most MSS. are in favor of the first; the sense favors the second. If we retain προσελθών, the *terminus ad quem* is wanting: unless there be a reference to drawing near to God in prayer, קָרַב. Luke uses an expression denoting separation.

[[2] Ver. 43.—After "Judas," A., D., K., Lachmann, Tischendorf read ὁ Ἰσκαριώτης.]

[[3] Ver. 45.—The second ῥαββί omitted by Lachmann after B., C.*, D., L., Vulgate.]

[[4] Ver. 51.—Lachmann, Tischendorf, after B., C.*, D., L., Syriac, Persian, Coptic, Itala, Vulgate, omit οἱ νεανίσκοι.]

EXEGETICAL AND CRITICAL.

1. *See* the parallel passages in *Matthew* and *Luke*. Peculiarities of Mark:—In narrating the sufferings of Christ in Gethsemane, Mark is the only Evangelist who gives the subject of Jesus' prayer,—that "the (dread) hour might pass from Him." The prayer, too, has with him a more earnest expression, with the "Abba," and "All things are possible unto Thee." In the passage recording the finding the three asleep, the reproof of Christ is directed especially to Peter, and Jesus calls him Simon, as He always does when He would remind him of his weakness and old nature. The modification of the first petition in the second, mentioned by Matthew, is omitted by him. Jesus prays, according to him, in the same words; that is, Mark will emphasize the wrestling importunity in this petition likewise, while Matthew gives prominence to the stronger manifestation of the resignation of Jesus. The third prayer is not introduced by Mark, but is nevertheless implied in his recital. In the remark: "For their eyes were heavy," he employs, according to Codd. A., B., (Lachmann,) the stronger term, καταβαρυνόμενοι. He also has the noteworthy statement: "Neither wist they what to answer;" which recalls the similar expression in the history of the Transfiguration. Strikingly characteristic is the short phrase: "It is enough" (ἀπέχει); which is addressed by Jesus to the sleep-oppressed disciples. According to Mark's representation, Judas stands suddenly before our Lord, like some unearthly appearance. The traitor had given to the enemy a distinct, previously appointed signal (σύσσημον), and commanded them to seize the Master with all possible care, and to lead Him away. With a twofold salutation, Rabbi, Rabbi, the traitor here approaches Jesus eagerly and with feigned friendship. Jesus' address to Judas is here passed over. Of the sword-stroke of Peter he speaks in milder terms, saying he had cut off the ὠτάριον (diminutive) of the servant. The command of Jesus to Peter is also omitted. On the other hand, we are indebted to Mark for the remarkable episode of the youth who changed so quickly from a follower of Jesus to a deserter.

Ver. 33. **To be sore amazed, and to be very heavy;** ἤρξατο ἐκθαμβεῖσθαι καὶ ἀδημονεῖν.—Matthew has λυπεῖσθαι καὶ ἀδημονεῖν. Luke, instead of either expressions: γενόμενος ἐν ἀγωνίᾳ (in a dreadful struggle or agony). This agony has its two sides, which are described with about equal force in the phraseology of Matthew and Luke; ἐκθαμβεῖσθαι is a stronger term than λυπεῖσθαι, and is given only by Mark; indeed, the word is only found in the passages, ch. ix. 15; xvi. 5, 6. Upon this point consult the *Commentary on Matthew*, xxvi. 37. The traitorous, false, despairing world, represented in Judas, fills Christ with sorrow to amazement; He shudders before it, before the infernal powers lying behind it, and before the abyss of wickedness in this spiritual hell; the impotent, poor, and lost world, which lay sleeping around Him, overcome with sorrow and devoid of all presentiment, as represented by the three sleeping disciples, gives Him the feeling of eternal abandonment, Isa. lxiii. 3. Comp. *Matthew*. Starke: ἐκθαμβεῖσθαι is used of fright at a peal of thunder, Acts ix. 3, 6; and before a phantom, Matt. xiv. 26:* from this some conclude that the most frightful phantoms may have presented themselves to Christ, etc.

Ver. 35. **The hour might pass from Him.**—Not His suffering generally, but that hour. The whole feeling of suffering and judgment, to be so betrayed by the one half of the world, and to be so forsaken by the other half. *See Matthew*. [The "feeling" cannot be entirely accounted for by the desertion of the creature merely; there was also to be the desertion of the Creator.—*Ed.*]

Ver. 36. **Abba.**—Most vivid narration. Citation of the actual words, as in the expression, *Talitha cumi*, and the exclamation on the cross. Meyer: "This address, among the Greek-speaking Christians, acquired the nature of a *nomen proprium*." Apart from the misunderstanding which would arise, the phrase *Talitha cumi*, and other expressions, speak against this opinion. Accordingly, ὁ πατήρ is certainly an explanatory addition. [Meyer remarks, *in loc.*, that the common view that ὁ πατήρ is a translation of *Abba*, is not congruous with the idea of earnest supplication; and refers to Romans viii. 15.—*Ed.*] —**Nevertheless not.**—We supply: "But do not this, as I will, as My feelings would have." Meyer: "Let this not be which I will." Matthew indicates by πλὴν οὐχ ὡς. Luke uses appropriately τὸ θέλημα (inclination of the will), not θέλησις (act of will). Accordingly, ἀλλ' οὐ τί is to be taken in rather a formal sense.

Ver. 40. **Found them asleep again.**—Luke: "For sorrow." Sorrow kept the Lord awake, but lulled the disciples to sleep.

Neither wist they what to answer.—Comp. ch. ix. 6.

Ver. 41. **Sleep on now, and take your rest.**—*See Note* upon *Matthew*. The ironical meaning, as conveyed by Matthew, is altered by Luke into a reproof: "Why sleep ye?" Mark presents an intermediate view: first irony, then the call to wake.—**It is enough** (ἀπέχει).—This is the opposite of οὐδὲν ἀπέχει: nothing stands in the way, nothing hinders. The meaning accordingly is, It has failed; it is no more of use, etc. "Meyer: "It is enough, = ἐξαρκεῖ." This is quite a derivative meaning, and an application of the word very remote indeed. (The Vulgate renders *sufficit*, &c.) Quite as untenable is another interpretation: "There is enough watching, ye have watched enough;" or, "My anguish is past."

Ver. 45. **Master, Master.**—Not merely an exclamation of excitement, but also of hypocritical reverence carried to its greatest height.

Ver. 51. **A certain young man.**—This forms an episode as characteristic of Mark as the Emmaus disciples of Luke; and given for similar reasons. That he was no apostle is evident from the designation: "A certain young man;" from the circumstance that he had already the night-dress on; and especially from the contrast he presents to the Apostles. He only presents himself after their flight, a youthful Joseph of Arimathea, and so a precursor of him Some have without reason settled upon John as the person (Ambrose, Chrysostom, Gregory the Great); others have selected, equally without ground, James the Just (Epiph. *Hæres.* 87, 13). That the youth belonged to a family standing in a relation of friendship to the Lord, we may safely assume; at least, he was himself an enthusiastic follower of Christ. On this account, it was natural to suppose a youth of the family where Jesus had eaten the Passover (Theophylact). In this case, however, we must assume that the young man had, on this occasion, bee-

* [In Matt. xiv. 26 the words employed are ἐταράχθησαν, and ἀπὸ τοῦ φόβου ἔκραξαν.—*Ed.*]

sleeping, or retiring to rest, in the house which belonged to the family, and which lay in the valley of the Cedron; for, that the young man had been startled from his sleep, or in preparing to retire to rest, in the neighborhood of Gethsemane (in some neighboring country-seat, says Grotius), is proved by his wearing the night-dress. Both circumstances might possibly be found united in Mark himself, whom we, with Olshausen, consider to be this "certain young man." (*See* Introduction.) Reasons: 1. The youth's picture agrees in every line with the character of Mark. 2. The circumstances of the youth agreed perfectly with those of Mark: the friend of the Lord, resting in this country-house for the night. 3. There is an analogical support of this view, in the fact that John also, by a mere hint, weaves himself and His mother into the Evangelical narrative (John i. 40, xix. 25); and probably Luke does the same thing (xxiv. 18). 4. The fact that this circumstance is related by Mark alone, which Meyer considers so very trifling, and Bauer holds to be a piquant addition.—**The young men.**—These certainly were not the temple-guards, nor yet the soldiery, but young persons who had of their own accord joined the company; partly from their interest in adventure. For this reason, they found themselves particularly tempted to make an attack upon this young man, their equal in years, in the night-dress, who wished to follow Jesus, clad in so ridiculous a manner.

Ver. 52. **And he left the linen cloth.**—The night-mantle, thrown about him, was easily loosed. Bengel: *pudorem vicit timor in magno periculo.* Whitefield has properly pointed out the action of this youth as the emblem of a late reception of Jesus, though others have praised it as the emblem of an early following of the Lord, as belief in youth. Both are to be found in it: a beautiful enthusiasm of belief, and a fanatical self-dependence and over-estimation of personal strength. Rather far-fetched is Guyon's allegory, that we must follow Jesus, stripping off all that is our own, and all that is false. This youth was a follower while he had the linen cloth; deprived of this, he became a deserter.

DOCTRINAL AND ETHICAL.

1. Comp. *Matthew.*

2. The suffering of Jesus in Gethsemane, and the treachery of Judas, stand in the most intimate relation to each other. The bringing about of His sufferings by means of the treachery which grew up in the midst of His disciples, and the spirit of worldliness, of worldly sorrow and worldly falseness, of self-disrespect and despair, manifested in this treachery, —this is, in the particular sense, the bitter cup which he had to drain; for it is the heaviest judgment of God, that sin itself must break forth in treachery proceeding out the disciple-circle; a fact, in which is revealed the full judgment of God upon the sin of the world in its faithlessness, and in its despair—upon the sin of that world which could break through the barriers separating the disciples of Christ from the world. In Christ's experience of this judgment, there are two points to be marked: the realization of His being perfectly deserted; the manifestation of the world's weakness, and of the imminent danger to which the wickedness of the world exposed Him even amid His disciples. That He must see Himself forsaken by His young Church, that He must grieve because of the apostasy in the midst of this Church: therein lies the bitter gall of His passion-cup, therein was judgment finished. He prayed that this hour might pass, if it were possible (ver. 35). And (ver. 41) it is said, The hour is come; behold, the Son of Man, etc. The betrayal marks and seals this hour.

3. The sleeping of the good disciples is contrasted with the watchfulness of the evil disciple. What was common to both parties, was the unspeakable sorrow. In the case of Judas, this has changed into absolute demoniacal distress, animosity, and rage; in the case of the Eleven, it is manifested in complete relaxation, cowardice, and indecision. On this account, Christ opposes to the sleep and indecision of the Eleven, the intensest agitation of soul and energy; to the fevered excitement of Judas, on the contrary, the most perfect quiet of soul.

4. The youth who follows the Lord in his night-garb, and then flees, is a striking picture of the pious resolutions of Jesus' disciples, which are dissipated in the night of great temptation.

HOMILETICAL AND PRACTICAL.

See Matthew.—The Lord's preparation as opposed to His enemies' preparation.—The unfathomable clearness of spirit in the agony of the Lord, and the unfathomable confusion of spirit in the agony of Judas.—The treachery of a disciple in Gethsemane, the Lord's secret place of prayer, forms a page black as midnight in the history of the world and of the Church.—God's providence has changed this terrific curse into a cup of blessing for the lost world, through Christ's obedience.—Jesus could pray twice or thrice almost the same words, yet make from them each time a new prayer (differently placed emphasis): 1. *Take* from Me this cup; 2. yet not what *I* will; 3. but what *Thou* wilt.—The chasm which opens between the Lord and His disciples, while He prays and they sleep: 1. Christ ever more wakeful, more calm, more sure of victory; 2. the disciples ever heavier with sleep, more confused, and undecided.—How the Lord Himself announces the hour of which He prayed that it might pass by: The hour is come; behold, the Son of Man is betrayed into the hands of sinful men.—Arise, let us go! lo, he that betrayeth Me is at hand.—Jesus' disciple as guide to the hostile band. —The kiss of Judas; or, here likewise is Antichrist concealed in the pseudo-Christ (a lying Christ).—Christ between the helpless assailants and the helpless defenders: 1. The assailants in their helplessness: *a.* the traitor, the soldiers; *b.* He grants them the might which they are allowed to have, according to the Holy Scriptures and God's providence, though it seems as if derived from human laws. 2. The defenders in their helplessness: *a.* the sword-stroke of Peter, the fleeing disciples, the fleeing youth; *b.* He grants them the might of His preserving grace.—There existed a natural relationship between this young man and the disciple Peter, as there existed a spiritual relationship between the Apostle Peter and the Evangelist Mark.—Christ betrayed and captured: 1. How all appears in this state of things to be lost; 2. how sin and Satan are thereby betrayed and captured.—By His bonds are we freed.

STARKE:—To pray is the best thing we can do in the hour of temptation.—QUESNEL:—God's will must be at all times dearer than our own, let it cost what it may to perfect it.—CANSTEIN:—Prayer is needed with watching, and watching with prayer. Both must go together.—Alas, if Israel's Shepherd should not be watchful, how evil would it be with us, from our lethargic security and sloth!—Judas sells Jesus. We should not consider the whole world a sufficient purchase-price for Jesus.—OSIANDER:—The wickedness of the world is so great, that the very persons who are appointed to administer justice persecute the just, and defend the unjust.—CANSTEIN:—Whosoever allures others into sin, sins himself, and loads himself with all the sin which the others commit.—OSIANDER: —Satan blinds men, that, when they do evil, they know not what will be its result.—CANSTEIN:—A good intention may lead to evil (the blow of the sword).—Hasty passions are dangerous; therefore, resist a blind zeal, which, the hotter it burns, displeases God the more.—HEDINGER:—Where the cross is, there is flight.

BRAUNE:—As Christ withdrew Himself, at the beginning of His public ministry, into the wilderness, so also now at the conclusion of His mission.—He addresses Himself to Peter at once, to do all that He could to bring him to see his weakness.—It is not the Scripture which makes the necessity of fulfilment: but the will of God, revealed in the prophets, causes the fulfilment of the Scriptures. The darkness, likewise, stands beneath God's light.—It is noticeable, that upon the spot where Jesus was seized by the band, Titus, the Roman commander, pitched his camp forty years after. The Turks, however, have walled the place where Judas kissed Christ, as an accursed spot.

BRIEGER:—Had Christ not been tempted as well from the side of terror as formerly from that of lust, the Scriptures could not say: He was tempted in all points.—Was that, perhaps, now fulfilled in His own person, which He prophesied of this time (Luke xxi. 26)? Then did that statement receive its accomplishment in Gethsemane: "I have trodden the winepress alone," Isa. lxiii. 3.—Rabbi, Rabbi. It was the last Rabbi his lips uttered.—The whole transaction (the arrest of Christ) presents itself as a drama arranged by the chief council. But all the pretence being destroyed, the leaders of the people stand before us as common criminals.—This terror could not have overmastered the disciples, had they not erred regarding the Lord. Being dissatisfied that Jesus did not deliver Himself from suffering, they held themselves bound to withdraw from danger.—GOSSNER, on ver. 27:—If thou canst not overcome sleep how wilt thou overcome death?—BAUER:—And these were the best of the disciples of Jesus!—Judas, accordingly, is there with his band already! He has been quick. Yes, sin runs a rapid race.

---

4. *Christ betrayed to the Jews, in the Palace of the High Priest, and before the Ecclesiastical Court. The False Witnesses. The Truthful Witness, and His sublime Testimony. The Sentence of Death. Peter's Denial.* VERS. 53-72.

(Parallels: Matt. xxvi. 57-75; Luke xxii. 54-71; John xviii. 12-27.)

A. Vers. 53-65.

53 And they led Jesus away to the high priest: and with him were assembled all
54 the chief priests, and the elders, and the scribes. And Peter followed him afar off,
even into the palace of the high priest: and he sat with the servants, and warmed him-
55 self at the fire. And the chief priests and all the council sought for witness against
56 Jesus, to put him to death; and found none. For many bare false witness against him,
57 but their witness agreed not together. And there arose certain, and bare false witness
58 against him, saying, We heard him say, I will destroy this temple that is made with
59 hands, and within three days I will build another made without hands. But neither so
60 did their witness agree together. And the high priest stood up in the midst, and asked
Jesus, saying, Answerest thou nothing? what *is it which* these witness against thee?
61 But he held his peace, and answered nothing. Again the high priest asked him, and
62 said unto him, Art thou the Christ, the Son of the Blessed? And Jesus said, I am:
and ye shall see the Son of man sitting on the right hand of power, and coming in the
63 clouds of heaven. Then the high priest rent his clothes, and saith, What need we any
64 further witnesses? Ye have heard the blasphemy: what think ye? And they all con-
65 demned him to be guilty of death. And some began to spit on him, and to cover his
face, and to buffet him, and to say unto him, Prophesy: and the servants did strike
him with the palms of their hands.

B. Vers. 66-72.

66 And as Peter was beneath in the palace, there cometh one of the maids of the high
67 priest: And when she saw Peter warming himself, she looked upon him, and said,
68 And thou also wast with Jesus of Nazareth. But he denied, saying, I know not, nei-

ther understand I[2] what thou sayest. And he went out into the porch; [and the cock
69 crew].[3] And a [the] maid saw him again, and began to say* to them that stood by,
70 This is *one* of them. And he denied it again. And a little after, they that stood by said
again to Peter, Surely thou art *one* of them: for thou art a Galilean, and thy speech
71 agreeth *thereto*.[4] But he began to curse and to swear, *saying*, I know not this man of
72 whom ye speak. And[5] the second time the cock crew. And Peter called to mind
the word[6] that Jesus said unto him, Before the cock crow twice, thou shalt deny me
thrice. And when he thought thereon, he wept.

[[1] Ver. 65.—Instead of ἔβαλλον, A., B., C., Lachmann, Tischendorf read ἔλαβον, "they took him" (away from the hall of judgment, into custody, *i. e.*).]

[2] Ver. 68.—We read, with Cod. A., &c., and the *Recepta*, οὐκ οἶδα, οὐδὲ ἐπίσταμαι. Certainly οὔτε, οὔτε is strongly attested by B., D., L., and is adopted by Tischendorf and Lachmann. We consider, however, this mode of expression too strong to be used in the circumstances. Matthew says, "I know not what thou sayest;" Luke, "I know Him not:" our reading, in what appears the original account, receives support from these two expressions.

[3] Ver. 68.—Καὶ ἀλέκτωρ ἐφώνησε, wanting in B., L., Coptic, bracketed by Lachmann; probably interpolated from the parallel passage in Matthew.

[4] Ver. 70.—Καὶ ἡ λαλια σου ὁμοιάζει, omitted in B., C., D., L., &c., and in the texts of Tischendorf and Lachmann. It is interpolated probably from Matthew.

[[5] Ver. 72.—Codd. B., D. have εὐθύς; A., C. have it not. Lachmann retains it; Tischendorf and *Recepta* reject it.]

[6] Ver. 72.—Τὸ ῥῆμα ὡς, A., B., C., L., Δ., Lachmann, Tischendorf.

* [The Greek runs: "And the maid (that kept the porch, *i. e.*), seeing him, again began to say," &c.]

EXEGETICAL AND CRITICAL.

See Matthew, and the parallel in *Luke*.—Mark gives the same account of the false witnesses as Matthew; but he is the only one who mentions the reason why the chief council obtained no false witness, viz.: the witnesses did not corroborate one another. Matthew selects two witnesses as testifying to Jesus' statement respecting the destruction of the temple; Mark says, a few. Matthew had in mind the legal number which must be present; Mark, the smallness of the number. In Mark's account, the false testimony is strongest on the point, "I will destroy this temple," etc.; at the same time, he notices the contrast between the temple made with hands and that not made with hands. Again, he brings into view the conflicting nature of the testimony. Perhaps even in Matthew the divergent testimony is alluded to, under "I am able to destroy," etc. According to Mark, the high priest comes forward into the midst. The silence is strongly marked. The adjuration of Jesus by the high priest is only implied in the remark, he interrogated Him. The testimony of Jesus is more strongly expressed than in Matthew, ἐγώ εἰμι. On the contrary, he does not report literally the sentence of death, as does Matthew. But, again, he gives us the distinct view of how the servants—probably the prison-warders—take Christ to lead Him to a place of safe custody till the next morning. Then he says that Peter was below in the entrance-hall (of the palace); and gives us, thus, to understand that the trial had taken place in an upper story, or at least in an elevated hall. The maid of the high priest calls Jesus, The Nazarene. The first statement of Peter is characteristically ambiguous. The first cock-crow is mentioned by Mark alone (according to the exact remembrance of Peter). The second attack, Mark again appears to place, contrary to Matthew, in the mouth of the same maid; but it is, without doubt, the portress of the προαύλιον that is meant. The ἕτερος here, alluded to by Luke, belongs to the bystanders, of whom Mark here informs us. The portress did not address Peter himself, but denounced him to those about: upon this, one of them laid hold of Peter. Of the second denial, Mark gives a shorter, and thus milder account, than Matthew; there is here no mention of the oath. Upon the second denial, immediately follows the second crowing of the cock. At the end, he marks, with a brief, forcible expression, ἐπιβαλὼν ἔκλαιε, the repentance of Peter.

Ver. 53. **And with him** (αὐτῷ) **were assembled.**—Of course it is the high priest who is meant. The meaning given by Meyer is quite foreign to the passage: They come, that is, they meet Jesus there all at the same time. The words might, literally taken, bear this explanation; but the thought of their meeting there at the same time must have been expressed more precisely; not to mention, that according to Luke, several members of the Sanhedrim had joined themselves to the band, and had gone to meet the party. It was only because there was a council at the palace of the high priest that matters happened in this way, although, no doubt, the αὐτῷ which follows immediately must relate to Jesus.

Ver. 54. **At the fire**, πρὸς τὸ φῶς.—It is an open hearth which lights and heats the hall at the same time, at which they warm themselves. The designation is employed to explain the circumstance, that Peter was recognized in the light of the fire.

Ver. 56. **Agreed not.**—Two witnesses at least must agree, Deut. xvii. 6; xix. 15. In the main, however, the witnesses must not contradict one another.

Ver. 58. **We heard Him say, I will destroy this temple.**—The variations, as respects Matthew, constitute no difficulty in this passage; since, as is remarked by the Evangelist, the testimonies did not agree. In the contrast,—made with hands, made without hands,—we have probably one of the most false declarations. Meyer: From this it is evident that the one witness was not examined in the presence of the other. Let the conduct of the judges in the trial of Susanna be compared with this.

Ver. 61. **Of the Blessed.**—The εὐλογητός, or הַבָּרוּךְ, in the absolute sense, is God. Undoubtedly this is a hypocritical expression of reverence in refraining from naming the name of God, intending to designate Christ's declaration blasphemy of God, of the Blessed. "The *Sanctus Benedictus* of the Rabbis is well known (SCHÖTTGEN *ad* Rom. 9, 5)." Meyer.

Ver. 63. **His clothes**, τοὺς χιτῶνας.—Comp. *Note* on Matt. xxvi. 65. He tore all his clothing, except that which was next his body. Winer: Persons of respectability, and travellers, sometimes wore two articles of underclothing.

Ver. 65. And some began.—Meyer: "The members of the Sanhedrim. The servants follow." Rather the temple attendants, who were surrounding the Lord in the hall (*see* John and Luke): those who afterwards took Jesus into custody, under the designation of servants, are prison-warders, as Matt. v. 25; hence servants in a special sense. Mark presents the scene of the mocking, which is given by Luke in detail, under the one aspect of abuse, which is in this way thrown out into stronger relief; and Matthew gives a similar view.

Ver. 66. **Beneath.**—This in opposition to the hall of trial, which was higher.

Ver. 68. **I know not**; or, it is unknown to me, not understood.—The double force in ὀυκ οἶδα οὐδὲ, κ.τ.λ., is difficult to express. If we translate, "I know not," this is too little; "I know Him not," this is too much; "I recognize not,"—then we have a phrase too decidedly unconnected.—**Into the porch,** or, according to Matthew, the entrance-hall. It is the same idea.

Ver. 69. **And a [the] maid.**—As soon as she noticed him. On the comparison between Matthew, and Luke, and Mark, consult the introductory remarks to this section. **And began to say again.**—As the other had begun. The first πάλιν relates a repetition of the denunciation to the bystanders, the second πάλιν to the second denial of Peter in the same circumstances; the third πάλιν implies that those around had already once laid hands upon Christ, and in this way substantiates the recital of Luke, ver. 58.

Ver. 70. **For thou art a Galilean.**—Not meaning: As Jesus is also; but among the other proofs that thou art one of them, is this, that thou art a Galilean.

Ver. 72. **And Peter called to mind the word.**—A similar important thought or self-recollection of Peter is related in ch. xi. 21.

And when he thought thereon, he wept.—It is extremely difficult to bring out clearly what ἐπιβαλὼν ἔκλαιε imports. For the various explanations, compare BRETSCHNEIDER's *Lexicon*, De Wette, Meyer, etc. Many consider it as the Vulgate, *cœpit flere;* but this is not grammatically correct. Others, he went out hastily (analogous to the phrases in Matthew and Luke); others, he threw a covering over his head; or, he cast his eyes upon the Lord; or, he continued to weep; or, according to Ewald, he interrupted with his weeping the sound of the crowing (that is, answering with loud sobbing the crowing of the cock); or, he took notice of that sound, bethought himself of the matter. (De Wette: 'Επιβαλὼν refers to the cock-crow; Meyer.) We find only three interpretations tenable: 1. He flung himself forth, that is, he involuntarily rushed out, as it were meeting the cock-crow as he hurried out, according to the narratives of Matthew and Luke. 2. Referring the phrase to the word of Jesus: he threw himself into it, under the condemnation of this word took it to heart), and wept. Or, 3. making the cock-crowing to be as it were Christ's waking call; and thereupon he threw himself out of the place (as though Christ had called him; *Leben Jesu*, iii. 334), and wept. First a rushing forth, as if he had an external goal to reach, then a bitter sinking down into himself and weeping. The turning-point between the carnal and spiritual mode of viewing the life. He hastened forth at the call; on the outside, he found the call went inwards and upwards, and he stopped and wept.

DOCTRINAL AND ETHICAL.

1. Comp. *Matthew.*

2. Peter has not extenuated his own fault; for from him, through Mark, we are informed that the first crowing did not suffice to recall him to his duty, but a second was needed.

3. In the three words, καὶ ἐπιβαλὼν ἔκλαιε, we have given to us the perfect revolution in Peter's view of the world. As he rushes forth upon the call, as though in his remorse he sought some object exterior to himself, his world-view (his opinion of the world) is still an external one; when he begins to weep, it becomes an inner view. His whole outer world has fallen in ruins; he has no longer an external object of pursuit; he has been thrown back into himself, and comes through his inner self to the Lord, who has now become to him a new Christ in the light of the Spirit. Judas could not attain to this change and revolution: he rushed out—to the associates of his guilt, the chief priests—and they gave him, in his despair, the final blow. In the case of Peter it was: "Against Thee, Thee only, have I sinned."

4. The maid mentioned in this passage, and Herodias, are the only examples of female wickedness, or enmity on the part of woman to what was good, recorded in the Gospels.

HOMILETICAL AND PRACTICAL.

See the parallel passages in *Matthew.*—The true Shepherd betrayed by a faithless disciple at the tribunal of a false world: 1. By the treachery of the false one; He stands as the Faithful One at the bar; 2. by the false judgment, He passes forth as the Faithful.—The false judgment passed by the world upon the Lord: 1. The false judges, who seek false witness against Him; 2. the false witnesses, who contradict one another; 3. the false judgment, which stamps the true praise of God as blasphemy, and represents blasphemy of God to be the judgment of God; 4. the false servants of God, who abuse, and make a mock of the prisoner entrusted to their guardianship.—As the sun bursts through mist and clouds, so breaks Christ triumphantly through all the false obscurations of His honor (by false judges, witnesses, judgments, guards).—So does God's truth, and work, break through all juggleries, deceits, and time-serving judgments, of sin and lying.—Christ's true testimony and confession is the only star of salvation in the awful night of human destruction and judgment.—Self-contradiction, the everlasting self-judgment of Satan, of sin, and of Christ's foes.—Christ the confessor, and Peter the denier (Christ was the divinely faithful friend to men, Judas the betrayer; Christ was He who held His ground, the disciples were the runaways).—The great and marvellous spiritual combat: 1. One strove against all, and yet for all; 2. He suffered as a lamb, yet conquered like a lion; 3. He is overcome, and yet He is the victor.—Contrast the powerful opponents of Christ and the weak opponents of Peter.—The difference between the Christ's confession, and Peter's Galilean dialect.—Mark how the chasm which bursts apart between Christ and His disciples unites them for ever: 1. The chasm which opens: Christ, the denied confessor; Peter, the positive denier. 2. Peter, now an actually humbled sinner; Christ, in the fullest sense, now his Saviour and Comforter.—The Lord's great discourse in His deep silence.—Christ's sublime silence at the world's tribunal a prediction of His sublime speaking at the future judgment of the world.

STARKE:—QUESNEL:—Let the world say what it will, how entirely different are things to the eye of faith, from what they seem to the eye of the world! What is more distinguished than this assembly? There at the same time sanctity, rank, and wisdom appear to collect and unite together; and yet it is nothing but a company of murderers, and a godless assembly (except, indeed, that it possessed a historic right, which was destroyed at Christ's crucifixion).—He who audaciously flings himself into danger, will soon find that he sinks continually deeper, till finally he cannot free himself.—CANSTEIN:—It is dangerous to be in the company of the wicked.—Alas! how much injustice is found in law-processes and contentions!—Envy.—*Nova Bibl. Tub.*:—Is it not to be deplored that many strive in behalf of the stones of the temple, and yet pull down and destroy the temple of the living God!—QUESNEL:—The greatest truths, when ill-understood, are often considered blasphemies, and furnish occasions for rage and tumult, Heb. xii. 3.—Keep silent (before the godless world's accusations).—Reply (to those who exercise authority).—One may mislead many.—As is the shepherd, such are the sheep [said in reference to the high priest. But this is only partially applicable].—When the higher classes condemn Christ, those beneath them mock Him. This is the effect of evil example. Oh! what an account is to be rendered!—Sufferings generally come in troops.—PETRUS:—Lies of necessity are not to be excused.—The cock which still crows, when we deny Jesus, is the conscience of each; ah, would that we heard its voice!—*Bibl. Wirt.*:—God uses every means to bring men to repentance.

BRAUNE:—Death was pronounced upon Christ: in the sight of God, the haters of the divine love had no right so to act; it was merely the seeming appearance of right before the people.—We never hear that these false witnesses were punished.—The first Epistle of Peter shows how changed his views regarding suffering and the cross had become. This change of view dates from his repentance.—BRIEGER:—His sitting at the right hand of God they were soon to find to be true (the founding of the Church, the Apostles' acts, the destruction of Jerusalem, etc.)—Jesus, although awaiting condemnation and death, subdued Satan in His people.—This we recognize in the repentance of Peter.—GOSSNER:—Before Pentecost, the disciples fled from death; after Pentecost, they rejoiced in death.—BAUER:—A fearful assembly.—On ver. 72. Alas! how lonely, how isolated, does sin leave us in the world!

---

5. *Christ, betrayed to the Gentiles, standing before Pilate at the Tribunal of Temporal Authority;* a. *The Examination. Christ and the Accusers. The Confession, the Accusations, and the Lord's Silence.* b. *The Judge's attempt to deliver. Christ and Barabbas. The Outcry of the Enemy, the Silence of the Lord. The Surrender. The Mocking.* CH. XV. 1–15.

(Parallels: Matt. xxvii. 1-26; Luke xxiii. 1-25; John xviii. 1-16.)

1 And straightway in the morning[1] the chief priests held a consultation with the elders
and scribes, and the whole council, and bound Jesus, and carried *him* away, and deliv-
2 ered *him* to Pilate. And Pilate asked him, Art thou the King of the Jews? And he
3 answering, said unto him, Thou sayest *it*. And the chief priests accused him of many
4 things; but he answered nothing. And Pilate asked him again, saying, Answerest
5 thou nothing? behold how many things they witness against thee. But Jesus yet
6 answered nothing: so that Pilate marvelled. Now at *that* feast he released unto them
7 one prisoner, whomsoever they desired. And there was *one* named Barabbas, *which*
lay bound with them that had made insurrection with him,[2] who had committed murder
8 in the insurrection. And the multitude, crying aloud,[3] began to desire *him to do* as he
9 had ever done unto them. But Pilate answered them, saying, Will ye that I release
10 unto you the King of the Jews? (For he knew that the chief priests had delivered
11 him for envy.) But the chief priests moved the people, that he should rather release
12 Barabbas unto them. And Pilate answered and said again unto them, What will ye
13 then that I shall do *unto him* whom ye call the King of the Jews? And they cried
14 out again, Crucify him. Then Pilate said unto them, Why, what evil hath he done?
15 And they cried out the more exceedingly, Crucify him. And *so* Pilate, willing to con-
tent the people, released Barabbas unto them, and delivered Jesus, when he had
scourged *him*, to be crucified.

[[1] Ver. 1.—Codd. B., C., D., Lachmann, Tischendorf read only πρωΐ.]
[[2] Ver. 7.—Codd. B., C., D., Lachmann, Tischendorf read στασιαστῶν.]
[[3] Ver. 8.—Codd. B., D., Lachmann, Tischendorf, ἀναβάς instead of ἀναβοήσας.]

EXEGETICAL AND CRITICAL.

Comp. the parallels in *Matthew* and *Luke*.—Mark, with Matthew, takes notice of the second formal council-meeting on the morning of the crucifixion: he, like Luke, brings more distinctly into view the circumstance that the whole Sanhedrim led Christ away to Pilate; and with him omits the end of Judas, recorded by Matthew, the dream of Pilate's wife, the washing of the hands, and the cry—"His blood be on us, and our children." Again, Mark, like Matthew, passes over the fact that Jesus was sent to the bar of Herod, which Luke records; the full examination before Pilate, omitted by all the Synoptics, related by John; and, finally, the repeated hesitations of Pilate in condemning. Mark merely notices what John and Luke relate very fully, that many additional accusations were raised against Jesus, regarding which He maintained an unbroken silence. He limits himself, like Matthew, particularly to the two chief features in the humiliation of Jesus before Pilate: His confession of His Messiahship (King of the Jews), and His being placed side by side with Barabbas. The characterization of Barabbas he gives more accurately, in a manner similar to Luke. He marks the decision of Pilate in a peculiar way, ver. 15. It is worthy of note that he, along with Matthew, represents the scourging and mocking of the Lord in Pilate's prætorium (Luke, on the other hand, relates the putting to shame of Jesus in the palace of Herod) to be part of the crucifixion-agonies; consequently, the second unsuccessful attempt of Pilate to release Him, which, according to John, he sought to effect by bringing forth the scourged One to the people, is passed over unnoticed. The assembling of the populace before the prætorium, and the more exact designation of the prætorium, are peculiar to Mark.

Ver. 6. **He released unto them one prisoner.**—This was a voluntary custom of the procurator.

Ver. 7. **In the insurrection.**—In which he had been captured. One of the numberless Jewish insurrections; not known more exactly. "Paulus refers to JOSEPH. *Antiq.* 18, 4." Meyer.

Ver. 8. **That had gone up.***—The stream of the populace comes, namely, back from the palace of Herod, whither Pilate had sent the Lord. Meanwhile the priests have prepared their people, have instigated and instructed them.

When he had scourged Him, to be crucified.—John, viewing matters from the psychological stand-point, mentions the scourging among the acts of Pilate, as the final attempt to deliver Jesus; Mark and Matthew, viewing the events from the historical stand-point, judge from this act that all is decided, and they look accordingly upon the scourging as the opening act in the awful tragedy of the crucifixion, παρέδωκε φραγελλώσας. Both are equally correct points of view. The scourging should have moved the people; it only led them to obduracy. And, as the matter issued, the crucifixion had already begun. In relating this circumstance, Matthew emphasizes the fact that the scourging resulted in the yielding up of Christ to the Jews (φραγελλώσας παρέδωκεν); Mark points out that the scourging was the opening scene in the crucifixion, and took place in consequence of the surrender.

DOCTRINAL AND ETHICAL.

1. Comp. *Matthew.*
2. Christ before Pilate, beside Barabbas, amid the soldiers: a threefold climax in the world's judgment upon the Judge of the world.
3. Barabbas, the murderer, a representative of the first murderer, the father of lies, as Christ stood there in the name of His Father.—The people's choice between the two: 1. The miscalculated and improper juxtaposition caused by the political party, a self-condemnation of worldly polity; 2. the evil advice of the chief priests, a self-condemnation of the hierarchical guardianship of the people; 3. the horrifying choice, a self-condemnation of the self-destroying populace.

HOMILETICAL AND PRACTICAL.

See Matthew.—The world assembled to judge the Lord: 1. Jerusalem (the chief council); 2. Rome (Pilate); 3. the whole wide world (the soldiery).—Jesus condemned as Messiah, as the Christ of God. As Christ: 1. Condemned by the chief council; 2. given over to judgment by Pilate; 3. mocked by the soldiery.—The surrender of the prisoner at the paschal festival (probably a Passover-drama to represent the atonement for the first-born of Israel) is here a judgment upon completed blindness.—Barabbas is made by the Jews to represent the first-born of Israel, Christ the first-born of Egypt.—Christ justified upon His trial by the hostile judges: 1. By the judge: he seeks to free Him; 2. by the accusers and the people: their petition for the release of Barabbas reveals the bitterness of their hate; 3. by the soldiers, who adorn Him with the symbols of His patience and His spiritual glory.—The very mockery of truth must witness, even by its caricatures, to the glorious original.

STARKE:—When superior judges act unjustly, they accumulate upon their heads much more guilt than the subordinate authorities; for in that case the oppressed have no further appeal.—QUESNEL:—The assembling of the magistrates is orderly and beautiful: but the more proper their appearance, the more sinful the abuse of their authority in the oppression of the innocent.—HEDINGER:—When innocence itself must appear and be accused before the judges, is it anything strange that Thou, precious Jesus, art persecuted by the devil, accused, slandered, and condemned?—*Nova Bibl. Tub.*:—Liars' mouths can devise much; enough, if thou art guiltless.—Envy is hateful in every man, especially in ministers of the Gospel, who should content themselves in God.—QUESNEL:—What envy did here against Christ, the Chief Shepherd, that it does still to His servants, and will not cease to do till the world's end.—*Nova Bibl. Tub.*:—If the rulers among the people, who should put a stop to evil, themselves instigate and make the people sin, then must Christ be crucified.—HEDINGER:—In the last day the heathen will put many Christians to shame.—QUESNEL:—Love of honor and the fear of the world may lead a judge (who is not firmly settled in his love to justice) to many sins.—One single sinful passion makes slaves of men.—Natural honor a weak shield against temptation.—*Nova Bibl. Tub.*:—The King of glory wears a crown of thorns, in order that He may take the curse away from the earth, and gain for us the crown of holiness.—The crowns of princes, also, have their thorns. Should they wear these to the honor of the crowned Jesus, then will they discharge aright the duties of their difficult office.—Hypocrites and the godless still insult Christ, though they even bow the knee at His name.

BRAUNE:—The deeper He went down in suffering, the less He pleased them.—All that God did to perplex the enemies of Jesus in their acts, was in vain (Peter's tears, the acknowledgment of Judas, the silence of Herod on the chief point, the witness of

* [Lange adopts the reading ἀναβάς in his translation. Luther's version does the same.—*Ed.*]

Pilate, the dream of Procula; the comparison between the insurrectionist and murderer Barabbas, and Jesus in His majesty and tranquil greatness).—BRIEGER:—Pilate did not concede the truthfulness of the accusations of the Jews, yet condemned the Son of God to death. He thereby fulfilled in two respects the wisdom of God:—First, that the Lord should be crucified, and not stoned: second, that Jews and Gentiles should unite in His death.—BAUER:—Sad is the scene which here meets our eyes; as it ever is when goodness has to protect itself by the votes of the masses.

---

6. *Jesus on Golgotha.—His Death, and the Death-signs* a. *The Mockings and the Lord's Silence.* b. *The Crucifixion; and Blasphemy against, and Silence of, the Lord.* c. *The World Darkened; the Anguish-cry, and the Silence of Victory; the Death-shriek, and the Death-silence of the Lord.* d. *The Rent in the Temple-vail, and the Silence of God upon the End of the Old Covenant.* VERS. 16–38.

(Parallels: Matt. xxvii. 27–53; Luke xxiii. 26–46; John xix. 17–30.)

A. Vers. 16–19.

16 And the soldiers led him away into the hall called Prætorium; and they call to-
17 gether the whole band. And they clothed him with purple, and platted a crown of
18 thorns, and put it about his *head*, And began to salute him, Hail, King of the Jews!
19 And they smote him on the head with a reed, and did spit upon him, and, bowing *their*
knees, worshipped him.

B. Vers. 20–32.

20 And when they had mocked him, they took off the purple from him, and put his
21 own[1] clothes on him, and led him out to crucify him. And they compel one Simon a
Cyrenian, who passed by, coming out of the country, the father of Alexander and
22 Rufus, to bear his cross. And they bring him unto the place Golgotha, which is, being
23 interpreted, The place of a skull. And they gave him to drink[2] wine mingled with
24 myrrh: but he received *it* not. And when they had crucified him, they parted his gar-
25 ments, casting lots upon them, what every man should take. And it was the third
26 hour; and they crucified him. And the superscription of his accusation was written
27 over, THE KING OF THE JEWS. And with him they crucify two thieves; the
28 one on his right hand, and the other on his left. And the scripture was fulfilled, which
29 saith, And he was numbered with the transgressors.[3] And they that passed by railed
on him, wagging their heads, and saying, Ah, thou that destroyest the temple,
30 and buildest *it* in three days,[4] Save thyself, and come down[5] from the cross.
31 Likewise also the chief priests, mocking, said among themselves, with the scribes, He
32 saved others; himself he cannot save. Let Christ the King of Israel descend now
from the cross, that we may see and believe. And they that were crucified with him
reviled him.

C. Vers. 33–37.

33 And when the sixth hour was come, there was darkness over the whole land until
34 the ninth hour. And at the ninth hour Jesus cried with a loud voice, saying, Eloi,
Eloi, lama sabachthani?[6] which is, being interpreted, My God, my God, why hast thou
35 forsaken me? And some of them that stood by, when they heard *it*, said, Behold,
36 he calleth Elias. And one ran and filled a spunge full of vinegar, and put *it* on a reed,
and gave him to drink, saying, Let alone; let us see whether Elias will come to take
37 him down. And Jesus cried with a loud voice, and gave up the ghost.

D. Ver. 38.

38 And the vail of the temple was rent in twain from the top to the bottom.

[[1] Ver. 20.—Codd. B., C., Lachmann, Tischendorf read αὐτοῦ instead of τὰ ἴδια (A., *Receptus*).]
[[2] Ver. 23.—Codd. B., C.*, L., Tischendorf omit πιεῖν.]
[3] Ver. 28.—This verse is wanting in A., B., C., D., X.; and Griesbach and Tischendorf have decided against it. But it is found in P., in Origen, Eusebius, and the Versions. The verse has probably been omitted, because it was supposed to involve a discrepancy between Mark and Luke, as in Luke xxii. 37 the quotation is referred to the apprehension of Jesus

Lange might have added, as supporting his view, L., Δ., 1, 13, 69. Alford's remark, [which Meyer also makes,] that Mark rarely quotes from prophecy, however, is deserving of attention.—*Trs.*)

[4] Ver. 29.—The best MSS. read οἰκοδομῶν τρισὶν ἡμέραις.

[[5] Ver. 30.—Codd. B., D., L., Δ., Lachmann, Tischendorf read καταβάς instead of κατάβα (*Receptus*).]

[[6] Ver. 34.—The words ἐλωΐ, &c., are differently-written in the MSS. Lachmann reads λεμὰ σαβαχθανί: Tischendorf, λεμὰ σαβακτανεί (ed. 1865); Fritzsche, λιμᾶ; *Receptus*, λαμμα σαβαχθανί.]

EXEGETICAL AND CRITICAL.

Comp. the parallels in *Matthew* and *Luke*.—Mark points out more distinctly the ironical consciousness with which the cowardly Pilate yielded to the demands of the populace. With Matthew, he employs φραγελλώσας παρέδωκε, in which the thought is involved that the surrender was decided in the scourging. In describing the mocking, he omits, like John, the mention of the reed, which the soldiers, according to Matthew, forced into the Lord's hand, or sought to force, and with which they struck Him (probably because He let it fall). Mark designates Simon of Cyrene the most particularly: he is the father of Alexander and Rufus. The address of the Lord to the daughters of Jerusalem, as they were following, which Luke reports, is omitted by Mark, as well as by Matthew. The bitter wine he names myrrh-wine. He makes the crucifixion to begin at the third hour. The quotation of Jesus from Isa. liii. 12, which we consider genuine, is given by him alone. The address of Jesus to Mary and to John, beneath the cross, is passed over by him as by the other Synoptics; also the repentance of the thief, in which he agrees with Matthew. He describes more graphically than the other Evangelists the mockery of the passers-by, using the word οὐὰ for this purpose; the derision and irony of the priests is given in their own words. He records in the original Syriac, Eloi, Eloi, etc. Of the man who gave the Lord vinegar to drink, he says indefinitely, "A certain one," and that he called to the others, "Let alone." Of the seven sayings of the Crucified, he records, like Matthew, only the Eli, Eli, and the last loud, piercing cry of Christ, without stating what the Lord expressed in it.

Ver. 16. **Into the hall** (within, into the inner court).—Comp. *Note* on Matt. xxvii. 27. They conducted Him into the palace-court, which we may easily suppose was surrounded by the neighboring buildings of the governor's palace, forming a kind of barracks.

Ver. 17. A scarlet military mantle (*see* on Matt. xxvii. 28) was made to represent the imperial purple; hence the designation *a purple* (πορφύραν), a purple robe, as Mark and John describe it. And because this is the symbolic import of the robe, there is no discrepancy. The scarlet military cloak no more required to be a real purple, than the crown of thorns required to be a real crown, or the reed a real sceptre; for the whole transaction was an ironical drama, and such a one, too, that the infamous abuse might be readily perceived through the pretended glorification. The staff must be a reed, the symbol of impotence; the crown must injure and pierce the brow; and so too must the purple present the symbol of miserable, pretended greatness: and this was done by its being an old camp-mantle.

Ver. 21. **And they compel.**—Upon the term ἀγγαρεύειν, comp. *Note* on Matt. v. 41.—**The father of Alexander and Rufus.**—These men must have been well-known persons in the then existing Church; and they testify to the personal, lively recollection and originality of Mark, as does his "Timæus, the son of Bartimæus." It is most natural to regard them as persons well known to the Church at Rome. On this account, Rufus, whom Paul greets, Rom. xvi. 13, may well be this Rufus. The Alexander, however, who is spoken of in the Acts of the Apostles, ch. xix. 33, appears not to have been a Christian, but to have belonged to the hostile Judaism. (LANGE's *Apostol. Zeitalter*, ii. p. 275 f.) Whether he was the same person as Alexander the coppersmith, who was the enemy of Paul, cannot be positively made out. Meyer: "But how common were these names, and how many of the then well-known Christians are strangers to us. In '*Actis Andreæ et Petri*' both are mentioned as the companions of Peter in Rome." They are, of course, here brought forth from the treasures of the evangelical tradition. —**Coming out of the country.**—Meyer will have it, that this fact, mentioned likewise by Luke, is a proof that Jesus was not crucified on the first day of the feast. But in this opinion, no attention is paid to the circumstances: 1. That the country, or the country-seat as it might be termed, from which Simon was coming, might have lain within an easy Sabbath-day's journey of Jerusalem (Meyer maintains,—If so, it must have been stated!); 2. that in case the Passover began with Friday, the *second* day, as Sabbath and Passover together, would be the chief festival-day; 3. that it is by no means historical to admit no contraventions of the Sabbath-law, and, furthermore, that it would be the very thing to turn the attention of the multitude to Simon, if there was anything remarkable, anything offensive, in his appearing at such a time. Such results are by no means uncommon in the similar instances of multitudes running together; so that the notice rather supports the view which adopts the first feast-day as the one. Jesus was crucified under the pretext that He was the great Sabbath-breaker. The people, in their witticism, might perhaps say, See, there comes another Sabbath-breaker from the country; let him suffer a little along with the other.

Ver. 22. **Golgotha.**—Meyer makes Golgotha genitive * (as if, Golgotha's place). Because the translation is κρανίου τόπος. But the question is, Has not τόπος in the first instance a more general import,—the place (Golgotha)? John retranslates κρανίου τόπος into Hebrew, Golgotha; Matthew also names the place, Golgotha; Luke simply, Skull. No doubt it is strange that Mark has τόπος following Golgotha. Probably the place was called sometimes Skull, and sometimes Place of a Skull, and Mark gives the more exact designation. *See* on Matt. xxvii. 33.

Ver. 23. **They gave Him**; that is, they offered Him myrrh-wine. This myrrh-wine cannot, from the different descriptions of Mark, be identical with the vinegar, or the wine-vinegar, of which a drink was at a later period given to Jesus. Most likely the wine was in each case the same, but the narcotic intermixture was omitted in the second instance.

Ver. 24. **Parted his garments.**—John gives the more exact description. The prevailing point of view among the first three Evangelists was the

* [Tischendorf (ed. 1865) reads ἐπὶ τὸν γολγοθᾶν —*Ed.*]

making the division an occasion for gambling. Comp. *Note* on Matt. xxvii. 35. The form of the play is not closely described. Meyer: "We must leave unsettled the question, Whether the lot-casting was performed with dice, or the lots were shaken in some vessel (a helmet), and that which first fell out decided in favor of him to whom it belonged."

Ver. 25. **And it was the third hour.**—Upon the apparent discrepancy between this declaration of Mark and Matthew, and the statement of John, ch. xix. 14, comp. *Note* on Matt. xxvii. 45. We cannot avoid, however, drawing attention to the striking relation subsisting between the third and the sixth hour. At the third hour, by the crucifixion of Jesus, the endurance of the cross for His people was decided, as it meets us in the superscription, The King of the Jews, and is represented in the crucifixion of the thief (and the later deridings of the chief priests, etc.). But when the sixth hour came, and the darkness spread over the whole land —literally, over the whole world and earth—then was the judgment of the whole world decided. The third hour was the dying hour of Judaism: in the sixth hour, the dying hour of the old world was present to the view in typical signs. We have here, also, to carefully note the relation between the superscription, which according to Mark was decided upon about the third hour, and the declaration of John, that it was about the sixth hour: "And he saith to the Jews, Behold your King! But they cried out, Away with Him, away, crucify Him." When the third hour had come, and it was advancing to the sixth, then was the crucifixion of Jesus decided in His being scourged, in accordance with the judgment of the people and of Pilate; but in this was, also, the crucifixion of the Jewish people themselves determined, which was first made apparent in the crucifixion of the two thieves in company with Jesus. About the sixth hour, according to John, the judgment of the world was decided along with that of Judaism—the presage of the *dies iræ* presented itself; that is to say, John has made this sign of the third hour to be the decisive, universal symbol, and has, on this account, probably brought it into connection with the sixth hour.

Ver. 27. **And with Him they crucify.**—As to the alleged difference between the accounts of Mark and Luke, consult *Note* on Matt. xxvii. 38, 44.

Ver. 34. **Eloi.**—*See Note* on Matt. xxvii. 46.

Ver. 36. **Let alone; let us see.**—According to Meyer, this is contradictory to the account given by Matthew, xxvii. 49. But it is not to be overlooked, that there is no reason why, in this moment of the intensest excitement, two divisions might not make the same exclamation, and that, too, in different senses,—the one mocking, the other speaking more earnestly. (Comp. the scene in SHAKESPEARE's *Macbeth* after the murder.) If this sympathizer meant it humanely with his cry, "Let alone," perhaps the idea shot through him, that Elias might interpose in the last extremity.

DOCTRINAL AND ETHICAL.

1. The death.—The death of humanity in its life-germ is here completed in the death of Jesus. Considered in this light, Christ's death is prophetical of the great dissolution of the world, to ensue at the end of all things. The extinction of the primary life: Christ condemned, His rights unacknowledged; derided, and by this derision looked upon by the world as destroyed; led forth, robbed, crucified, and in this act rejected in His person, and with His work, as the curse of the world; blasphemed, and so made to pronounce sentence of death upon the obdurate; Christ dead upon the cross. Hence there is announced, in presages, the future extinction of the derivative life, (*i. e.*, the death of the world): The sun of the old world darkens at mid-day; the holy of holies of the divine ordinance in the old human world vanishes like a vision of the night, when the temple-vail rends asunder. All is now over with the old world; it has but to live out its remnant of life. It has judged itself; and in that self-condemnation lay God's condemnation,—a condemnation which nothing but the conquering love of Christ could turn into a blessing.

HOMILETICAL AND PRACTICAL.

See Matthew; also the preceding reflections.—Christ was, notwithstanding, the King of the Jews the whole crucifixion through. This is seen: 1. In the accusation of His enemies; 2. in the impression produced upon Pilate, and in his decision; 3. in the kingly ornaments which the soldiers placed upon Him; 4. in the train which bore Him forth with them out of Jerusalem; 5. in the superscription on the cross; 6. in the terror which breaks forth in the blasphemy of His foes; 7. in the miracles accompanying His death.—The great dying on Golgotha: 1. There dieth the King of the Jews; 2. there dieth the Son of God; 3. there dieth the old world; 4. there dieth old sin; 5. there dieth old death.—Simon of Cyrene and his sons; or, the everlasting memory of the cross-bearers and their children.—Simon; or, how man becomes unconsciously separated from his commonplaceness, and involved in the great history of the cross.—The terrifying world-darkness at bright midday forms a symbol of the terrifying world-darkness spread over mankind by their blindness of heart.—Christ the clear light of the world in this night of the world.—His heart and His eye are fixed most earnestly on God during this world-judgment; and that preserves the world, which is lost in itself, from sinking into the abyss.—The unholy and the holy Golgotha: 1. The unholy: men of violence, drunkards, gamblers, thieves, blaspheming priests. 2. The holy: the great Sufferer, the temperate One in holy clearness of soul and knowledge, the Laborer, the Warrior of God, the Supplicant.—[The potion rejected and the potion accepted, or holy refreshment in the conflict of suffering enjoyed after the example of Christ: 1. As refreshment at the right time; 2. in the right place; 3. in the right measure; 4. in the right consecration.]—The despair in the seeming triumph, and the triumph in the seeming despair: 1. In the conduct and mockery of the enemies; 2. in the supplicatory cry of the Lord: My God, etc.—The signs of hellish madness in the blasphemies with which the chief priests end their work.—Let alone, let us see; or, how, at the life-flame of the dying Jesus, a new life has kindled in the dying world: 1. From the horrors of His death springs the horror of the world; 2. from His trust in God, the world's belief; 3. from His pity, the compassion of the world. —Let alone, let us see: or, this history is not yet completed; it is only beginning at the time when it seems to approach its completion.—The death-shriek of the Lord is the great waking call to a new life for the world of man.

STARKE:—QUESNEL:—Christ, by becoming the derision of His creatures, has atoned for the criminality of the creatures in mocking God and religion. —Many would willingly pass by the cross of Christ; but, before they are aware of it, they are laid hold of, and forced into companionship with Christ in suffering.—Participation with Jesus in the cross, is that which alone makes our name in truth eternally renowned, and prevents it from passing into forgetfulness.—At the end, the world is bitter as gall, but heaven is sweet.—HEDINGER:—View, O my soul, in faith this picture of martyrdom!—Christ has been reckoned with the transgressors; hence we may console ourselves, that we shall come to God's blessed companionship, and the company of the holy angels. —The understanding, in its wisdom, is offended at the cross of Christ.—He succeeds ill in the faith, who must *see* (John xx. 29), and who will believe when he pleases (John vi. 44).—Christ died for thee; be thou ready to die for Him.—When the true Lamb of God was offered, all the Levitical offerings found their completion.

BRAUNE:—They caught him, and cast him out of the vineyard, and slew him, Matt. xxi. 39.—God's wrath is heavier to bear than Christ's cross.—Isa. liii. 12.—"My God," etc. Let us imitate Him in the employment of the Holy Scriptures; also, that, when in the anguish of our hearts we cannot pray any more in our own words, we may allow the Spirit, whose work the holy word is, to represent us with groanings that cannot be uttered.

BRIEGER:—*And they that passed by.* So thoroughly helpless was Jesus upon the cross, that this crowd easily persuaded themselves that all was deception that they had seen and heard of Jesus.—*The chief priests.* So spake Satan, too, in the wilderness: If Thou be the Son of God, command that these stones, etc. To self-help he there challenged the Holy One of God: here he does the same through his well-approved servants.—Ps. ii. 5.—*The darkness.* God must witness against these murderers.—In the destruction of the holy of holies, Jehovah destroyed the temple itself. The Most Holy was taken forth from the city of Jerusalem and laid outside the gate upon Golgotha. There, too, was a vail rent, even the flesh of Christ (Heb. x. 20).—GOSSNER, on ver. 30:—Self-help.—One might often free oneself by a mere word. But if the truth and the honor of God suffer by that word, one may not speak it.—His death was the rising sun for the spirit-world; and therefore the world's natural sunlight veiled itself before Him. (LAMPE:—The sun set over Christ, and rose for me.)

---

7. *The Descent of Jesus into the Realm of Death. His Death, and the Tokens of the New Life.* VERS. 39–47.

(Parallels: Matt. xxvii. 54–66; Luke xxiii. 39–56; John xix. 31–42.)

39 And when the centurion, which stood over against him, saw that he so cried out,[1]
40 and gave up the ghost, he said, Truly this man was the Son of God. There were also
women looking on afar off: among whom was Mary Magdalene, and Mary the mother
41 of James the less and of Joses, and Salome; (Who also, when he was in Galilee, fol-
lowed him, and ministered unto him;) and many other women which came up with
42 him unto Jerusalem. And now, when the even was come, (because it was the prepara-
43 tion, that is, the day before the sabbath,)[2] Joseph of Arimathea, an honourable counsel-
lor, which also waited for the kingdom of God, came, and went in[3] boldly unto Pilate,
44 and craved the body of Jesus. And Pilate marvelled if he were already dead: and,
calling *unto him* the centurion, he asked him whether he had been any while dead.
45 And when he knew *it* of the centurion, he gave the body[4] to Joseph. And he bought
46 fine linen, and took him down, and wrapped him in the linen, and laid[5] him in a sepul-
chre which was hewn out of a rock, and rolled a stone unto the door of the sepulchre.
47 And Mary Magdalene, and Mary *the mother* of Joses,[6] beheld where he was laid.[7]

[1 Ver. 39.—Codd. B., L., Tischendorf omit κράξας; Lachmann retains it with *Receptus*.]

[2 Ver. 42.—A., B., Lachmann read πρὸς σάββατον (Meyer: only an error of the copyist); Tischendorf reads with the *Receptus* προσάββατον.]

[3 Ver. 43.—A., B., C., Lachmann, Tischendorf read ελθών instead of ἦλθεν.]

[4 Ver. 45.—B., D., L., Lachmann, Tischendorf read πτῶμα (corpse) instead of σῶμα.]

[5 Ver. 46.—B., D., L., Lachmann, Tischendorf read ἔθηκεν; *Receptus*, κατέθηκεν; Cod. A., κάθηκεν.]

[6 Ver. 47.—Cod. A. reads Ἰωσήφ; B., Δ., Lachmann, Tischendorf read Ἰωσῆτος, which is merely the Greek form of Ἰωσῆ.]

[7 Ver. 47.—A., B., C., Lachmann, Tischendorf read τέθειται; *Receptus*, τίθεται.]

EXEGETICAL AND CRITICAL.

See Matthew and *Luke*.—In the account of the centurion's exclamation, Mark harmonizes with Matthew: the occasion of it he makes, characteristically, to have been the loud cry of the expiring Jesus. The three women beneath the cross, he mentions, like Matthew; also Salome by name, adding many other women, whom he does not specialize. Still more generally and comprehensively is this sorrowing circle alluded to by Luke. Like the other two Synoptics, Mark is less full in his narration of the burial than John; nevertheless he declares with exactness, as do John and Luke, the day to have been the παρασκευή. Nicodemus is missing here; Joseph of

Arimathea is described as the disciple of Jesus in words different from Matthew, and more explicitly than Luke: "Who waited for the kingdom of God." In this, the Petrine idea of the kingdom appears. That the step of Joseph was a bold one; that Pilate called the centurion, and assured himself of the certainty of Jesus' death: these are features which are peculiar to Mark.

Ver. 39. **Said, Truly this man.**—Comp. *Note* upon *Matthew.*—The noticing of the motive of the centurion's cry, viz.: that he saw that Christ οὕτω κράξας ἐξέπνευσεν, is peculiar to Mark, and is strikingly characteristic of him. The Lion of Judah is, even in His departing, a dying lion. The expression of a wondrous power of life and spirit in the last sign of life, the triumphant shout in death, was to the warrior, who had learned to know death from a totally different side upon the battle-fields, a new revelation. Theophylact: οὕτω δεσποτικῶς ἐξέπνευσε. De Wette, following some others, gives but a weak conception: He saw in the speedier death of Jesus a favor from the gods. As to the monstrously gnostic explanation of the passage given by Baur, consult Meyer.

Ver. 40. **James the Less.**—Meyer makes this remark apply solely to the stature. Comp., on the contrary, Judges vi. 15. No doubt it points to a second James, rather than to James the disciple in the stricter sense, since James the son of Alpheus, as he is elsewhere termed, was not the brother of James the Greater. Comp. *Note* on *Matthew.* That this Mary the mother of James the Less and of Joses is identical with Mary the wife of Alpheus, is proved by John xix. 25.

Ver. 42. **And now, when the even was come, because.**—We cannot construe this passage: Because it was even, Joseph came. Reasons: 1. The Jews, indeed, who, according to John, prayed Pilate to remove the bodies, had no other ground for the request than that the next day was the Sabbath. Joseph, on the contrary, had quite a different motive. He wished to entomb the Lord's body with respect, and for this purpose could only employ the circumstance that the Jews themselves wished it removed. The connection of the words, ἐπεὶ ἦν, κ.τ.λ., with ἐλθὼν Ἰωσήφ, κ.τ.λ., would be, notwithstanding all that is said to the contrary, very clumsy; and the correction ἦλθεν, moreover, goes to prove this. 3. Then had Joseph in a legal sense come too late. He must come before the evening. Accordingly, we understand the passage thus: between ὀψία and ὀψία there was a difference (sunsetting, and twilight); upon the evening preceding a feast, the earlier ὀψία was observed. About this time Joseph appeared upon Golgotha, and then he went to Pilate.—**Was the preparation, that is, the day before the Sabbath.**—*See Note* on *Matthew.* Meyer says: "Here, accordingly, there is not a trace that this Friday was itself a festival." The trace is given fully, ch. xiv. 12. If the day mentioned there was the 14th Nisan, then the following day must have been the 15th Nisan. Besides, we know that upon a Passover-feast, where the second day of the feast was at the same time a Sabbath, upon this day, according to the Jewish ideas of the Sabbath, the chief feast fell, as is distinctly shown in John xix. 31. *See* WIESELER, *Chron. Synop.* p. 386. By the Sabbath occurring upon the second day of the feast, the first feast-day became the preparation, the day before the Sabbath.

Ver. 43. **Came, and went in boldly.**—He had come; had seen what occurred as the bones of the crucified were broken; knew that Jesus was [illegible] to be taken down; and now he felt that th[illegible] no time to be lost, and hence he dared to ask

Ver. 44. **Whether He had been any while (already long) dead,** πάλαι.—Before the return of the centurion. He wished to be sure as to what he did.

Ver. 45. **Gave the body.**—Joseph being known as a wealthy man, we might have expected, from the character of Pilate, that he would have extorted money, because the bodies were frequently sold (*see* the quotations in Meyer). This generosity was the mark of a strange state of mind. Probably he was glad to hear that Jesus was really dead, because the Saviour in His higher nature had grown awful to him.

Ver. 47. **Where He was laid:** ποῦ τέθειται.—From this time onward, there appears to have been a relation of confidence and friendship between the old disciples (the women), and the new disciples (Joseph and Nicodemus). In consequence of this new-born confidence and friendship, the Galilean women enter without hesitation the garden of the rich counsellor, and kneel down before the grave. According to Mark and Luke, their intention was at the same time to mark accurately the grave; already they were thinking of the anointing after the Sabbath. Bauer: It was not always the custom in Israel to employ a shroud in burying, and the shortness of time on this occasion did not admit of it.

DOCTRINAL AND ETHICAL.

1. *See* the parallel passages in *Matthew.*
2. The signs of the new life, which present themselves in the death of Jesus.
3. The Lord's death-cry, as expressing the might of His life and spirit, was the awakening of the heathen captain. Death is swallowed up in victory, 1 Cor. xv. The death of believers is henceforth a new death, the prospect of a new world, the presentation of a new world for contemplation.

HOMILETICAL AND PRACTICAL.

The last word of the Jewish priest: He was a blasphemer, is contradicted by the first word of the heathen soldier: He was the Son of God.—Golgotha becomes changed by the Lord's death: 1. The enemies, mockers, and blasphemers have vanished; 2. the friends, confessors, and worshippers appear.—The alternation of life and death in the dying hour of Christ: 1. While He still lived, all sank in death; 2. when He died, all awoke to a new life.—With Christ's death, the presentiments of His resurrection spring up in the minds of believers.—The miraculous workings of the death of Jesus upon those who come under its influence, so different and yet so uniform: 1. So different: the heathen, Roman warrior, the emblem of the Roman Empire shattered to its foundations; the timid Jewish women transformed into heroines; the honorable Jewish counsellor, a Christian grave-digger to the Lord; Pilate, the proud man of the world, himself overcome by the spirit of mildness. 2. So uniform: all agree in the self-forgetful manifestation of their homage, and in an expression of readiness to do or to suffer, evidencing the beginning of a new life.—The soft sleep of the Saviour, and His sacred watchers: two female disciples on Good Friday, two angels on Easter morning.—The little congregation at the grave of Jesus, the germ of all Christian congregations. — All Christian Churches are Churches of the Holy Sepulchre.

STARKE:—Christ is also the heathen's Saviour.—*Nova Bibl. Tub.*:—Even in the assembly of the wicked, and in a godless council, there may be a pious councillor; therefore beware of impious judgments.—QUESNEL:—God knows where to find persons who will carry out His plans, how dangerous soever they may be.—What appears to be destroyed, will turn out well at the end. Therefore despair not, dear Christian; believe and trust.—Whosoever hazards anything for the Lord, God will enable that venturer to succeed.—The counsel of the godless never succeeds; that of the righteous stands sure.—Look more to Christ's glory than to self-interest and personal praise.—It is a beautiful work of love when the rich bury the poor.—Let the grave be as deep and as well-guarded as it may, the omnipotence of God will open it, and bring forth the dead.—BRAUNE:—The Head, like the members, was carried to resurrection through the grave.

BRIEGER:—The pious confessors (the first, the penitent thief; the second, the captain) condemn the chief council and all the people, Isa. liii. 9. He was to have been buried, like other transgressors, on Golgotha. The heavenly Father had decreed otherwise.—BAUER:—From this time forward, God's witnesses for the crucified Jesus come forward into view.

PART FIFTH.

THE Resurrection of the Lord. The Great Victory, and the Appearance of the Victor in the Company of the Apostles, to bring to Completion the New Church. His Ascension (Last Withdrawal) to complete His Conquest of the World.

FIRST SECTION.

THE RISEN ONE AS CONQUEROR ON BEHALF OF THE CHURCH; OR, THE INTRODUCTION OF THE BELIEF IN THE RESURRECTION OF THE BODY. THREE EASTER MESSAGES: THE ANGEL, THE WOMAN, THE TWO MEN.

CHAPTER XVI. 1–13.

(Parallels: Matt. xxviii. 1–15; Luke xxiv. 1–35; John xx. 1–18.)

1. *The Resurrection. The Angelic Message, and the Women.* CH. XVI. 1–8.

1 And when the sabbath was past, Mary Magdalene, and Mary the *mother* of James,
2 and Salome, had bought sweet spices, that they might come and anoint him. And
very early in the morning, the first *day* of the week, they came unto the sepulchre at
3 the rising of the sun. And they said among themselves, Who shall roll us away the
4 stone from[1] the door of the sepulchre? (And when they looked [up], they saw that the
5 stone was rolled away,) for it was very great. And, entering into the sepulchre, they
saw a young man sitting on the right side, clothed in a long white garment; and they
6 were affrighted. And he saith unto them, Be not affrighted. Ye seek Jesus of Naza-
reth, which was crucified: he is risen; he is not here: behold the place where they
7 laid him. But go your way, tell his disciples and Peter that he goeth before you into
8 Galilee: there shall ye see him, as he said unto you. And they went out quickly, and
fled from the sepulchre; for they trembled and were amazed [trembling and ecstasy
held them]: neither said they anything to any *man*; for[2] they were afraid.

[[1] Ver. 3.—Codd. A., B., Tischendorf read ἐκ; *i. e., upwards* from the descending entrance. With this corresponds the reading ἀνακεκύλισται in B., L., Tischendorf.]
[[2] Ver. 8.—Codd. B., D., Lachmann, Tischendorf read γαρ instead of δε.]

EXEGETICAL AND CRITICAL.

See the parallel passages in *Matthew* and *Luke.* —This portion, considered in itself, is manifestly a fragment; for no treatise, especially no Gospel, can conclude with ἐφοβοῦντο γάρ. Upon the critical question, as to the authenticity of the following part, compare the Introduction. In this section, we have followed the remarkable division of the Pericope; but we would point out that this part might most properly be united with the following, under the common idea with which we have designated the section. Mark gives the day of the resurrection in such a way as to supplement the other Gospels. The early morning is termed by him the sunrising. He is the most accurate in the account of the women who came to anoint Christ's body, stating their number to be three, and giving their names. He agrees with Luke, in saying that the women came for the purpose of embalming the Lord's body. The representation of the moment of the resurrection, and the revelation to the women as they were returning from the grave, of which Matthew gives the details, is omitted by him; and we find here, moreover, but a brief notice of the meeting of the risen Lord with Mary Magdalene. He alone remarks upon the anxiety of the women, as to how the stone was to be rolled from the door of the sepulchre. Only *one* angel, according to his account, appears to the women; and the same is true of Matthew. This was the first appearance, whereas Luke and John relate a later appearance (*see Matthew*). In describing the return of the women from the grave, the Evangelists differ the most from one another. Matthew states: "And they departed quickly from the sepulchre with fear and great joy, and did run to bring His disciples word." Luke similarly. Mark, on the contrary: "And they said nothing to any man; for they were afraid." The circumstances, however, are different. These women who were afraid, are Mary the mother of James, and Salome, who had gone into the grave after Mary Magdalene had hurried forth on finding the grave empty. The women, however, who departed quickly with great joy to declare what had taken place to the disciples, form a larger group, composed of those who had been the first at the grave with the materials for embalming, and of those who had followed them. (*See Matthew.*) Mark omits this fact in order to introduce the separation of Mary Magdalene from the other two women. And yet he makes it appear that the first impression produced on the women was a mingling of fear and ἔκστασις.

Ver. 1. **And when the Sabbath was past.**—That is, on Saturday evening, after sunset. Luke says, xxiii. 56: After their return (when they came back), they prepared spices and ointments; and rested the Sabbath day, according to the commandment. It is not said, "and thereafter," but, "and of course rested;" so that it is intended as a special explanation of the preceding. We have no contradiction, accordingly, between Luke and Mark, as Meyer would make out. The antecedent embalming, John xix. 39, is not excluded by this. Neither is the fact excluded, that some of the women purchased the spices as early as Friday evening, before sundown; only the two Maries had remained too long at the grave to do so, and hence they could not make their purchases till the Sabbath had passed. (*See* LANGE'S *Leben Jesu*, ii. 3, p. 1623.)—**Spices,** ἀρώματα.—"Aromatic herbs to mix with ointment." Meyer. The ἀρώματα are not necessarily dry substances. "The ointments were seldom *simplicia* (*e. g.*, the nard); they were generally composed of various substances (Job. xli. 22; Plin. 29, 8),—of olive oil (that much-praised product of Palestine), and various fragrant, especially foreign (Ezek. xxvii. 22), vegetable extracts,—namely, oils and resins, such as nard and myrrh. Such ointments were, in part, very expensive, and special articles of luxury. Amos vi. 6." Winer.

Ver. 2. **When the sun had begun to rise.**—We translate thus somewhat singularly, because De Wette (and, following him, again Meyer) maintains that ἀνατείλαντος τοῦ ἡλίου can only mean, when the sun *had risen*, not, as it *was rising*.* The words, "very early," immediately preceding, contradict this view. But between the beginning of the sunrise and its ending is a considerable interval, as between "eve" and "evening;" and according to this distinction has Mark conceived of the matter, as he previously distinguished the two evening seasons. The sunrise, accordingly, had begun: *oriente sole.* Meyer discovers in this passage not only a discrepancy between Mark and John, who indeed says it was still dark, but in a certain measure between the statements of the Evangelist Mark himself ("very early, when the sun had risen").—Beza's conjecture, οὐκέτι ἡλίου ἀνατ., is quite unfounded.

Vers. 3, 4. **From the door of the sepulchre... when they looked up... rolled away... it was very great.**—These are all accurate statements, which are characteristic of Mark's clear view of things. The stone was lying in the hollow cut deep into the rock, so as to form the door, and must accordingly be rolled forth from this recess outwards; hence "rolled away." The rock-tomb, however, itself lay upon a height; hence the women saw the stone when they looked up. That upward glance, accordingly, does not form a mere contrast to the supposed circumstance, that before this "their eyes were cast down to the ground." And because the stone was very great, they could even from a great distance see it lying. This latter explanation of Meyer, respecting the stone, is to be preferred to the reference (by Cod. D., and Wessenberg) of the clause, "for it was very great," to the clause, "who shall roll us away the stone?"—although this conveys a natural meaning.

Ver. 5. **A young man.**—The angel is described in these terms, because of his external appearance. Similarly does Luke express himself: "Two men in shining garments." The facts, as they occurred in point of time, must be distinguished in the following way: First, the appearance of *one* angel *in* the tomb, who showed himself to the two Maries after Mary Magdalene had hurried forth to inform Peter and John (Mark); then, two angels who manifested themselves to her upon her return (John). These two appearances of the angels are given only generally by Luke, (they appeared "to the women which came with him from Galilee.") Finally, we have the appearance of the angels before the tomb upon the stone, which was seen by the larger group of women who assembled in the garden at a later period (Luke xxiv. 1: "And certain with them"). This construction commends itself, if we adopt the view that Luke's account is not designed to give an exact description. The first point then is, that there are three women who are witnesses: Mary Magdalene hastens back to

* [The English version agrees with Lange's: "At the rising of the sun."—*Ed.*]

tell the disciples, and the other two Maries see an angel in the sepulchre. The second point to be considered is that the Magdalene sees two angels in the tomb, then the Lord, while the two Maries wait irresolutely for the other women, or go to meet them. The third point is, that the assembled women, among whom also is Johanna, first see the angel upon the stone (or two angels,—one of them in the sepulchre); then, as they are returning, the Lord Himself.

Ver. 6. **Be not affrighted.**—In the liveliness of the words, we find by asyndeton the copulatives omitted.

Ver. 7. **And Peter.**—Especially. Meyer (following De Wette): "Because of his superiority, not because Peter as denier required a mark of forgiveness (as is the common opinion)." But the superiority of Peter had ceased for a time. It must be first, according to John xxi., restored to him. So it is, accordingly, a gracious token to unfortunate Peter. —**He goeth before you.**—Ὅτι introduces the message.—**As He said unto you.**—*See* ch. xiv. 28. Upon the apparent contradiction between this announcement, that Jesus would precede the disciples, and His appearing unto them so shortly after, consult the commentary on *Matthew*. The first message applied especially to the Galilean disciples in a body. They, as such, first saw the Lord in Galilee again. Secondly, it was in a more special sense a preparation of the disciples for the approaching appearance of the Lord, which was by no means excluded by the message. And thirdly, the return of the disciples to Galilee was delayed, contrary to the wish of the Lord: first, through their own unbelief; secondly, through the unbelief of Thomas. *See Leben Jesu*, ii. 3, pp. 1664–5–6.

Ver. 8. **They trembled and were amazed.**—The term εἶχε δὲ is intended without doubt to express the idea, that, even when out of the sepulchre, their former feelings held fast possession of them. These feelings were the opposing sentiments of trembling and ἔκστασις, which latter cannot be possibly conceived of as horror. It is the parallel to the phrase in Matthew: With fear and great joy. The ecstasy indicates always, that one is not master of oneself; and here it indicates such a state of feeling, in opposition to the extreme measure of fear, τρόμος. It is a state of transition from trembling and amazement; and while this play of feeling continues, men find it impossible to act.—**Neither said they anything to any man.**—De Wette maintains that this is contradicted by Matthew and Luke. It certainly does not mean simply, that they said nothing to any one by the way (Grotius), nor yet to any man beyond the circle of the Apostles; but, nevertheless, there is no contradiction. The intention of Mark was to lay hold of the fact of their indecision, and to unite it to the two following manifestations of hesitating unbelief. The women did not act upon the message of the angels, the individual disciples did not act upon the women's message, the assembled Apostles did not act upon the message of the men and of the disciples who had been met upon the way to Emmaus. The intention of our history is this, to bring out prominently the barriers which unbelief throws up, by which the ever-increasing urgency of the pressing messages is repelled. In the first instance, the weak faith of the two Maries prevented them from fulfilling their mission. The Magdalene met them in this state, and they did not allow themselves to be cheered by her information till they had met the other women (*see Luke*), and with them had seen the Lord. Now, their message was naturally a new and different one. Meyer distinguishes thus: They *related* the message at a later period, but it is self-evident that they had not *fulfilled* it. We distinguish thus: They did not fulfil their original commission, but, at a later period, the related, along with the other women, the earlier and later occurrences in one united narrative.—**They were afraid.**—This can only mean: The occurrence was so new to them, great, unheard-of, that they ventured not in the full confidence of faith to publish it, and that they, still more, did not expect to find any faith among the disciples.

DOCTRINAL AND ETHICAL.

1. Consult the parallels in *Matthew*.

2. The entire chapter in its one central idea: Christ risen in perfect certainty and in the might of His resurrection, the destroyer of all unbelief in His people, and thereby the destroyer of the kingdom of darkness throughout the world; or, Christ appearing in His triumphal glory, able to redeem to the uttermost by that unlimited power which He acquired through His victory.

3. The three grand divisions of the chapter are:—the Risen One as Conqueror *for* the Church, *in* the Church, *with* the Church.

4. The contrast in the chapter: The annunciations of the resurrection of the Lord to the Church, by the angels, by the women, by individual disciples, are not sufficient to overcome fully the unbelief of the disciples; *the circle of disciples becomes a believing Church only when Jesus Himself reveals Himself personally in their midst.* And this is, indeed, the thought underlying the entire Gospel of Mark, which is founded upon the mission of Peter—of that Peter whom man would and will make the head of a new Church in which, by the tradition of an Apostle, angel-voices, holy women, and visions to women, should be made to represent Christ Himself.

HOMILETICAL AND PRACTICAL.

Upon the whole chapter, consult the superscription and the *Doctrinal Reflections.*—*Upon the Section*, vers. 1–16: The Church has not arrived at the full belief in a risen Saviour by even the most glorious messages, but by the personal revelation of the Risen One Himself.—*Upon the Section up to* ver. 13: The three Easter-messages of Jesus to His Church in their progressive effect: 1. Through the angels to the women; 2. through the women to the amazed disciples; 3. through the two amazed disciples to the assembled company.—*Upon the Section before us:* The [Jewish] Sabbath is passed away, the [Christian] Sunday has appeared; or, a new arrangement of the periods of rest and labor has been made by Christ. Man proceeds no more to the holy day from his labor, but from the holy day to his labor. 1. So is it in the life of the glorified Christ: first sitting at the right hand of God, then ruling, then coming again. 2. So is it in the life of the Church: first Sunday, then the consecrated working-day.* 3. So in the life of the believer: first justification, then sanctification. Conclusion: In this form, Christianity is the beginning (the principle) of the glorified world.—Our conversa-

* *Sonntäglicher Werketag:* a secular day into which the spirit of Sunday is carried.

tion is in heaven.—The walk of the three women to the grave is a symbol of the separation between the old and the new world in the history of the Passover: 1. The three women with their solicitude [Mary Magdalene in the deepest emotion; the others, two mothers of five Apostles, two aunts of Jesus of Nazareth, calmer, quieter]; their unconsciously-entertained hopes of life, and their ointments for the dead corpse. 2. The rising sun, but the heavy stone of their anxiety. 3. The angel appears, but the Lord has disappeared. 4. The resurrection of Christ declared, in the distant prospect of His re-appearance, out of the mouth of the grave. 5. The delightful commission to proclaim these good tidings; but their souls are oppressed by the overmastering feelings of fear and joy.—"And Peter" [Peter could never forget this addition, and hence Mark records it].—How the sinner ever thinks of the word which shows that the Saviour thought of him.—The first Easter-message, a message from the Prince of Life given by angelic lips to the women who wished to anoint the dead.—This message is not carried to its destination; but in the contending feelings of the women, between their fear and joy, is left unfulfilled.—Why the female disciples, even now, do not come up to that evangelizing faith which the message enjoins: 1. They are not yet able to give themselves up to that obedience of faith, because the fact overcomes their feelings [could not believe for joy]. 2. They cannot yet give themselves up to the confidence of faith, because their feelings amid the signs of the fact are not yet stilled [they cannot believe for fear; they miss the Lord, whom they have not seen; and they are still afraid of finding among the disciples no faith to receive their great news]. 3. They cannot yet give themselves up to the peace of faith, because these conflicting feelings are contending in their hearts.—As Christ is elevated above the angels, so is the certainty of the resurrection elevated above the testimony of the angelic appearance.—Since Christ died, a new heavenly activity is demanded, which lies far above all the visions of the old economy.

STARKE:—*Nova Bibl. Tub.*:—What does not love do, when it is strong?—Through woman was life lost at first; by women must it be first sought, found, and revealed.—(The stone.) Hindrances in the way of salvation.—Men often make to themselves unnecessary anxieties: before they actually meet them, the Lord has helped them already.—If we look with believing eyes into Christ's grave, all our anxiety falls into it; for Christ's resurrection is our resurrection.—God will comfort the penitent, and will make their anguished hearts joyful again.—Christ's heart is as compassionate after, as before, His resurrection—God's promises pass certainly into fulfilment, and that too more gloriously and sooner than their mere form would lead one to expect.—OSIANDER:—Untimely fear often hinders from fulfilling one's office.

BRAUNE:—No shrine is made of the grave, and no worship from the contemplation of it; but the women are bidden to carry the good news and to awaken faith.—Weak sentimentalism avails nothing in the kingdom of God which has been established in the earth by the death of Jesus.—BRIEGER:—The resurrection, which is also a birth, is a mystery, like every birth. It is also an act of God's omnipotence, like every other birth.—If we are because of sin related to death, which is so foreign to our being, much more are we related to life.—HEUBNER:—The morning of the resurrection of Jesus: 1. Distinguished by heaven itself; 2. bringing a glorious reward to Jesus Himself; 3. fearfully condemnatory as regards His foes; 4. joyfully quickening as regards the disciples of Christ.—DIETZSCH:—The mingling of fear and hope which the thought of death and immortality is wont to awaken in us.—SCHULTZ:—The first witnesses of Christ's resurrection: 1. They were strong [their love is manifested in their going to the grave]; 2. they were weak [their sorrow, their fear].—THIESS:—The cross of Calvary illumined by the rays of the Easter-sun.—RAUTENBERG:—Easter at the graves: 1. The stone of the curse is rolled away; 2. angels inhabit them; 3. the dead are risen.

---

2. *Mary Magdalene and the Two Disciples.* VERS. 9–13.

(Parallels: Matt. xxviii. 9–15; Luke xxiv. 9–35; John xx. 11–19.)

9 Now, when *Jesus* was risen early, the first *day* of the week, he appeared first to
10 Mary Magdalene, out of whom he had cast seven devils. *And* she went and told them
11 that had been with him, as they mourned and wept. And they, when they had heard
12 that he was alive, and had been seen of her, believed not. After that he appeared in
13 another form unto two of them, as they walked, and went into the country. And they
went and told *it* unto the residue: neither believed they them.

EXEGETICAL AND CRITICAL.

See Matthew and *Luke*.—According to Meyer, the apocryphal fragment of some other evangelical writing begins here. Compare the Introduction on this point.* The epithet apocryphal, would not be appropriate, even if the section were an addition taken from another Evangelist's narrative. The narrative contained in our Gospel comprehends within its very brief hints the detailed statement of John regarding the

* [The reasons for assuming that vers. 9–20 are an original portion of Mark's Gospel much outweigh those to the contrary. 1. They are found in the Uncial Codd. A., C., D., X., Δ., E., G., H., K., M., S., U., V.; as well as in 33, 69, and the rest of the Cursive MSS. which have been collated. They are in copies of the Old Latin, in the Vulgate, Curetonian Syriac, Peshito, Jerusalem Syriac, Memphitic, Gothic, and Æthiopic. 2. Irenæus (*Cont. Hær.* iii. 10, 6) recognizes their existence; as do also Hippolytus, Cyril of Jerusalem, Ambrose, Augustine, Nestorius. Scholz also claims that Clement of Rome, Justin Martyr, and Clement of Alexandria sanction the passage; but Tregelles regards this as an error. The chief argument against the genuineness of this section is found in the fact, that it was wanting in *some* of

Easter-message of Mary Magdalene, and the still more detailed account by Luke of the Easter-message sent by the disciples met on the road to Emmaus. Mark groups both accounts under the single head of two duly-authorized embassies, which do not meet with full credence. The first and second halves of this chapter are, however, united into an inseparable unity in the one fundamental thought, that the risen Saviour is the absolute and universal conqueror of unbelief, which was already, even in the circle of disciples, throwing obstacles in the way of Jesus; and that Christ, as the subduer of this unbelief, stands raised above all the messages of men and angels.

Ver. 9. **Was risen early.**—The manifestation of the Risen One by the angels had been preceded by His own personal appearances. The first day of the week is again named, of course, for the purpose of bringing into prominence, even at that early period, the Christian day of rest. We would translate: Upon the first of the seven days (τὸ σάββατον indicating here, as frequently, the week, after the later and more extended custom of the Jewish language). Upon this day He appeared to the Magdalene, out of whom He had cast seven devils. Christ, as the Risen One, has sanctified the week as a holy period; and at the beginning of the holy week, He reveals Himself to one who was preëminently sanctified and susceptible, because He had cleansed her from seven demons. The Evangelist has, accordingly, not merely before him the contrast,—the risen Saviour revealing Himself to a poor woman,—but the spiritual relationship,—she who had been freed from seven devils stands especially near to the conqueror of demons on the morning of His great triumph, and she is peculiarly fitted in spirit to be the first to see Him, and to announce to the disciples His resurrection. Accordingly, in this revelation we have the activity of the Saviour, in His conquest over devils, set over against the passivity of the pardon-seeking woman, who had been freed from the seven devils. Meyer considers this remark concerning Mary as not belonging to this passage. We view the expulsion of *seven* devils in connection with the sacred number seven, and regard the term symbolic of a glorious deliverance out of the great snares which Satan had prepared. (Comp. Matthew.) Mark is wont to employ ἐκβαλλειν in other passages to express strongly a glorious redemption. It is questionable whether the words, "early on the first day of the week," go back to ἀναστὰς δέ (Beza, Ewald, etc.), or are to be construed with ἐφάνη (Grotius and others). We prefer the first construction, because the second mention of the resurrection as having occurred upon the first day of the week appears to point at the sanctification of that period. In verse second, μία σαββάτων had reference to Jewish customs; but here the allusion is to the renewed week, the πρώτη σαββάτου.

Ver. 10. **And she went.**—That is, even she. It must be conceded that Mark employs πορευεσθαι to express a solemn proclamation of the Gospel only in this place (ver. 15 excepted). By this, however, he reminds us of the mode of expression employed by his teacher, Peter: 1 Pet. iii. 19.*—**Them that had been with Him.**—This also is a peculiar expression to indicate the disciples in a wider sense. It indicates, however, their scattered condition, their present despairing state, as opposed to their former blessed communion with Him. The expression itself is not an unusual one with Mark; *see* ch. i. 36.—**A they mourned and wept.**—Comp. Luke vi. 25 This has undoubtedly a special reference to the sorrowful and weeping Peter. To bring prominently out that Jesus revealed Himself to Peter, after the message given to Mary, consists not with the matter-of-fact disposition of Mark.

Ver. 11. **And had been seen of her,** ἐθεάθη.—A strong expression. "That θεᾶσθαι is not found elsewhere in the Gospel by Mark, considering how frequent is its use by others, is one of the marks of a strange hand." Meyer. Hermeneutics might, we think, have taught him: *new facts, new words.*

Ver. 12. **In another form.**—An explanation of the expression in Luke xxiv. 16, but by no means a condensation of Luke xxiv. 13–35, as Meyer would represent. Jesus' form was, on the one hand, changed. different clothes (John xx. 15), traces of the sufferings during the crucifixion: on the other hand, more sublime in its appearance, Jesus being in the transition-state from humiliation to glorification.

After that.—The three specifications, πρῶτον, μετὰ δὲ ταῦτα, ὕστερον; relate manifestly to one another. Hence it cannot be at all remarkable that μετὰ ταῦτα is not elsewhere to be found in Mark (comp. ch. xiii. 24).—**Of them**—of the unbelieving disciples in a wider sense.

Ver. 13. **Neither believed they them.**—Even they did not gain credence. Meyer: "A different tradition from that given in Luke xxiv. 34." It is certain that no interpolator would have allowed this manifest appearance of a discrepancy. But the Evangelist, who was writing from the stand-point of a special idea of the resurrection, was not afraid to employ it. And Luke gives the means of knowing what is meant. The Eleven knew for a certainty, in the evening, that Christ had appeared to *Simon*, and were consequently for the moment believing. Now the Emmaus disciples arrive, and declare that Jesus had revealed Himself unto *them*. Not being able to comprehend this new mode of existence on the part of Christ, that He now is here, and now there, new doubts fill them. The thought of a spiritual apparition occurs to them; and hence they are affrighted when Jesus at length appears in their midst, and imagine that a ghost is present. And now the Lord must convince them as to the truth of His new corporeality. The point brought forward by Mark testifies, accordingly, to an exceedingly accurate, and moreover, a perfectly independent, knowledge of the facts of the resurrection. The expression is, of course, explained by Luke xxvi. 34, without, however, referring to it (Schulthess). And so it is unnecessary to suppose, with Augustine, that the λέγοντες were certain believing disciples, to be distinguished from certain who did not believe; or to say, with Calvin, "At first they doubted, then they believed." The situation of affairs was of such a nature as to lead them into new difficulties on hearing the message of the Emmaus disciples, instead of strengthening them in their belief. Because, as yet they were not in possession of the idea of a glorified body; and hence

the early copies of Mark's Gospel. This is attested by Eusebius, Gregory Nyssa, Victor of Antioch, and Jerome. But this is certainly an insufficient reason for affirming its spuriousness in the face of the strong testimonies upon the other side. *See* TREGELLES on the Printed Text of the Greek Testament, p. 246 *seq.* Its genuineness is affirmed by Simon, Mill, Bengel, Matthæi, Eichorn, Kuinoel, Hug, Scholz, Guericke, Olshausen, Ebrard, Lachmann; is denied by Griesbach, Rosenmüller, Schulz, Fritzsche, Paulus, Wieseler, Ewald, Meyer, Tischendorf.—*Ed.*]

* [Lange seems to have in his eye the objection of Meyer (*in loc.*) to the genuineness of the section, drawn from the fact that the word πορεύω occurs three times in it.—*Ed.*]

they thought very naturally, that if the Lord had appeared to Simon in Jerusalem, He could not at the same time have appeared unto others at a distance from the city. Not to speak of this, that several of the Eleven might very reasonably have thought: Why should He reveal Himself to these two at Emmaus earlier than to us at Jerusalem?

DOCTRINAL AND ETHICAL.

1. *See Matthew* and the parallels in *Luke* and *John:* also the foregoing *Note* on ver. 13.

2. The Easter-embassy of the angelic world to the human world has been replaced by the message of the resurrection passing from man to man, at first from the female disciples to the male disciples, then the message passing between individual disciples and the disciple-band. The Risen One has destroyed, in His resurrection, the bands and bolts of the grave; He must now destroy, likewise, the doubts, the weak faith, the unbelief of His own, in order with them to destroy in like manner the unbelief of the world. The certainty of His resurrection presses gradually forward; but the Church comes only to perfect knowledge when He reveals Himself in her midst.

3. The appearing and disappearing of Jesus in the circle of disciples is a type of His appearance in, and of His disappearance from, the Church.

HOMILETICAL AND PRACTICAL.

See Matthew, and the parallel passages in *Luke* and *John.*—The risen Saviour presents Himself to be recognized by one who stood especially near to the kingdom of heaven and of the Unseen, because He has freed and cleansed her heart from seven devils.—Mary Magdalene, the much-forgiven sinner, sent as a comforter to the weeping Peter, to the sorrow-laden and mourning disciples.—The two Maries, who had remained with Jesus beside His grave, late into the night of His dying day, are to be the first to see Him on His resurrection morn.—The distinction made in the case of the two disciples going into the country: 1. Because they, like Magdalene and Peter, especially required consolation; 2. because they united in going before the Lord as two messengers and witnesses unto the Church.—The risen Saviour brings His own at once together again.—Jesus appearing in another and new form, as the Prince and Pledge of another, new world: 1. In the form of one who had passed through death; 2. with the glorified crucifixion-marks; 3. with the signs of the new life (even the Magdalene did not at once recognize Him).—The threefold form of the unbelief which departed not, even from the community of believers, without assistance: 1. They cannot conceive to themselves the mysterious majesty in which Christ caused an angel to represent Him; 2. they cannot conceive to themselves the greatness of the grace, in consequence of which He appears to Mary Magdalene first; 3. they cannot conceive to themselves the might of His exaltation, by reason of which He appears now here, now there.—Neither the angels, nor the women, nor the two Evangelists, satisfy their faith: they wish to be assured of His actual existence by His own appearance.—Not having yielded themselves to faith in His prediction, they find it difficult to believe in its fulfilment.

Starke:—As the woman was the first to sin, so hath Christ, after finishing salvation, chosen to reveal Himself to a woman first.—The most despised in the opinion of the world are often the most precious in the eyes of God.—Quesnel:—God delights in blessing those who have remained faithful to Him in persecution, and have not been ashamed of the cross.—Christ imparts His grace according to the need for it, Matt. v. 4.—Jesus ever, even upon our journeyings, with us.

Braune:—The intelligence brought by Mary and the women concerning the resurrection of the Saviour is believed neither lightly nor superstitiously; and hence we see that their belief, and their testimony, is the more firmly founded, and the more trustworthy.

SECOND SECTION.

THE RISEN LORD AS VICTORIOUS IN THE CHURCH, DESTROYING UNBELIEF, PERFECTING FAITH, AND PREPARING THE CHURCH TO GO FORTH WITH THE GOSPEL MESSAGE.

Chapter XVI. 14–18.

(Parallels: Matt. xxviii. 9–20; Luke xxiv. 36–49; John xx. 19–21, 25.)

14 Afterward[1] he appeared unto the eleven as they sat at meat, and upbraided them
with their unbelief and hardness of heart, because they believed not them which had
15 seen him after he was risen.[2] And he said unto them, Go ye into all the world, and
16 preach the Gospel to every creature. He that believeth, and is baptized, shall be saved;
17 but he that believeth not shall be damned. And these signs shall follow them that believe:
In my name shall they cast out devils; they shall speak with new tongues;
18 They shall take up serpents; and if they drink any deadly thing, it shall not hurt them;
they shall lay hands on the sick, and they shall recover.

[1] Ver. 14.—C., D. add δέ to ὕστερον.

[2] Ver. 14.—Ἐκ νεκρῶν, supported by A., C., X., Δ., 1, 33.

[3] Ver. 17.—The omission of καιναῖς by C., L., Δ. is not decisive against it.
[4] Ver. 18.—Codd. C., L., M.**, X., Δ., the Coptic, Armenian, and Syriac versions, read before ὄφεις, καὶ ἐν ταῖς χερσὶν but it is probably a mere explanatory addition.

EXEGETICAL AND CRITICAL.

See the parallel passages in *Matthew* and *Luke*.—The section before us is another of those peculiar passages which are so characteristic of Mark. The object sought in it is to show the full persuasion of the Apostles of the truth of the resurrection,—the complete subduing of their hard-heartedness, so often brought out by the Evangelist (ch. vi. 52; viii. 17), and of their unbelief. This is with him the decisive point; and hence he connects all further information with the manifestation made by Christ of Himself in the midst of the disciples upon the evening of the first day after the resurrection. In the account of this manifestation, contained in ver. 14, he agrees with Luke and John. But while Luke brings prominently forward the pains Jesus was at to free His disciples from all fear, through convincing proofs of His bodily presence, Mark gives prominence to the fact, that Christ blamed their unbelief; and also to the facts of the completion of the disciples' training, of their deliverance from hard-heartedness, and of their being brought at last to a full belief. Luke's account is not, however, wanting in the points which go to corroborate the Lord's reprimand, vers. 38, 44, and especially ver. 45. John relates this revelation of Jesus from the other side,—from the side of the solemn perfecting of the disciples' faith. Mark then brings forward in this connection, ver. 15, the apostolic commission, which Matthew represents to have been issued on the mountain in Galilee. As to this point, we have only to remark, that he connects the anticipatory re-installation of the Apostles upon the first Easter evening, of which we are informed by Luke and John, with the sending forth of the Apostles from Galilee, and gives to the whole the solemn expression of the latter commission. In doing this, he selects a stronger term than Matthew, "Preach the Gospel *to every creature*;" this is the phrase corresponding to "Disciple all nations." Mark alone, in accordance with his energetic character, gives the alternative, "He who believeth and is baptized," etc.; and he combines in the brief expression, "and is baptized," both the words, "make disciples of," and the baptismal formula contained in Matthew. Very strong, and peculiar to him, is the promise given by the Lord to the Apostles; and it is a grand thought, that He gives it to the Apostles for all who believe, vers. 17 and 18. It is the full, the last unfolding of the *charisma*, which the Lord (according to ch. iii. 15; Matt. x.) has imparted to the Apostles; the wonderful proclamation through them of the forgiveness of sins, the institution of absolution recorded by Luke and John, and also the promise of Jesus given by Matthew, "Lo, I am with you alway."

Ver. 14. **Afterward.**—By ὕστερον we are, certainly, not to understand, lastly; still it marks here the later, the personal revelations of Christ in the circle of the disciples, which succeeded His former isolated manifestations, and which established the fact of His resurrection. The confusions, which Meyer discovers in the account now following, rest upon critical prejudices, and upon the absence of details in the narrative of the Evangelist, which last characteristic also appears in the final chapter of Luke.—**And upbraided them with their unbelief.**—Upbraiding, the original form which Christ's contest took with the weak faith, the doubting, and feeble yielding to the influences of the evil one. (*See Leben Jesu*, ii. 1. p. 295.) And these are the causes of Christ's last upbraiding among His disciples.—**And hardness of heart.**—Comp. ch. viii. 17 *seq.*

Ver. 15. **And He said unto them.**—Thus Mark, exactly as Luke xxiv. 45, passes over to a general conclusion.—**Preach the Gospel to every creature;** πάσῃ τῇ κτίσει, the entire creation.—We find no reason to limit, with De Wette, this phrase to the conception, "all men" ["literally, all creatures, that is, all men, as also the Jews use בְּרִיּוֹת:" Lightfoot, Wetstein]. Comp. Rom. viii. 21. Because the miraculous gifts of the Christians, here mentioned, point to a glorification of all nature through the Gospel. *See* Isa. xi. Still less is the phrase to be restricted with Lightfoot and others, to the heathen, who were contemptuously termed by the Rabbins הבריות; for, as Meyer remarks, this would be in opposition to vers. 16 and 20.

Ver. 16. **He that believeth.**—Expressed from the stand-point of Christ, as He who was one day to return in the capacity of the world's Saviour and Judge, for the purpose of giving the due recompense. Baptism is not named along with faith as in itself an indispensable matter, but as the natural, certainly, also, necessary consequence of faith; because baptism indicates the entering of the believer into the communion of the believing Church. There is no occasion for the distinction made by Meyer between the newly converted and the children of Christians, because the antithesis runs, ὁ δὲ ἀπιστήσας; and it is not self-evident that baptism was not dispensed to such children. It is manifest that Jesus, according to Mark, has made the damnation depend upon a positive, personal disbelief, or rejection of the Gospel. But the Gospel is to be proclaimed to every creature, without exception. In this we have a connection opened between this passage, and the passages 1 Pet. iii. 19; iv. 6.*

Ver. 17. **Signs.**—Σημεῖα is first brought forward, the term indicating that miracles of all kinds should accompany them, should make their testimony trustworthy; but these signs Christ will specify.—**That believe** (that have believed).—That is, who have become believers, have adopted the faith. This promise holds good not merely of the Apostles and the Seventy (Kuinoel), but also of all Christians, without exception. Meyer: "Finally, Jesus does not mean that each of these signs should manifest itself with each believer, but this miracle with one, that with another." In entire Christendom, however, all of them; and, apart from their original, miraculous form, these signs were always to be more and more glorious and potent in their action, as the forces which are transforming the world.—**Follow;** παρακολουθήσει.—Literally, to follow in company, to proceed along with. *See* the expression, Luke i. 3.—**In My name.**—The miraculous power by which they were to effect all the succeeding wonders. To the expulsion of demons corresponds speaking with new tongues, and to the taking up of serpents the drinking of anything deadly; and, finally, to the laying of hands upon the sick, their recovery. The first

* [These passages, however, speak only of *human* creatures.—*Ed.*]

division indicates, negatively, the overthrow and expulsion of ethical evil (the casting out of devils); positively, the new form taken by the ethical world in the life of believers (speaking with new tongues). The second division indicates, negatively, the destruction of what is physically injurious, and its transformation into what is beneficial for the world (to take up serpents); positively, the overcoming of all that is physically injurious, through the strengthening of the life of Christians. The third division (laying hands upon the sick) indicates, negatively, the removal of all ethico-physical sufferings from others; positively (they shall recover), the return of the perfect, natural feeling of health to those who believe. These six members represent a proclamation, by means of facts, of that Gospel which is designed for every creature, or better, for the whole creation.—**Cast out devils.**—Employed in the most extensive sense, and with the deepest meaning. Purification of the new, divine world from all evil spirits.—**Speak with new tongues.**—This statement is to be restricted neither to the form under which "the speaking with tongues" showed itself at Pentecost, nor to the more general form of the Corinthian gift of tongues, obtaining commonly among the new converts of the apostolic era (Acts x. 46; xix. 6). For the statement of Christ applies to Christians generally, and to all time. The germ of this promise, of speaking with new tongues, lies in the instructions to the Apostles, ch. xiii. 11; comp. Matt. x. The new form which the spiritual world assumes, under the teaching of the Spirit, is here revealed by means of a symbolic expression; and we have an indication of the miraculous development of that world when the apostolic gift of tongues appeared. Meyer declares that there is a reference in this passage to the Apostles speaking with tongues under the influence of ecstasy (a state as entirely different from the Montanist conception, as the free, ethical inspiration is from pathological somnambulism); that tradition has explained this "speaking," with reference to what occurred at Pentecost, as speaking in foreign tongues, —the fact being that Mark, influenced by traditions, conceived of the matter in a mythical way, and went far beyond Luke's idea. But, holding such opinions, Meyer is on the high road to a mythological explanation of the passage, and only obscures a statement which is to be received as an exalted expression, symbolical in character, but in meaning most fully accordant with the Bible.

Ver. 18. **Take up serpents.**—By αἴρειν may be understood destroy, drive forth (Luther), or exterminate (Theophylact). This explanation would give a good sense, and might find support from some other passages of the Scriptures (Luke x. 19): nevertheless, to express such an idea, no such peculiar expression would have been selected; and moreover the conception we obtain thus is too trifling, for Hercules had already proved himself able to exterminate serpents. The word may, however, have another meaning: throw into the air (and so mediately destroy the reptiles), as Paul did with a serpent (Acts xxviii. 5). But to express this idea, the term before us is not sufficiently clear. Or it may signify, to draw forth by means of some potent conjuration; an idea that savors too much of heathenish magic arts. Or, finally, it may mean, to set up on a pole, as a token of victory. Commentators have hitherto passed over unnoticed this signification of αἴρειν, to lift up, or elevate as a σημεῖον or signal upon some pole or staff, and yet it is a force properly belonging to the verb; and it leads our thoughts back to the lifting up of the brazen serpent in the wilderness as a symbol of victory. The expression ἱστάναι ἐπ σημείον, Num. xxi. 9, is of the same import as αἴρειν, for which John employs (ch. iii. 14) ὑψοῦν for a particular reason. The special reference of that brazen serpent was to Christ, who was elevated upon the cross in the character of a heretic and transgressor, rejected by the old world, and so formed a type of the arch-enemy, and yet was made by God Saviour of, and means of life to, all that looked up to Him. Still, the more general reference was this, that the deadly and horrible serpent was not only overcome, but that its image was made to be a standard of victory. And this is accordingly a type which has been fulfilled to the fullest extent in Christianity: serpents are not simply overcome, destroyed; they are lifted up on high as ensigns of victory, with healing efficacy. What was in itself injurious has been serviceable to the interests of God's kingdom, as we find represented in the Gothic cathedrals. And this occurs not merely in a typical manner, but with actual serpents,—of course according to their symbolic signification. The fact that Christ only represented a serpent (that is, represented a deceiver and destroyer of the people dying on the cross, by whom the world was delivered from ruin), does not prevent our adopting the more general explanation, according to which actual serpents, the signs of death in the world, are changed into signs of life. Meyer, in his remarks on this passage, far surpasses De Wette, when the latter says, "If Mark had before his mind the serpent-charmers so common in the East (MICH. *Mos. Recht*, § 255), the account is apocryphal." Meyer puts this view aside with the one hand, and with the other takes it back again, with many additions. This conversion of the symbolism of the Bible into obscure, mythical allusions is now altogether antiquated. [The simplest explanation is the most rational. The "taking up of serpents" is immediately connected with the "drinking of any deadly thing," and denotes that their lives would be preserved by the miraculous power of God, whenever the exertion of such power was needed. The extension of the statement to believers generally, in every age of the church, is not warranted by anything in the text, and introduces confusion. This was a promise to the Apostles, and the apostolic age.—ED.] —**And if they drink any deadly thing.**—This expresses symbolically the restoration of life to such a degree as to be actually inviolable. De Wette thinks that the apocryphal story of John having, without injury, drunk a poisoned cup, and the similar story regarding Barnabas, related by Eusebius, *Hist. Eccl.* iii. 39, gave origin to this passage. Meyer has good reasons for opposing this view; but he is somewhat inconsistent, since he considers this section to be an apocryphal addition. The remark has more force, that the custom of condemning a criminal to drink a cup of poison suggested the idea. And why should this custom not have occurred to Christ? yea, why may He not have thought of the condemnation of Socrates, and then have declared, "The poisoned cup shall not harm My people;" primarily, of course, in a symbolic sense (just as the cup of hemlock hurt not the soul of Socrates)? But also in a typical sense the life of believers should grow more and more able to overcome all injurious influences, and often *literally* to overcome these influences in a miraculous manner. The passage Matt. xx. 23 is the most general, the passage Matt. xxvi

39 the most special, Christological conception of the similar thought in a symbolic form.—**Sick.**—Miraculous cures. Also a symbolical expression of the removal of sickness. — **They shall recover.** — Guided by the two preceding parallels, we consider this last sentence to refer to believers themselves. They are, on their side, to enjoy perfect well-being.

DOCTRINAL AND ETHICAL.

1. Comp. the parallel passages in *Matthew*, in *Luke*, and *John*.

2. By the first appearance of Jesus in the full assembly of the disciples, on the first evening after the resurrection, the certainty of His having risen is decided for the Church, and so mediately for the world. This first revelation of the risen Christ stands opposed to the last rising of the unbelief of the disciples. They have sinned, in respect to His resurrection, through unbelief; and hence His appearing is accompanied with an upbraiding of their want of faith, which wakens shame in them. The last remnant of unbelief is now actually driven forth by rebukes with this departing unbelief, the hard-heartedness disappears, the spiritual life of the disciples becomes free and active; they can now yield themselves up to the perfect revelation of His glory, and all succeeding revelations of that glory, with full confidence, and with an ever-growing soul-life. This upbraiding of the unbelief, which passes over into a blessing, marks the perfected triumph of the Lion of the tribe of Judah, and so gives the concluding thought of Mark, through whose entire Gospel the contest of Christ against the unbelief and hardness of heart of His disciples is found running as the fundamental thought. Least of all could the Gospel by Mark conclude, as a Gospel of fear, with the little faith of the disciples. In the belief, however, of Christ's absolute glory through His victory, the spiritual glory of the Church is also declared. According to the Gospel of Peter, the Church of Christ must go on from one degree of faith to another, till it attains unto perfection. It cannot, like the Romish phantom of Peter, remain amazed for ever upon the first step of faith; it must advance with the almighty administration of Christ, must grow and work in the fulness of spiritual life, till the Gospel be preached to every creature.

3. *The Gospel to every creature.* — Out of the demon-polluted, the enslaved, the fear-ruled world, shall arise an evangelized, freed, glorified world of faith, of peace, of life. The glorification of the world through the Gospel is an idea and a promise which runs through the whole of Holy Writ (Deut. xxviii.; Song of Sol.; Isa. xi.; ch. lxv. 17; Rom. viii.; Rev. ii. 1): and Christ here makes this promise to take the form of an institution. What His resurrection is in fact,—a proclamation of the Gospel to every creature: this the apostolic preaching is to make known to the world, to bring about, and to seal by the sacraments. And every true, living, earnest preaching of the word is consequently a proclamation of that Gospel, the aim of which is to free all creatures from their subjection to vanity, a power conducing to that regeneration which the great *palingenesis* is to bring about, and which shall appear along with the world's end. This thought of the great regeneration of the world rests altogether upon views peculiar to Peter: Acts ii. 20; iii. 20, 21; 2 Pet. i. 4; ch. iii. 13.

4. *He that believeth.*—With the Gospel, accordingly, begins the great crisis, the separation, which comes to view at the end of the world. *See* John iii. 19, 36. Belief and unbelief form the grand distinction in the new history of the world; and they are operating to bring to its completion the separation of the eternal, divine world from the territory of death and of the devils' torment; and they will continue to act thus until judgment begins. That the believer, as such, is at once baptized, that is enters under the sacramental seal of his faith into the communion of the believing Church, is a self-evident presupposition; therefore, whoso believeth and is baptized. The promise of salvation, of deliverance, is not annexed to baptism in itself, but to the faith which receives its completion in baptism. Hence, on the other hand, want of baptism is not followed by damnation, but the want of faith, which may undoubtedly evidence itself, even though baptism be lacking.

5. Upon the doctrine of baptism, consult the dogmatic systems.

6. *The accompanying miracles.*—The new birth of creation is completed in three stages: 1. The personal stage, preaching the Gospel: 2. the social stage, the sacrament; 3. the cosmical stage, the cures, as they enter into the natural life, and lead it on to its transformation, by working on the one hand to purify, on the other to liberate. Compare the preceding observations on the single miracles. Heubner: "Promise of miraculous powers. How far does it extend? Many commentators maintain that it extends to all time, and in a very wide sense; *e. g.*, Grotius. He says, we are to blame that the χαρίσματα have ceased (so also Lavater, Hess). But have, then, the later Christians,—*e. g.*, from the third century down, the most spiritual of the Christian Fathers, the Reformers,—had no faith, because they wrought no miracles? Augustine says: The miraculous gifts continued so long as they were needed, until firm ground was laid for the Church to rest upon; they could be dispensed with, when the Church became firmly established (comp. *De Civ. Dei.* x. 7)." According to Mark, however, this promise is given in as universal a form as the sending of the Gospel into all lands, for all times. The elder theology was wanting in the defined conception of the Church as an organic whole; otherwise, it would have seen that the miraculous signs continue, though the forms are not the same,—least of all, do the forms at the beginning correspond with those to obtain at the last end.

7. The festival of the Ascension.—It was from the first, undoubtedly, celebrated within the great Quinquagesima period, between Easter and Pentecost. After the fourth century, it assumed the form of a special festival, and was celebrated when the fifty days began to end.

HOMILETICAL AND PRACTICAL.

See Matthew, and the parallel passages in *Luke* and *John*.—*This section*, vers. 14–18. Not until after the personal appearance and presence of Christ in the Church, did the belief of the Church in the resurrection become perfect: 1. The personal revelation as opposed to the earlier, preparatory revelations; 2. the belief in the resurrection as opposed to those degrees of faith, at which the hardness of heart remained stationary.—With the personal announcement of Christ in the Church comes the Spirit and spiritual life, in which all hardness of heart ceases.—The last upbraiding of Christ in the circle of His disciples changes into a blessing.—Lo, the Lion of the tribe of Judah had prevailed!—The last death-cry of the Lord upon the cross, and His first life-word in the Church, in their great and ceaseless efficacy.—The Easter-period, the great turning-point at which the Church of the disciples became the Church of the Apostles.—The Lord's upbraiding in the Church; or, the seven thunders which from time to time resound in her (Rev. x.): voices of reformers, which affright the demons, and predict new summer-seasons.—The expulsion of unbelief from the hearts of the disciples is succeeded by their being sent into all the world.—The Gospel of faith: 1. From the faith; 2. in the faith; 3. for the faith.—The Gospel in its unlimited appointment: 1. To the end of the world—all creatures; 2. to the end of all time—blessed or damned; 3. appointed to work till all imperfection in the kingdom of God is ended [the miracles].—The Gospel in its threefold attestation: 1. By itself; 2. by the sacrament; 3. by miracles.—The miracles which accompany the Gospel: 1. In the world of spirit: *a.* the evil spirits expelled; *b.* the good spirits praise the Lord [new tongues]. 2. In the external world of nature: injurious things overcome, the evil in life made serviceable, life triumphing over death. 3. In the personal life, as soul and body: diseases removed, the restored rejoicing in a new existence.—Christianity remains a continuous miracle of curing and of life till the new, great signs of the world's glorification.—*The Lesson for Ascension Sunday*, vers. 14-20. *See* the following section.—The ascended and glorified Christ, in His perfect victory over the world's unbelief: 1. In the Church [vers. 14, 15]; 2. by the Church [vers. 16-18]; 3. above and along with the Church [vers. 19, 20].—The exaltation of Christ, how it was unfolded in the resurrection and ascension of the Lord: 1. The resurrection, the beginning of His ascension; 2. His ascension, the completion of His resurrection.—The last retreat of the Lord into concealment the ground of His victorious advance into, and progress through, the entire world: 1. He retires from view, in order to advance again into the light as the risen Lord; 2. He retires to heaven, in order to advance again as He who had been raised to the glory of heaven.—Preaching faith is an upbraiding of unbelief to the end of the world.—The upbraiding of unbelief in the Church and the world, the sweetest message of highest love and grace.—The Lord's glorious upbraiding: 1. Glorious in the storm and the thunder-peal; 2. glorious in the law; 3. still more glorious in the Gospel. Or, 1. Fearful only to devils, opposed only to them; 2. to all susceptible, pious hearts a greeting of peace.—Whosoever cannot rebuke in the spirit of Christ, can expel no demons.

STARKE:—*Bibl. Wirt.*:—We must willingly and pleasantly receive even the denunciatory statements of God's word. They proceed from the purest love, to effect our salvation.—LUTHER:—The words of Christ are words of majesty; for that may well be termed majesty, by virtue of which these poor beggars are commanded to go forth and preach this new truth, not in one city or country, but in all the world, in every principality and kingdom, and to open their mouths freely and confidently before all creatures, so that all the human race may hear this preaching. This was most assuredly stretching the arm far out, grasping on all sides, and lading itself with a great burden. This is a command so strong and powerful, that no injunction of earth has surpassed it.—Those alone can preach repentance who have repented, and are truly humble.—*Nova Bibl. Tub.*:—Lo, Jesus has instituted the ministerial office for the benefit of all the world. The portals of grace stand open to all: oh! let us enter, and not delay!—OSIANDER:—God will exclude no one from eternal blessedness, who does not exclude himself through unbelief.—Faith is enjoined upon all, but given only to those who do not obstinately oppose themselves.—*Nova Bibl. Tub.*:—Mark well, my soul, how blessed thou mayest be, and escape damnation! One way alone leads to heaven, faith; one way alone to hell, unbelief.—Unbelief is the sole ground of damnation.

GERLACH:—Although no man can be saved except through Christ, nevertheless Christ declares him alone damned who has refused the salvation offered to him.—All miracles which accompany the proclamation of the divine word are signs: they point to that internal wonder of salvation and the new birth which the word effects, and only in so far have they value.—LISCO:—He who is ashamed of such a confession of Christ [baptism] should think of Matt. x. 32, 33.—In the name of Jesus, in faith upon Him, empowered by His might, for the furtherance of His ends, were these signs to be wrought.

BRAUNE:—From Rieger: "Wonder not, although in thine own case faith is a constant overcoming of unbelief."—BRIEGER:—The command of Christ ["Go ye," etc.] given to the Church, which came into prominence at Pentecost.—The Gospel is for all.—The state of a Church may be seen in what it does for missions.—After the signs which accompanied belief have ceased, the ascension of the Son of God can be evidenced only in that which manifests itself as the life of faith [and this is the sign of the regeneration of the world; a sign, no doubt, manifesting itself ever under new forms, while the divine power remains ever the same].

The Lesson. HEUBNER (compare, in addition, Luther's explanation, Works ix. 2546-2747):—Unbelief is blameworthy, is dependent upon the heart, upon being willing or not willing. Were it otherwise, Christ could not rebuke.—The world is the theatre for the display of the Gospel.—Christianity is a matter for humanity.—It is a duty continually to spread the Gospel.—We must profess the faith we have in our hearts (baptism).—Faith is necessary for all without exception, would they be saved. To disbelieve is very different from not knowing the Gospel (unbelief and ignorance are two essentially distinct ideas): unbelief is rejecting an offered, an understood Gospel, which has to some degree influenced one. Unbelief is chargeable, when it is a positive, determined rejection. The heathen cannot be charged with (deliberate) unbelief.—The revelation of the glory of Jesus in the moment of His parting from His disciples.—The departure of Jesus from the earth: 1. The description itself; 2. how edifying for us.—The power of faith in the heavenly majesty of Jesus.

SCHLEIERMACHER (*Predigten*, Bd. ii., 1834, p. 204): The close of our Lord's appearance upon earth compared with its beginning.—GRUNEISEN (*Pred.* 1842, p. 280):—Upon the blessing of the exalted Redeemer.—HEILENREICH:—The ascension of the Lord, contemplated from the stand-point of faith.—ILLGEN:—How heaven appears to us in the light of Christ's ascension: 1. As our eternal fatherland; 2. as the land of our spiritual perfection; 3. as the place of our highest blessedness.—VON KALM:—Let the entrance of Jesus into glory strengthen us during the period of probation; let it strengthen, 1. Our faith in heaven; 2. our longing for heaven; 3. our striving to attain heaven.—UHLE:—What Christ in His exaltation is to men upon the earth.—RAMBACH: —If we look into the hearts of the disciples of Jesus, upon His exaltation to heaven, we see the deepest reverence for His divine majesty, living faith in His promises, heart-longings after the better world, joyous zeal to fulfil His commission, courage undaunted by consequences.—REINHARD:—The connection between true Christians and the Church above.—RAMBACH:—Seek the things above.—The ascension of Jesus in its power to elevate the heart.—REINHARD: —Our unbroken communion with the perfected of our race.—KUMMICH:—Our Lord's ascension shows us the way to heaven.—HOSSBUCH:—Our Lord's ascension is the real completion of His work on earth. —HERBERGER:—The ascension, the last miracle; with it the Lord closed His visible sojourn on earth: a blessed termination of Christ's entire journey, as St. Bernard says.—KAPFF:—The ascension of Jesus shows us heaven now standing open.—DIETZ:—The ascension of Jesus contemplated as His entrance upon government as the King of God's earthly kingdom.—HARLESS:—The Gospel being preached to every creature is the best testimony of Christ being raised to the right hand of God.—BENGEL:—With the ascension, the kingdom begins to extend on all sides.—GENZEN:—The Lord ever continues to bless His Church.—AHLFELD:—The last expression of the will of our Lord Jesus Christ.—KEM:—Not till His ascension did He become properly our Saviour [*i. e.*, the most remote distance becomes the most immediate contiguity].—FLOREY:—The disciples' pain and consolation in the departure of the Lord.—BURK:—Consider how Jesus, by His ascension, has opened all that formerly was closed: 1. The human heart to faith; 2. the whole earth to the Gospel; 3. heaven for all to enter who believe on Him

---

THIRD SECTION.

THE RISEN SAVIOUR IN HIS ASCENSION, AS CONQUEROR WITH THE CHURCH, GIVING POWER TO THE MESSAGE OF SALVATION THROUGHOUT THE ENTIRE EARTH.

CHAPTER XVI. 19, 20.

(Parallels: Luke xxiv. 50–53; Acts i. 4–12.)

19 So then, after the Lord[1] had spoken unto them, he was received up into heaven, and
20 sat on the right hand of God. And they went forth, and preached everywhere, the
Lord working with *them*, and confirming the word with signs following. Amen.

[1] Ver. 19.—After κύριος stands Ἰησοῦς in Codd. C., K., L., Δ. Lachmann adopts this reading. (Lange renders literally: "The Lord Jesus, after he had spoken thus unto them, was raised," &c.—*Trs.*)

EXEGETICAL AND CRITICAL.

Comp. the parallels in *Luke* and *Acts;* also the comments upon the conclusion of *Matthew.*—Mark's account of the ascension possesses a noble simplicity; and so conveys to the mind a comprehensive idea of Christ's majesty and rule, which consists most fully with the character of this Gospel. The ascension, described accurately by Luke, is here briefly sketched: the exaltation of Christ in the words, "and sat on the right hand of God," implies the supreme rule of Christ, as related by Matthew; while the last verse is analogous to the end of the Gospel by John, and expresses in a word the essence of all contained in the Acts.

Ver. 19. **The Lord Jesus.**—Term of reverence.—**After He had spoken.**—Augustine and the majority of commentators understand this to refer to the forty days; but Meyer will not concede this. According to him, this account and the lapse of forty days are quite irreconcilable. It is only when the Gospels are treated as mere *chronicles*, in which an exact sequence of all events in time is expected, that it becomes impossible to reconcile them with each other.

He was received up.—Taken up. Meyer properly combats the representation given by Strauss and Bauer, that Christ ascended to heaven from the room where they had supped. Yet, if we must not interpret this passage literally regarding *the place*, Meyer has as little right to insist upon a literal view as to *the time*. The account of the ascension is in every point to be supplemented by that of Luke, with whom Mark stands in no contradiction.—**And sat on the right hand of God.**—An account, resting partly upon the direct vision of the disciples (Acts i. 19), partly upon a revelation (Acts i. 11), partly upon the words of Christ (John xiv. 3), and upon the lively inference of faith, especially from the events occurring at Pentecost, Acts ii. 33. The fact is itself, on the one hand, local—that is, the being seated upon that throne of glory where the self-revelations of God take place, and in the midst of that majesty whence the manifestations of His power proceed; and, upon the other hand, is symbolic of Christ's royal dominion, Phil. ii. 10.

Ver. 20. **Everywhere.**—As it is probable the Evangelist wrote in Rome, and had been in Babylon, he knew that the Gospel was extending over the earth.—**The Lord working with them.**—*See Matthew*, close; Eph. i. 19.—**With signs following.**—The previously-promised powers to work these signs have been conferred; the miracles have appeared in striking forms, and conveying their symbolic import in their more general working. We see here the Gospel's absolute power to conquer in the might of the Lord. From this we perceive how close the connection between the closing of this Gospel and its beginning, and its every statement. Each

Evangelist concludes in a manner peculiar to himself, but with each the common topic is the glory and the kingly rule of Christ. The view peculiar to Mark is the forthputting of Christ's power by His servants on earth, to free the world and remove all demoniacal powers by which the earth was polluted.

DOCTRINAL AND ETHICAL.

1. *See* the conclusion of *Matthew* and the parallels in *Luke.*—We find the explanation of the circumstance, that Mark has combined the ascension in his Gospel narrative, in the fundamental principle of his Gospel, viz.: Christ, the omnipotent conqueror bursting through all barriers, the Lion in His retreat and advance. On this principle he was led to briefly mention the last withdrawal of Christ, the ascension; but then, only as the basis for the last forthcoming of Christ in His people, in their preaching of the Gospel and their working of signs in all places. Matthew presents Christ as a spiritual, invisible, theocratic King, beneath whose jurisdiction the present and the future worlds both lie, and whose administration over His people is in this present world universal, and of a specially spiritual character. By John, the universality and the present manifestation of Christ's glory are still more strongly emphasized. The typal form of this administration of Jesus is to be seen in the activity of a John and a Peter; that is, in contemplation and profound meditation combined with earnest labor and constancy in faith. Respecting Christ Himself, it is only hinted by John that He goes and comes again. According to Mark and Luke, Christ is with equal distinctness characterized as King of both worlds; but He works individually and personally from the other world outwards: and hence both these Evangelists present the ascension as a link, connecting Christ's life on earth with His work in and from heaven. In addition to this, however, Mark, like Peter, makes the rule of the exalted Christ in and with His people to prevail, because it is a work of the exalted Jesus which success will certainly crown; while Luke, with Paul, makes this prevalence result from the exalted *state* of the working Jesus.

2. When we estimate the resurrection properly, and consider that it was not the return of Jesus to His old, His first life, but His exaltation to His second, His new life, we see at once that the ascension must be joined to the resurrection as its necessary consequence. Christ's last departure from His disciples must have therefore, in any case, been termed His ascension; nevertheless, it consisted with His glory, that His return home should be an imposing and sublime ascension.

3. The doubts of critical writers as to the history of the ascension rest upon a mistake, often alluded to, regarding the nature of the Gospels, which are held to be memorabilia collected from various sources, instead of being received as individual, graphic life-pictures and views, organic in form, and Christological in character. The doubts of writers upon dogmatics are to be connected with their doubts regarding the resurrection itself, the divine dignity of Christ, the eternal continuance of personality, and the reality of a future state in heaven. In each of these two points the Apostles agree, as witnesses of the ascension, in their testimony with one another.

4. The theologians of the Lutheran school have thrown as much obscurity around the historical ascension, as those of the Reformed school around Christ's descent into hell (the Heidelberg Catechism). The Reformed Church has gone too far in its teaching regarding the glorified Christ's spiritual, omnipresent working; and the Lutheran, in its views upon the distinct localization and extension of Christ, now exalted. (Luther upon the Supper.) But the descent into hell and ascent to heaven must not be separated; and the localization of the exalted Redeemer in heaven must be held, along with His omnipresent manifestation. "That He reveals Himself in one way only in heaven amid the blessed, and that He in some other sense is everywhere present, are not contradictory propositions." SPENER, *Katechismus-Predigten*, 2 Bd. p. 914.

5. When we represent the ascension as the triumph of Christ and His Church, let us not forget the sad, earnest side for the Church in her human weakness. But as death is swallowed up in victory, so human sorrow is swallowed up in divine joy.

6. For the accounts given in Church history, and for the various traditions regarding the apostolic labors in preaching the Gospel, *see* LANGE's *Apost. Zeitalter*, 2 Bd. p. 401.

HOMILETICAL AND PRACTICAL.

See Matthew and *Luke.*—Christ's exaltation the great turning-point in His life and work.—The exaltation of Christ to heaven, a sign of the completion of His work on earth ("After the Lord," etc.).—The union of the Father and the Son seen in the ascension: as He had been *sent*, and yet *came* freely,—as He had *finished* the work *given Him* by the Father, and *unfolded His own secret life*, was *given up* to the death, and *resigned* His life,—as He *was raised* from the dead, and *rose* by His own power,—so *He is exalted* by the Father, and yet *ascends* by virtue of His own might.—The degrees of Christ's exaltation shadowed forth in the ascension: 1. It points back to His descent into hell, and His resurrection; 2. it points forward to His being seated upon the throne of glory at the right hand of God.—Christ's ascension: 1. A return home; 2. an exaltation; 3. a never-ending march of triumph.—The import of Christ's exaltation for His people. It settles, 1. the ascension of the members in Him, as the Head; 2. the ascension of the members after Him, in the spirit; 3. the final ascension of the members at the coming of the Lord.—Christ's seat at the right hand of God, the goal of His pilgrimage; or the point of rest between His two great careers: 1. His career through all the misery of the world; 2. His career through all the salvation of the world.—Because Christ is the highest above all heavens, He is the nearest to His people in all their depths: In their depth, *a.* of struggling, *b.* of suffering, *c.* of want, *d.* of death and the grave.—The Lord's rest causes the activity of Apostles, and of the members of Christ's body.—From the tranquil, rejoicing, divinely-human heart above, proceeds every pulsation of the new life throughout the entire world—All Christ's Apostles are Apostles of His royal authority.—The blessed consciousness of Christ's glory, the motive power of the Gospel in the hearts of believers.—The preaching of Christ is a preaching for all places.—Human proclamation of salvation confirmed by the divine manifestations from the Lord.—The truth of the faith established by the signs of love.—The Lord was one with them in the power of the Spirit.—The ever-blessing and victorious efficacy of the Gospel, a witness for Christ's everlasting administration of blessing and conquest. —Christ above all; Christ here, too, in His people. —Lo, the Lion of the tribe of Judah hath prevailed! —Our faith is the victory which overcometh the world.—Christ's seat, His throne: 1. The unceasing rest and festival in heaven; 2. unceasing work on earth; 3. unceasing rule in both kingdoms.—At the right hand of God, working in concert with Him; or, the revelation of the Trinity in Christ's exaltation (as at His birth and baptism, in His death and resurrection).—Where the exalted Christ appears, there doth heaven appear: 1. Where He is throned, there *is* heaven; 2. where He works, thither heaven *comes* (the spiritual, glorified world; the inheritance incorruptible, undefiled, that fadeth not away, 1 Pet. i. 4; 2 Pet. i. 4, 11).—We are with Christ, transferred to the heavenly state.

STARKE:—Let each see that he hold his confidential interview with Jesus, ere he leave the earth. —God is gone up with a shout, Ps. xlvii. 6.—The ascension of our Jesus is our after-ascension. Where the Head is, there are the members. "Where I am, there shall My servants be, that they may see My glory."—The heavens stand open: we are certain of our salvation. Even so come, Lord Jesus!—The presence of Christ in the earth has not ceased with His ascension; it is rather established, being combined with His session at the right hand of God.—HEDINGER:—Be faithful and industrious in thy calling; God will add His blessing and success.—If believers are not able to see Christ with their eyes, yet they feel His working in their hearts (proof sufficient that He is with and in them).—OSIANDER:—Jesus is to the present day with the preachers of the Gospel. —When the spiritually blind are enlightened, the spiritually dead quickened, the spiritually deaf and dumb made to hear devoutly and speak piously, the spiritually lame made to be righteously industrious and active, and the spiritually leprous are cleansed from sins, these are greater signs and wonders than physical changes.

LISCO:—He wished to depart from them in such a way that they, seeing whither He had gone, could not imagine that they had lost Him: rather should the thought that He lived and was in heaven be ever present to them, that they might testify courageously of Him, and labor for Him, as though they had Him by their side.—They should know Christ no more after the flesh (2 Cor. v. 16), but as the exalted Son of God, whose glorious elevation filled them with the most blessed hopes and opened to them the most blessed prospects.—BRAUNE:—A close of the activity of the visible, personal Redeemer, that corresponds perfectly with the beginning. Not more mysterious than the birth and resurrection of the Saviour is His ascension.—Christ, having conquered death, could not die, and so ascended to heaven.—BRIEGER:—Ps. lxviii. 19; Eph. iv. 8: Christ, to manifest His victory over the devil and his angels, returns as a conqueror to heaven, Col. iii. 1, 2; Heb. viii. 1.—We are the subjects of the Heavenly (the second Adam), who is transforming us more and more into His likeness.—BAUER:—Holy, holy, holy is the Lord of hosts, the whole earth is full of His glory.